STOLEN CITY

OWEN TOEWS

ARP

OWEN TOEWS

STOLEN CITY

RACIAL CAPITALISM AND THE MAKING OF WINNIPEG

Copyright ©2018 Owen Toews

ARP BOOKS (Arbeiter Ring Publishing)
205-70 Arthur Street
Winnipeg, Manitoba
Treaty 1 Territory and Historic Métis Nation Homeland
Canada R3B 1G7
arpbooks.org

Cover and interior design and layout by Urbanink.
Printed and bound in Canada by Friesens on paper
made from 100% recycled post-consumer waste.

Second printing, February 2020

ARP BOOKS acknowledges the generous support of the Manitoba Arts Council and the
Canada Council for the Arts for our publishing program. We acknowledge the financial
support of the Government of Canada through the Canada Book Fund and the Province of
Manitoba through the Book Publishing Tax Credit and the Book Publisher Marketing Assistance Program of Manitoba Culture, Heritage, and Tourism.

LIBRARY AND ARCHIVES CANADA CATALOGUING IN PUBLICATION

Toews, Owen, author
    Stolen city : racial capitalism and the making of
Winnipeg / Owen Toews.

Includes bibliographical references.
Issued in print and electronic formats.
ISBN 978-1-894037-93-8 (softcover).--ISBN 978-1-894037-95-2
(EPUB)

    1. Urbanization--Manitoba--Winnipeg--History. 2. City
planning--Manitoba--Winnipeg--History. 3. Winnipeg (Man.)--
History. 4. Winnipeg (Man.)--Race relations--History. I. Title.

HT384.C32W55 2018   307.76097127'43   C2018-900488-6
                                            C2018-900489-4

CONTENTS

ACKNOWLEDGEMENTS

This book started with the generosity and thoughtfulness of the brilliant fighting, caring, teaching community that is Winnipeg's city centre. From my days as a young student, veteran community organizers—as well as those in other lines of activity and stages of their lives—in Winnipeg's city centre have taken the time to reflect with me on the deep-running origins, uneven power dynamics, and oppressive and promising realities of life in Winnipeg. Much love, respect, and gratitude to Leslie Spillett, Duncan Mercredi, Joan Hay, Kathy Mallett, Diane Roussin, Carol Moar, Kemlin Nembhard, Erika Wiebe, Lucille Bruce, Margaret Ormond, Sandra Guiboche, Sonia Prevost-Derbecker, Tom Simms, Kristin Fontaine, Warren Goulet, Cheyenne Chartrand, Sharon Allard, Dilly Knol, Annette Champion-Taylor, Cheyenne Henry, Valerie Garneau, Robert Neufeld, Kathleen Shellrude, Shayla Elizabeth, Elaine Bishop, Linda Williams, Rain Greyeyes, Janet Sarson, Rita Richard, Kathleen Mico, Jill Ramsay, Sandy Dzedzora, Sandra Leone, Gord Dong, Don Mediema, Damon Johnston, Karen Mediema, Jamil Mahmood, Pat Macklem, Greg Macpherson, Kathy Downs, Kathryn Mackenzie, George Munroe, Lawrence Houle, Sam Medd, Barbara Romanik, Elizabeth Treidler, Rosa Cerda, Trevor Greyeyes, Wayne Helgason, Lawrence Barkwell, JD Ormond, Christa Bishop, Jackson Duong, Milena Placentile, Iain Brynjolson, Ashlyn Haglund, Karen Glugosh, Kate Sjoberg, Matt Gemmel, Crystal Dawn Greene, Alice, Elvis, Charles, Mary, Melissa, and Eli. Thank you to Jesse Green and Vanda Fleury-Green for making and allowing me to cite their mighty documentary film, *Brown Town Muddy Water*. I am solely responsible for any mistakes in this book, and for its specific analyses and arguments, but nothing here would exist without this community.

The Preserving Aboriginal Institutional History in Winnipeg project—which completed many lengthy videotaped interviews with long-time community organizers at the same time as I was researching this book—provided an invaluable source of reflection on the rich history of Indigenous community organizing in Winnipeg. Big thanks to Darrell Chippeway, Louise Chippeway, and Evelyn Peters for providing me with the videotaped interviews and welcoming me to draw on them for this project. Utmost respect and gratitude to those who participated in the project as interlocutors, including Marion Meadmore, Janet Fontaine, Doris Young, Louise Champagne, Mary Guilbault, Wayne Helgason, Larry Morrisette, Vern Morrisette, Louise Chippeway, Albert McLeod, and to Darrell for his remarkable interviewing.

I am grateful for those who generously read parts of the book before publication: Duncan Mercredi, Janet Fontaine, Doris Young, Louise Champagne, Kathy Mallett, Trevor Greyeyes, Gord Dong, Elizabeth Treidler, and Leslie Spillett.

The way this book thinks, feels, and acts owes a very great deal to the mentorship of Ruth Wilson Gilmore, who schooled me in dialectical materialism and guided me through years of studying race, place, state power, infrastructure, consciousness, and capitalism. Ruthie introduced me to Clyde Adrian Woods's *Development Arrested*, and transformed this book by helpfully informing me, in typically incisive style, that "What you are really talking about is racial capitalism." Ruthie's dazzling insights are indispensable, they course through this book, and are one of its essential foundations. Audra Simpson provided crucial mentorship in the early stages of this project, offering a brilliant course in settler colonialism and introducing me to the vital work of many contemporary scholars in Native American and Indigenous studies. More than anyone, Audra helps us think about what Canada is, and she remains one the most committed, generous, and supportive people I have ever met. This book would not have been written without my incomparable PhD dissertation advisor, Setha Low, who kept me on track, regularly and gently steering me away from doubt, depression, and half-baked ideas toward purpose, form, and clarity. Across five years and hundreds of pages of field notes, she helped me see the forest for the trees. I must also thank her for her genuine interest in my hometown, something that remains difficult for me to wrap my head around, except that it epitomizes the noble devotion to her students that so sets her apart.

A number of other professors in the City University of New York (CUNY) Graduate Centre orbit during my time there shaped this book significantly, including David Harvey, whose courses on Capital Volume 1 and the Grundrisse provided me with an essential understanding of the basic dynamics of capitalism. Kandice Chuh offered careful feedback and support for the project—including advising me to "go big," something I took to heart—in her writing workshop and introduced me to the inspiring work of scholars engaged in revolutionizing American studies. I am indebted, too, to Neil Smith, Jenna Loyd, Cindi Katz, Rupal Oza, Vinay Gidwani, Mary Louise Pratt, and Don Mitchell.

The ex-department store on 34th Street and 5th Avenue can be a special place, in large part because of the students' own culture of solidarity, mutual aid, disdain for petty competition, and genuine commitment to changing the world. This book is a product of that environment and of the radical CUNY students who forged it, especially those in the Earth and Environmental Sciences department, the Space Time Research Collective, and seminars led by Setha Low and Ruthie Gilmore. Big thanks to Laurel Mei-Singh, Hunter Jackson, Annie Spencer, Jack Norton, Héctor Agredano, Keith Miyake, Jessica Miller, Rachel Goffe, David Spataro, Jesse Goldstein, Steve McFarland, Manissa Maharawal, Amanda Matles, Denisse Andrade, Amanda Huron, Naomi Adiv, Stephanie Wakefield, Esteban Kelly, Malav Kanuga, Maggie Ornstein, Katie Gill, Tommy Wu, Terri Bennett, Alyson Spurgas, Cindy Gorn, Bradley Gardener, Morgan

Buck, Rafael Mutis, Erin Siodmak, Lalit Batra, Stephen Boatright, Kareem Rabie, Dominque Nisperos, Einat Manoff, Fang Xu, Zoltán Glück, Conor Tomás Reed, Peng fei Li, Hillary Caldwell, Benjamin Haber, Jen Jack Gieseking, Christian Anderson, Desiree Fields, Chris Eng, Lydia Pelot-Hobbs, Neil Agarwal, Edwin Mayorga, Elizabeth Sibilia, Michelle Billies, Pilar Ortiz, Jane McAlevey, Sara Martucci, Ujju Aggarwal, Jen Tang, Francesca Manning, Marnie Brady, Colin Ashley, Erin Michaels, Brenden Beck, Josh Scannell, Caroline Loomis, Frances Tran, Jenny LeRoy, Aidah Gil, Gaurav Jashnani, Robin McGinty, Greg Narr, and Albert de la Tierra.

Back in Canada, several wise and generous scholars offered feedback and support at different stages. Jim Silver, my undergraduate advisor at the University of Winnipeg, was the first to help me think through the forces shaping the city and to offer me the opportunity to be a researcher and writer. Jim showed me what it means to do dedicated, community-based scholarship, and he provided tremendous support to get me into graduate school. I am similarly indebted to Shauna Mackinnon and Lynne Fernandez at the Canadian Centre for Policy Alternatives–Manitoba Office. Helmut-Harry Loewen, Tom Carter, Doug Smith, and Jim Freeman provided generous early mentorship. Since finishing my doctorate, I have been grateful for the support of Adele Perry, Niigaan Sinclair, Evelyn Peters, Bruce Erickson, and Chris Andersen. I received valuable feedback during later stages of this project from Adele Perry, Doug Owram, Gerald Friesen, and Aimeé Craft. Throughout the process, my ideas were sharpened by wonderful students in classes I taught at Brooklyn College, Hunter College, and the University of Manitoba.

I am grateful to have been able to workshop versions of parts of this book with comrades and colleagues at the annual meetings of the American Association of Geographers, Critical Ethnic Studies Association, Black Canadian Studies Association, University of Manitoba Native Studies colloquium, the 2013 Whose Winnipeg? workshop, the Fulbright Canada Canadian Studies Colloquium, and the Northeast Regional Space Time Workshops. I am grateful for the collegiality and friendship of Toronto-based geographers I first met at the latter workshops, especially Shiri Pasternak, Jen Ridgley, Katie Mazer, Patrick Vitale, Paul Jackson, David Hugill, Brett Story, Martine August, and Heather Dorries. Scholarly communities at the annual conferences of the Native American and Indigenous Studies Association and the American Studies Association have been especially generative of the ideas in this book.

An assortment of libraries and archives contributed to the research, including the City of Winnipeg Archives, Provincial Archives of Manitoba, Manitoba Legislative Library, University of Manitoba Archives & Special Collections, Winnipeg Public Library Local History Room, Winnipeg Free Press Archives, University of Winnipeg Library, Institute of Urban Studies Library, The People's Library at the Manitoba Indigenous Cultural Education Centre, the Toronto Reference Library, and the City of Winnipeg City Clerk's Department. Much gratitude to archivists Shelley Sweeney, Linda Eddy, Martin Comeau, Sarah Ramsden, Julianna Trivers, Michelle Swanson, and Jody Baltessen. I am indebted to a number of interlocutors at other institutions who met my inquiries with generosity and openness, including Alissa Brandt, Rose Passante, Rudy Friesen, Edith Friesen, Garry Hilderman, Paula Mitchell, Ramona Mattix, Annitta Stenning, Loretta Martin, Britanny Shewchuk, Patty Nero, Russ Tychonic, Matt Dryburgh, Fabian Suárez-Amaya, and Michael Foster.

Funding for the research and writing of this book came from a CUNY Graduate Teaching Fellowship, a CUNY Instructional Technology Fellowship, CUNY Doctoral Student Research Grants, a CUNY Advanced Research Collaborative Knickerbocker Award for Archival Research in American Studies, a Canada-US Fulbright Student Award, a Social Sciences and Humanities Research Council of Canada doctoral fellowship, and a University of Alberta Notley Postdoctoral Fellowship.

Finishing the book with ARP Books has strengthened the manuscript immensely. Editor Linda Preussen guided me with impressive patience and determination to write about complex ideas with accessibility, simplicity, and directness. Irene Bindi steered the manuscript through peer review, selection of photographs, book design, and countless other processes. Thanks to Josina Robb for believing in the book, to Jessica Antony for copy editing, and to Todd Besant for running the show.

Years of talk and action with friends and comrades in Winnipeg, Montréal, and New York City have shaped this book. I am grateful for the friendship and solidarity of Bonnie-May Wadien, Rowan Moyes, Alex Stearns, Chandel McAuley, Jon Benson, Stéphane Doucet, Alannah Zeebeck, Buck Doyle, Jordyn Null, Weston Smith, Kendra Ballingall, Laura Simms, Shelagh Pizey-Allen, Les Sabiston, Janis Maudlin, Macho Philipovich, Joel Ferguson, Colin Smith, Paula Ducharme, Kim Parry, Caitlin Hutchison, Sarah Fox, Jacquie Nicholson, Rob McGregor, Alex Paterson, Chuck Wright, Thor Aitkenhead, Anlina Sheng, Andrea Derbecker, Krystal Payne, Claudia Scott, Scott Price, Vera Coppola, Aviva Cipilinski, Craig Settee, Kevin Settee, Charlie Crow, Cam Scott, Jenny Heijun Wills, Bruno Cornellier, Todd Scarth, Esyllt Jones, Peter Ives, John K. Samson, Christine Fellows, Teddy Zegeye-Gebrehiwot, Monique Woroniak, David Camfield, Matthew Brett, Shimby Zegeye-Gebrehiwot, Lenard Monkman, Jesse Hajer, Sarah Cooper, Jonathan Hildebrand, Brigette DePape, Natalia Ilyniak, Maurice Williams, Emily Leedham, James Wilt, Aruna Krishnakumar, Maeve Johnston, Audrea Lim, Manu Mei-Singh, Maggie Schreiner, Suzanna Collerd, Juan Pablo Galvis, Gretchen Virkler, Hannah Mermelstein, Freddy Burgos, Josh Pavan, Sarah Pupo, Teres Knoppers, Bridget Simpson, Ana Leventhal, Kandis Friesen, Danielle Holyk, Sissy Hall, Patrick DeDauw, and Naomi Lightman.

I have benefitted a whole lot from a very solid family of friends in Winnipeg who sustain me, crack me up, and lighten my load. Big thanks to Cale Smith, Jordan Kovacs, Aaron Challis, Ellen Friesen, Jessica Howison, Margaret Howison, Amy Wilkinson, Ryan Trudeau, Noni Brynjolson, Patrick Dunford, Ben Johnson, Megan Donald, Blair

Cardigan-Smith, Justin March, Hailey March, Caitie Thomas-Dunn, Kalev Anniko, Kat Kolar, Lindsay Duthoit, Jon Challis, Lisha Mehta, Will Barr, Lin Howes Barr, Al Scott, Renee Scott, Kieran Rice-Lampert, Malcom McPherson, Trent Fennell, Keith Arigo, Nick Smith, Dominic Kovacs, Paul Goldstone, Kelli Goldstone, Shea Youngdahl, and Claire Friesen.

This book would not exist without two Mennonite women who migrated to Winnipeg's city centre from southern Manitoba in the late twentieth century, making me a first-generation Winnipegger: My mother, Miriam Toews, who moved downtown to be a punk, waitress, writer, and mother, and my father's mother, Irene Rempel, who moved to the North End to be a teacher and a single mother to four boys. I owe everything to their courage, hustle, and commitment to subversive ideas. For a sense of where I came from as a descendant of Russian Mennonites, a sense of how frontier occupation and its afterlife was lived and felt on the prairies in the twentieth century, and for a special kind of buoyant love, I am endlessly thankful for my mother's mother, Elvira Toews. Much love to my father Neal Rempel, my sisters Georgia Toews and Anastasia Chipelski, Marjorie Toews, Ben Rempel, Basil Hatte, T.H. Hatte, Kajia Eidse-Rempel, Savannah Eidse, Carol Loewen, Jacque Basker, Erik Rutherford, Meredith Potter, Sean Richens, Mark Boucher, Courtney Slobogian, Cole Ferencz, and David Schlaikjar. Huge thanks to Wendy Land, Victor Dobchuk, and Megan Dobchuk-Land, who give so much love, support, insight, and inspiration. Thank you to my baby daughter Silvia Dobchuk, for teaching me a wild new kind of love. Finally, I am forever indebted to Bronwyn Dobchuk-Land, for sharing her enormous capacities for love, solidarity, curiosity, intellectual work, style, humour, and good times with me. Everything in this book comes from the paths we've taken together and the reflections we've shared along the way.

ICEBERGS

On a chilly evening in February, a coalition of community organizers in Winnipeg's Indigenous[1] North End convened one of their regular meetings; the details of that night's agenda are difficult to reconstruct, in part because the group meets so often, about so many things. As the organizers took their seats, one of them passed around the morning's newspaper, bringing the group's attention to a small item on the front page. White Christian missionaries none of them knew were set to receive free land and $6 million dollars from the government to construct a large youth recreation centre for North End children. Somehow, the matter had reached City Council—who would vote in only six days' time—without a single one of the organizers hearing about it, despite nearly all having worked for decades on grassroots programs for North End youth. Because they were well organized, because they had a history of taking control over this aspect of their neighbourhood, and because state funding had always fallen pathetically short of what they needed—to which Canadian politicians had replied, over and over, that their cupboards were simply bare—the news sparked instant, highly productive anger. The group formed a sub-committee to research the situation. They registered to speak at the city council meeting. They published an essay outlining their position. They made a list of potential allies—fellow neighbourhood organizers, youth service providers, and Indigenous activists—and started rallying support.

Four days later, a coalition aligned in resistance to state funding for the missionaries packed Winnipeg's city council chambers. The coalition made sixteen speeches condemning the project for reviving a mode of colonialism—the state-sponsored Christianization of Indigenous children—that was supposed to be, finally, thank goodness, officially dead. In addition to the Prime Minister's 2008 Indian Residential Schools apology, two longstanding local political traditions were invoked: the struggle for Indigenous community control over urban education and youth programming; and the struggle for Indigenous community control over urban planning and development of the city's Main Street strip, the North End, and Winnipeg's broader city centre.[2] Indigenous Winnipeggers had worked for decades to wrest control over these aspects of their lives from often well-intentioned Canadians. They had marched in the streets, made endless speeches, written volumes of essays, pulled off myriad direct actions, and achieved—hadn't they?—a hard-won agreement that Canadians would no longer muscle in on these worlds. Armed with these powerful traditions, impressively mobilized, and struggling on new cultural terrain that they themselves had worked to shape, and in which the thing they opposed was now officially unacceptable, the coalition seemed well-positioned to win.

The question of why they did not win—why a four-storey, 100,000-square-foot, steel-and-glass, state-financed "contemporary, altered form of the residential school experience" now casts its shadow every morning over Indigenous Winnipeg—begs the question, what exactly was the coalition up against that day?[3] This question demands more than pat answers about the same old Canadian ignorance, Prairie racism, and the timeless evils of "colonialism," "capitalism," and "the state."[4] While these forces are certainly the culprits, the point is that they are now functioning in new ways. Indeed, Canadian colonialism, racism, and state power have been renovated into new institutions and structures—including structures of feeling[5] and explanation—that confront various places in specific ways.[6] In fact, the coalition at City Hall that day was up against a new kind of institutional power that was in the process of pursuing an agenda much broader than that single parcel of land, meaning that the assault on the community that claimed and continues to claim that land was not an exceptional, one-off controversy. The missionaries were, in fact, the tip of the iceberg. Lurking underneath the waterline was a recent urban agenda set on perpetrating a new round of theft in a city defined by serial dispossession.

WINNIPEG

Winnipeg—a provincial capital of nearly one million people in the Canadian North-West,[7] internationally known for Indigenous social, cultural, and political power, and for anti-Native racism—is a Native city. It is home to 100,000 Indigenous peoples, the second largest urban Indigenous population on Turtle Island.[8] More than simply a location or a container of Indigenous life, however, Winnipeg is a place that Indigenous peoples have collectively and strategically decided to remake in order for their families, communities, and nations to survive and thrive in resistance to colonial occupation. Not surprisingly, these efforts defy both the colonially recognized boundaries of Native space—such as the Indian reserve system—and the requirements of post-industrial capitalism. Today, Indigenous peoples' decolonial claims to urban land, space, and resources are systematically denied, displaced, and dispossessed by an urban redevelopment agenda that is deemed necessary for regional survival in a globalized, post-industrial, potentially post-suburban world.[9] In this sense, social relations in present-day Winnipeg are produced not only by past colonialism, nor by colonial dispossessions occurring outside of the city, but by a specifically urban mode of colonialism that is happening right now.

Winnipeg, by some measures the coldest city in the world, is often portrayed as a forgotten place, a tendency that is at times fed by anti-Native racism. For places accustomed to being the butt of bad jokes—even places where money and jobs are not particularly rare—anxiety about regional survival can become a powerful force. CentreVenture, a city-centre redevelopment authority that Winnipeg's City Council established in 1999 and that has persisted—no small feat—into 2018, is an institutional expression of this unease. It has been a major player in shaping the city's post-industrial future. The most immediately striking thing about CentreVenture is that it exhibits the peculiar hallmarks of what has been called neoliberal governance, attributes that have come to dominate cities worldwide in recent decades: it is a private corporation created and financed by the state, with little in the way of public accountability; it privatizes public land, money, and buildings, redistributing these resources upward and outward to millionaire and billionaire developers for the production of the most profitable kinds of space those developers can come up with—for the most part, exclusive spaces for affluent people—under the pretense of trickle-down economics; and it utilizes recent, convoluted innovations in urban governance—tactics such as "enterprise zones" and "tax increment financing" (TIF)—to do so. In this sense, CentreVenture is a typical cog in the overall class strategy, most infamously advanced by Ronald Reagan and Margaret Thatcher in the 1980s and still triumphant today, known as neoliberalism. In short, neoliberalism is a strategy for transferring social wealth from everyday working people to a wealthy few by insisting that markets and private ownership are the most beneficial way to distribute the world's resources.[10] Privatization of public land, infrastructure, and resources—a process sometimes referred to as "accumulation by dispossession"—is integral to it.[11]

CentreVenture was the landowner and the biggest player pushing City Council to fund the missionaries' North End outpost. Youth For Christ (YFC) is a multinational corporation in the business of accumulating souls, not money. Nevertheless, public land and money flowed into its megaproject—and *not* into local people's social, cultural, and economic visions, most notably Indigenous-controlled projects—because it is a wealthy organization with millions to spend on urban development and thus fit CentreVenture's neoliberal requirements. While CentreVenture is a strictly neoliberal institution on paper, in practice, as the YFC project exemplified, its decisions about who may access land and resources play into a longstanding colonial tradition. The authority's tendency to destroy Indigenous peoples' spaces and jettison their development plans demonstrates that neoliberal approaches to urban governance are among the latest means by which Canada dispossesses Indigenous peoples.[12] At the same time, the inherited racist structures associated with the area's long history of settler colonialism have greatly facilitated the rise of neoliberal schemes. In this basic sense, there is a mutually supportive relationship between neoliberalism and settler colonialism. Although this combination is somewhat specific to Winnipeg, and likely to the Canadian North-West as a whole, the overriding way that power operates is not unique. The braid of neoliberalism and settler colonialism is, in fact, a particular example of the inseparability of capitalism and racism encapsulated by the concept of racial capitalism. To make sense of what is going on in Winnipeg and the world, a grasp of racial capitalism is indispensable.

WHAT IS RACIAL CAPITALISM?

Stolen land and stolen labour are the essential requirements of capitalism. Thinking about how most of the world has actually experienced capitalist expansion quickly reveals the crucial and persistent role of theft by coercion, colonization, fraud, genocide, and captivity in capitalist society. Starting from this understanding, the concept of racial capitalism conveys the fact that capitalism, rather than homogenizing, rationalizing, and demystifying social relations (as Karl Marx predicted), has continuously tended, as political scientist Cedric J. Robinson wrote, "to differentiate—to exaggerate regional, subcultural, and dialectical differences into 'racial' ones."[13] Racism naturalizes the socially manufactured attacks and inequalities that capitalism requires, making them seem proper, inevitable, and just.[14] As Winnipeg's past and present demonstrate, racist thinking is used to excuse capitalist inequality in many different ways, from straight-up vilification of oppressed groups to more cunning ways of feeling that promote the sense that oppressed groups, perhaps through no fault of their own, are not quite ready to enjoy self-determination or a humane standard of living. The persistence of colonial activity in Winnipeg is therefore not surprising, given how essential racism is to capitalist development everywhere.

Getting the specific historical relationship between capitalism and racism right is crucial to understanding how they function together in the present and what to do about it. While capitalism depends on racism and has always been racial, capitalists did not invent racial ways of thinking. In fact, racialism was a key aspect of European society before capitalism—Robinson called it an "ordering idea" of Western civilization—and it provided a supportive foundation for the rise of capitalism.[15] This cultural groundwork was bolstered, not demolished, as capitalism took hold. This means that while capitalist structures are not solely responsible for racism in our society, neither are they passive inheritors of it, as if racism was simply human nature. Rather, capitalist structures, such as CentreVenture, actively renew, renovate, and entrench racial hierarchies, feelings, and practices.

Thinking about today's world as the product of racial capitalism helps us keep in mind the full breadth of differently dispossessed working people and places whose land and labour have been taken from them through different means and to different extents. It encourages us to think about how different groups of working people relate to each other, and how they relate to capitalists.[16] Racial capitalism is not only about capital stealing land and labour, it is also about how some dispossessed people accept goods that have been stolen from others. Indeed, capitalism depends on racial hierarchies that encourage some working people—usually those who are encouraged to see themselves as white—to align with capitalists in return for a share of the spoils. Racialism encourages these people to think of themselves as inherently more adept and deserving than others and, as such, to support racial capitalist structures to the detriment of all working people including, ultimately, themselves.[17] Feelings of national belonging and the bundling of nation and state are glaring examples of such alliances. As some workers are welcomed into the Canadian nation, for example, they are encouraged to cosign the conquest, captivity, and dispossession meted out by the Canadian nation-state. This setup was fundamental to Canada's initial occupation of the North-West by farm workers who saw themselves as white Canadian settlers, and it remained crucial, in modified forms, to the region's urbanization, suburbanization, and gentrification.

While racism has a life of its own apart from capitalism, racism has shaped the entire historical development of capitalism, and capitalism, in turn, has profoundly shaped the character of racism as it has shaped the world.[18] Understanding this, one can see that there are no eternal or universal laws of racism or capitalism, only an interlocking array of specific racial capitalisms in specific times and places.[19] The first upshot of this is that events in the present are never usefully understood as pure extensions of the past. "Though [racism] may draw on the cultural and ideological traces which are deposited in a society by previous historical phases," cultural theorist Stuart Hall wrote, "it always assumes specific forms which arise out of present—not past—conditions and organization of society."[20] This means that in order to figure out what is going on in Winnipeg, we can't rely entirely on universal truths about colonialism. Dispossession, captivity, and genocide are still with us; the task is to figure out how they've survived in new times, what exactly they have become, and what they are doing now.

The second upshot is that racial capitalism in one place is never identical to racial capitalism elsewhere.[21] In fact, agendas around capital accumulation, labour attraction, land acquisition, and so on are often coordinated by local interests who establish distinct racial hierarchies, structures, and narratives in particular places.[22] The way local powerbrokers build alliances to control regional resources and justify their uneven redistribution is crucial to the dynamic spatial life of racial capitalism.[23] In Winnipeg, regional planning has been dominated by shifting blocs of local capitalists and their allies who have persistently created new world-making structures: CentreVenture is simply one of many.

This runs against the grain of the popular notion that we live in a "globalized" world, increasingly shaped by top-down processes that are making every place look the same.[24] In fact, regional regimes are crucial mediators between global economic restructuring and the social life of various places.[25] Globalization, like capitalism, racism, and the state, is not a universal logic or something imposed from on high, but something that local powerbrokers meaningfully shape and respond to. "What is missing [from the prevailing idea of globalization] is a discussion of how dominant—and dominated—economic/ethnic blocs in each region respond to the restructuring process," geographer Clyde Adrian Woods wrote. "Once we lift the veil off the restructuring process, we can more clearly see the specifically regional practices of ethnic supremacy."[26] CentreVenture is a good example of the kinds of regional planning authorities that have popped up all over in recent decades—authorities that renovate local racial traditions in their attempts to manage the fallout of globalization.[27]

An awareness of the role of regional blocs demonstrates that urban and regional planning is not merely a technical matter of improving places or maximizing profits; it is also a political strategy to preserve domination and subordination, re-entrench inequality, and silence alternative visions.[28] Reflecting on the political function of urban and regional planning, especially its capacity to silence alternatives, is crucial. For one thing, it reveals that capitalists—despite their efforts to have us believe otherwise—are forever dependent on state assistance. More importantly, it allows us to realize that "community organizing" is a politically neutral term: both dominant and dominated groups simultaneously build alliances, structures of power, social explanations, and plans for regional futures. But as Woods noted, "Blocs, agendas, and movements that challenge the dominant regime are often eliminated from the historical record and from popular memory by the normal workings of the dominant institutions."[29] This insight is key to seeing through dominant explanations of the persistence of poverty in places, like Winnipeg, that produce immense wealth. "Responsibility for the coexistence of great poverty beside great wealth rests squarely at the feet of a dominant regional bloc that has fought every effort to expand the parameters of social, economic, and cultural justice," Woods wrote.[30] Rejecting dominant explanations of poverty—liberal or illiberal—that blame past trauma, lack of education, risky behaviour, or cultural deficiencies, this approach emphasizes the dominant mobilizations that have persistently thwarted the creation of socially just regions. The events surrounding the creation of CentreVenture demonstrate just this, as the authority came on the heels of, and silenced, city-centre peoples' own radical 1990s counter-plan for the future of the city.

WHAT IS SETTLER COLONIALISM?

Settler colonialism is one of the most impactful forms of racial capitalism shaping present-day Winnipeg. To see beneath the surface of the city, it is very helpful to have a grasp of the abstract workings of power that first set the stage for industrial capitalism on the Prairies and that persist in different guises today. Settler colonialism is a specific, but not unique, mode of racial capitalism that describes Canada's relationship to Indigenous peoples. In other words, settler colonialism is characterized by certain tendencies that resemble, but do not duplicate, those that define other processes of racial capitalist acquisition.[31] Settler colonialism may be one of the biggest forces preventing people in a given place, and Winnipeg is certainly one of these places, from piecing together whole selves and worlds—whatever they want to call that wholeness—but it is only ever one of many interwoven modes of racial capitalism operating simultaneously.[32] Perceiving that settler colonialism is one expression of racial capitalism helps us to understand the particular class interests—real estate developers, financiers, merchants, industrialists, and so forth—that orchestrate and benefit the most from settler-colonial ventures. It allows us to observe that settler colonialism, which is typically understood to define countries such as Canada, Australia, New Zealand, the United States, and Israel, is only one aspect of the larger system that is remaking the *entire* world. And it helps us keep in mind that *all* working people—including non-Indigenous peoples in settler-colonial contexts—have been dispossessed, in qualitatively and quantitatively different ways, by diverse expressions of the same force, even while participating unevenly in each other's dispossession. For example, settler-colonialism's tendency to prioritize the theft of Indigenous land rather than Indigenous labour, one of its primary characteristics, is possible only in relation to capitalists' ability to mobilize other forms of racism to achieve the hyper-exploitation of non-Indigenous labour. In Winnipeg's early development, for instance, apartheid and genocide made Indigenous peoples unavailable to industrialists seeking an urban workforce, prompting them to establish a new rung in the city's racial hierarchy for migrant industrial workers.[33]

What distinguishes settler colonialism from other modes of racial capitalism? Yes, it is similar to other forms insofar as capital accumulation is the objective; force, fraud, and theft are the methods; and white supremacy is the justification.[34] But settler colonialism needs to be understood in and of itself. For a start, settler colonialism explains a relationship in which stealing peoples' land tends to take precedence over stealing their labour, and struggles against settler colonialism continue to take aim primarily at the dispossession of land.[35] Closely related to this dynamic is the way that settler colonialism aims for the total destruction and replacement of people's collectivities—nations, laws, economies, identities—with new regimes on the same lands. Settler-colonial power is based on the persistent suppression of Indigenous peoples' right to access lands according to their own economic and political systems, and the overwhelming imposition of settler structures over and above those of Indigenous peoples.[36] Renewing Indigenous dispossession is how settler-colonial nation-states express their sovereignty and attempt to guarantee the fast, reliable, and easy access to land that capitalists require. From Canadian invasion to the CentreVenture era, Winnipeg's development has turned on different expressions of this dynamic.

It is important to emphasize, however, that land is at the centre of settler colonialism not merely as a thing to be kept or taken away, but as a social relation, a way that relationships between people play out.[37] Theft of land is achieved by enforcing certain social relationships—Western ideas of territorial sovereignty, capitalist private property, and commodification, for instance—through which people are excluded from accessing land in ways they deem necessary to the survival of their nations, communities, families, and the world itself. These social relationships, enshrined in law and feeling, are justified as superior, progressive, and necessary based on racist ideas about the inferiority, backwardness, and impossibility of Indigenous sovereignties and social relations, which Coulthard summarizes as "respectful, nondominating, [and] nonexploitative."[38] As Michi Saagiig Nishnaabeg scholar Leanne Simpson has said, the Indigenous opposite of dispossession is not possession—in the capitalist sense—but connection.[39] Coulthard explains this idea by referring to Dene leaders who, in their opposition to the Mackenzie Valley Pipeline, differentiated their reluctance to share land with "those few people who are the richest and most powerful in the world" from their eagerness to share it with "the poor people of the world."[40] Indeed, the struggles that have made and remade Winnipeg have not simply been fights over who will get land, jobs, and housing, but what visions, principles, and ways of relating will govern urban life.

This understanding of settler colonialism is particularly important because it does not accommodate a politics of mirroring colonial partitions—such as those that mythologize the mixture of blood and soil to suggest that some belong while others do not—but of implementing the radically egalitarian ways of relating to the world that racial capitalism has attempted to destroy. In this spirit, Tonawanda Seneca scholar Mishauna Goeman offers the concept of "(re)mapping" as a way of moving toward contemporary alternatives to settler colonialism: "(re)mapping is not just about regaining that which was lost and returning to an original and pure point in history, but instead understanding the *processes* that have defined our current spatialities in order to sustain vibrant Native futures."[41] This insight can help to identify a much broader range of geographical processes that sustain settler-colonial dispossession than we might otherwise have been able to. To name Indigenous dispossession in this manner is not necessarily to refer only or simply to the theft of national territories mapped out with reference to past Indigenous economies and ways of life, but to understand the diversity of present-day tactics through which people are robbed of their lands, bodies, and loved ones. Processes such as these not only destroy traditional Indigenous lands and economies, but also arrest the development of future Indigenous economies and ways of life, including those that rely on urban land and which all working people would ultimately benefit from.

If, as Coulthard writes, "settler colonial formations are *territorially acquisitive in perpetuity*," the shape of settler-colonial acquisition is never permanent.[42] Understanding that settler colonialism is a specific expression of racial capitalism helps us to think dynamically about the shifting racial orders, blocs, agendas, feelings, and institutions that have remade settler colonialism on Turtle Island since the earliest invasions. For instance, it has been widely demonstrated that settler structures continue to construe Indigenous communities as out of place in Canadian cities and to erase Indigenous urban land claims through a logic of *urbs nullius* (the idea that cities are empty of Indigenous rights to land and self-determination).[43] Building from this work by tracing the specific political and economic alliances, agendas, and capacities mobilized to achieve that outcome again and again—something that Indigenous resistance makes far from inevitable—might lead to a more strategic understanding of the dynamic life of *urbs nullius*. It is possible to think about regional accumulation regimes as forces that draw on and reshape settler colonialism, for instance, by looking at how settler-colonial domination and resistance unfold through struggles over urban development.[44] Capitalist struggles to remake cities, regions, and countries, in other words, are processes where the contemporary character of settler colonialism—including the character of race and state—is renovated.[45]

Despite the delusions of liberalism, in which history begins anew each morning—expressed by the popular settler-colonial plea to "get over it"—every effort to reshape the world must contend with the accumulated material conditions, structures, habits, and ideas of the past. As geographer Ruth Wilson Gilmore writes, "we make places, things, and selves, but not under conditions of our own choosing."[46] In Winnipeg, parallels can clearly be drawn between present-day dynamics and classic late-1800s settler colonialism. However, in order to achieve a true understanding of the present, it helps to go beyond such comparisons to trace how successive schemes to remake the city since 1870 have responded to conditions—crises, contradictions, intended and unintended effects—generated by previous agendas.[47] There is a dynamic interrelatedness to each dominant development agenda, and counter-agenda, that is much more than mere repetition.

By retracing the steps of Winnipeg's settler-colonial development tradition, we can see that it has been shaped by resistance at every turn.[48] A series of alternative economic development plans for Winnipeg—largely but not exclusively crafted by Indigenous peoples—have contributed invaluable critiques of dominant agendas and built up a revolutionary alternative development tradition defined by an emphasis on land reform, community control, and prioritizing basic needs. From the Canadian invasion of the North-West to the most recent gentrification frontier, people living at the confluence of the Red and Assiniboine Rivers have repeatedly plotted and fought for alternatives to capitalist development and the deadly inequalities it requires. Following Woods' approach in *Development Arrested: The Blues and Plantation Power in the Mississippi Delta*, specifically Woods' chronology of dominant regional development plans and buried counter-plans, we can trace a series of successive development plans in Winnipeg, examining how they operate(d) as tools of domination, consolidating the power of small alliances over an entire region, modifying the character and function of racism, and thwarting, silencing, and dispossessing the alternative development tradition. Woods' structure is particularly well-suited to tracing the persistence of settler-colonialism. Applying it to Winnipeg enables us to incorporate the effects of classic settler colonialism—its dispossessions, accumulations, and apartheid geographies—into understandings of urban history and contemporary urban processes, challenging the dominant tendency to keep these histories apart, and opening our eyes to the urban colonial present.[49]

1   *Indigenous*, *Aboriginal*, and *Native* are used interchangeably in this book to refer to First Nations, Métis, and Inuit peoples.

2   This book defines Winnipeg's city centre as the area that suffered most significantly from postwar suburbanization. This includes the North End; the West End (including West Broadway); the area in between the North End and the West End, including the neighbourhoods of Centennial, Central Park, and West Alexander; and the Downtown. "City centre" is used in lieu of "inner city" throughout for two reasons: first, to avoid connotations of intense separateness or pathology that the trope of the "inner city" sometimes conveys (see Chapter 4; for more, see Gregory, *Black Corona*, 5). Second, to reject the artificial separation of the residential "inner city" from the commercial "downtown," which is often used to dismiss city-centre residents' claims to the latter (see Chapter 5).

3   Nahanni Fontaine, quoted in City of Winnipeg, "Hansard of the Council of the City of Winnipeg Wednesday, February 24, 2010." For a lengthier discussion of contestations over state funding for Youth For Christ in Winnipeg's North End, see Chapter 6 and Hugill and Toews, "Born Again Urbanism."

4   Theorists such as Audra Simpson and Glen Coulthard demonstrate the importance of charting, as Patrick Wolfe put it, the "continuities, discontinuities, adjustments, and departures" through which settler colonialism "transmutes into different modalities, discourses, and institutional formations" across space and time (Wolfe, "Settler Colonialism and the Elimination of the Native," 402).

5   Williams, *The Long Revolution*.

6   "For researchers, purpose and method determine whether one reifies race and state—chasing down fetishes—or, rather, discovers dynamic processes that renovate race and state" (Gilmore, "Fatal Couplings of Power and Difference," 16).

7   The region between the Rocky Mountains and the Great Lakes north of the forty-ninth parallel, as referred to in the 1869 *Declaration of the People of Rupert's Land and the North-West*.

8   *Turtle Island* is used throughout to refer to the continent also known as North America (see Norma Jean Hall's discussion of the term's origins at https://hallnjean2.wordpress.com/resources/note-on-place-names-red-river-settlement-assiniboia-ruperts-land-the-north-west/). New York City, home to 111,749 Indigenous people, is the largest urban Indigenous population on Turtle Island (Canadian Broadcasting Corporation, "Winnipeg's Indigenous population highest in Canada, but growth rate is slowing"; Schwartzkopf, "Top 5 Cities With the Most Native Americans").

9   I use the terms *development vision*, *development agenda*, and *development plans* interchangeably to avoid repetition.

10   Harvey, *A Brief History of Neoliberalism*.

11   Harvey, *The New Imperialism*.

12   I use the terms *Canada* and *Canadians* primarily to refer to the Canadian nation-state and to people who actively support its white-supremacist agenda, as opposed to referring to a place or to the people who live there.

13   First used by members of the Black Consciousness movement in South Africa to explain the durability of apartheid, the concept of racial capitalism was most thoroughly elaborated and extended both geographically and historically by Robinson in his 1983 book *Black Marxism: The Making of the Black Radical Tradition* (Murch, "History Matters," 35. Robinson, *Black Marxism*, 26).

14 Racialism is "the legitimation and corroboration of social organization as natural by reference to the 'racial' components of its elements" (Robinson, *Black Marxism*, 2).

15 Robinson, *Black Marxism*, 2.

16 By *working people*, I mean the vast majority of people on earth who must work for a living and do not have the option of living off the avails of capital investment. "Race is the modality in which class is lived," Stuart Hall wrote, elaborating the point by stating that, "racism is also one of the dominant means of ideological representation through which the white fractions of the class come to 'live' their relations to other fractions, and through them to capital itself" ("Race, articulation and societies structured in dominance," 341).

17 Robinson points to Du Bois' analysis in *Black Reconstruction*, whereby the failure of white labour to align with Black labour in the US south, due to a culture of white supremacy promoted by capital, kept the planter class dominant and resulted in oppressive conditions for all workers (*Black Marxism*, 202).

18 As Jodi Melamed writes, "procedures of racialization and capitalism are ultimately never separable from each other" ("Racial Capitalism," 77).

19 Robinson insisted that the character of racism shifts in relation to new agendas of oppressive expropriation: "The comprehension of the particular configuration of racist ideology and Western culture has to be pursued historically through successive eras of violent domination and social extraction" (*Black Marxism*, 66).

20 Hall, "Racism and Reaction,"146.

21 Geographers of racial capitalism such as Clyde Adrian Woods, Ruth Wilson Gilmore, and Bobby Wilson build on Hall's theorizing by insisting that, as Wilson writes, "We must situate race, not only in a historical context, but in a historical-geographical context" (Wilson, "Critically Understanding Race-Connected Practices", 37).

22 "A critical geography of race-connected practices requires sensitivity to the way in which regional regimes of accumulation transform racial practices" (Wilson, "Critically Understanding Race-Connected Practices", 37).

23 Woods, *Development Arrested*, 26.

24 The late 1990s and early 2000s scholarship of Woods, Gilmore, and Bobby Wilson addressed the rise of "globalization" specifically and is the source of this observation.

25 "A dynamic conception of how various regional blocs respond to, and anticipate, the general processes of uneven development must be utilized" (Woods, *Development Arrested*, 26).

26 "The state and capital are often depicted as abstract, nameless, and faceless entities. Globalization then becomes the essentialized working out of capitalist rationality" (Woods, "Life After Death", 64).

27 The Lower Mississippi River Delta Regional Commission is the example Woods studied in *Development Arrested*.

28 Woods' concept of the "dominant regional bloc" often refer to formations sometimes known as "growth coalitions" or "growth machines." Woods' framing is more accurate for two reasons. First, it directs our attention toward the conservation of social relations of dominance, whereas "growth coalition" tends to stress only the pursuit of profits, leaving aside the relationship of the coalition to the rest of society. Second, it indicates the continuity of power over time and the reproduction of regional conditions and power dynamics, whereas "growth machine" tends to highlight a post-1970s "entrepreneurial turn" in urban governance as an historical rupture (Gregory et al., *The Dictionary of Human Geography*, 320).

29   Woods, *Development Arrested*, 27.

30   Woods, *Development Arrested*, 40.

31   Lowe, *The Intimacies of Four Continents*, 10.

32   Saldaña-Portillo and Goldstein, "The Settler Colonialism Analytic: A Critical Reappraisal."

33   Recognizing the diversity of racial capitalisms at play, this book is only a partial view into the racial capitalist remaking of Winnipeg because it examines the city's racial order primarily from the vantage point of settler colonialism.

34   In Canada, "colonial domination continues to be structurally committed to maintain—through force, fraud, and more recently, so-called 'negotiations'—ongoing state access to the land and resources that contradictorily provide the material and spiritual sustenance of Indigenous societies on the one hand, and the foundation of colonial state-formation, settlement, and capitalist development on the other" (Coulthard, *Red Skin White Masks*, 7).

35   "The history and experience of *dispossession*, not proletarianization, has been the dominant background structure shaping the character of the historical relationship between Indigenous peoples and the Canadian state," Coulthard writes. "Just as importantly, I would also argue that dispossession continues to inform the dominant modes of Indigenous resistance and critique that this relationship has provoked" (Coulthard, *Red Skin White Masks*, 13). It should be noted that struggles against stolen lives and loved ones—such as movements against the mass murders of Indigenous women, child theft, and police mistreatment—are also often land-based struggles.

36   "Settler-colonialism, in particular, refers to contexts where the territorial infrastructure of the colonizing society is built on and overwhelms the formerly self-governing but now dispossessed Indigenous nations," according to Coulthard. "Indeed, settler-colonial polities are predicated on maintaining this dispossession" (Coulthard, *Red Skin White Masks*, 184).

37   Pasternak, *Grounded Authority*; Goeman, *Mark My Words*, 3.

38   Coulthard, *Red Skin White Masks*, 60.

39   Simpson, "The Misery of Settler Colonialism. Roundtable on Glen Coulthard's *Red Skin, White Masks* and Audra Simpson's *Mohawk Interruptus*."

40   Coulthard, *Red Skin White Masks*, 62.

41   Goeman, *Mark My Words*, 3. My emphasis. Parenthesis in the original.

42   Coulthard, *Red Skin White Masks*, 125. This dynamic conception of settler colonialism is inspired by Coulthard's *Red Skin White Masks* and Audra Simpson's *Mohawk Interruptus* among others. Wolfe described the necessity of charting the "continuities, discontinuities, adjustments, and departures," through which settler colonialism "transmutes into different modalities, discourses, and institutional formations" (Wolfe, "Settler Colonialism and the Elimination of the Native," 402).

43   Scholars who have demonstrated this include Jean Barman, Amber Dean, Sherene Razack, Kara Granzow, Glen Coulthard, Nicholas Blomley, Jordan Stanger-Ross, and The New B.C. Indian Art and Welfare Society Collective. "*Urbs nullius*" was coined by Glen Coulthard in *Red Skin White Masks*, 176.

44   In this sense, this book is less an authoritative account of Winnipeg's past and present and more an effort to open up new ways of thinking about how racism and capitalism have shaped them.

45   Gilmore "Fatal couplings of Power and Difference," 16.

46   Gilmore, *Golden Gulag*, 242.

47   This observation is indebted to Clyde Woods' work in *Development Arrested*. Positioning the gentrification frontier not only as a continuation of the 'ethic' of settler colonialism, but as a continuation of its material force, is incisive because it goes beyond the common tendency to compare the "class war" of gentrification to settler-colonial conquest in the abstract (see Smith, *New Urban Frontier*). In Native cities, gentrification *is* Indigenous conquest, and the erasure of working people's geography and history *is* the erasure of Indigenous geography and history.

48   Winnipeg's alternative development tradition is integral to this book, but it is not at all a comprehensive history of that tradition.

49   This tendency, which places an imaginary barrier between industrial and pre-industrial Turtle Island, implies the disappearance of Indigenous peoples after industrialization and does not perceive Indigenous politics as integral to industrial society. See McCallum, *Indigenous Women, Work, and History, 1940-1980*, 10.

PART 1

FOUR VISIONS

CHAPTER 1

SOWING APARTHEID: THE EXPORT-AGRICULTURAL VISION

How did they get our blueberry meadows
our spruce and willow groves
our sun clean streams
and blue sky lakes?
How did they get
Their mansions on the lake
Their cobbled circle drives
with marbled heads of lions on their iron gates?

How did they get so rich?
How did we get so poor?

—Emma LaRocque, "My Hometown Northern Canada South Africa"

The radical transformation of the human geography of the North-West—the vast segment of northern Turtle Island between the Great Lakes and the Rocky Mountains—between 1870 and 1900 remains one of the most intense regional reconstructions in the history of the continent. In just a single generation, this historical pivot—described by Métis scholar Adam Gaudry as "the moment of a settler-colonial transition" and by Dene scholar Glen Coulthard as "the transition between mercantile and industrial capitalism"—turned the political and economic life of the North-West upside down.[1] More than any other period, these 30 years established the groundwork of the current racial order. It can be summarized very simply: Canada stole virtually all of the lands of the Indigenous peoples of the North-West and gave them to white men. The two questions posed by Métis scholar and poet Emma LaRocque in the epigraph are not merely rhetorical—they are urgent, practical, and crucial to any understanding of racism today.[2] This is the case not only because the original theft reverberates, but also because it established conditions and structures—including cultural traditions of conquest and anti-colonialism—that subsequent regional remakings would be forced to confront.

INDIGENOUS CITY

The North-West was a predominantly Indigenous space in the mid-1800s, home to a complex network of Indigenous nations engaged in sophisticated and longstanding economic and political structures. With its network of forts and trading relationships, the Hudson's Bay Company (HBC) was the primary European player in the area, having been given so-called jurisdiction over the North-West by the King of England in 1670 and merging with its rival North-West Company (NWC) in 1821. Within this context, the city of Red River, at the confluence of the Red and Assiniboine Rivers, emerged as a major economic, political, and cultural hub. Located 70 miles north of the forty-ninth parallel, where eastern woodlands meet western plains, Red River was home to 12,400 residents—9,900 Métis, 1,000 First Nations, and 1,500 Europeans—living in 24 distinct neighbourhoods, or parishes, and many thousands more Anishinabe, Cree, Oji-Cree, Dakota, and Dene peoples who made the city an important part of their lives and traditional territories.[3] It was truly an Indigenous *city*, at more than half the size of Ottawa and approximately three times the size of Victoria, British Columbia, at the time.[4]

Red River was the epicentre of the historic homeland of the Métis nation, an Indigenous nation that emerged in the 1800s through political resistance to the HBC.[5] The emergence of the Métis nation was not a biological outcome of marriage between First Nations women and European men, as it has often been described, but a product of a distinct political consciousness that developed through specific events, the first of which was the 1816 Battle of Seven Oaks.[6] Collective memory of these events fostered a sense of peoplehood in resistance to oppression. The political consciousness at the heart of Métis identity is encapsulated in the term *Otipemisiwak*, meaning "free people" or "people who own themselves."[7]

A city without landlords or bosses. Red River, ca. 1857. Archives of Manitoba, Can. Exploring Expeditions, 1857, 1858, The Red River at Pierre Gladieux's, ca. 1857, 11. (Courtesy of Archives of Manitoba)

By the mid-1800s, Red River was a powerful self-governing community.[8] Democratic governance structures directed the buffalo hunt, months-long Red River cart journeys, and international diplomacy and self-defence, among other activities.[9] No matter how badly it tried, the HBC was not able to enforce its own regime of law and order at Red River without deliberate Métis consent. When the people of Red River found HBC laws unfair, they organized to make sure they could defy them without being punished.[10] Pierre Falcon, known as "The Bard of the Prairie Métis," parodied the colonial assumptions of Thomas Douglas—the so-called Lord Selkirk—in poetry commemorating the Battle of Seven Oaks.[11] "Like a lofty lord he tries to act," wrote Falcon. "Bad Luck, old Chap! A bit too hard you whacked!"[12]

In addition to its political traditions, Red River had its own distinct economic structures. The distribution of resources was governed by cooperation and based on need rather than competition and greed. "[R]ealizing maximum profit," writes Red River historian Norma Jean Hall, "was not as important to producers as was meeting their household needs and maintaining the community's pattern of social relationships through sharing and reciprocal support."[13] It was common for Red River women to do work that hetero-patriarchal Europeans—HBC officials included—considered inappropriate for women, such as farm labour and bookkeeping.[14] A system of property rights determined who could use what land for what purpose, based on verbal agreements and a traditional practice of distributing long, narrow lots—known as Red River Lots—radiating from the river to ensure equal access to the water.[15] Land was freely available for hunting and for subsistence agriculture, and workers generally owned their own means of production and reproduction.[16] In addition to the traditional hunting economy, thousands of acres were under cultivation in and around Red River in the 1860s.[17] It was extremely difficult, if not impossible, to become a landlord or a boss. When, on occasion, an enterprising resident attempted to do so, the people of Red River refused to cooperate.[18] In many ways, then, economic structures of feeling; gender, property, and hierarchy at Red River were radically different from those emerging from industrial capitalism. More than two thousand kilometers away, however, across the expanse of the Great Lakes, events were in motion that would transform Red River forever.

THE RISE OF THE CANADIAN EXPANSIONIST DEVELOPMENT VISION

In 1857, the Crown Lands Department of the Province of Canada released a new map entitled "Map of the North West Part of Canada."[19] As Canadian historian Doug Owram writes in his 1992 book *Promise of Eden*, the map was groundbreaking for a number of reasons. First, the vast segment of Turtle Island it depicted—the whole area between the Great Lakes and the Rocky Mountains, north of the forty-ninth parallel, also known as Rupert's Land or simply the North-West—belonged at the time, in the eyes of the Queen of England, not to Canada at all but to the HBC. Second, the map's creator, Thomas

Devine, had never actually set foot in the area. He based his creation not on first-hand knowledge of the West, nor on knowledge generated by geographers employed by the Crown Lands Department, the Province of Canada, or even by the British Geographical Society. Instead, he drew on existing second-hand information from US sources. Third, despite a total absence of new evidence, the 1857 map was drastically different from the Department's previous representations of the North-West. The most striking new feature was a litany of glowing geographical assessments of the region—casting, for instance, "the scenery of these fertile valleys as magnificent, and the banks of the rivers on either side luxuriant beyond description"—that the Department had not openly held until this point.[20] The map, then, introduced two new and powerful ideas into the Canadian geographical imagination: first, that the North-West was a place of fertility and luxury where Canadians could thrive; and second, that the North-West already belonged to Canada.

The 1857 "Map of the North West Part of Canada" emerged from and emboldened a settler-colonial subculture that Owram calls the "Canadian expansionist movement."[21] "Centred in Toronto and along the Ottawa valley," Owram writes, "these individuals were a loose collection of people who began to look westward in their search for the destiny of the United Canadas."[22] They consisted mainly of capitalists, politicians, and newspapermen—including the editor of the Toronto *Globe*—but also included geographers, cartographers, civil servants, and entire government departments. Geographical knowledge and technocratic assessments of the North-West were integral components of the movement. "[Devine's] map was," writes Owram, "as much a product of the expansionist impulse as was any editorial in the *Globe*." While expansionists tended to be young and more likely to be associated with the Reformers than the Conservative party, they came from a wide cross-section of Canadian society. "What linked them was the cause itself," says Owram, "visions of a Canadian empire of the West within a grand imperial context."[23] Many, too, were linked by an interest in ideas of racial superiority.

Canadian expansionists drew on a 300-year-old European intellectual tradition that sought to justify the dispossession and governance of the Indigenous peoples of Turtle Island without their consent. In *Aristotle and the American Indians: A Study in Race Prejudice in the Modern World*, Lewis Hanke traces the origin of anti-Native racism in the Americas to Aristotle's doctrine of natural slavery, as cited by Spanish scholar Juan Ginés de Sepulvéda in the mid-1500s. At the dawn of the first colonial assault on the Americas, the King of Spain commissioned Sepulvéda to provide a philosophical answer to the question, "How can conquests, discoveries, and settlements be made to accord with justice and reason?" Drawing on Aristotle's idea that certain segments of humanity were born to be enslaved by others, Sepulvéda answered that the Indigenous peoples of the Americas could be justly and reasonably conquered due to "the rudeness of their natures, which obliged them to serve persons having a more refined nature." The counter-idea, however, that the Indigenous peoples of the Americas are inherently equal to Europeans, also has a long-standing history in European thought, most prominently espoused at the time by Sepulvéda's intellectual rival Bartolomé Las Casas.[24]

Nevertheless, Sepulvéda's idea of Indigenous Americans persisted through various shifts within European thought, into the so-called Enlightenment. "Western scientific thought simply took its place as the latest formal grammar for the expression of a racial metaphysics," political scientist Cedric J. Robinson wrote. "Indeed, during much of the nineteenth century, one of the most persistent projects for which Western science was employed was the attempt to demonstrate what was already understood to be the natural order of the races."[25] In the 1800s, Sepulvéda's concept of racial refinement resonated with Canadians who believed, as John Stuart Mill did, that "the English are farther from a state of nature than any other modern people...They are, more than any other people, a product of civilization and discipline."[26] This belief prompted Canadians to think of themselves as having a racial monopoly on political self-determination, and therefore having a right to impose their rule on lesser races. As historian Carl Berger pointed out, this constituted a "racial basis of liberty" within Canada's political foundation.[27] As Gaudry writes, "[F]or Canada to be able to sweep aside preexisting Indigenous political authority, it must rely on a fantasy of sovereignty, predicated on an inherent inferiority of Indigenous political formations that could easily be unhinged from their territories and replaced by foreign systems of power."[28] Without the idea that Indigenous peoples were inherently inferior to Europeans there could be no just or reasonable basis for Canadian expansion into the North-West.

In the build-up to expansion, a new variety of toxic white supremacy sprouted within the Canadian culture. The Canada First movement, a moneyed, white male literary subculture of the mid-1800s, provided a spark to Canadian expansion by promoting ideas of racial manifest destiny over northern Turtle Island. Kanucks, as members of the movement called themselves, were prominent young members of Canadian society—including Alexander Morris, Henry Morgan, Charles Mair, John C. Schultz, George Taylor Denison, William Foster, Robert Haliburton, and D'Arcy McGee—and included poets, scholars, journalists, capitalists, and militia men. Haliburton, an amateur ethnologist, wrote a Canada First bible of sorts, entitled *Men of the North and Their Place In History*. Haliburton toured the book across Canada, promoting the idea that Canadians possessed a superior masculinity unique to the so-called northern races—which he often referred to as Aryans or Caucasians—that made it their destiny to rule over the northern climates of the Earth, particularly the vast expanse of northern Turtle Island. "For these men who had known Canada only as a narrow strip of territory along the St. Lawrence," writes Berger, "the prospect of acquiring the North-West territory generated an indescribable sense of liberation from the past and faith in the future."[29] For bored, insecure Canadian men, who could identify as neither Britons nor Yankees, stealing the North-West would prove to the world "that we will be as our ancestors have always been, the dominant race."[30] Crucially, however, the idea of white supremacist manifest destiny over the North-West—beyond tantalizing Canadian egos—took root within an economic system of racial capitalism long reliant on cultures of racial superiority. White supremacy flowered in the mid-1800s in part because it was used to drum up working-class support for collective action deemed necessary to prevent a set of emerging, concrete crises from afflicting Canadian capitalism.

The material momentum for the expansionist movement came from two sources: first, a worldwide overaccumulation of capital and subsequent search for new markets; and second, the related, growing spectre of a complete US takeover of Turtle Island, which would erase Canadian capitalists' special access to markets and force them to compete directly with US firms. Indeed, events in Britain in 1846–47 set off a period of unprecedented overaccumulation of capital at a global scale. "The outcome," geographer David Harvey explains, "was a sudden paralysis of the economy, in which surpluses of capital and labour lay side by side with apparently no way to reunite them in profitable and socially useful union."[31] The crisis of 1846–47 set capitalists around the world on missions of territorial expansion as a solution for capital and labour surpluses. "The vast expansion of foreign trade and investment after 1850 put the major capitalist powers on the path of globalism," Harvey wrote, "but did so through imperial conquest and inter-imperialist rivalry that was to reach its apogee in World War I—the first global war."[32] While interest in formal empire within European countries and settler colonies varied from decade to decade in the late 1800s, the global economic context of overaccumulation made imperial conquest—formal or informal—a capitalist necessity.

The Canadian expansionist movement emerged from this worldwide search for new markets. Adding to the momentum, the British Empire ceased its policy of "imperial preferences" in the 1840s, cutting off a geographical outlet for trade and investment that had been crucial to Canadian capitalists.[33] With the rest of the British Empire increasingly off the table, most Canadian capitalists turned to the US for trade and investment opportunities. But the overall reduction in available markets boosted Canadian capitalists' interest in colonizing the North-West. The Toronto Board of Trade expressed its interest as early as 1856, viewing the region, as historian Donald Swainson writes, "as a huge extractive resource, designed to provide profit for the businessman, land for the farmer, and power for Toronto."[34] Some even considered it a lucrative trade route to China.

The production of Canadian geographical knowledge about the North-West accelerated exponentially in the years after the British Empire's abolition of imperial preferences for investment. Until the 1850s, little was known in Canada about who or what lay west of the Great Lakes, but it was not generally thought to be promising for Canadian purposes. Especially after 1821—when the two dominant fur-trading corporations, the HBC and the NWC, merged—Canada had very few social, political, or economic ties to the region. "The impression came to prevail that the West was an irreclaimable waste," economist Ruben C. Bellan writes, "too arid for grain growing, exposed to recurrent frosts and grasshopper plagues, fit only for Indians, half-breeds and fur traders."[35] Such racist Canadian views of the North-West as Native space—and, therefore, degraded, worthless, and backwards—were a key obstacle to expansionists who sought to rally their countrymen around the opposite view: that the North-West could be a prosperous, comfortable home for white people.

Expansionists pounced on rumours that a special sub-region of the North-West, a segment referred to as the "fertile belt," held particular value as farmland. In the settler-colonial 1800s, a place's suitability to European-style agricultural production was the primary measure of its potential for so-called civilization and white occupation. In 1856—a year before Devine's map was published—the Toronto *Globe* broke the news to Canadians that "there is a stretch of country [between Lake Superior and the Rocky Mountains] containing probably over two hundred million acres of cultivable land."[36] After circulating a series of glowing yet unsubstantiated reports about the region's agricultural geography, expansionists arranged for Canada to deploy special geographical expeditions to the North-West in order to produce scientific backing for their claims. Two official expeditions were organized in 1857—one Canadian and one British (sponsored by the Royal Geographical Society)—to assess the region's potential for European-style agricultural methods.

The 1857 expeditions were part of a wider Canadian trend of staking claim to the North-West in the 1850s. Also in 1857, a Select Committee was established to investigate the HBC's capacity to carry out the new export-agricultural development vision. The hearings were early rehearsals for Canadian officials who wanted to assert their sovereignty over the North-West. The supposed key to such claims was the Doctrine of Discovery, which Select Committee officials, specifically William Henry Draper, used to argue that Canada justly possessed the North-West. "The Select Committee created a political space for the North-West, or at least its 'fertile belt,' to be imagined as a settler-colonial space," Gaudry writes. "Regardless of the accuracy of Draper's argument, with its underlying assumption that Indigenous political authority did not matter, Canada's fantastical claim to the North-West was adopted as the creed of settler-colonial expansion and the fantasy was disseminated through the expansionist press to the general public back in Canada."[37] The fantasy of Canadian sovereignty over the North-West powerfully guided the politics of Canadian exploration, and therefore Canadians' image of the region.

As such, the 1857 expeditions were deployed for the very narrow purpose of gathering information about the potential profitability of the North-West for eastern capitalists. As laid out in the expansionists' development vision, such profitability depended specifically on the mass-viability of European-style agricultural methods in the region. Moreover, the Canadian vision of transforming the region required the creative destruction of the existing fur trade-based human geography. This meant that mid-1800s Canadian knowledge of the North-West completely ignored, erased, and dismissed the existing predominantly Indigenous social, political, and economic geography of the region. "Both [the British and Canadian expeditions] were instructed to look specifically at those economic questions raised by the idea of expansion," as Owram puts it. "The instructions led to an examination of the potential of the region rather than its present state." Canada's settler-colonial export-agricultural development vision for the North-West heavily influenced the findings of Canadian geographers. "The West was no longer seen through the eyes of the fur trader or the missionary," Owram writes, "but through those of the potential farmer."[38] This was conquest geography.

British and Canadian geographers returned from the North-West with maps of the region's wheat-growing lands, hay-producing marshes, and cattle-feeding pasturelands, analyzed according to soil quality. Many geographers were highly skeptical of the prospects for agricultural production in the "fertile belt." But others, as geographer John Langton Tyman put it, seemed "optimistic to the point of indiscretion."[39] Tyman refers specifically to Simon Dawson, of the British expedition, who seems often to have recorded observations more poetic than scientific, such as this one from just west of Lake Winnipegosis: "It required no great effort of the imagination in weary travellers to see civilization advancing in a region so admirably prepared by nature for its development...to plant cottages among groves which seemed but to want them."[40]

Geographical findings such as these proved sufficient for the purposes of Canadian expansionists, who effectively reversed long-held Canadian perceptions of the North-West as a hopeless wasteland. Alongside the propaganda of the Canada First Kanucks, the 1857 expeditions turned the North-West's supposed fertile belt into one of the British Empire's trendiest frontiers. "In the years after 1857," Owram writes, "the North West became almost fashionable as a destination for the young and adventurous tourist... well-to-do young men from Britain headed to the far west in search of new game and new adventures."[41] The emphasis on exploration and popular depictions of the North-West offers two key insights into processes of conquest, past and present. First, settlers' desires for better lives tend to be channelled toward specific frontiers by those who stand to benefit most from their occupation. Second, as will become even more evident shortly, the state tends to be the first one in; despite popular mythology, the frontier is not the spontaneous product of enterprising settlers but of intense, prior public expenditure to make a capitalist market possible there.

It would take the geopolitical events of the 1860s—namely, the acceleration of the colonial scramble for Turtle Island—to push Canadian expansionism to the top of the agenda. The American Civil War of 1861–65 made the US a much more risky place for Canadian capitalists to invest, and immediately after the War, in 1866, the US terminated its economic reciprocity agreement with Canada altogether. It was only at this point that capitalists in the Dominion of Canada came to view expansion as the best solution to the crisis of overaccumulation. With the closing of trade opportunities in both the US and the rest of the British Empire, Canadian capitalists began to view the forcible creation of a new market in the North-West under direct Canadian control as the most viable path toward continued profitability.[42]

The expansionist movement fomented Canadian fears of a US takeover in the 1860s, casting Canadian Manifest Destiny over the North-West as crucial self-defence against US Manifest Destiny over the entire continent. Without a strong Canadian presence from coast to coast, expansionists argued, the US could seize the North-West to create a contiguous American territory while isolating Canada from British Columbia and making the prospect of total US domination much more likely. Expansionists positioned their development agenda for the North-West as crucial to the future of the entire Dominion of Canada, and thus became increasingly involved in the movement to create a Canadian nation-state with independence from both the British Empire and the United States.

"Canada First" ascended in the late 1860s as more and more Canadian politicians began to make grandiose statements about the inevitability of western conquest. George Brown, a so-called Father of Confederation and editor of the Toronto *Globe*, described the North-West as "the vast and fertile territory which is our birthright—and which no power on earth can prevent us occupying."[43] In response to the HBC's requests to retain almost half of Rupert's Land, the Colonial Office in London replied: "the whole progress of the Colony depends on the liberal and prudent disposal of the land...Colonists of the Anglo-Saxon race look upon the land revenue as legitimately belonging to the community."[44] The creative destruction of the old fur trade landscape—and the Indigenous, French, and Catholic lives central to it—had finally ascended to prominence in Canada, in no small thanks to growing feelings of white supremacy.

Canada's first prime minister, John A. Macdonald, made Canadian expansion a central part of his platform in the new Dominion's first election in August 1867, and reiterated it as a top priority in his legislative program. Macdonald's fellow so-called Fathers of Confederation continued to amplify their expansionist rhetoric. "The future of the Dominion depends on our early occupation of the rich prairie land," avid expansionist D'Arcy McGee warned his countrymen.[45] Canadian expansion soon became the central project of Macdonald's National Policy, and is described by historian John Herd Thompson as "the overall development strategy underlying [Canadian] Confederation."[46] The build-up to the Canadian invasion of the North-West provides another key insight into processes of conquest that would be born out over the region's next 150 years. While territorial acquisitiveness, silencing of Indigenous land claims, and white supremacy are perpetual aspects of settler-colonial societies, the most intense rounds of capitalist conquest are kicked off when political and economic circumstances come together in just the right way. In the case of the North-West, a surplus of capital combined with a foreclosure of outlets for that surplus, which in turn led to the breakdown of agreements between powerful competing interests, and a power struggle resulting in an aggressive round of redevelopment.

After Canadian resolutions on the issue were approved, an "Address to the Queen from the Senate and House of Commons" was issued to request the official transfer of possession over the North-West from the HBC to the Dominion of Canada.[47] The request was approved and negotiations began in London for the termination of the 1670 Charter granting Rupert's Land to the HBC. While the deal signalled the end of the HBC's economic monopoly over Rupert's Land, as well as the beginning of a forcible transition from a fur-trade to an export-agricultural economy in the North-West, the HBC benefitted tremendously from the restructuring. London granted the HBC property rights to 45,000 acres of land around its 120 trading posts, in addition to seven million acres—or 20 percent—of the region's fertile agricultural lands, all without the consent of the people actually living on these lands. In the sense that the HBC never justly owned the homelands of the Cree, Dakota, Anishinabe, and Métis in the first place, the deal mirrored the British decision to pay reparations to former slave owners—rather than formerly enslaved people—as compensation for abolishing slavery in 1833. From the outset, the HBC—one of the largest and oldest racial-capitalist corporations in the world—was one of the biggest winners of late-1800s Canadian nation-state formation and the vast process of accumulation by dispossession that inaugurated it.

COUNTER-PLAN I: THE MÉTIS MANITOBA TREATY DEVELOPMENT VISION

Red River was a city in flux in the 1860s, a situation that created, as historian Adele Perry writes, "a time of radical possibility."[48] The 200-year-old fur-trade economy was in crisis. By the 1840s, buffalo and fur-bearing animals were disappearing rapidly as a result of technological innovation, the region's extended incorporation into worldwide markets, and the genocidal US policy of exterminating the Plains buffalo in order to weaken the Indigenous peoples of the area. In only ten years, buffalo would virtually disappear from the northwestern plains. Entire ways of life that had supported Indigenous peoples, French and English fur traders, and the HBC's profit margin for generations were fast becoming unsustainable.

Living conditions were correspondingly dire. As the HBC became more interested in real estate speculation than in fur trading, it abolished its social safety net for Indigenous fur-trade workers. Gone was a system of credit for people unable to work due to sickness, injury, or old age.[49] In 1868 and 1869, drought and plagues of grasshoppers, thick "as snow in the air and as flakes of snow upon the ground," spoiled the crops.[50] Famine resulted, making residents susceptible to illness and disease; a Central Relief Committee at Red River counted 2,342 people in need of emergency assistance.[51] A smallpox epidemic in 1869 and 1870 killed 3,500 people on the northwestern plains.[52]

Canadian expansionists minimized the importance of the conditions in the North-West. In 1868, Canada First poet Charles Mair visited Red River. In response to the desperate conditions in the community, the young Ontario tourist wrote, "The half-breeds [sic] are the only people here who are starving...it is their own fault—they won't farm."[53] Mair's comments fomented a growing culture of anti-Native racism that would govern the economic restructuring of the North-West in the decades to come. Racist thinking such as Mair's would emerge as an effective way to exclude existing inhabitants from the new development agenda, to dismiss their political and economic claims to the territory, and to ensure the future of the region belonged to white Anglo-Saxon men from Ontario.

Wilful geographic ignorance combined with racist contempt to dictate the expansionist Canadians' actions toward the existing inhabitants of the North-West. The geographical expeditions of the 1850s intentionally learned little about the existing human geography of the region. "In the language of western expansionists," Thompson writes, "the land had to be 'opened' to commercial agriculture and 'filled' with white settlers—as if it had been 'closed' and 'empty' before."[54] The reports of the official expeditions—with their focus on the agricultural potential of soil and climate—gave scientific weight to this sense of regional emptiness and left Canada ill prepared for the actual human geography it would attempt to upend.

Deliberately little thought was given to any potential opposition existing inhabitants might pose to outsiders attempting a dramatic takeover of the region. "We are in utter darkness as to the state of affairs there; what the wants and wishes of the people are—or, in fact, how the affairs are carried on at all," Prime Minister Macdonald admitted.[55] Indeed, Macdonald's first move after compensating the HBC was to deploy land surveyors directly to the North-West. The priority was to make the region's natural resources—rather than its people—legible to the Canadian state through what historian Rod Bantjes has called the "imperial panorama" of the Dominion Lands Survey, the largest land survey in the history of the world.[56]

Indigenous resistance to Canadian expansion was swift. Anishinabe and Métis communities organized patrols in and around Red River in the late 1860s to locate Canadian land surveyors and aspiring settlers and take direct action to prevent them from stealing the land. Métis leaders at Red River confronted Mair when he began to pace out lots himself in June of 1869.[57] And on October 11, 1869, when Canadian surveyors began to measure land belonging to André Nault, Nault crossed the Red River by boat to get his cousin, Louis Riel. Upon arriving at the scene, Riel stepped on the surveyors' chain, informed the surveyors that the land belonged to the people of Red River and not to Canada, and ordered them to leave.[58] The next day more than 600 Red River residents gathered to enforce the end of the Canadian survey.[59] Soon after, Red River residents mobilized to prevent William McDougall—the Ontario Member of Parliament chosen to be the so-called Lieutenant Governor of the North-West—from entering the city. The people then occupied the HBC's Upper Fort Garry and established a provisional government. This uprising would become known as the Red River Rebellion. Building from the Métis tradition of resistance to the HBC, this movement—in combination with the Anishinabe development vision that would be articulated during the negotiation of

Treaty 1—inaugurated the modern tradition of radical anti-racist counter-planning in the area now known as Winnipeg.

The Rebellion was based on the simple yet radical belief that the people of Red River and the North-West had the right to decide the fate of their own community. First and foremost, as the emphasis on land surveying demonstrates, the people of Red River insisted that they continue to determine for themselves how access to land would be distributed. Riel, as the elected leader of the provisional government, emphasized "ancient surveys, land marks, boundaries and muniments [sic] of title" that established existing residents' land claims.[60] Alternative claims to these lands made by people living 2,000 kilometers away were viewed as ridiculous, illegitimate, and violently non-consensual. "We refuse to recognize the authority of Canada," the provisional government of Red River stated in its 1869 *Declaration of the People of Rupert's Land and the North-West*, "which pretends to have a right to coerce us and impose upon us a despotic form of government."[61] *The New Nation*, the provisional government's newspaper, got the point across with satire, comparing McDougall to Don Quixote and McDougall's assistant, Colonel J.S. Dennis, to Sancho Panza.[62] The opinion in Red River, that so-called Canadian sovereignty over the North-West was nothing but a delusion, was an extension of the self-determination exercised by Métis Red River residents against the supposed authority of the HBC for the past 50 years.[63] The HBC did not have a right to rule the people of Red River, so Canada certainly could not buy such a right from the HBC in a London boardroom.

More solemnly, Red River residents critiqued Canadian colonialism as a form of attempted captivity and observed that colonizers' failure to seek consent was based in troubling ideas of racial superiority. "[B]efore seeing our country coerced into slavery," the *Declaration* stated, "we shall employ every means of defence that Divine Providence has placed at our disposal."[64] The critique of colonial captivity drew on Red River traditions of economic equality to oppose the enslaving power of money and property. "I will break the bonded cage/That your moneyed reign affords," wrote Riel. "From the people's boundless rage/Naught will protect your lords."[65] The feeling of being held captive stemmed from being deemed categorically unworthy of participating in the community's future. The *Declaration* criticized Canada and the HBC for negotiating the future of the North-West "by transactions with which the people were considered unworthy to be made acquainted."[66] Deepening his opposition to structures of racial unworthiness, Riel later wrote of "seeing our people daily insulted, and hearing threats by these foreign officials of extermination, in order to make room for the 'incoming intelligent man,' Canadian."[67] Based on this critique, the people of Red River crafted their own radical anti-colonial plan for the future of the North-West.

The plan called for the North-West to remain an autonomous territory—under the new name of Assiniboia—with Red River as the capital city.[68] In November 1869, the people of Red River elected 24 representatives—one from each parish, three-quarters of whom were Métis—to the first assembly of the provisional government of the territory, referred to at the time as the Convention of the People of Rupert's Land and the North-West, and later as the Legislative Assembly of Assiniboia, On December 1, 1869, the members of the Assembly adopted a bill of rights outlining the conditions under which the people of the North-West would consent to join Canada. This list included: the right to approve or reject Canadian legislation affecting the North-West; the continued absence of any Canadian military force in the North-West; respect for the rights of all Indigenous nations; respect for all existing resource management and land-use systems; and support for infrastructure including schools, public buildings, railroads, and other roads.[69] While the assembly was strictly opposed to invasion, its vision for the North-West was open and inclusive. "We will have an influx of strangers here," said Reverend Noël Ritchot to cheers from the assembly. "We want them, and will be glad to receive them."[70] Riel and other members of the assembly concertedly rejected the racist hierarchies being used against them and welcomed the people of the world to the North-West.

Planners of an anti-colonial North-West. Louis Riel and Council, Back row: left to right, Charles Larocque, Pierre Delorme, Thomas Bunn, François Xavier Pagée, Ambroise Lépine, Jean Baptiste Tourond, Thomas Spence; centre row: Pierre Poitras, John Bruce, Louis Riel, William Bernard O'Donoghue, François Dauphinais; front row: Hugh F. O'Lone and Paul Proulx. Red River, ca. 1869. Archives of Manitoba, Zachary M. Hamilton fonds, Louis Riel and Council Bennetto Photo, ca. 1869, Hamilton 1. (Courtesy of Archives of Manitoba)

Canada's response to the now unavoidable fact that people actually lived in the North-West, cared about its future, and were determined to decide it for themselves was to mobilize the "scheme of armed emigration" for which Canada First Kanucks clamoured.[71] In May 1870, Macdonald deployed an expedition of 1,400 troops led by General Garnet Wolseley—a veteran of British imperial conquest in Burma, India, and Sudan—to overthrow the Legislative Assembly of Assiniboia and occupy Red River. Macdonald justified his actions through the classic logic of English colonialism, by implying that Indigenous resistance to expropriation was nothing more than savagery.[72] "In another year," said Macdonald, dismissing the uprising, "the present residents will be altogether swamped by the influx of strangers who will go in with the idea of becoming industrious and peaceable settlers."[73] Racial swamping, more than simply a turn of phrase, would become a key geographical tactic of Canadian settler colonialism.

Meanwhile, the assembly in Red River had sent delegates to Ottawa on February 10, 1870 to communicate its terms to Canada. On June 24, the delegates returned and reported that Canada was willing to follow the assembly's orders. Satisfied with this, the Legislative Assembly of Assiniboia ratified the Manitoba Act—which they referred to as a treaty between nations, and which some contemporary scholars refer to as the Manitoba Treaty[74]—and joined Canada as a new province called Manitoba, with boundaries forming a 260-square-kilometre rectangle around Red River. But Wolseley's troops continued west and the people of Red River, with a force of only 800 troops, were significantly outnumbered.[75] The Anishinabe community at Rainy Lake, to the east of Red River, offered to destroy Wolseley's army by filling the rapids of the Winnipeg River with logs while the expedition tried to cross, but the Legislative Assembly of Assiniboia refused. The assembly hoped the Canadian army would be respectful, but scouts sent to Rat Portage to gauge the expedition's intentions reported that the camps were full of anti-Native feeling, stoked by Wolseley himself.[76] By the morning of August 24, 1870, as Wolseley's expedition marched down Main Street to Upper Fort Garry, Métis troops and leaders had already retreated. Wolseley entered the fort and the Canadian occupation of Red River was officially underway.

Canadian occupiers unleashed a reign of terror on the Métis of Red River, designed to break the spirit of a people committed to self-determination and to expel them from the homes they so vigorously sought to protect. "Wolseley, on the same day of the capture of Fort Garry," wrote Riel, "paid off his men, gave them three days license, thus letting them loose upon our people, whom they abused in their intoxication and disorder, in the most brutal manner."[77] As Wolseley's mercenaries were paid in looted land and settled in Red River permanently, days of terror turned into years. Canadian troops and their civilian allies—Kanucks like Schultz and Mair who got rich by speculating in looted lands[78]—carried out armed raids and evictions while raping, assaulting, abducting, and lynching Métis residents of Red River with impunity for years after the invasion.[79] Residents of Red River who were lynched by invading Canadians include Elzéar Goulet,

James Tanner, Francois Guilmette, and H.F. O'Lone. Canadians chased André Nault out of Red River and left him for dead on the open prairie, although he survived and found refuge with a nearby Métis family.[80] Schultz and three other men raided the *New Nation*, assaulted editor Thomas Spence, and shut down the press.[81] Members of the Legislative Assembly of Assiniboia were imprisoned, including Pierre Poitras, François Xavier Pagé, and François Dauphinais.[82]

The occupation turned Red River into a militarized zone. Most of Wolseley's troops settled to the west of the Red River and to the north of the Assiniboine River—the area that now encompasses downtown Winnipeg. A system of urban apartheid was established as Métis residents were forced east of the Red and south of the Assiniboine, and were met with hostility and violence when they travelled to the other side.[83] Métis residents of Red River during this period organized armed forces, sometimes as large as 200 people, to resist the Canadian occupation.[84] But the ratio of occupying troops to local residents was extremely high, at more than one Canadian soldier for every ten residents. It would take an occupation of 80,000 troops to achieve that ratio in Winnipeg today. Soon after the invasion, Canada established its first military base in the North-West at Red River, and the city functioned as a strategic military stronghold for the Canadian takeover of the region. Thirty-five thousand Ontarians migrated to Red River in the 1870s, fulfilling Macdonald's swamping strategy and transforming the city.[85]

The reign of terror against the Métis people of Red River—which Canada implicitly authorized and encouraged—betrayed the promises of land and self-determination contained in the Manitoba Treaty. Canada delayed the promise of self-determination, sometimes referred to as "responsible government," for the people of Manitoba for years, until Macdonald was able to swamp the Métis majority with Ontarians. Macdonald feared that if the majority Métis province were given full political rights it would elect a majority Métis legislature, perhaps with Riel as premier, that would guarantee Métis land rights at the expense of Ontarians. Instead, Macdonald ruled the province indirectly for four years via a series of lieutenant governors he appointed himself.[86] Only in 1874, after thousands of Ontarians had arrived, was Manitoba permitted provincial self-government.[87] Canadian democracy was racial democracy: Canadian-sanctioned self-determination was effectively for white communities only.[88]

The most important promise in the Manitoba Treaty was Section 31, which supposedly ensured that the Métis people of the North-West would retain rights to 1,400,000 acres of land in and around Red River. This land was to be distributed in the form of "scrip"—vouchers for plots of land to be redeemed by Métis families. But Canadian administrators systematically disregarded the treaty and distributed land based on anti-Métis views, such as those held by Chief Justice Wood, who advocated that settler land grants take priority over Métis scrip so that Manitoba "would fill up quickly with an Ontario population and would yield a profitable return for the money expended on it."[89] According to historian Sarah Carter, most independent Canadian historians (as opposed to those hired directly by the Canadian government) agree that Canada deliberately violated the Manitoba Treaty. "Judicial roadblocks were placed in the way of the Métis who wished to get title to their land," Carter points out. "On nine occasions between 1872 and 1880, the Department of Justice revised what should have been an unalterable agreement." As Justice Wood's comments indicate, Canada viewed Métis land ownership as counter to the new racial-capitalist order. "The Métis were perceived as a strong military people," Carter writes, "and thus a potential threat to profit and to the goal of changing the ethnic face of the province."[90] "There is plentiful evidence," Thompson adds, "that federal politicians and bureaucrats shared the racist contempt that virtually every white Canadian felt towards people of Native ancestry."[91] In the face of a hostile colonial government and bureaucracy, military occupation, and white terror, even those Métis people who did receive scrip often abandoned it and fled west. Through a thinly veiled form of looting, speculators—known at the time as "land sharks"[92]—capitalized on the situation and made off with 800,000 acres of Métis land.[93]

COUNTER-PLAN II: THE ANISHINABE TREATY 1 DEVELOPMENT VISION

The Anishinabe[94] people were not included in the Manitoba Treaty. Several had signed the Selkirk Treaty of 1817 with Thomas Douglas, but this only allowed a small colony of Scottish settlers to occupy limited tracts of land along the Red and Assiniboine Rivers. The Anishinabeg, like the Métis, were navigating a pre-existing regional economic crisis at the same time as they navigated the crisis of Canada's military occupation and preparations for mass invasion. In order to ensure that their nations survived and thrived through a new set of social, political, and economic arrangements developed in response to this double crisis, the Anishinabeg demanded that Canada obtain their consent before developing the region any further. Through a well-organized campaign of petitions and direct actions to obstruct Canadian surveying, wood cutting, cattle raising, and construction of telegram lines, the Anishinabeg forced Canada to come to terms with them in the summer of 1871.[95]

Two thousand Anishinabe people gathered at Lower Fort Garry in Red River on July 27, 1871, to negotiate Treaty 1 with a handful of Canadians representing the British Crown.[96] The Anishinabeg viewed the treaty negotiations as the beginning of a respectful, reciprocal, ongoing relationship with Canada that would be "constantly fostered, re-defined, re-examined, and re-negotiated" as conditions shifted.[97] Over the course of the week's negotiations, the Anishinabeg articulated an extensive, detailed development plan for the region's future. This plan was driven by a desire to maintain access to *aeindauyaun* ("a place that belongs to me and where I long to be") in order to ensure *mino-bimaadiziwin* ("a good life").[98] At the same time, they were guided by Anishinabe principles of inclusivity, equality, and reciprocity in their openness to sharing their territory with Canadians.[99] This spirit of openness, however, had firm limits delineated by the Anishinabe principle of non-interference.[100] Anishinabe negotiators welcomed

Canadians to enjoy their lands as long as this did not obstruct Anishinabe land use. They welcomed Canadians to govern themselves, as long as they didn't interfere with ongoing Anishinabe self-government. In accordance with this principle, the Anishinabe chiefs refused to negotiate Treaty 1 until Canada released the Anishinabe people imprisoned at the fort.[101] "I can scarcely hear the Queen's words," said Chief Ayee-ta-pe-pe-tung at the start of negotiations:

> An obstacle is in the way. Some of my children are in that build-ing (pointing to the jail). That is the obstacle in the way which prevents me responding to the Queen's words…I want my young men to be free, and then I will be able to answer.[102]

The Anishinabe development plan put forth during the negotiation of Treaty 1 stipulated the future of property law, land distribution, economic activity, and standards of living in the region surrounding Red River. With respect to property law, the Anishinabeg dictated that land was never to be bought or sold, never acquired or surrendered, but only shared. "The Anishinabe did not surrender their land in the Treaty One nego-

Planning a future absent of Canadian interference. Anishinabe Treaty 1 negotiators at the Stone Fort, ca. 1871. Archives of Manitoba, Events 243, Signing Treaty #1, Lower Fort Garry, ca. 1871, 2. (Courtesy of Archives of Manitoba)

tiations," explains Anishinabe-Métis legal scholar Aimeé Craft in her analysis of the agreement. "It was not in their power to do so, as they did not own it." When the Anishinabeg asked things of Canada, they did not ask for payment in return for land acquisition, but simply included Canada within the web of reciprocal relations inherent in using the land. "In return for the sharing of the land," Craft continues, "the mother [the Queen of England] had obligations of love, kindness, and caring toward her children, which entailed listening to their wants and providing for their needs, in order for them to have *mino-bimaadiziwin* (a good life)."[103] Anishinabe elders today refer to Treaty 1 as a "sharing treaty" and compare it to the relationship of two people eating from the same plate simultaneously, rather than dividing up the plate into two separate sections. "Let us be clear that sharing," Craft concludes, "did not mean giving up land and resources, but, rather, it meant using the land and resources together."[104]

According to this mode of property law, when Canadian negotiators pushed the Anishinabe to map the lands they wished to retain access to, the Anishinabe outlined nearly two-thirds of Manitoba.[105] Henry Prince, Chief Peguis's son, insisted on retaining the lands guaranteed to his father by the Selkirk Treaty. "Again," said Prince, "I wish to say that nearly the last words my father said before dying were—There is the line—keep it; and we want to retain it."[106] Wa-sus-koo-koon, who represented the Anishinabe people between Pembina and Fort Garry, insisted on ensuring access not only to enough land for the existing Anishinabe population, but for the much larger Anishinabe population that would exist seven generations into the future.[107] The tiny amount of land—approximating the 0.38 percent of Manitoba that came to be controlled by First Nations by the mid-twentieth century[108]—suggested by Canadian negotiators was unimaginable for Anishinabe negotiators. "After I showed you what I meant to keep for a reserve, you continued to make it smaller and smaller," said Chief Ayee-ta-pe-pe-tung. "I have turned over this matter of a treaty in my mind and cannot see anything in it to benefit my children."[109] Such extensive access to land was viewed as a necessary requirement of a diversified Anishinabe economy that would seek to expand existing agricultural production while maintaining longstanding hunting, fishing, trapping, and harvesting production.[110]

This was an economic vision that refused total assimilation into the Canadian export-agricultural vision while embracing new agricultural techniques in so far as they allowed the Anishinabe to confront economic crisis. This was also a refusal of assimilation into Canadian capitalism and an insistence on maintaining traditional systems of production for use rather than exchange.[111] "People were to take only what they needed," according to Craft. "Simple ownership without use was meaningless." As such, Anishinabeg negotiators agreed to set aside smaller plots of land for agricultural production. "[R]eserves were understood to be for use as agricultural lands (if they chose to engage in agriculture)," according to Craft, "while not limiting their other existing resource use."[112] Similarly, Anishinabe negotiators agreed to share their lands with Canadians for agricultural purposes only, and only in a way that would not interfere with ongoing traditional Anishinabe economies.[113]

In order for Canadians to be welcomed and incorporated into the region's web of social relations, and based on the principles of equality, sharing, and reciprocity, the Anishinabe required Canadians to commit to maintaining a certain basic standard of living for the Anishinabe people. Anishinabe negotiators ordered Canada to share in the responsibility for ensuring that everyone had access to the means of both hunting and agricultural production, housing, education, and children's clothing. "Each man is to be supplied with whatever he sees for hunting, and all his other requirements, and the women in the same way," Wa-sus-koo-koon told the Canadian Treaty 1 negotiators. "Whenever an Indian wants to settle, a house is to be put up for him fully furnished, and a plough, with all its accompaniments of cattle, etc. complete, is to be given him."[114] In this way, the Anishinabeg established a minimum standard of living that Canada would be required to guarantee in order to share the land.

This was the Anishinabe development vision put forth by negotiators in the summer of 1871: land was to be shared and not surrendered, enclosed, or commodified; the Anishinabeg would retain access to roughly two-thirds of the land for whatever mix of hunting, fishing, trapping, harvesting, and agriculture they so desired; and basic standards of living for the Anishinabe people, including housing, clothing, education, and means of production, were to be guaranteed. After a full week of discussion, the Anishinabe negotiators—fed up with the Canadian negotiators' stubborn failure to agree to these terms—were prepared to walk away. "Now, I will go home today, to my own property, without being treated with," said Chief Aÿee-ta-pe-pe-tung on August 2, 1871.[115]

There is no evidence that the Canadian negotiators changed their terms in the 24 hours that followed, and yet, on August 3, 1871, the Anishinabe signed Treaty 1. "We cannot know what induced the Anishinabe to change their minds and conclude the treaty after they had announced their departure," Craft writes about the unexplained reversal, "other than to speculate that they were reassured by McKay that their position would be protected."[116] While Canada's written version of Treaty 1 contains the terms "cede," "surrender," "extinguish," "yield and forever give up all rights' and titles," the Royal Commission on Aboriginal Peoples found that "discussion of the meaning of these concepts is not found anywhere in the records of treaty negotiations." "[T]he fact remains that the Anishinabe were never recorded to have agreed to a complete surrender of land," Craft concludes.[117]

After signing Treaty 1, the Anishinabeg continued to claim most of their lands, in accordance with the development vision articulated during negotiations. Whenever Canadian officials attempted to restrict their land use, Anishinabe leaders resisted. In the 1870s, these leaders sent many letters to Canadian officials disputing Canada's interpretation and implementation of Treaty 1.[118] When, five years after the negotiations, Canadian officials tried to force the Anishinabe people at Portage to map out a reserve within which their access to the land would be restricted, they outlined half of Manitoba.[119]

STEALING THE NORTH-WEST: CONQUEST, GENOCIDE, APARTHEID

The Canadian development vision for the North-West radically opposed the Anishinabe plan of sharing, reciprocity, and ongoing relationships between equal nations; instead, it was a vision of racial capitalism built on conquest, genocide, and apartheid. By disregarding both the Anishinabe plan and the Manitoba Treaty and opting instead for armed occupation, Canada commenced a modern tradition of racist conquest at Red River that persists to this day—one in which anti-Native violence came to be felt as key to regional and national well-being. "Negotiations satisfactory to two parties are not possible when power is unequally distributed between them," Métis scholar-activist Howard Adams points out, noting that "Ottawa officials were bargaining from a position of state power, backed by the mounted police and the combined military force of Canada and England," as well as the general economic crisis in the North-West at the time.[120] Indeed, Canada's development agenda of armed emigration and export-agriculture allowed no room for the Anishinabe plan. Instead, it required eliminating Anishinabe claims and access to virtually all of their lands; replacing the region's existing hunting, fishing, trapping, harvesting, and farming economy with farming only; limiting the Anishinabeg to Indian reserves and establishing a regime of private property to criminalize the sharing of the land; and lethally ignoring the resulting decline in Indigenous standards of living. Canada's plan was a radical settler-colonial pivot away from the long history of "mutually beneficial associations...between equal nations," as political scientist James Tully explains, "to the coercive imposition of a structure of domination...in which Aboriginal peoples and their cultures were treated as unequal and inferior."[121]

Apartheid—the forcible containment of Indigenous peoples on Indian reserves—was the ultimate geographical expression of this development vision.[122] For over a decade prior to invading the North-West, Canada had been preparing to formalize a racial geography within its borders. The Gradual Civilization Act of 1857, as historian Sarah Carter writes, "singled out Indians as a race apart, placed them on settlements remote from non-Indians, and provided them with a special administrative agency that would serve Indians only," thus establishing the legislative foundations of Canadian apartheid.[123] Through racial principles, Canada sought to partition the plate that the Anishinabe, based on principles of equality, intended to share as a whole. This was the typical colonial impetus to create, as the French anti-colonial theorist Frantz Fanon famously put it, "a world divided into compartments." Without consent, Canada aimed to butcher the North-West into a non-Native world speckled with small hold-outs of colonially recognized Native space.[124]

This racial geography of apartheid was considered an economic necessity.[125] Canada viewed Indigenous peoples' extensive spatial networks—the distribution of Indigenous lives, minds, hearts, economies, and political formations throughout the entire North-West—as incompatible with both the coming private-property grid and the injunction to maximize the exploitation of the land inherent to export-agricultural and industrial capitalism. Whereas Indigenous spatial networks had been immensely valuable to fur-trade capitalism—the HBC relied on the independent labour and established trade networks of Indigenous peoples[126]—the new economic vision saw them as obstacles to be removed from the path of development, like rocks from a prairie field.

It comes as no surprise, then, that the specific geographical arrangements of Canadian apartheid in the North-West have been called a process of "ethnic cleansing."[127] Canada sought to locate Indian reserves away from areas that colonial administrators considered most desirable for white settlement, such as the so-called fertile belt of the southern prairies and the sites of incipient settler cities. Indigenous nations were able to negotiate the locations of reserves to some extent, but the imperative to push Indigenous peoples away from white settlement dictated Canada's approach to the negotiations. Colonial officials deployed racial logics to justify this, based on the genocidal idea that the reserves should function as "laboratories of transformation." "It was believed that [Indian reserves] would best succeed if they were remote from the rest of civilization," Carter writes, "as it was felt that native [sic] people adopted only the worst characteristics of the surrounding white society."[128] This priority was pursued for decades via reserve location and relocation, as Canada forcibly displaced established Indian reserves wherever white development encroached on them.[129]

In order to achieve apartheid in practice, Canada resorted to the use of force, thereby turning Indian reserves into prison-like spaces. While the Anishinabe were never totally confined to reserves and continued to access a much broader economic and cultural geography in spite of apartheid, the number of sites accessible to Indigenous peoples and the length of time they were able to spend at them was significantly decreased.[130] "We are collected here/Like raindrops in a bucket," wrote Minahikosis (Little Pine), Chief of the Plains Cree, critiquing the new Canadian landscape:

> The piece of parchment says
> We are to stay here
> Like stones that do not move.
> We are to wait for rations
> Like a dog or beggar.[131]

Minahikosis deftly summarized the Canadian pass system, which required Indigenous peoples to obtain Canadian permission to leave the space of the reserve. A network of surveillance administrators called Indian Agents and a newly established police force called the North-West Mounted Police (NWMP) physically enforced the pass system. Canada's new legal and cultural regime of private property outside of Indian reserve boundaries—what geographer Cole Harris calls the "disciplinary power of the land system"[132]—further enforced those boundaries by legally criminalizing Indigenous peoples as trespassers and culturally casting Native peoples as out of place beyond the reserves. Moreover, Canada lethally enforced apartheid by leaving Indigenous peoples outside of reserves to die, refusing them access to emergency relief such as food during famines and medicine in the midst of epidemics.[133]

Imprisonment through apartheid, in addition to pursuing the direct economic goal of Indigenous dispossession and removal from the land, was an integral part of Canada's political strategy for suppressing Indigenous resistance. With Indigenous uprisings and direct action—especially against the construction of the Canadian Pacific Railway (CPR)—increasingly challenging Canadian expansion, exploitation of the violent possibilities inherent in incarceration became a key tactic of Canadian colonialism. In addition to spectacular displays of violence, such as executing eleven Indigenous resistance leaders in the high-profile legal lynchings of 1885, Canada sought to "pacify" Indigenous resistance by breaking the bodies, minds, and spirits of the people it held captive on reserves. This included sexual violence, shows of force intended to terrorize, and the intentional withholding of food and medicine that allowed famine, malnutrition, and disease to kill thousands of Indigenous peoples between 1870 and 1900.[134]

Apartheid also attempted to conquer Indigenous peoples politically by dividing their nations and isolating them from one another. In a 1994 article entitled "Reservation Geography and the Restoration of Native Self-Government," geographer Robert White-Harvey demonstrates the extent of the isolation of Canadian Indian reserves as contrasted with the situation in the US. Whereas "whole tribes, and in some cases several tribes, were relocated onto single reservations" by the US, Canada chose to recognize "only small individual subdivisions of larger tribes, and left these small bands dispersed across thousands of tiny and isolated reserves."[135] In addition to being allocated far less land in total than Indigenous peoples in the US, the result for Indigenous peoples colonized by Canada was a more carceral experience. Adams elaborates on the consequences for Indigenous organizing and worldviews:

> Under these conditions it was easy for white authorities to propagate suspicions and beliefs among native communities that served to ossify their culture. Each Indian reserve and half-breed community was encouraged to think it was alone in its struggle, that problems were unique to each community and of their own creation.[136]

Apartheid further disfigured settler imaginations of Indigenous peoples and fostered anti-Native racism within the emerging settler culture of the North-West. Adams argues that Indian reserves intentionally hid Indigenous peoples from the settler population, making it easier for Canada to spread lies about Indigenous peoples to settlers. In particular, apartheid made believable the genocidal myth that Indigenous peoples would soon disappear forever. The social distance achieved through segregation legitimized the paternalistic domination of Indigenous peoples—including attempts to eradicate Indigenous identity altogether through Christianization and incarceration of children in church-run residential schools—in the eyes of most settlers, according to Adams.[137] While Canada feigned an interest in supporting Indigenous agricultural production, apartheid and genocide took priority. A series of Canadian policies designed with the latter goals in mind arrested Indigenous agricultural development by curtailing Indigenous access to agricultural land, technologies, and markets.[138] Rather than exploit Indigenous labour in the mode of franchise colonialism, Canada looked elsewhere for the bulk of the agricultural labour required by the new development vision.[139] The importation of non-Indigenous agricultural labour—that eastern banks, commodity traders, and railway companies could exploit for immense profits—therefore became a major function of Canadian state power in the colonization of the North-West.

An essential aspect of Canadian settler colonialism in the North-West was its attempt to lure, rather than enslave or indenture, agricultural labour to the region through promises of land ownership, citizenship, and cultural superiority to Indigenous peoples. Canada's primary method for doing so was the Dominion Lands Act (DLA), introduced in 1872 and designed to match and compete with the 1862 US Homestead Act and to formalize a Canadian practice, established since 1869, of giving free 160-acre sections of land to white men in return for their promise to live on and cultivate the land. While a vast amount of land surveyed by Canada in the North-West was in fact redistributed to large capitalist corporations—in particular the HBC, which received seven million acres, and the CPR Syndicate, which received 32 million acres—the Canadian state gifted over 70 million acres to individual white male settlers through the DLA between 1870 and 1930.[140] The administration of the DLA and the recruitment of settlers to the region were crucial infrastructural functions carried out by the Canadian state on behalf of the eastern capitalists who sought to profit from the export-agricultural development vision.

Canada gave free land to settlers in order to generate a critical mass of white land-owning Canadian farmers in the North-West that would benefit eastern Canadian interests in at least three ways. First, their labour would produce value in the form of cash crops through which eastern financiers and railway companies would profit in various ways. Second, with money from selling their crops, settlers would become a new market for eastern manufactured goods. Third, and perhaps most importantly, property-owning Canadian citizens would establish a radically new cultural geography in the North-West where people who depended on and supported Indigenous dispossession, Canadian law and order, private property, markets, white supremacy, patriarchy, capitalist modes of relating to both the human and non-human world, and a range of other colonial institutions and power structures would outnumber— or "swamp," to use Macdonald's language—those who did not.

On this last point, many historians agree that enclosure and commodification of land in general was the primary function of late-1800s colonial development agendas for Turtle Island. Frances W. Kaye suggests that the US Homestead Act and the Canadian DLA were not primarily geared toward turning so-called unproductive land into family farms, but toward transforming state-owned lands into private property. Bantjes similarly posits that Canada's actions were primarily "designed to open prairie space to the flow of capital." "One of the central achievements of the imperialism of the 19th century was the transformation of communal property in land and resources to state ownership and then its privatization to individuals and firms," political economist John Warnock writes. "This was one of the central features of [Canada's] National Policy." Settlers, therefore, in addition to creating value by mixing their labour with the land, performed an extremely important legal function by privatizing the land and inducting it into the capitalist market. They also helped to establish a culture of liberal capitalism in the North-West in which people "ordered their lives in ways that made further accumulation possible," according to historian Kurt Korneski, whereby people bought into economic arrangements that coerced them "into allowing a net transfer of their productive powers."[141] By embodying private property in living, breathing— and feeling—settlers, the state could more effectively destroy and prevent alternative non-capitalist ways of relating to land and each other.

This logic is evident in Canada's attempts to exclude non-Indigenous migrants who practised economies of sharing, equality, and reciprocity similar in some ways to those of the Anishinabe and the Métis. Canada refused to include provisions in the DLA for collective land ownership despite an enormous number of applications for such arrangements from interested groups of settlers around the world, including Mennonites, Mormons, Icelanders, and Doukhobors. The prospect of non-Indigenous collective land ownership in the North-West was demonized by Canadian politicians and newspaper editors as a threat to the country's aspirations for coast-to-coast liberal capitalism. Once again, economic differences were formulated as racial ones, as Canadians cast collective land ownership as a racial threat to the proper white Anglo-Saxon character of the nation.[142]

At times, however, Canada's desperation to "swamp" militant Indigenous populations near Red River overshadowed its commitment to individually owned private property. Macdonald, initially a strident opponent of both non-Anglo-Saxon immigration and collective land ownership, capitulated in the 1870s and gave a number of "block grants" to various settler ethnic groups, including Icelanders and Mennonites, who wished to own the land collectively.[143] These groups' ability to materialize Indigenous dispossession and to practice "peaceable" loyalty to Canadian authority mattered more to Canada in that moment than their particular form of industriousness.[144] Canadian officials subsequently justified block grants as an effective way to manage non-Anglo-Saxon immigration, portraying them as "laboratories"—like Indian reserves—that would facilitate Canadian surveillance and assimilation of non-Anglo-Saxon settlers while preventing race mixing.[145] The Canadian anxiety to "swamp" Indigenous resistance in the 1870s by any means necessary thereby created a distinctive non-Anglo-Saxon geography in southern Manitoba—now home to some of the largest concentrations of Icelanders and Mennonites in the world—that endures to this day.

Settlers were slow to migrate to the Canadian North-West. As a result, Canada worked exceptionally hard to advertise the North-West and recruit settlers from around the world. Much of this work took the form of propaganda that popularized and embellished the findings of the 1857 geographical expeditions and attempted to overcome hundreds of years of European and Canadian depictions of the North-West as a frozen, isolated, unpredictable, Indigenous-dominated wasteland.

Canadian propaganda drew on a tradition of exaggerating the region's charms in order to tantalize settlers into migrating there. In the early 1800s, for example, the HBC attempted to lure a handful of Scottish farmers to the region (to provide food security to the company's employees). The company relied on outlandish claims—that the area was "an Edenlike environment in which groves of bananas and other tropical fruits flourished"—to deceive settlers who in fact experienced sub-zero temperatures, winter famines, and plagues of grasshoppers in the summer.[146] Many of these first settlers quickly abandoned the region in favour of the US or Ontario. Similarly, late-nine-

Luring Anglo-Saxons. The Canadian immigration office in London, England, ca. 1911.
Library and Archives Canada, Ref. No. C-063257. (Courtesy of Library and Archives Canada).

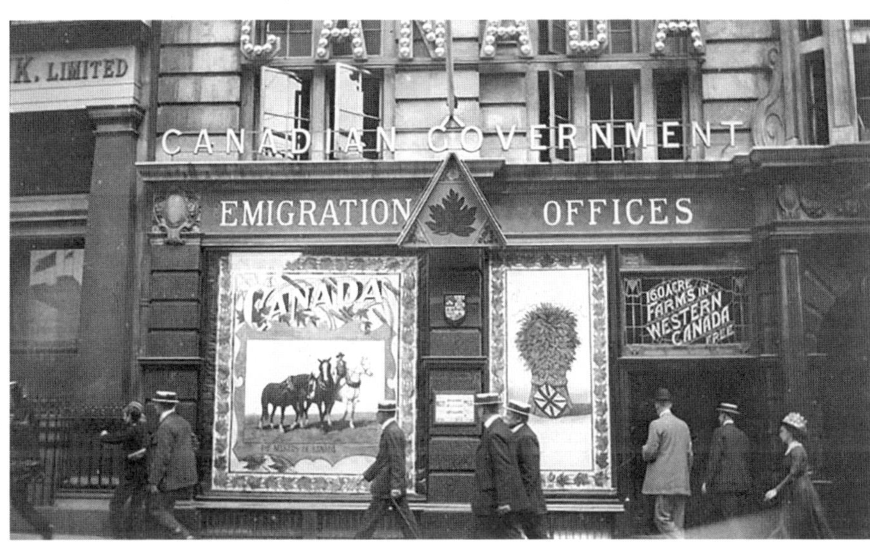

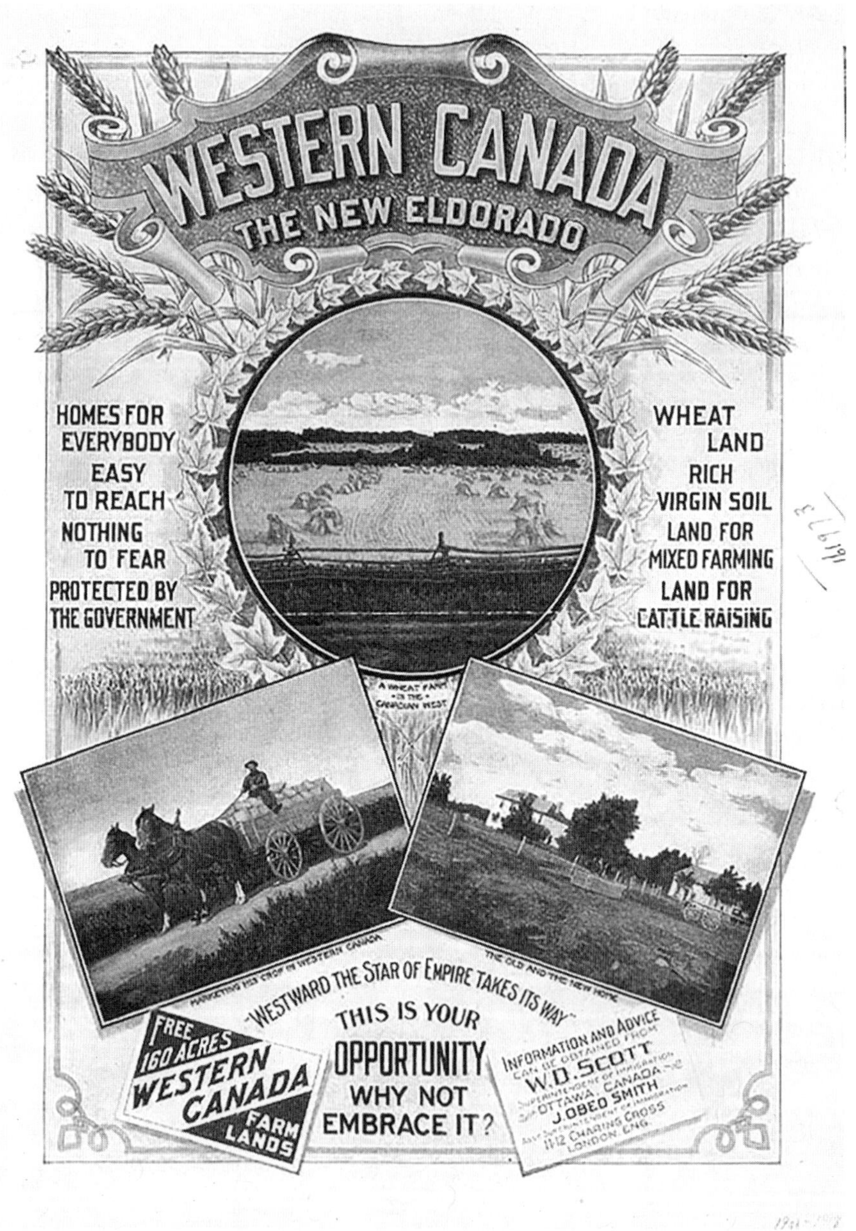

Making settlers. Canadian immigration advertisement, ca. 1908. Library and Archives Canada, Ref. No. C-085854. (Courtesy of Library and Archives Canada).

teenth-century Canadian attempts to engineer the mass-settlement of the region, while not going so far as to present the area as a tropical paradise, did advertise the Canadian North-West as the superior destination of footloose European agriculturalists in the midst of global upheaval and the rise of industrial capitalism.

Government publications from the period promoted European migration to the North-West as a solution to the supposed twin surpluses of European labour and Turtle Island land. "The continuous emigration from the old settled countries of Europe, principally from the United Kingdom and Germany," an 1874 Canadian Department of Agriculture publication began, "to new countries in different parts of the world within the last fifty years, is one of the most remarkable features of modern civilization." "There is crowding in the labour markets, and a large amount of pauperism," the publication, entitled "Information for Intending Emigrants," continues. "Emigration relieves both, while it builds up powerful and prosperous and happy communities in hitherto waste places of the world."[147]

Within this context, officials in Ottawa made their case to European settlers, pitting the North-West against the colonial frontiers of the rest of the world, especially the US. "Information for Intending Emigrants" uses official testimony from the US consul in Manitoba and a Winnipeg-based collector of customs to establish that Manitoba's soil is "of unsurpassed richness...So rich and inexhaustible is the soil, that wheat has been cropped off the same place for forty years without manure, and without showing signs of exhaustion." According to the collector of customs, "The soil [of Manitoba] is believed to be better than that of Minnesota. I believe there is no country where the soil is equal to it." Relatively sober assessments such as these were marshalled to make spectacular claims about the future of the region and of the Canadian nation. "The climates of...the lands open for settlement are among the most pleasant and healthy in the world, and favourable to the highest development of human energy," the Department of Agriculture went on. "The Dominion of Canada must, therefore, from these facts, become in the not distant future, the home of one of the most populous and powerful peoples of the earth...Every immigrant will have an inheritance in the great future of the Dominion, and help to build it up."[148] This type of propaganda, it is clear, was strongly influenced by the white supremacist stylings of the Canada First movement.

With statements such as these, expansionist officials circulated images of a glorious regional/national future for potential settlers, promising them that migration to the North-West meant participation in the ascendance of a powerful, healthful, superior people. One way of doing this was to brand the North-West as the latest frontier of the British Empire. Advertisements deployed British imperial language and imagery in order to foster a sense of white security and connectedness to a distant, unknown, and uncertain Indigenous place. The CPR published maps announcing "FREE HOMES FOR ALL" along "THE IMPERIAL HIGHWAY FROM COAST TO COAST," that featured a collared hand stretching from Great Britain to lay its index finger on Manitoba.[149] Armed with such propaganda, Canada sent immigration agents on overseas junkets and subsidized settlers' transportation costs in order to entice them to the North-West.

The notion that settling the North-West would make Canada one of the "most populous nations on earth" was a pipe dream. In 1883, almost fifteen years after Macdonald promised to "swamp" the region's existing residents, Canada's Surveyor General complained that the area's dearth of settlers posed a serious risk to the very existence of the survey grid. Wooden survey posts, according to the Surveyor General, were being incinerated in prairie fires, carried away by melting snowdrifts, and repurposed by Indigenous peoples (most often for use as fire wood) at an alarming rate.[150] Without a certain viscosity of settlers economically and emotionally invested in the survey grid, the reliability of land tenure—a key infrastructural task of the state—could not be guaranteed.

Canada counted settlers compulsively in the decades after expansion became official policy, accumulating a wealth of census and homestead entry statistics for Manitoba and the rest of the North-West. Before 1900, in an effort to find new owners for the remaining lands, Canada introduced easier conditions on homesteads than those in the US, reducing the age limit to 18, reducing the residence requirement from three years to three months, and making it easier for settlers to annex adjacent lands to existing homesteads.

Even well after the completion of the CPR, Canada was desperate to drum up settlers for the North-West. In 1909, the minister of the interior released *Letters from Satisfied Settlers*, a collection of interviews with actual Canadian settlers, such as this typical exchange with Francis Green, who moved to Minnedosa, Manitoba, from Driffield, East Yorkshire, in 1908:

> Q: Are you satisfied with your prospects in Canada?
> A: Above satisfied. I think Canada a great country.
> Q: Would you advise British agriculturalists to come to Canada?
> A: Certainly, if they be young men who have been farm hands
>   same as we were, and mean to work. They can't help but
>   succeed. There are two chances here to one there is in England.[151]

As the above example hints, expansionist officials made the task of attracting settlers to the North-West much more difficult for themselves by focusing predominantly on a tiny segment of potential migrants from Great Britain, Ontario, and the US, and adhering to a strict racial hierarchy of "suitable settlers." The introduction of a head tax in 1885 on Chinese migrants was the most famous of Canada's officially racist immigration policies in this period, but expansionist officials were openly prejudiced against most of the world's population, citing supposed racial characteristics to explain the unevenness of their activities to promote or discourage the migration of different peoples to Canada.

To justify barring people of colour from the North-West, Canada relied on the same mythical Aryan racial requirements of agricultural capitalism it had employed to rationalize apartheid for Indigenous peoples. According to Canadian thinking at the time, the vast majority of humanity—over three-quarters of the earth's population were people of colour in the late 1800s[152]—was inherently unfit for capitalist agricultural production. Thus, as historian D.J. Hall writes of Canada's most famous minister of the interior, Clifford Sifton, "in his opinion Blacks, Italians (and most other southern Europeans), Jews, Orientals, and the English city-dweller were equally useless because he believed they simply would not be successful prairie farmers."[153] Under direct advice from Canadian Prime Minister Wilfrid Laurier, Sifton drafted memoranda instructing immigration officials to discourage certain racial groups—at times referred to as the "uninvited races"—from migrating to Canada. The following anti-Semitic order was typical: "Our desire is to promote the immigration of farmers and farmer labourers...Experience shows that the Jewish people do not become agriculturalists."[154] Thus, whiteness was associated with a set of practices—sobriety, industriousness, beef eating, and grain growing, for example—that was cast as essential to the dominant regional development vision, and people of colour were systematically barred from the North-West on this basis.

The anti-Blackness of Canada's redevelopment of the North-West was especially egregious given the geopolitical events of the time. By the end of the 1870s, four million Black people on the other side of the US border were being dispossessed and disenfranchised of significant gains won over the previous twelve years of Black Reconstruction. Above all else, according to W.E.B. Du Bois, formerly enslaved African Americans in the late 1800s desired "land which they could own and work for their own crops."[155] So when a resurgent planter class blocked African Americans' access to agricultural land in the south, many migrated to the north and to the west in search of agricultural land. But rather than welcome this mass migration of experienced agricultural workers—landless, persecuted, whose own government was willing to sponsor their emigration[156]—Canada's reaction was to stifle African-American attempts at reaching the border.

While Canada did not impose overtly anti-Black immigration laws, it "effectively throttled" African American migration to the North-West, writes historian Valerie Knowles, "by discouraging private schemes for black settlement and by instructing its agents in the United States to withhold assistance from individual blacks who wanted to emigrate to Canada."[157] Canada paid Black doctors in Oklahoma and Kansas to advise African Americans not to migrate to Canada, took out advertisements to the same effect, and paid border guards a bonus for each Black person turned away at the border.[158] When African Americans did manage to arrive in the North-West—the Black population of the region reached more than 1,500 by 1911[159]—Canadian officials openly wished for them to fail. "The Negro problem which faces the United States...is one in which Canadians have no desire to share," stated Canadian Superintendent of Immigration William Scott. "It is to be hoped that climatic conditions will prove unsatisfactory to those new settlers, and that the fertile lands of the West will be left to be cultivated by the white race only."[160] Canadian statesmen of all political stripes, therefore, applied the myths of the planter class—including the myth that 200 years of slavery had made African Americans unfit for democracy[161]—to their vision for the North-West.

The regional settler culture that emerged from Canada's redevelopment vision for the North-West reflected the white supremacist social engineering with which it was crafted. "The English-speaking Protestant Ontarians who formed the largest and most influential group of white settlers in Manitoba and the territories," Thompson writes, "had no intention of allowing the North-West to become a 'multicultural mosaic.'"[162] After establishing a white settler geography in the North-West, Canada took pains to maintain white supremacy and racial divisions. When, in the 1870s and 1880s, Indigenous nations in the North-West forged strong alliances with white settlers—themselves disillusioned with the lies Canada had told them, and frequently dispossessed by corporate land grabs—Canada strategically divided such alliances by making concessions to white farmers while simultaneously fomenting Indigenous frustrations. This strategy, according to Adams, was crucial to marshalling settler affinities to Canada's side—and selling myths of Indigenous savagery—during the 1885 uprising at Batoche.[163]

Settlers at Red River were similarly encouraged to view themselves as enemies of Indigenous peoples and Indigenous resistance movements. On Dominion Day, July 1, 1885, settlers hung an effigy of Louis Riel on Main Street in Winnipeg alongside a banner reading, "EITHER SHOOT THE WRETCH OR HAVE HIM HUNG." White settlers at Red River possessed, according to Lieutenant Governor Archibald, "a frightful spirit of bigotry...[they] talk and seem to feel as if the French half-breeds [sic] should be wiped off the face of the globe." Fostering a culture of anti-Native racism among settlers at Red River helped to ensure the ascendance of a small, white, Anglo-Saxon Protestant ruling bloc. "After 1889," Thompson writes, "English-speaking Protestants began to ruthlessly assail the political and educational rights that the Manitoba Act and the North-West Territories Act guaranteed to [the Métis]." "By 1920 they had succeeded in eliminating those rights," Thompson goes on. "What was striking about the Prairie West at the end of the nineteenth century was how much it had come to resemble the other English-speaking provinces."[164]

A DOMINANT REGIONAL BLOC EMERGES IN WINNIPEG

"Probably no better idea of the prosperity of the country can be obtained than may be gained by a visit to the city of Winnipeg, to which it seems impossible for writers to do justice in ordinary terms of phrase," the Department of the Interior announced in a 1905 Atlas of Western Canada published "For the Guidance of Intending Settlers." "In commercial possibilities Winnipeg is great," the Department went on. "It has electric railways, wide streets, well-kept boulevards, fine pavements, and the best of other

A new landscape of accumulation.
The first grain elevator in
the North-West, Niverville,
Manitoba, ca. 1879. (Courtesy of
Mennonite Archives of Ontario)

improvements. During the present year about $10,000,000 worth of buildings will be erected, a record which is surpassed only by such cities as Chicago and New York."[165] Although Canada was not able to recruit nearly as many settlers to the North-West as it had envisioned—the number never approached that of the northwestern US—it lured enough of them to eventually transform the area into one of the greatest grain-growing regions in the world. Encompassing much of what used to be Red River, Winnipeg emerged as the capital of the new agricultural empire: buying, selling, and processing the region's agricultural exports and supplying the litany of commodities required by settlers on the northwestern frontier. As the Department of the Interior's atlas indicates, creating a settler metropolis in the North-West was a key requirement of Canadian occupation and a priority for Canadian officials eager to promote their settler-colonial achievements in the region.[166] As such, Winnipeg's urban history has always been intimately caught up in the history of Canadian colonialism.

Canada invested heavily in Winnipeg's built environment in the 1870s and 1880s in order to establish military, political, and administrative headquarters—or a so-called gateway city—for the colonization of the North-West. Substantial federal spending on the military, NWMP, new departmental offices, public works, and subsidies to the new Manitoba government made up much of Winnipeg's 1870s economy.[167] Federal investment in Winnipeg's infrastructure, in turn, created the urban space necessary for a new stage of capitalism in the North-West—one characterized by the emerging dominance of large independent merchants, financiers, and rentiers, and the declining significance of the HBC. Enormous banks, warehouses, and trading floors for wheat and real estate were erected alongside, and often towered over, Canada's new political and administrative buildings.

By the turn of the twentieth century, Winnipeg was home to a ruling bloc of millionaire financiers, speculators, rentiers, and manufacturers—historian Alan Artibise calls it the city's "commercial class"—who dominated the political life of the region.[168] These men, and not the small prairie homesteaders, were the true Wheat Kings of the North-West: investors who bought and sold wheat on the Grain Exchange in Winnipeg for huge profits, railway men who reaped exorbitant transportation fees from small farmers, and the land sharks who speculated in stolen Indigenous lands.

Winnipeg capitalists glorified Colonel Wolseley, the Canadian conquest of the region's Indigenous peoples, notions of frontier progress, and British imperialism. Winnipeg streets were named for Wolseley and for people such as the Scotland-born Donald Smith, who invaded Red River with Wolseley and became one of Manitoba's first millionaires in large part through Winnipeg real estate transactions. To position the city within the British Empire, the dominant bloc named schools, streets, and parks after British imperial figures, erected monuments to British imperial figures and events, and distributed Union Jacks to city residents.[169]

At the same time, Winnipeg's dominant bloc deployed municipal state power—primarily through the police force but also via more mundane authorities such as the health department—to drive Indigenous peoples out of the city. The dominant bloc's apartheid geography cast Indigenous peoples as "inappropriate in the city and constructed their bodies culturally to represent dangers to be controlled and eliminated." Urban areas that Native people frequented most often were the Winnipeg Police Service's (WPS) biggest targets from its inception in 1874. To keep urban Indigenous peoples in their place, the WPS was known to shackle Native people to a 25-pound ball-and-chain or to banish them from the city entirely.[170]

Members of the dominant bloc keenly understood that their vast fortunes depended on colonial violence. Unlike their descendants, Winnipeg's earliest businessmen did not attempt to clean the blood from their money or hide its racist origins behind screens of tolerance and benevolence. Walter Begg, a prominent Winnipeg merchant, foregrounded

Half-Breed Lands In Manitoba

It is probable, according to announcement of the Dominion Government, that during the Summer of 1876, the Half-Breed Reserves in Manitoba (plots of 190 acres each) some 54 Townships, or

One Million Four Hundred Thousand Acres

will be patented to the grantees   These plots, lying near the Red and Assiniboine Rivers, as far as Poplar Point Westward, beyond Selkirk to the North, and near Emerson on the South, make in all the most valuable tract of land in the North-west

The allotment of Scrip (160 acres each) about

200,000 Acres !

to the Half-Breed heads of families and old settlers, which may be located anywhere on Government lands, will also, it is promised, be distributed to them without delay   The greater part of this immense acreage will then be thrown upon a market unable from its limited capacity to absorb it, and consequently will be sold at absurdly low prices   It is probable that these lands may then be purchased at from 30 to 50 cents per acre

A W Burrows, Winnipeg, Manitoba, will undertake, for intending investors, the purchase of these lands, after the issue of Scrip and Patents, and guarantee satisfaction   For this he possesses unusual advantages in his extensive acquaintance with the settlers, through his former connection with the Land Office in Manitoba, when the original census of the Half-Breed and Old Settlers was revised by personal attendance for the basis of these grants   He is also fully acquainted with the value and quality of all the land referred to

CITY LOTS in Winnipeg and outside TOWN PLOTS, also RIVER FRONT, and quarter section FARMS for sale on favourable terms

References :

MESSRS MORPHY, MORPHY & MONKMAN, Barristers, Toronto
MESSRS WALKER & PENNOCK,   Barristers, Ottawa
MESSRS GILMORE & HOLTON,   Advocates, Montreal
MESSRS J H FLOCK, Esq   Barrister, London

Winnipeg land sharks. Advertisement by A.W. Burrows, Winnipeg, ca. 1876.
(Courtesy of Manitoba Métis Federation)

the connection between war and profit in the opening lines of his popular history of Winnipeg, published only nine years after the Red River Rebellion:

> On the morning of Tuesday, the 23rd August, 1870, Col. Wolseley, at the head of the 60th Rifles, entered Fort Garry [occupied by Métis forces during the rebellion]; Riel and O'Donohue had only left a few minutes previous to the entrance of the troops, and thus barely escaped capture. This was the closing scene of the Red River Rebellion and the march of progress was from that time commenced, by the then small village of Winnipeg. The arrival of the troops infused confidence amongst the people; trade which was almost dead suddenly revived, and money became very plentiful.[171]

In this spirit, capitalists took to the *Manitoba Free Press* and the *Winnipeg Telegraph* to encourage popular understandings of the settler city as a crowning achievement of ethnic cleansing on Turtle Island. This narrative positioned Winnipeg, and all settler cities, as the literal outcome of Indigenous death and disappearance. Placing a romantic touch on his article about Winnipeg's rapid economic growth, Winnipeg-based Ontarian E.F. Hutchings, one of the largest leather goods manufacturers in the British Empire, quoted an 1878 poem that reads:

> Behind the scared squaw's birch canoe,
> The steamer smokes and raves;
> And city lots are staked for sale
> Above old Indian graves.
>
> I hear the tread of pioneers
> Of nations yet to be;
> The first low wash of waves, where soon
> Shall roll a human sea.
>
> The rudiments of empire here
> Are plastic yet and warm;
> The chaos of a mighty world
> Is rounding into form![172]

Many members of the dominant bloc had in fact participated directly in the filling of so-called Indian graves, and viewed the city, as well as their bank accounts, as something for which they had literally fought. A handful—such as J.H. Ashdown, John Christian Schultz, George Bryce, and Donald Smith—had been directly involved in military conquest. But it was common for all members of Winnipeg's dominant bloc to swap stories of Indigenous resistance—from Indigenous peoples' demands during treaty negotiations to their direct actions against land-survey parties—that attempted to dismiss Indigenous development agendas, strip Indigenous peoples of their humanity, and reaffirm the inevitability of conquest.[173] They were British-Ontarian conquistadors, armed with toxic ideas of white supremacy and Indigenous inferiority, and perceiving open resistance to their authority as an invitation to violence. When resistance was more muted, they built an ideology of assimilation that blamed Indigenous peoples' circumstances on cultural inferiority and aimed to lift them up the racial hierarchy to the level of white settlers, a philosophy taken to its extreme by the Indian Residential School system.

Because so many turn-of-the-century Winnipeg millionaires forged the "settler-colonial transition in the North-West"[174] with their own hands, their biographies read like allegories of conquest. Take Duncan Steele Curry, who retired—on the avails of extensive Winnipeg real estate holdings—from Winnipeg to San Diego, California, in 1907. After finishing his private-school education and a stint at a coal and railway company in Nova Scotia, Curry travelled to Winnipeg in 1874 and quickly joined the NWMP, pacifying Indigenous resistance and enforcing apartheid. After quitting the NWMP, Curry helped to partition vast sections of Cree, Anishinabe, and Métis lands into private property for settlers as a Dominion Lands surveyor. In moments when he was unoccupied by the survey, Curry found work building Canada's first inter-oceanic railway, the CPR, which upon completion precipitated a boom in Winnipeg real estate prices. In 1884, Curry capitalized: he was named comptroller of the newly incorporated City of Winnipeg and began investing aggressively in local real estate. By 1910, a few years into his California retirement, the *Winnipeg Telegraph* counted Curry among Winnipeg's nineteen millionaires.[175] The Curry Building, named in his honour, still stands on Portage Avenue in downtown Winnipeg today.

Settlers like Curry lived during the most intense and formative period of colonial conquest and economic restructuring thus far in the history of the North-West. In just ten years, Curry participated in almost every aspect of the Canadian expansionist agenda, uncannily laying the foundations—apartheid, survey grid, railroad—for his eventual fortune, which sprouted directly from his involvement in the settler-state apparatus. The final two decades of Curry's life symbolize how a small class of Anglo-Saxon men was able to accumulate vast fortunes through a development agenda that relied on military force, Indigenous apartheid, white settler agricultural labour, and narrow elite control over regional political life. These fortunes, inherited by generation after generation of white settlers, demand a central place in any discussion of the legacies of colonialism.

By the first decade of the twentieth century, the Canadian expansionists' vision had come to fruition. An enormous new market, seized by Canadian businessmen through decades of exploration, propaganda, military occupation, genocide, apartheid, and border violence—a laborious process that would, astoundingly, come to be considered inevitable—was yielding steady returns. Crucially, relations between classes under the new economic system were lived according to a fresh racial calculus.[176] Newly imported agricultural workers were enfranchised and given a small piece of the stolen pie based on a racial identity of white masculine superiority. Thus, they were encouraged to align as white men with the architects, wardens, and primary beneficiaries of Indigenous dispossession: the fathers of confederation, the HBC, the CPR syndicate, and local blocs of millionaires such as the one emerging in Winnipeg. Even as the latter exploited the former in myriad ways, this racial solidarity—combined with the physical segregation of apartheid—kept the new agricultural workers from aligning themselves with those who had proposed alternative economic agendas that would have benefited them more in the long run.

This is the crux of what settler-colonialism did for capitalism in the late 1800s: support for economic systems based on radical commitments to reciprocity, consent, local autonomy, collective well-being, and a right to basic needs such as food, housing, and medicine—non-capitalist economies—was blocked by the nominal inclusion of the new agricultural workers in systems of property and governance premised on supposed white superiority and inferiority of Indigenous peoples and people of colour.[177] Soldiers and police arrested the proponents of these development agendas, but the creation of a landscape of people who had been convinced to accept stolen land and therefore to accept racial superiority, guaranteed that those agendas would remain buried.[178]

With the defeat of the radical development agendas proposed by the Métis and the Anishinabe during the negotiations of the Manitoba Treaty and Treaty 1, respectively, the possibility of a free, just, and humane North-West waned profoundly. It is difficult to imagine the enormity of this crossroads, just 150 years later. In *Black Reconstruction in America, 1860–1880*, Du Bois asks if it is possible to truly imagine another late-1800s radical transformation of the human geography of Turtle Island. "Can we imagine this spectacular revolution?" Du Bois asks, recalling the sudden freeing, in 1865, of four million enslaved Black people in the US South. "Not, of course, unless we think of these people as human beings like ourselves," he answers. "Not unless, assuming this common humanity, we conceive ourselves in a position where we are chattels and real estate, and then suddenly in a night become 'thenceforward and forever free.'"[179] A simi-lar, if reversed, strength of imagination is necessary in order to conceive the depth of unfreedom established almost overnight in the North-West. It was the unfreedom of living in a vast, free world that had—relatively speaking—been vast and free forever, and one morning being invaded by a foreign army, driven away, confined to a tiny patch of land, kidnapped by priests, and monitored by foreign agents while the rest of the world is fenced-off into other tiny rectangles and, to top it off, filled with strangers who are unfathomably hostile. Meanwhile, as the Anishinabe and the Métis struggled under conditions of such extreme captivity, Winnipeg's dominant bloc began to plan a new round of accumulation that would renovate the regional racial order and spark its own radical counter visions.

1   Gaudry, "Fantasies of Sovereignty: Deconstructing British and Canadian Claims to Ownership of the Historic North-West," 47; Coulthard, *Red Skin White Masks*, 12.

2   I follow Ruth Wilson Gilmore's definition of racism as "group-differentiated vulnerability to premature death" ("Abolition Geography and the Problem of Innocence," 439).

3   Swan, "Robert A. Davis: 1874–1878"; Aimeé Craft, personal communication.

4   Wilson and Center, *Frontier Farewell*.

5   Andersen, "*Métis*," 109.

6   Andersen "*Métis*," 111.

7   Hall, *A Casualty of Colonialism*, Introduction.

8   Andersen, "*Métis*," 124.

9   Howard, *Strange Empire*, 112.

10   Friesen, et al., "Justice Systems and Manitoba's Aboriginal People."

11   MacLeod, *Songs of Old Manitoba*, 8.

12   Falcon, "The Battle of Seven Oaks" (in MacLeod, *Songs of Old Manitoba*, 8).

13   Hall, *A Casualty of Colonialism*, Chapter One.

14   Hall, *A Casualty of Colonialism*, Chapter One.

15   Burley, "The Emergence of the Premiership, 1870–1874," 19.

16   Hall, *A Casualty of Colonialism*, Chapter One.

17   Daschuk, *Clearing the Plains*, 95.

18   Hall, *A Casualty of Colonialism*, Chapter One.

19   High resolution image of Devine's map under Creative Commons license is available here: http://digitalarchive.mcmaster.ca/islandora/object/macrepo%3A32263.

20   Owram, *Promise of Eden*.

21   Owram, *Promise of Eden*.

22   Owram, "The Promise of the West as Settlement Frontier," 4.

23   Owram, "The Promise of the West as Settlement Frontier," 5; 4.

24   Hanke, *Aristotle and the American Indians*, 41.

25   Robinson, *Black Marxism*, 76.

26   Mill, *The Subjection of Women*, as quoted in Valverde, *The Age of Light, Soap, and Water*, 105.

27   Berger, *The Sense of Power*, 118.

28   Gaudry, "Fantasies of Sovereignty," 47.

29   Berger, *The Sense of Power*, 52.

30   Mair Papers, Denison to Mair, March 10, 1869, as quoted in Berger *The Sense of Power*, 56.

31   Harvey, *The Condition of Postmodernity*, 260.

32   Harvey, *The Condition of Postmodernity*, 264.

   33   Friesen, *The Canadian Prairies*, 163.

34   Swainson, "Canada Annexes the West," 65–66.

35   Bellan, *Winnipeg, First Century*, 4.

36   Owram, "The Promise of the West as Settlement Frontier," 5.

37   Gaudry, "Fantasies of Sovereignty," 57, 61.

38   Owram, "The Promise of the West as Settlement Frontier," 11.

39   Tyman, *By Section, Township and Range*, 11.

40   Ibid.

41   Owram, "The Promise of the West as Settlement Frontier," 9.

42   Sarah Carter explains that Canadian expansion was designed primarily as a scheme for capital accumulation "conceived by a predominantly commercial elite in central Canada who wished to see the West exploited as a means of ensuring the viability of their own region" (*Lost Harvests*, 22).

43   Canadian Broadcasting Corporation, "Canada Buys Rupert's Land."

44   Martin, *Dominion Lands Policy*, 217.

45   Wilson and Center, *Frontier Farewell*, 32.

46   Thompson, *Forging the Prairie West*, 51.

47   Wilson and Center, *Frontier Farewell*, 32–33.

48   Perry, *Colonial Relations*, ix.

49   Daschuk, *Clearing the Plains*, 93; Ray, et al, *Bounty and Benevolence*, 46–47.

50   Begg, *Begg's Red River Journal*, 188.

51   Stanley, *Louis Riel*, 50.

52   Daschuk, *Clearing the Plains*, 80.

53   Owram, "The Promise of the West as Settlement Frontier," 10.

54   Thompson, *Forging the Prairie West*, 51.

55   Wilson and Center, *Frontier Farewell*, 50.

56   Bantjes, *Improved Earth*.

57   Stanley, *Louis Riel*, 55; Morris, *The Treaties of Canada with the Indians*, 25–26.

58   MacLeod, *Songs of Old Manitoba*, 32

59   Riel, October 3, 1870, in Huel and Stanley, *The Collected Writings of Louis Riel, Volume 1*, 112.

60   Riel, letter to US President Ulysses S. Grant on October 3, 1870, in Huel and Stanley *The Collected Writings of Louis Riel, Volume 1*, 111.

61   Representatives of the people in Council assembled at Upper Fort Garry, *Declaration of the People of Rupert's Land and the North-West*, 1.

62   *The New Nation*, "Our Canadian Heroes."

63   Gaudry, "Fantasies of Sovereignty," 60.

64   Representatives of the people in Council assembled at Upper Fort Garry, *Declaration of the People of Rupert's Land and the North-West*, 1.

65   Riel, "You Are Like the Trembling Seed."

66   Representatives of the people in Council assembled at Upper Fort Garry, *Declaration of the People of Rupert's Land and the North-West*, 1.

67   Riel, letter to US President Ulysses S. Grant on October 3, 1870, in Huel and Stanley, *The Collected Writings of Louis Riel, Volume 1*, 111.

68   Riel, 4 March 1870, in Oliver, *The Canadian North-West, its early development and legislative records*, 914.

69   Howard, *Strange Empire*, 130–131.

70   Hall, *A History of the Legislative Assembly of Assiniboia*, 23.

71   G.T. Denison, as quoted in Berger, *The Sense of Power*, 57.

72   Robinson, *Black Marxism*, 187.

73   Wilson and Center, *Frontier Farewell*, 51.

74   Craft, *Breathing Life into the Stone Fort Treaty*, 42; Gaudry, "'Free Men Consenting to Unite with Canada': Métis-Canadian Negotiations and the Manitoba Treaty of 1870."

75   MacLeod, *Songs of Old Manitoba*, 56.

76   Howard, *Strange Empire*, 206, 202

77   Riel, October 3, 1870, in Huel and Stanley, *The Collected Writings of Louis Riel, Volume 1*, 116.

78   Stanley, *Louis Riel*, 55.

79   Howard, *Strange Empire*, 210; Riel, October 3, 1870, in Huel and Stanley, *The Collected Writings of Louis Riel, Volume 1*, 116; Hall, *Aftermath: The 'Reign of Terror.'*

80   Riel, October 3, 1870, in Huel and Stanley, *The Collected Writings of Louis Riel, Volume 1*, 116; January 3, 1873, in Huel and Stanley, *The Collected Writings of Louis Riel, Volume 1*, 250; and Howard, *Strange Empire*, 210.

81   Hall, *Aftermath: The 'Reign of Terror.'*

82   Hall, *A History of the Legislative Assembly of Assiniboia*, 21.

83   Swan, *Robert A. Davis: 1874–1878*, 32.

84   Bumsted, "The Emergence of the Premiership, 1870–1874," 9.

85   Swan, *Robert A. Davis: 1874–1878*, 51.

86   Swan, *Robert A. Davis: 1874–1878*, 34.

87   Burley, *The Emergence of the Premiership, 1870–1874*, 4.

88   The term *Herrenvolk* democracy—in which a master race possesses democratic rights while dominated races are ruled tyrannically—applies here.

89   Chartrand, *Manitoba's Metis Settlement Scheme of 1870*, 7.

90   Carter, *Aboriginal People and Colonizers of Western Canada*, 109.

91   Thompson, *Forging the Prairie West*, 57.

92   Burley, *The Emergence of the Premiership, 1870–1874*, 20–21.

93   Carter, *Aboriginal People and Colonizers of Western Canada*.

94   *Anishinabe* is a broad term that encompasses multiple nations and communities. While late-1800s Red River was also Cree, Oji-Cree, Dakota, and Dene territory, the Indigenous negotiators of Treaty 1 all came from nations and communities now known as Anishinabe. It is important to recognize that Treaty 1 and Manitoba Treaty negotiations with Canada took place in the context of Anishinabe and Métis peoples' pre-existing diplomatic relations with the other Indigenous nations present in and around Red River (Aimée Craft, personal communication).

95   Miller, *Compact, Contract, Covenant*, 153–156; Morris, *The Treaties of Canada with the Indians*, 25–26.

96   Craft, *Breathing Life into the Stone Fort Treaty*, 48.

97   Craft, *Breathing Life into the Stone Fort Treaty*, 113; Borrows, *Negotiating Treaties and Land Claims*, 191.

98   Johnston, *Honour Earth Mother*, 147

99   Brown and Grey, *A. Irving Hallowell—Contributions to Ojibwe Studies*, 451; Pratt et al, *Untuwe Pi Kin He—Who We Are*, 13 and 30.

100   Craft, *Breathing Life into the Stone Fort Treaty*, 60.

101   Craft, *Breathing Life into the Stone Fort Treaty*, 82.

102   As quoted in Craft, *Breathing Life into the Stone Fort Treaty*, 75.

103   Little Bear, Aboriginal Rights and the Canadian 'Grundnorm,' 247; Brown and Grey, *A. Irving Hallowell—Contributions to Ojibwe Studies*, 150; Craft, *Breathing Life into the Stone Fort Treaty*, 60, 112.

104   Craft, *Breathing Life into the Stone Fort Treaty*, 61; Courchene, "Treaty 1"; Craft, *Breathing Life into the Stone Fort Treaty*, 110.

105   Hall, "'A Serene Atmosphere'? Treaty One Revisited," see record of Treaty One negotiations in appendix.

106   Craft, *Breathing Life into the Stone Fort Treaty*, 58.

107   Craft, *Breathing Life into the Stone Fort Treaty*, 56; Courchene, "Treaty 1."

108   Manitoba Indian Brotherhood, *Wahbung*.

109   *The Manitoban* 1871, 30.

110   Craft, *Breathing Life into the Stone Fort Treaty*, 51.

111   Pratt et al, *Untuwe Pi Kin He—Who We Are*, 29; Brown and Grey, *A. Irving Hallowell—Contributions to Ojibwe Studies*, 451.

112   Craft, *Breathing Life into the Stone Fort Treaty*, 97, 111.

113   Craft, *Breathing Life into the Stone Fort Treaty*, 61; Courchene, "Treaty 1"; Nelson, "RCAP submissions," 213.

114   As quoted in Craft, *Breathing Life into the Stone Fort Treaty*, 59.

115   *The Manitoban* 1871, 30.

116   Craft, *Breathing Life into the Stone Fort Treaty*, 112.

117   Royal Commission on Aboriginal Peoples, *Report of the Royal Commission on Aboriginal Peoples, Volume 1*; Craft, *Breathing Life into the Stone Fort Treaty*, 112.

118   Craft, *Breathing Life into the Stone Fort Treaty*, 103.

119   Morris, *The Treaties of Canada with the Indians*, 129.

120   Adams, *Prison of Grass*.

121   James Tully, "Aboriginal Peoples: Negotiating Reconciliation," 419.

122   Nearly a century later, the architects of South African apartheid looked to Canadian apartheid for inspiration. See Bannerji, "Geography Lessons: On Being an Insider/Outsider to the Canadian Nation."

123   Carter *Lost Harvests*, 25.

124   Fanon, *Wretched of the Earth*, 3; Harris, *Making Native Space*, xxiv.

125   Coulthard, *Red Skin White Masks*, 12.

126   Perry, *Colonial Relations*, 28.

127   Daschuk, *Clearing the Plains*, 123.

128   Carter, *Lost Harvests*, 24

129   Daschuk, *Clearing the Plains*, 123; Stanger-Ross, "Municipal Colonialism in Vancouver"; Tough, *As Their Natural Resources Fail*, 151.

130   Harris, *Making Native Space*, 289.

131   As quoted in Scofield, *Louis: The Heretic Poems*, 51.

132   Harris, *Making Native Space*, 289

133   Daschuk, *Clearing the Plains*, 122.

134   Daschuk, *Clearing the Plains*, 108, 185, 156.

135   White-Harvey, "Reserve Geography and the Restoration of Native Self-Government," 590.

136   Adams, *Prison of Grass*, 35.

137   Adams, *Prison of Grass*, 37.

138   Carter, *Lost Harvests*; Vowel, *Indigenous Writes*, 206.

139   Coulthard, *Red Skin White Masks*, 12.

140   Lambrecht, *The Administration of Dominion Lands, 1870–1930*.

141   Kaye, *Goodlands*; Bantjes, *Improved Earth*; Warnock, "The National Policy and 19th Century Imperialism and Colonialism," 148; and Korneski, "Britishness, Canadianness, Class, and Race," 174.

142   Eyford, *White Settler Reserve*, 55, 62

143   Eyford, *White Settler Reserve*, 66

144   Antwi, *Faithful Bodies and their Affective Currencies in the Black Atlantic*.

145   Eyford, *White Settler Reserve*, 10, 56.

146   Manitoba, *The Red River Settlement*, 10.

147   Department of Agriculture, "Information for Intending Emigrants," 7.

148   Department of Agriculture, "Information for Intending Emigrants," 46, 50, 11.

149   Thompson, *Forging the Prairie West*, 54.

150   Bantjes, "The Dominion Survey as Imperial Panorama: Inscriptions and Counter-Inscriptions," 5.

151   Minister of the Interior, "Prosperity Follows Settlement in Any Part of Canada: Letters from Satisified Settlers," 8.

152   Du Bois, *Black Reconstruction in America, 1860–1880*, 197.

153   Hall, "Clifford Sifton: Immigration and Settlement Policy, 1896–1905," 295.

154   Maynard, *Policing Black Lives*, 36, 296.

155   Du Bois, *Black Reconstruction in America, 1860–1880*, 123.

156   Ibid., 149.

157   Knowles, *Strangers At Our Gates*, 118.

158   Maynard, *Policing Black Lives*, 35.

159   Knowles, *Strangers At Our Gates*, 118.

160   Scott cited in Knowles, *Strangers At Our Gates*, 118.

161   Knowles, *Strangers At Our Gates*, 117.

162   Thompson, *Forging the Prairie West*, 69.

163   Adams, "Causes of the 1885 Struggle," 79.

164   Thompson, *Forging the Prairie West*, 61, 57, 69.

165   Minister of the Interior, "Twentieth Century Canada And Atlas of Western Canada," 8–9.

166   Also see Perry, *Aqueduct*.

167   Bellan, *Winnipeg, First Century*, 9.

168   Thirty-seven of Winnipeg's first 41 mayors were business owners, and the other four were classified as "professionals." In 1910, the majority of Winnipeg's nineteen millionaires held positions at city hall. All but five of over 500 elected officials between 1874 and 1914 were Anglo-Saxon Protestants. Virtually all resided in the city's wealthy south end (see Toews, "Winnipeg Free for All," 4).

169   Korneski, "Britishness, Canadianness, Class, and Race," 166.

170   Burley, "Rooster Town," 10, 11.

171   Begg and Nursey, *Ten Years in Winnipeg*, 3.

172   Whittier, *Poems of John Greenleaf Whittier*, 141.

173   Korneski, "Britishness, Canadianness, Class, and Race," 172, 178.

174   Gaudry, "Fantasies of Sovereignty," 47.

175   Bumsted, *Dictionary of Manitoba Biography*, 61; Bryce, *A History of Manitoba*, 402.

176   "Race is the modality in which class is lived" (Hall et al., *Policing the Crisis*, 394).

177   Cedric J. Robinson called these the "paltry dividends" of white supremacy (Robinson, *Forgeries of Memory and Meaning*, 126).

178   "The purpose of racism is to control the behavior of white people, not Black people. For Blacks, guns and tanks are sufficient" (Otis Madison, quoted in Robinson, *Forgeries of Memory and Meaning*, 82).

179   Du Bois, *Black Reconstruction in America, 1860–1880*, 121.

CHAPTER 2

RECONSTRUCTION: CONQUERING THE RED URBAN INDUSTRIAL VISION

At the dawn of Canada's subjugation of the North-West, the first city of the new era emerged at the edge of the plains, engulfing the well-worn paths, fresh ashes, and surviving traces of the Red River settlement. The new frontier town, dubbed Winnipeg, functioned as the local capital of the occupation: the place where aspiring settlers gathered, colonization was administered, and the spoils of conquest were bought and sold. Almost immediately, however, a new economic agenda would add to this palimpsest and transform both the city and the regional racial order.

Winnipeg's first dominant bloc, though it emerged from the eastern capitalists who designed the Canadian expansionist agenda, soon crafted a local agenda that diverged from the original expansionist vision in one important respect: rather than merely providing a rural market for goods produced in eastern cities, the regional bloc would industrialize the North-West, manufacture the commodities itself, and capture profits that would otherwise have flowed east. Executing this vision hinged on the bloc's ability to restructure Winnipeg from a mercantile and administrative centre to an industrial city. Industrializing Winnipeg was viewed as the key to expanding profits not only for those who would become factory owners, wholesalers, and railroad magnates, but also for those invested in finance, real estate, and virtually all other modes of capital accumulation in the region.

The crucial first step in this vision was to ensure that the proposed transcontinental Canadian railway would cross the Red River at Winnipeg. Winnipeg's merchants, land speculators, financiers, and industrialists envisioned Winnipeg as a central hub—"the Chicago of the North"—in the emerging continental rail network. The settlement's strategic position at the eastern edge—"the gateway"—of the Prairie West would enable it to provide all the goods required for the westward occupation of settlers; in turn, Winnipeg would process the grain and other exports produced by prairie farmers, sending it eastward around the world.[1]

The dominant bloc's first organized efforts were thus directed at attracting the main line of the Canadian Pacific Railway to Winnipeg. In 1874, Prime Minister Alexander Mackenzie announced that the CPR would not cross the Red River at Winnipeg but at Selkirk. The City of Winnipeg was incorporated as a municipality in the same year, and local powerbrokers soon put their new powers of taxation toward lobbying Ottawa and the CPR Syndicate (a group of eastern capitalists awarded the federal contract to build a transcontinental railroad) for a route change. A Citizen's Railway Committee was formed to draft petitions and send businessmen and the mayor to Ottawa to plead Winnipeg's case. The committee promised the CPR Syndicate a suite of publicly financed incentives, and in the end paid a significant price: "exemption from taxation forever to all Canadian Pacific Railway property, the grant of free land for a passenger station and $200,000 in cash, as well as the construction of a $300,000 bridge over the Red River."[2] The CPR Syndicate held Winnipeg hostage, in effect, for free land, free infrastructure, a big grant, and massive tax breaks, and Winnipeg capitalists—who stood to profit immensely—were happy to pay the ransom with public money, foreshadowing a long tradition of transferring public wealth into the accounts of distant investors.

The arrival—at least on paper—of the CPR mainline "has given an impetus to our progress, has enhanced greatly the value of every foot of real property in Winnipeg and has encouraged us to spend over one million dollars on building operations within the last year," the Winnipeg-based *Manitoba Free Press* announced. Indeed, after the CPR announcement, the city experienced a real estate boom that made landowning members of the dominant bloc instant millionaires. Rumours of Winnipeg's new millionaire dandies—donning $5,000 sealskin coats and bathing in champagne—spread quickly. In 1872, "the poorest inhabitant seemed willing to give anyone a lot or an acre," according to W.J. Healy, Associate Editor of the *Manitoba Free Press*. "And now land on Main Street, and the streets adjoining, is held at higher figures than in the centre of Toronto; and Winnipeggers in referring to the future, never make comparisons with any city smaller than Chicago."[3]

RENOVATING THE RACIAL ORDER

Following the completion of the railroad, Winnipeg transitioned rapidly from a small merchant-based economy to a booming manufacturing and wholesaling economy for which an industrial city of factories and warehouses was constructed around Winnipeg's new rail yards. With the railroad in place and surplus capital in abundance, all Winnipeg industrialists required were workers. In Winnipeg, as in the rest of the Americas, Indigenous genocide and apartheid forced capitalists to go to great lengths to find and import new sources of labour.[4] Since the Prairie export-agricultural agenda depended on providing free land to white working-class settlers, strictly limiting Black and Asian immigration, and allowing Indigenous peoples to die from disease and starvation while forcing survivors to remain on Indian Reserves—all of which worked directly against the creation of an urban proletariat—Winnipeg industrialists looked elsewhere for a new urban working class. Their search was aided by the arrival of a key ally in Ottawa.

In 1896, Brandon, Manitoba-based land speculator, money lender, and newspaper owner Clifford Sifton (with a summer home in the Lake of the Woods and a position in the Winnipeg-based Manitoba Legislative Assembly) became the first member of the new Prairie West elite to become the federal minister of the interior. He was placed in charge of national immigration policy, Indian policy, and Dominion Lands policy, arguably making him the single human being with the most power over the future of the region.

Sifton was an impassioned regional booster and leader of a new generation of western expansionists with actual ties to the region. Sifton's biographer, D.J. Hall, writes that Sifton "saw himself partly as a missionary called to renew eastern Canada's faith in the possibilities of the West." [5] In this sense, Sifton and others like him sought to convince eastern Canadian powerbrokers of their responsibility to follow through on the decision made by their fathers to conquer and annex the west. For Sifton, this meant major investment in repopulating the Prairie West through immigration.

While WASPs from the UK and US remained the immigrants of choice for nearly all Canadian politicians and businessmen, this thin slice of humanity was not sufficient to meet growing regional and national demands for labour. Sifton, like most of his peers, was a virulent white supremacist: he supported a $250 "Oriental head tax"; language tests designed to eliminate Asian immigration to Canada; and the 1897 Alien Labor Act, which he used to turn away Italian Americans, among others. But Sifton primarily used unofficial means to encourage immigration from certain parts of the world and not others. The hiring of private "shipping agents"—immigration recruiters—from specific parts of the world became a powerful means of carrying this out. Outside the UK and US, Sifton focused most of his attention on Central and Eastern Europe, hiring recruiters in Russia, Ukraine, Poland, Germany, Austria, Romania, France, and northern Italy, among other places. For Sifton, peoples from Central and Eastern Europe occupied a second-class category of whiteness, not as desirable as UK and US WASPS but superior to peoples from Asia, Africa, or the Americas.

The effects of Sifton's strategy were felt within a matter of years in the Prairie West: in 1899, 6,000 new immigrants arrived in Winnipeg from the UK and US combined, while 6,900 arrived from the Ukraine and 7,400 from Russia. [6] Sifton was criticized in the Manitoba Legislative Assembly and in the Sifton-owned *Brandon Sun*, as well as other Prairie newspapers, for welcoming Slavic peoples and other non-WASPs into the country. These criticisms—and the white supremacist ideology they bolstered—were in fact economically useful to Sifton and the rest of the dominant regional bloc. Sifton used this xenophobic rhetoric to justify allocating the worst prairie farm lands to Central and Eastern European immigrants and to deny them government assistance while they attempted to set up farms, except in a few instances where "assistance" took the form of a lien on the settler's property. Publicly, Sifton remarked that only agricultural settlers—"stalwart peasants...born to the soil"[7]—would be welcome in Canada, but his policies had the opposite effect. During Sifton's time as Minister of the Interior, 70 percent of immigrants to Canada became urban industrial workers rather than rural farmers.[8] By creating an additional category of racism for Slavic peoples—fit enough to work but not to enjoy full participation in the social, political, and cultural life of the nation—the new racial order suited the requirements of industrial capitalism perfectly: a new wave of immigrants would be assisted in coming to the Prairie West based on their supposed capacities for whiteness, but, based on their supposed otherness, they would be subsequently dispossessed, pushed into cities, and forced to sell their labour under hyper-exploitative conditions.

The industrial city. Winnipeg, ca. 1912. Archives of Manitoba, Winnipeg – Views, ca. 1912, 1. (Courtesy of Archives of Manitoba)

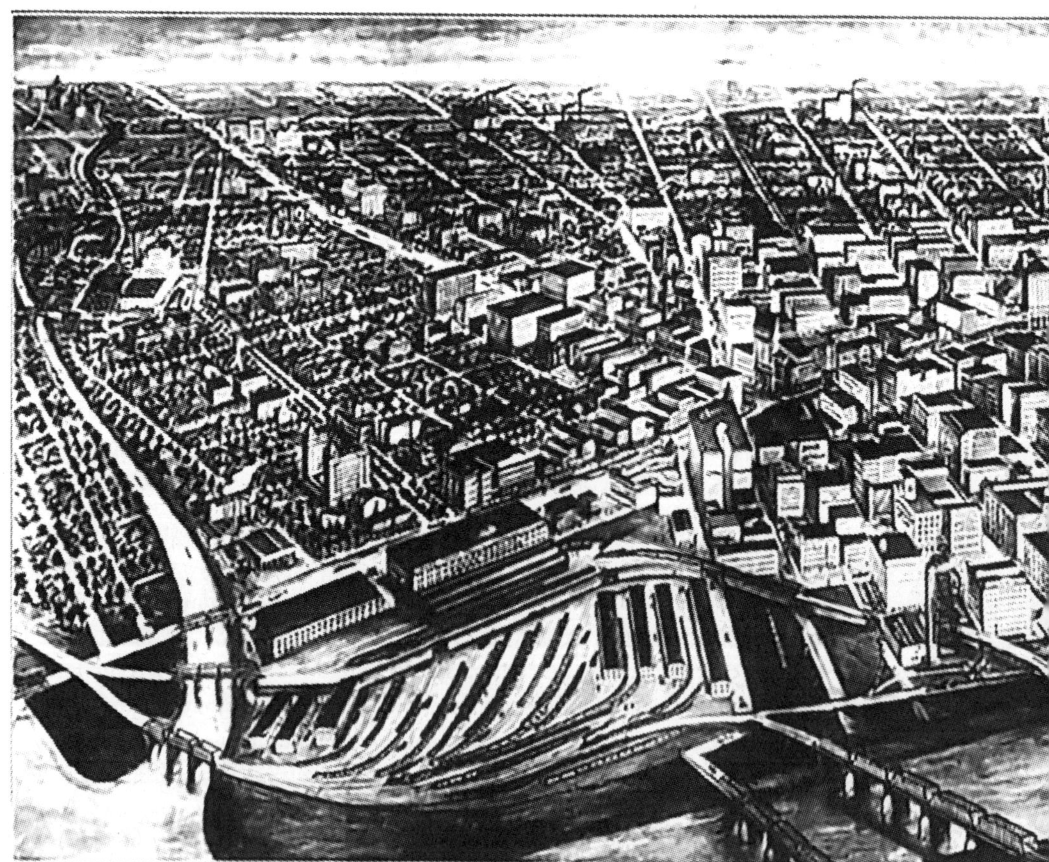

Sifton's policies delivered an immense labour force to Winnipeg industrialists. The city's population quadrupled from 42,000 to 163,000 between 1900 and 1915.[9] The number of manufacturing workers quadrupled between 1901 and 1911, while the number of manufacturing firms in the city also quadrupled from just over 100 in 1901 to over 400 in 1921.[10] By 1911, Winnipeg accounted for half of all manufacturing in the Prairie West and ranked behind only Toronto, Montreal, and Hamilton among Canadian cities. But the manufacturing of commodities in the city took second stage to the processing and distribution of wheat. By 1909, Winnipeg was the greatest grain distribution centre on the continent: the city processed 88 million bushels of wheat that year, compared to 81 million for Minneapolis, 61 million for Buffalo, 26 million for Chicago, and 23 million for New York City.[11] The Canadian Pacific Railway employed nearly 4,000 workers in Winnipeg, making it the largest single employer in the city.

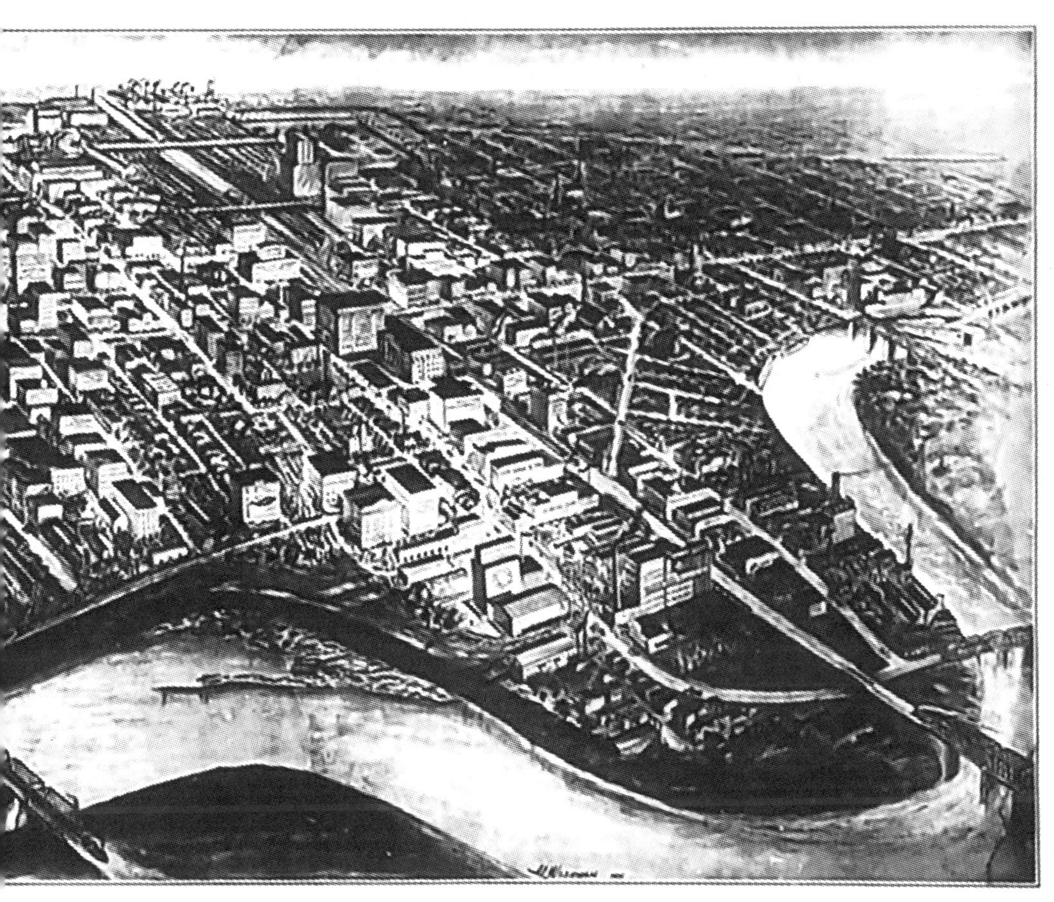

The workers who gave life to the vision of an industrial Winnipeg did not share in the massive wealth it generated. Newly arrived immigrants and their families settled in neighbourhoods constructed as quickly and as cheaply as possible amidst the city's emerging rail yards, warehouses, and factories. Multiple families often crowded into individual dwellings while single workers crammed into boarding houses. Many families lived in what health inspectors at the time described as "shacks," "cottages," and "hovels"[12]—often converted barns, stables, or sheds—heated by wood stoves and lacking running water, sewer connections, or proper ventilation. Under such conditions, preventable illness, disease, and death were tragically common.

Unprotected by even the most basic labour regulations, workers logged gruelling hours for little pay. Manitoba labour and factory legislation technically limited workers (in establishments employing five people or more only) to twelve-hour workdays and six-day workweeks, but enforcement was uneven. In 1913, most full-time industrial workers in Winnipeg earned between 17 and 20 cents per hour, well under the 45 cents per hour considered necessary to cover basic human needs in Winnipeg at the time.[13] Child labour laws were weak and rarely enforced; children often left school to work in factories, breweries, and stores, and in offices as messengers and assistants.[14]

Making space for industry. Main Street near the CPR yards, ca. 1904. Construction of subway looking north. Archives of Manitoba, Winnipeg – Railway Yards – CPR 17 – 22 Aug. 1904. (Courtesy of Archives of Manitoba)

North End workers. All Peoples Mission, Sutherland Avenue, Winnipeg, ca. 1921. Archives of
Manitoba, L.B. Foote fonds, Foote 1452, Mothers & babies, All Peoples Mission, Sutherland Ave
– 23 June 1921. (Courtesy of Archives of Manitoba)

At the same time, the city's capitalist, managerial, and professional classes profited
and prospered in wealthy enclaves. Exclusionary zoning enforced minimum lot sizes
and building costs, effectively keeping the working classes out of wealthy South End
areas such as Wellington Crescent, Armstrong's Point, and Roslyn Road.[15] The city's elite
financed their own infrastructure of exclusive institutions. Private schools such as St.
John's-Ravenscourt; country clubs such as St. Charles, Pine Ridge, and Lakewood; and
men's establishments such as the Manitoba Club and the Canadian Club ensured that
well-off residents lived in a world apart from those who created their wealth. Trains to
the nearby beaches of Lake Winnipeg did not operate on Sundays—workers' only day
off—turning summertime resorts into exclusive domains of the wealthy.

The industrial vision required race prejudice to keep wages low. The same anti-Slavic racism that pushed—or kept—many Central and Eastern European immigrants landless and in Winnipeg to labour for industry also helped keep them in a subordinate position within the urban hierarchy and suppressed the position of the working class as a whole. The city's predominantly Anglo-Saxon industrialists and politicians frequently demonized its Eastern European immigrant population—which numbered 36,000 compared to 116,000 Anglo-Saxons in 1921[16]—casting them as "aliens" unfit for full participation in civic life. "There are few people who will affirm that Slavonic immigrants are desirable settlers, or that they are welcomed by the white people of Western Canada," wrote the *Winnipeg Telegram* in 1901, littering the page with anti-Slavic epithets.[17] But open white supremacy such as this was not the only way for the dominant bloc to blame the urban poor for their own conditions.

A social scientific explanation of "slum" conditions emerged at the turn of the twentieth century, built around the idea that the massively unequal cities of industrialized Turtle Island could be explained by the supposed moral failings—closely linked to supposed racial inferiority—of the urban poor. As historian Mariana Valverde points out, a growing moral reform movement oriented around "ideals of purity, whiteness, and cleanliness" made a strong impact on the emerging fields of sociology and urban planning. Scholars in Winnipeg came to the forefront of this "surveillance of the immoral," establishing the first sociology department in Canada in 1906 at Winnipeg's Methodist Wesley College.[18]

Members of Winnipeg's dominant bloc—including millionaire merchant and real estate capitalist J.H. Ashdown, also known as "the Merchant Prince of Winnipeg," and a former opponent of the Red River Rebellion[19]—who did bother to express concern over workers' living conditions in the North End did so through the lens of the moral reform movement. Ashdown and other elites supported an agenda of racial uplift for the "alien" working classes, with an emphasis on education and assimilation into Anglo-Saxon society. Sifton sometimes turned to this mode of explanation when justifying his role in promoting Slavic immigration. "The Anglo-Saxon is itself a conglomerate race, and every century and every generation it becomes more so," he remarked. "It has never failed to absorb all elements that come within its influence."[20] By design, the moral reform agenda did not translate into a critique of the existing economic structure, Anglo-Saxon supremacy, or a challenge to the dominant bloc's rule over the city.

COUNTER-PLAN III: RED RECONSTRUCTION

By the first decades of the twentieth century, however, North End workers had built a formidable infrastructure of working-class culture and politics and crafted their own analysis of urban living conditions that directly challenged the position of the city's wealthy dominant bloc. The new workers brought not only their labour power to Turtle Island, but also their radical consciousness from revolutionary struggles in England, Russia, Ukraine, Hungary, Germany, and other European countries. Winnipeg's first labour union formed in 1872—before the city had even been incorporated—and in 1884 several Winnipeg labour unions combined to establish a central Labour Council and publish Manitoba's first working-class newspaper, the *Winnipeg Labour Call*.[21] By the 1900s, the North End boasted an array of working-class institutions, including labour temples, community newspapers, educational societies, mutual aid organizations, musical and dramatic societies, and political clubs, structures that often arose from specific national or ethnic radical traditions. There were, for instance, three branches—one each for revolutionary Marxists, socialists, and anarchists—of the Arbeiter Ring, a radical Jewish umbrella organization with 48,000 members across Turtle Island and its base in the Liberty Temple at Pritchard Avenue and Salter Street. By 1911, a little more than 8,000 of Winnipeg's 11,705 wage earners were unionized.[22]

Throughout the 1900s and 1910s, strikes at individual shops were common in all sectors—from manufacturing to retail to public service—but almost all were unsuccessful. Winnipeg earned the nickname "Injunction City" for the frequency with which employers sued unions to break strikes, a practice outlawed in the UK but still legal in Canada at the time. Employers regularly installed replacement workers, in at least one case under the protection of troops armed with machine guns.[23] Increasingly frustrated, Winnipeg workers soon scaled-up their struggle.

In early 1919, negotiations between labour and capital broke down in Winnipeg's "big three" building and metal manufacturing firms—Vulcan Iron Works, Manitoba Bridge and Iron Works, and Dominion Bridge Company. On May 13, 1919, in solidarity with the city's ironworkers, Winnipeg union members voted overwhelmingly for a citywide general strike. Thirty-five thousand workers struck, with 95 of the city's 96 unions joining the action (police were asked to remain on duty by the Strike Committee).[24] Based on a three-person family per striking worker, the strikers represented 105,000 people,

---

Factory action. Vulcan Iron Works, Winnipeg, ca. 1915. Archives of Manitoba, L.B. Foote fonds, Foote 1383, Group of [Vulcan Iron Works] – [ca. 1915]. (Courtesy of Archives of Manitoba)

more than half of Winnipeg's population at the time.[25] The strike made international headlines—including one written by Italian socialist Antonio Gramsci—and has been referred to as "one of the most complete withdrawals of labor power ever to occur in North America," as well as "one of the greatest ruptures between the workers and the upper classes in the history of commercial society."[26]

But the 1919 Winnipeg General Strike was more than a high-profile flashpoint in the struggle between labour and capital for a share of the wealth generated by industrial capitalism, and more than a refusal—as crucial as that refusal was—on the part of workers to participate in an unfair economic system. While the strikers' immediate demands for the right to collective bargaining and a living wage were relatively modest, and while historians have debated the extent to which Winnipeg's strikers were revolutionary, many Winnipeg workers struck as part of a larger struggle to radically reconstruct the political and economic foundations of the city and the world.[27]

Winnipeg workers were emboldened to broaden the imagination of their struggle by two distinct yet related historical currents. First, they struck just as visions of post-WWI "reconstruction" were capturing the imaginations of many. This moment of crisis—in which there emerged broad consensus about the unsustainability of current economic relations built around war—created fertile terrain in which new visions of society could take root. Second, revolutions and revolutionary movements already taking place around the world—especially in countries such as Russia, Germany, and Hungary, where many Winnipeggers of the time maintained strong ties—powerfully inspired the local labour movement. The *Western Labor News*, widely read in Winnipeg, published a regular column on revolutions and general strikes from around the world throughout the 1910s.[28] Winnipeg workers clearly took these revolutions to heart in their organizing. In 1918, 1,700 Winnipeg workers attended a mass meeting co-sponsored by the Winnipeg Trades and Labour Council and the Socialist Party of Canada at the Walker Theatre (now the Burton Cummings Theatre) to announce their support for the 1917 Russian Revolution.[29]

Newspapers and mass assemblies such as these provided a stage on which Winnipeg workers could put forth a vision of urban society that fundamentally challenged dominant explanations of economic inequality. While workers' analyses were diverse, many prominent strikers tried hard to show that urban poverty was not a moral or racial failing but rather an inevitable result of capitalist progress. Minister, researcher, and author J.S. Woodsworth was an early luminary of the moral reform movement, and would later become a key leader of the Winnipeg General Strike. According to his research, the industrial development vision itself—and not the moral failings of the poor—was the key source of deepening poverty, including the advent of homelessness as a new social reality. "Our industries and our constructive works call for large armies of unskilled workers," Woodsworth wrote in his 1911 book *My Neighbour*. "The very nature of their work, seasonal, shifting and intermittent, demands that they be more or less a mobile force without the encumbrances of a fixed home and family...This ill-paid, aimless, roving life reacts upon the men and is creating a large and well-recognized class—'the homeless man'," he argued. Strike leaders echoed this understanding at mass meetings held in the lead-up to the strike. "As time passed, much improvement in machinery and method took place, bringing more land, forests, and also mineral deposits into the realm of property," carpenter George Armstrong told workers assembled at Winnipeg's Majestic Theatre on January 10, 1919. "The increase of wealth being enormous, wage slaves became more plentiful, and poverty presented itself in our large cities."[30]

Strikers translated such analyses into their own reconstruction vision. Playwright and cleaner Samuel Blumenberg, speaking at the same Majestic Theatre assembly, applied these critiques to reconstruction plans—largely borrowed from US capitalist J.D. Rockefeller, Jr.—then being promoted by the local dominant bloc. "When you reconstruct a building you do not do it on an old foundation, as, if you did, the plaster would crack and the shingles fall off, and you would find yourself in the same position as before," Blumenberg told the crowd. "They tell you that we are going to have prosperity, but let me tell you that capitalist prosperity means poverty for the working class."[31]

Indeed, many strikers endorsed a radically new vision. "[T]he abolition of the present system of production for profit and the substitute therefore of production for use" became the first resolution at the Calgary Conference of Labour, a regional gathering attended by a large Winnipeg contingent in March of 1919. Strikers vehemently opposed the institution of private property—in land or anything else. "Property is the corner-stone of all capitalistic constitution," letter carrier Bill Hoop told the Walker Theatre crowd during the celebration of the Russian Revolution. "There can be no salvation for the common people until they know the nature of property and with that intelligence seek to abolish it."[32] Workers at the Calgary conference imagined "the transformation of capitalistic private property to communal wealth" as the cornerstone of a new North-West.[33]

Winnipeg strikers imagined—and began to create—political as well as economic transformations of the region. Many viewed Canada's British-style parliamentary system as fundamentally rigged against the majority of the people, prompting strikers to imagine more democratic structures. Workers at the Calgary conference proposed a new mode of democratic governance based on the "selecting of representatives from industries."[34] In the same spirit, speakers at the Calgary conference emphasized the need to build autonomous worker power as an alternative to petitioning the state, resolving to "no longer plead for legislation to improve the lot of labour...but rather to build up 'an organization of workers on industrial lines for the purpose of enforcing, by virtue of their industrial strength, such demands as such organizations may at any time consider necessary for their continued maintenance and well-being.'"[35]

In fact, many saw the Winnipeg General Strike as prefiguring just such a transformation. "We are going to run this city," Blumenberg declared in the run-up to the

Talk and action. Mass meeting of the Winnipeg General Strike in Victoria Park, ca. 1919. Archives of Manitoba, L.B. Foote fonds, Foote 1681, Winnipeg General Strike, crowds at Victoria Park – 1919. (Courtesy of Archives of Manitoba)

General Strike—and they did.[36] Represented by the Strike Committee, the city's workers took direct control over nearly every aspect of urban life, from the distribution of food and water to the public telephone and transportation systems. Bosses lined up at the North End Labor Temple to ask permission to operate during the strike. Essential services operated with placards reading "PERMITTED BY AUTHORITY OF STRIKE COMMITTEE."[37] "The government of the city has been shifted from the City Hall to the Labor Temple," one of the strike leaders was reported to have said, "and we mean to keep it there."[38]

Winnipeg strikers also developed a fierce anti-militarism and opposition to capitalist imperialism around the world. Strikers' visions of reconstruction most often opposed the rush to war that created the necessity of reconstruction in the first place. According to historians Mildred and Harry Gutkin, leaders of the Winnipeg General Strike were united in their "total rejection of the European militarism that led to the Great War of 1914–1918...[strikers] denounced the war as a struggle between imperialistic powers, and all the more so when Britain and the Allies turned against the successful Bolsheviks in the Russian Revolution."[39] Most Winnipeg General Strike leaders critiqued the era's global military conflicts as wars waged by capitalists and fought by workers. Their class analysis highlighted the absurdity of workers killing their fellow workers in the interests of capital.[40]

Thus, it might be said that Winnipeg workers, struggling to forge a new North-West from the contradictions of the booming industrial city, fiercely opposed two of the three "triple evils"—capitalism and militarism—of the modern world that Martin Luther King Jr. identified 50 years later.[41] But the strikers of 1919 treated King's third "evil," racism, with far more ambivalence. This failure would presage important trends in Winnipeg's development.

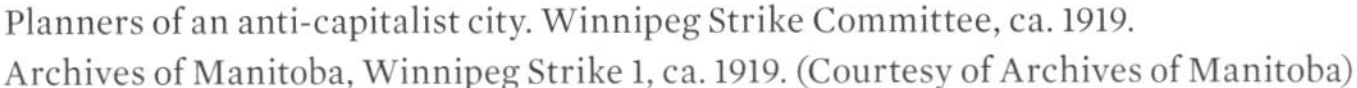

Planners of an anti-capitalist city. Winnipeg Strike Committee, ca. 1919.
Archives of Manitoba, Winnipeg Strike 1, ca. 1919. (Courtesy of Archives of Manitoba)

RACISM AND THE GENERAL STRIKE

In order to discuss the race politics of the strikers, it is necessary to understand the racial strategies of capital at the time. Surfacing in perhaps its most transparent guise ever as the officially anonymous yet practically obvious "Citizens' Committee of 1,000," the dominant bloc attempted to discredit the strike by portraying it in racial terms. Much has been written about the committee's anti-Slavic racism, but less is known about the broader regional history of racism from which it sprang. Despite ongoing interest in both the Winnipeg General Strike and the history of settler colonialism in the North-West, virtually no account of the strike has connected the Committee of 1,000—or the racial dynamics of the strike, or even of capital-labour relations in the region generally—to the process of colonial conquest that reached its most violent depths in the North-West just three decades earlier. Only 34 years separate the rebellion in Batoche from the rebellion in Winnipeg, yet the traditional reticence to discuss them together implies the two belong to fundamentally separate stories. Broadly, this seems to indicate the persistence of colonial modes of history that rigidly separate industrial and pre-industrial Turtle Island, and in doing so imply the disappearance of Indigenous peoples after industrialization. It also shows how the history of Winnipeg, and of modern urban Turtle Island, has been severed from regional histories of ongoing settler colonialism.

To correct this mistake, it is necessary to understand that export agriculture and urban industry were designed by the same people for the same purpose. Urban industry was devised to preserve the obscene wealth and power seized through the region's settler-colonial transition and, as such, required similarly massive levels of human sacrifice and produced similarly fierce resistance. Crucially, as the dominant bloc turned their energies primarily from stealing land to stealing labour, they inevitably brought specific ways of thinking, feeling, planning, and acting forged in their attempted conquest of Indigenous peoples to their attempted exploitation of industrial workers. When Winnipeg workers struck, the dominant bloc made use of settler-colonial legacies to preserve urban industrial accumulation. This was more than a coincidence and more, even, than a tradition inherited by the 1919 dominant bloc from its fathers.

Many of the key figures involved in suppressing the Winnipeg General Strike had themselves participated as young men in the conquest of the Métis and First Nations peoples of the North-West. Examples include: A.J. Andrews, leading lawyer and spokesman of the Committee of 1,000, and a former Winnipeg mayor who fought at the age of 20 under Lieutenant-Colonel Thomas Scott during the 1885 North West Rebellion; D.J. Dyson, a prominent Committee of 1,000 member, pickle manufacturer, and former mayor of Winnipeg, who travelled west of Ontario for the first time at the age of 21 to fight alongside Andrews at Batoche; General Huntley Ketchen, leader of the eventual Canadian military offensive against the strikers in Winnipeg, who was born in India to a British Imperial Army major, joined the Imperial Army himself at the age of 18, came to Winnipeg at 22 to serve in the NWMP, and later served as a lieutenant in the Boer

War;[42] Hugh F. Osler, a real estate, oil, and shipping capitalist and director of Great West Life Assurance, whose uncle Britton Osler prosecuted Louis Riel in 1885;[43] and factory owner E.F. Hutchings, known to glorify "Indian graves" as a symbol of regional progress (see Chapter 1), a prominent member of Winnipeg's dominant bloc during the strike.

Even without a full historical investigation of the ties between Indigenous conquest and working-class suppression in the Prairie West, these biographical details broaden our view of the early twentieth-century urban business elite to the imperial context in which they were raised and in which they vigorously participated, and allows us to see their response to militant urban workers as part of a regional tradition of violent racial capitalism. A racial and national sense of belonging—a belief in the righteous mixing of Anglo-Saxon blood and Turtle Island soil to create a British settler colony—was no less instrumental for the stealing of labour than for the stealing of land in the Prairie West. Once again, the dominant bloc deployed this particular alchemic fantasy in an attempt to dehumanize those who stood in the way of its latest accumulation strategy and to avoid the necessity of respectful negotiation aimed at a more equitable distribution of regional power and resources.

The spirit of colonial conquest surviving into the industrial era. Reunion of North West Rebellion Veterans, Winnipeg, ca. 1935. Archives of Manitoba, Zachary M. Hamilton fonds, 2, Reunion of North West Rebellion veterans [Winnipeg, 1935?]. (Courtesy of Archives of Manitoba)

As soon as the Winnipeg General Strike began, the Committee of 1,000 published ads in the *Free Press, Tribune,* and *Telegram* casting strikers as part of a sub-human race—bearers of an inferior brand of European civilization—and urging the federal government to deport "the undesirable alien and land him back in the bilge waters of European Civilization from whence he sprung." Committee of 1,000 supporters began to wear Union Jacks on their coats as an anti-strike symbol and marched in the streets under the banner "TO HELL WITH THE ALIEN ENEMY."[44] Labour agitation, a revolutionary spirit, and any number of radical political and economic ideas were marked as racially "other" by the dominant bloc—intrinsically unreasonable and beyond the pale of white British-Canadian society. "I.W.W. IDEALS DON'T APPEAL TO WHITE MEN," read the cover of the May 21, 1919, *Winnipeg Citizen,* the Committee of 1,000's special anti-strike newspaper.[45] The city's "Ironmasters"—owners of Winnipeg's big-three metal factories, where the general strike began—publicly lamented the overtaking of "responsible" Anglo-Saxon labour leaders by "unskilled workmen of alien origin, permeated with...socialistic and anarchistic theories."[46]

Just as in their nineteenth-century conquest, however, the dominant bloc's violence was more than rhetorical. Even before the General Strike, the Winnipeg Board of Trade and Citizens Protective Association repeatedly incited attacks on the city's non-Anglo-Saxon communities. North End ethnic clubs, businesses owned by non-Anglo Saxons, and the Socialist Party of Canada offices were all vandalized in the years leading up to the strike. In January 1919, German and Jewish businesses in Winnipeg's North End were attacked after workers called for a public assembly in Market Square to commemorate the passing of assassinated German revolutionaries Rosa Luxemburg and Karl Liebknecht.[47]

From the outset of the strike, the Committee of 1,000 took a hard line of non-negotiation and successfully closed ranks—every boss in the city refused to negotiate with strikers.[48] Non-negotiation was backed up with physical force. The presence on city streets of "hired thugs and gunmen (the usual policy of capitalism all over the world)," was soon noted in the strikers' newspaper, the *Strike Bulletin.* A few weeks into the strike, these individuals—presumably under the direction of the Committee of 1,000—announced themselves as "The Specials" and were reportedly patrolling the city armed with baseball bats, pipes, and chains, "brutally attacking any person who voices any opinion favorable to the strikers."[49] Meanwhile, wealthy South End residents organized armed neighbourhood patrols to keep out the striking rabble.[50] These were half-measures, however, until the dominant bloc could marshal the full force of the Canadian state against the strikers.

On Saturday, June 21, 1919, Winnipeg capitalists took their racist-inflected position of non-negotiation to its ultimate conclusion. On their urging, General Ketchen ordered a combined force of Canadian military troops, NWMP officers, and The Specials to march on a group of strikers demonstrating along Main Street in the city's warehouse district. After being pelted with stones and bottles, the anti-strike forces, armed with

Prairie gangsters. Manitoba Club members shooting guns, ca. 1930s. University of Manitoba Archives & Special Collections, The Manitoba Club 100 Years, 1874-1974, by Mary Lile Benham. (Courtesy of University of Manitoba Archives & Special Collections)

machine guns—Canada's weapon of choice at Batoche as well—opened fire on the strikers. One striker, described as a "foreigner" by General Ketchen in his report, was killed in the attack that would come to be known as Bloody Saturday.[51] Strikers were arrested en masse following the attack, labour temples and offices were raided, and the city was put under military occupation, effectively ending the Winnipeg General Strike. Strike leaders were taken from their homes in the middle of the night, imprisoned in Stony Mountain federal penitentiary, and threatened with deportation.[52] Once again, Canadian state violence was deployed against the people of the North-West to guarantee capitalism's future in the region.

With the settler-colonial foundations of the twentieth-century Prairie West in mind, and with attention to a dominant regional bloc turning its energies from colonial to industrial conquest, it is possible to discuss the race politics of the Winnipeg strikers in its necessary context. The Winnipeg General Strike is sometimes mythologized as a struggle between WASP bosses flying the Union Jack and Slavic workers aspiring to the hammer and sickle. But this is a regurgitation of the dominant bloc's propaganda. In fact, strikers took pains to play into the dominant bloc's racist and nationalist narrative of the strike, regularly striving to dispel the idea that they were anything but loyal, white, empire-loving British subjects.

The guns that took Indigenous peoples in 1885 came for industrial workers in 1919. Canadian military occupation of Winnipeg, ca. 1919. Archives of Manitoba, Robert Maxwell Dennistoun family fonds, Photographs of the Winnipeg Strike including some with Robert Peel Dennistoun pictured, 1919, P7909/12. (Courtesy of Archives of Manitoba)

For this purpose, it helped that virtually all members of the Winnipeg General Strike Committee—and labour union leaders in the early 1900s Prairie West generally—were white Anglo-Saxon Protestant men who followed the same path west from Britain and Ontario during the previous three decades as virtually all members of Winnipeg's dominant bloc had.[53] With their roots in the factory cities of northern England and Scotland, strike leaders tended to craft their social and geographical vision within the parameters of the dominant settler-colonial framework that aspired to make Canada a "Better Britain."[54] Strikers regularly placed the Union Jack at the front of marches, while the phrase "BRITONS NEVER SHALL BE SLAVES" became a popular rallying cry in the strikers' fight for collective bargaining rights. In Ottawa, the pro-strike Member of Parliament for Winnipeg Centre declared that the Winnipeg "strikers are as loyal citizens as Canada ever had."[55]

While the strategy of presenting the strike as a WASP movement did not make much room for it, the necessity of anti-racist alliances was noted—and even celebrated—from time to time during the strike. "For the workers of Winnipeg, the barriers of color, race and creed had been torn down and are now beyond hope of being rebuilt," said one striking worker. "Which is as it should be." Many workers also saw through the dominant bloc's strategic xenophobia. "The bosses have no quarrel with the rich alien, no quarrel with the unorganized alien," one worker pointed out, while an assembly of strikers at the time resolved, "this body of workers recognize no alien but the capitalist."[56] More often, however, Winnipeg strikers reiterated the dominant bloc mythology that partitioned humanity into deserving and undeserving subjects based on race and nationality.

Strikers often resorted to anti-immigrant and anti-Black rhetoric. Strike parades featured banners with anti-immigrant messages, including calls to "DEPORT ALL UNDERSIRABLES." "[W]e are opposed to any wholesale immigration of workers from various parts of the world," one group of strikers wrote at the time of the strike, and especially those "who would be brought here at the request of the ruling class." At times, strikers appealed directly to notions of whiteness, white supremacy, and anti-Blackness in articulating their demands. When Winnipeg City Council asked City workers to sign a pledge promising not to unionize, strike leaders responded: "ONLY A SLAVE COULD SIGN IT. A FREE MAN, A WHITE MAN—NEVER!"[57] In the aftermath of Bloody Saturday, when strike leaders were imprisoned and threatened with deportation, their fellow strikers expressed outrage by asking—in reference to recent events in England, in which participants in "negro" uprisings had been protected from deportation—in the *Western Labor News*, "Have Scotchmen, Englishmen, and Canadians in Canada less rights than negroes in England?"[58] The anti-Black racism of the Winnipeg General Strike came during a time of highly visible Black labour organizing in Canada. The United Negro Improvement Association (UNIA), in particular, had an active Canadian membership among both domestic and factory workers in the 1910s. In Winnipeg in particular, Black train porters were extremely well organized.[59] Neither was it unheard of for mostly-white industrial workers' organizations elsewhere on Turtle Island to concertedly align themselves with Black workers in these years.[60] Thus, the racism of Winnipeg's WASP and Slavic workers cannot be written off as a "product of the times." To do so would be to erase both the labour organizing of people of colour and the anti-racist consciousness of many white workers at the time, and to risk downplaying the reality that people also shape their times.

It is noteworthy too, that revolutionary workers in Winnipeg apparently remained silent while Indigenous peoples were also sacrificed for the industrial agenda. Strikers in 1919, for instance, failed to pursue a relationship of solidarity with the Anishinabe people of Shoal Lake, whose lands were being stolen and disfigured without their consent for the construction of the Winnipeg aqueduct—a key infrastructural requirement for Winnipeg's industrial economy—at the very same time as the Winnipeg General Strike. Strikers were keenly interested in the aqueduct—they organized educational tours that presented it as a marvel of modern progress and engineering—but showed little interest in the people at the other end of the pipe.[61] In a time and place of such intense solidarity and opposition to industrial capitalism's disregard for human life, the lack of solidarity shown to Shoal Lake by Winnipeg workers reveals just how much Winnipeg's dominant bloc relied on anti-Native racism to divide and conquer.

The important point is that as Canadian development of the North-West produced two powerful social and historical negations of capitalism within the same country—Indigenous peoples and migrant workers—the barriers of apartheid, genocide, and anti-Native racism and the lure of white supremacy prevented them from joining forces. Rather than making common cause with all other peoples dispossessed and exploited by the dominant bloc, too many migrant workers in Winnipeg were successfully encouraged to formulate their right to freedom in terms of white racial superiority, either implicitly or explicitly. These workers failed to transcend the racial terms of belonging imposed on the North-West by Canadian occupation, which granted a modicum of political and economic freedom to "industrious and peaceable" white men.[62] Winnipeg's ironworkers, carpenters, and cleaners, in other words, sought their freedom through the racist channels they knew white farm workers had used to obtain it a generation earlier. Whereas Indigenous peoples' political consciousness drew on their own autonomous cultures and traditions, the consciousness of European-descended workers was imbued with the values and habits of the European-descended ruling class, including its strong tendency toward racial thinking.[63] This led the European-descended workers away from the opportunity of drawing on powerful, prior regional radical traditions established by the Anishinabe and the Métis. They were simply unable to see such political traditions as such, and therefore unable to see the Anishinabeg and the Métis as likely allies in struggle, clouded as their minds were by the supposed naturalness, inevitability, and desirability of Indigenous death and disappearance.

By refusing subordination specifically on the basis of being "Britons," "Scotchmen," "Englishmen," "Canadians," and "white men"; by remaining silent and keeping their distance from the matter of industrial capitalism's predations against Indigenous peoples; by fomenting anti-Black racism; and by performing loyalty to British and Canadian colonizers, Winnipeg's industrial workers instead tended toward a racial socialist future whereby workers would gain control over the means of production via whiteness. Other working people from whom it had been stolen—Indigenous, Black, Chinese, and other people of colour—would remain dispossessed according to this formulation. While Winnipeg's early-twentieth-century industrial workers established a radical anti-capitalist tradition, the tradition's tendency to embrace many of the cultural feelings—including the racial and settler-colonial spirit—of the established order fatally weakened it and made it vulnerable to co-optation. It was the bosses, not the workers, who were primarily responsible for the racist ideas circulated during the strike. But it is worth noting that one of the most forceful—and fondly commemorated—emancipatory social visions in the history of the North-West missed a tremendous historical opportunity by failing to oppose the white supremacist and settler-colonial underpinnings of capitalism in the region. Indeed, the white supremacist tendency of Winnipeg's working classes and their drive for inclusion within the ruling WASP society would remain important forces in the city's development for the next century.[64]

1   Korneski, "Britishness, Canadianness, Class, and Race: Winnipeg and the British World, 1880s–1910s," 166.

2   Artibise, *Winnipeg: An Illustrated History*, 26.

3   Healy, *Winnipeg's Early Days*, 2.

4   Robinson, *Black Marxism*, 128.

5   Hall, *Clifford Sifton Vol.1: The Young Napolean 1861–1900*, 128.

6   Ibid., 262.

7   Knowles, *Strangers At Our Gates: Canadian Immigration and Immigration Policy, 1540–2006*, 91.

8   Ibid., 86.

9   Artibise, *Winnipeg: An Illustrated History*, 200.

10   Ibid., 199–200.

11   Artibise, *Winnipeg: A Social History of Urban Growth, 1874–1914*, 283.

12   Woodsworth, *My Neighbor: Urban Ills and Urban Reform*, 70.

13   Woodsworth, *Report on Living Standards, City of Winnipeg, 1913*.

14   Woodsworth, *My Neighbor: Urban Ills and Urban reform.*, 60–62.

15   Kramer and Mitchell, *When the State Trembled: How A.J Andrews and the Citizens' Committee Broke the Winnipeg General Strike*, 32.

16   Woodsworth, *My Neighbor: Urban Ills and Urban Reform*, 207.

17   *Winnipeg Telegram*, May 13, 1901.

18   Valverde, *The Age of Light, Soap, and Water*, 129.

19   Riel, December 7, 1869.

20   Hall, *Clifford Sifton Vol.1: The Young Napolean 1861–1900*, 268.

21   Bercuson, *Confrontation at Winnipeg: Labour, Industrial Relations, and the General Strike*, 7.

22   Bercuson, *Confrontation at Winnipeg: Labour, Industrial Relations, and the General Strike*, 8

23   Kramer and Mitchell, *When the State Trembled: How A.J Andrews and the Citizens' Committee Broke the Winnipeg General Strike*, 12, 45.

24   Bercuson, *Confrontation at Winnipeg: Labour, Industrial Relations, and the General Strike*, 186, 116.

25   Kramer and Mitchell, *When the State Trembled: How A.J Andrews and the Citizens' Committee Broke the Winnipeg General Strike*, 11.

26   Bercuson, *Confrontation at Winnipeg: Labour, Industrial Relations, and the General Strike*, 176; Kramer and Mitchell, *When the State Trembled: How A.J Andrews and the Citizens' Committee Broke the Winnipeg General Strike*, 11.

27   "Those of us who are serious about transforming our society—socially, culturally, and polit-
      ically—need to clarify what we mean by 'revolution'… Many leftist ideas of revolution have
      nothing to do with the actual process by which real human beings, confronted with real and
      seemingly intractable problems, make decisions and exercise their capacities to create new
      ways of living," Grace Lee Boggs wrote in *The Next American Revolution*, 48. Indeed, since the
      mid-twentieth century, the meaning of the word *revolutionary* has shifted away from the idea
      of overthrowing the government and seizing state power, toward making power from below
      through horizontal alliances and coalitions, Boggs wrote in "Nothing Is More Important than
      Thinking Dialectically," 3. Inspired by this insight, by Gilmore's (*Golden Gulag*, 242) call to
      conceive a break with the old order as "something both short of and longer than a single cata-
      clysmic event," and by Louise Champagne's use of the word in reference to Indigenous housing
      and worker co-ops, this book refers to activity as "revolutionary" when it opposes essential
      characteristics of racial capitalism, attempts to shrink the reach of racial capitalist structures,
      and/or embodies radical alternatives.

28   Bercuson, *Confrontation at Winnipeg: Labour, Industrial Relations, and the General Strike*, 96.

29   Kramer and Mitchell, *When the State Trembled: How A.J Andrews and the Citizens' Committee
      Broke the Winnipeg General Strike*, 23.

30   Woodsworth, *My Neighbor: Urban Ills and Urban Reform*, 60–62; Penner, *Winnipeg 1919: The
      Strikers' Own History of the Winnipeg General Strike*, 17.

31   Ibid., 20.

32   Ibid., 23, 11.

33   Bumsted, *Winnipeg General Strike of 1919: An Illustrated History*, 23.

34   Penner, *Winnipeg 1919: The Strikers' Own History of the Winnipeg General Strike*, 28.

35   Bumsted, *Winnipeg General Strike of 1919: An Illustrated History*, 24.

36   Kramer and Mitchell, *When the State Trembled: How A.J Andrews and the Citizens' Committee
      Broke the Winnipeg General Strike*, 94.

37   Bumsted, *Winnipeg General Strike of 1919: An Illustrated History*, 31.

38   Gutkin and Gutkin, *Profiles in Dissent: The Shaping of Radical Thought in the Canadian West*,
      158.

39   Ibid., 5.

40   Bumsted, *Winnipeg General Strike of 1919: An Illustrated History*, chapter 2.

41   King Jr., *Where Do We Go From Here: Chaos or Community?*

42   Manitoba Historical Society, *Memorable Manitobans: Alfred Joseph Andrews (1865–1950)*; *David
      John Dyson (1863–1949)*; and *Huntley Douglas Brodie Ketchen (1872–1959)*

43   Howard, *Strange Empire*, 512.

44   Kramer and Mitchell, *When the State Trembled: How A.J Andrews and the Citizens' Committee
      Broke the Winnipeg General Strike*, 125–26, 95.

45   Dupuis, *Winnipeg's General Strike: Reports from the Front Lines*, 44.

46   Bercuson, *Confrontation at Winnipeg: Labour, Industrial Relations, and the General Strike*, 106.

47   Kramer and Mitchell, *When the State Trembled: How A.J Andrews and the Citizens' Committee
      Broke the Winnipeg General Strike*, 22.

48   Ibid., 52.

49   Penner, *Winnipeg 1919: The Strikers' Own History of the Winnipeg General Strike*, 114, 136.

50   Bercuson, *Confrontation at Winnipeg: Labour, Industrial Relations, and the General Strike*, 122.

51   Kramer and Mitchell, *When the State Trembled: How A.J Andrews and the Citizens' Committee Broke the Winnipeg General Strike*, 193.

52   Bercuson, *Confrontation at Winnipeg: Labour, Industrial Relations, and the General Strike*, 173, 164–165.

53   Ibid., 4, 125.

54   Korneski, "Britishness, Canadianness, Class, and Race: Winnipeg and the British World, 1880s–1910s."

55   Penner, *Winnipeg 1919: The Strikers' Own History of the Winnipeg General Strike*, 102, 115, 106.

56   Penner, *Winnipeg 1919: The Strikers' Own History of the Winnipeg General Strike*, 78, 29.

57   Ibid., 115, 29, 83.

58   Kramer and Mitchell, *When the State Trembled: How A.J Andrews and the Citizens' Committee Broke the Winnipeg General Strike*, 190.

59   Maynard, *Policing Black Lives*, 39. Prominent Canadian UNIA members included Malcolm X's parents Louisa Langdon Norton and Earl Little Sr., who started a Montréal branch in 1917 (Marable, *Malcom X*, 16).

60   Robinson, *Black Marxism*, 217. The American Communist Party, for instance, worked very closely with the African Blood Brotherhood (ABB) in the years immediately following the founding of the ABB in 1919.

61   Perry, *Aqueduct*; Perry, "Drinking Dispossession: Winnipeg, Water, and Settler Colonialism, 1913–1919."

62   John A. Macdonald as quoted in Wilson and Center, *Frontier Farewell*, 51.

63   Cedric J. Robinson (1983, 275) observed that, "Capitalism had produced its social and historical negations in both poles of its expropriation: capitalist accumulation gave birth to the proletariat at the manufacturing core; 'primitive accumulation' deposited the social base for the revolutionary masses in the peripheries. But what distinguished the formations of these revolutionary classes was the source of their ideological and cultural developments. While the European proletariat had been formed through and by the ideas of the bourgeoise ('the ruling ideas,' Marx and Engels had maintained, 'were the ideas of the ruling class'), in Haiti and presumably elsewhere in slave populations, the Africans had constructed their own revolutionary culture."

64   Just as a thorough investigation of the connections between Indigenous conquest and suppression of the Prairie West's industrial working class remains to be written, so too does an in-depth examination of the racist and colonial underpinnings of the Winnipeg General Strike and the non-Indigenous labour movements of the Prairie West. My intention here is simply to situate urban industrial social relations within their settler colonial context and to indicate important potential implications of this—a framing that in and of itself is still too rare.

CHAPTER 3

INVENTING MALL PEOPLE: THE SUBURBAN VISION

The mall was invented in Winnipeg.

—Tomson Highway, *Kiss of the Fur Queen*

The conquest of Winnipeg's industrial workers was a resounding success for the domin-ant bloc.[1] Through their military occupation of the city, the city fathers regained a steel grip on industrial wealth and city governance, and maintained it with little interrup-tion: The Citizens' Committee of 1,000 morphed over the years into several political organizations that controlled Winnipeg's City Council, including the Citizens' League of Winnipeg (1919–21), the Civic Progress Association (1929–32), the Winnipeg Elec-tion Committee (1936–59), and the Independent Citizens' Election Committee (1971–1983).[2] As was the case in the wake of its late-1800s conquest, the early-1900s dominant bloc was keenly aware of—and made little effort to hide—the fundamental violence that made their fortunes possible. Winnipeg businessmen openly admired the rise of fascism in Europe, particularly the violent attacks perpetrated by Benito Mussolini and his blackshirts against trade unionists and socialists in Italy. Their hold on local state power helped ensure that the radical visions of Winnipeg's workers remained unrealized and that poverty, misery, and unliveable conditions persisted in the city into the 1940s.[3]

Global events beyond their control, however, severely decelerated industrial capital accumulation for Winnipeg's dominant bloc. In fact, Winnipeg's strategic position in the world economy was already in decline by 1919. The opening of the Panama Canal in 1914—which created a much cheaper shipping route than the trans-continental rail network—set in motion a longstanding period of "slow growth" in the city. It would be only a few decades until Vancouver, Calgary, and Edmonton began to eclipse Winnipeg as the premier economic centres of the Canadian West. Winnipeg transitioned from a "gateway" to a "central place" city in this period, wrote historian Alan F.J. Artibise. "While Winnipeg's once vast hinterland was severely and permanently reduced in size," according to Artibise, "the city remained the largest metropolitan center in the prairie region," and became the economic capital of a circumscribed hinterland that Artibise mapped as "Manitoba, northwestern Ontario, and most of Saskatchewan."[4]

While the boom days of the industrial vision were long over, Winnipeg remained an industrial city into the 1950s. Indeed, the percentage of Winnipeg workers employed in manufacturing rose from 17 percent in 1921 to 25 percent in 1951, the highest percentage of any sector. But deindustrialization began to set in during the 1950s, in part due to the declining significance of rail transport and in part due to the worldwide migration of manufacturing investment to the global south. Winnipeg lost over 5,000 manufacturing jobs between 1951 and 1971, as many large firms, including Air Canada and John Deere, moved operations out of the city.[5] By this time, however, the dominant bloc had set their sights on an entirely new regional development agenda.

The accumulation strategy that emerged in the late 1940s had less to do with the production of commodities—neither agricultural nor industrial—for export, and more to do with the production of new built environments oriented around consumption. Planning for the obsolescence and abandonment of the old city, the new agenda envisioned a world of fresh business opportunities in the migration of industry, residences, and commerce to new suburban complexes along the outer edges of the city. This regional shift was part of a much broader global restructuring of capital, which moved away from the global north as a location for the production of value, as the industrial vision had done, and toward the global north as a location for the realization of value through consumption.[6] For Winnipeg investors and boosters awakening from dreams of a "Chicago of the North," suburbanization was fresh salvation. But unlocking new fortunes on the urban edge would, as usual, require the dominant bloc to first leverage massive state subsidies in the form of new infrastructure.

EXPRESSWAYS: THE NEW RAILWAYS

By the start of the Second World War, landowners, speculators, and real estate developers had given up hope that Winnipeg would continue to grow at the same rate as it had during the industrial boom years. After buying up immense amounts of land near the city in a frenzy of speculation, investors had abandoned much of it in the 1920s and 1930s.[7] A striking map published by the newly minted Winnipeg Metropolitan Planning Committee displays this dynamic in stark black and white, showing a thick swath of tax-forfeited lands encircling Winnipeg in 1946. The amount of abandoned land on the city edge is at least as great as the amount of privately owned land in the city.[8]

Land without an owner—that is, an owner legible under the rubrics of liberalism and capitalism—is a recurring Achilles heel of the settler-colonial capitalist state. In an effort to find new owners for this suburban land—in other words, to make suburban growth profitable—Winnipeg became a leader among Canadian cities in pursuing regional-scale urban planning and governance. In 1949, the government of Manitoba approved a new Metropolitan Planning Commission for the entire Winnipeg urban region, encompassing over ten separate municipalities. This was the first time that a comprehensive planning process was attempted for the entire Winnipeg metropolitan region.[9]

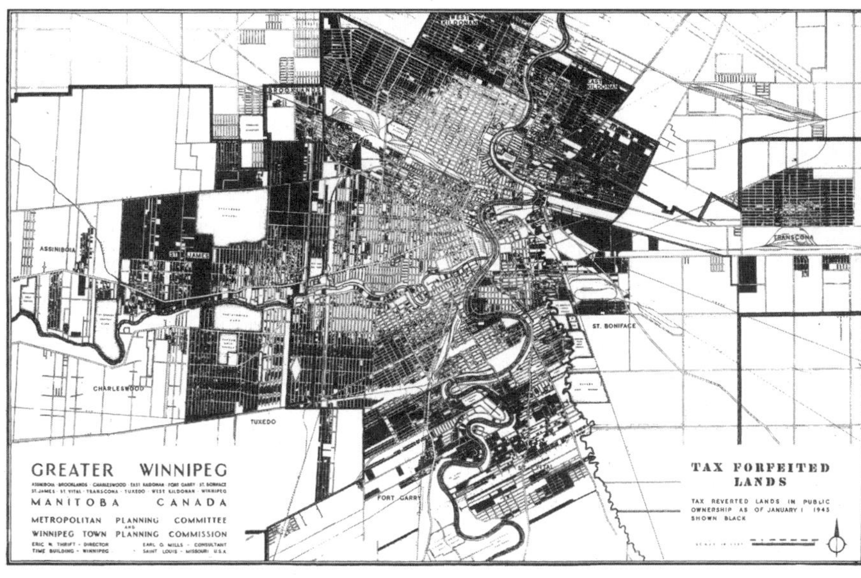

Publicly-owned suburbia.
Greater Winnipeg Metropolitan Planning Committee map of Tax Forfeited Lands, ca. 1946.
flickr.com/photos/manitobamaps/3130341037/sizes/l Manitoba Historical Maps ⓒⓒ

One of the key tasks of the Metropolitan Planning Commission was to answer the dominant bloc's calls for construction of new intra-urban freeways connecting suburbs to each other and to the city centre. As early as 1950, the Winnipeg Chamber of Commerce (WCC), lamenting growing levels of automobile congestion, urged Winnipeg City Council—controlled at the time by the WCC-aligned Winnipeg Election Committee—and the "Metro Commission" to build a network of new metropolitan roadways, citing the US interstate system as a model and submitting its own detailed plans for future roadways. City Council in turn convinced the Province of Manitoba and the Government of Canada to finance the Chamber's plan, in part by ensuring that the federal government's new Trans-Canada Highway would pass through Winnipeg.[10]

A massive 55-mile loop road surrounding the entire metropolitan area, dubbed the Greater Winnipeg Perimeter Highway, was the centrepiece of an updated Chamber of Commerce plan submitted to City Council in 1954. By 1955, the Province of Manitoba began to purchase extensive swaths of suburban Winnipeg land for the highway's construction. In 1957, the provincial and federal governments announced they would finance the majority of the $25 million project. The "broad aim of the plan," reported the *Winnipeg Free Press* at the time, "is to enable through traffic to bypass Winnipeg altogether."[11] The Perimeter Highway was the centrepiece, in other words, of an intentional, highly organized, and well-funded plan to forsake the old City of Winnipeg by enabling a new economy based on suburb-to-suburb transportation.

To build on this momentum and to increase the technical sophistication of its suburban planning, Winnipeg City Council hired Wilbur Smith—a traffic guru from New Haven, Connecticut—to draft an extensive plan for the city's suburban future. After seventeen months of research, Smith—described in the local media as "the foremost traffic authority on the North American continent today"[12]—called for the construction of massive suburban automobile infrastructure including three metropolitan expressway systems and thirteen new bridges, along with a metropolitan governance model to coordinate the plan. Praising the city's brand new Perimeter Highway, Smith's plan stressed the importance of additional "circumferential" expressways enabling motorists to travel even more easily between suburbs without passing through the city centre.[13]

Local media instantly fell in love with the plan and urged Winnipeggers to embrace it as the official vision of an efficient, convenient modern city. "Just imagine you are driving downtown along Salter street in Winnipeg—and you want to reach St. Vital in a hurry," the *Free Press* conjured:

> If [Smith's] suggestion comes true, you would turn on to an
> elevated expressway near Salter street bridge at Logan and Alex-
> ander avenues. And from there you would travel—at speeds of up
> to 50 miles an hour—in a circular route. The expressway might
> even have eight lanes of traffic, four in each direction. You would
> hit St. Mary's road in no time. No fuss, no bother. No intersections
> to worry about. No stops.[14]

Speeding in one's car from downtown to the suburb of St. Vital, according to the *Free Press* and the Metropolitan Planning Commission, would be an early phase of Space Age urban living. "The Wilbur Smith report is a blueprint for years to come, perhaps even the year 2000...Said one metro official this week: 'Maybe we will all be piloting helicopters by then.' But if we are not, he added, something will have to be done, and now is the time to plan for it."[15]

In order to win resources for its suburban vision, the dominant bloc manipulated popular understandings about the order in which private and public investment were taking place in the suburbs. To justify its outsized requests for state subsidies, that is, the dominant bloc claimed that large-scale suburbanization was already happening. Smith's plan was crucial to the dominant bloc's ability to sell this claim since it added a scientific sheen to the dominant bloc's keystone idea of "the growing problem of traffic congestion." Three questionable predictions—for which Smith provided many elegant graphs and tables—formed the basis of his recommendations: rapid population growth of the Winnipeg metropolitan area; the nearly total concentration of population growth in the city's suburbs; and significantly increasing rates of car ownership. The upshot of these predictions, for Smith, was that "suburban areas will generate over ten [daily automobile] trips for each one presently recorded."[16] The *Free Press*, reading this, envisaged catastrophe: if expressways were not built, "Winnipeg could be swallowed up in one tremendous traffic jam."[17] Rather than highlighting the obvious alternatives to freeway construction as a response to population growth—densification of the existing city and investment in public transportation—local media were led by the dominant bloc, via Smith's supposed scientific expertise, to conclude that expressways were the city's only option.

On certain less-publicized pages of his plan, Smith admits that construction of suburban infrastructure will in fact be a catalyst for, rather than a response to, suburbanization. "Development of major new highway facilities will have an important influence on future urban growth," Smith advised. "In the same way that railroads, years ago, encouraged settlement along their rights of way, express highway facilities radiating from the central city will speed the development of rural areas beyond present limits of urbanization."[18] With Smith's report in hand, local state planners and politicians evidently understood suburban expressways to be catalysts of regional growth and inducements—rather than responses—to urbanites and real estate capital to settle the suburbs.

Just weeks after the release of the Smith report, the Province of Manitoba announced its most ambitious commitment to date to regional expressway construction. The province committed $40 million ($350 million in today's dollars) to construct over 1,650 miles of new highways in the province, with a strong emphasis on bridges, overpasses, and interchanges in metropolitan Winnipeg.[19] Two years later, Manitoba premier Duff Roblin introduced the Metropolitan Winnipeg Act, giving the Metropolitan Corporation of Greater Winnipeg broad powers over regional-scale infrastructure.[20] From 1960 to 1971, the Metropolitan Corporation coordinated a massive suburbanization agenda, widening and extending suburban roadways; building new suburban bridges, overpasses, and underpasses; creating thousands of acres of new suburban parks, golf courses, and parking lots; erecting hundreds of new suburban elementary schools and high schools; extending water mains, sewers, and energy infrastructure; constructing new suburban sewage treatment plants, reservoirs, and pumping stations; providing planning assistance for the development of large regional shopping centres; and grading over 52 million square of feet of land for new development.[21] These investments, far from benefitting all suburbs equally, leaned heavily toward expansion of the South End.[22]

In 1972, the city took a final, major step toward realizing the dominant bloc's suburban vision. This was the year that Winnipeg finally followed through on Wilbur Smith's recommendation and became the first urban region in Canada to amalgamate under a single metropolitan government, often referred to as "Unicity." Eleven formerly separate municipalities joined the old City of Winnipeg in the scheme, shifting the balance of power on Winnipeg City Council to the new suburban constituencies. The new suburban-dominated Winnipeg City Council—now controlled by the dominant bloc under the banner of the "Independent Citizens' Election Committee"[23]—pursued an even more aggressive agenda of suburbanization through rezoning and extensive spending on the same types of infrastructure the Metropolitan Corporation had prioritized.

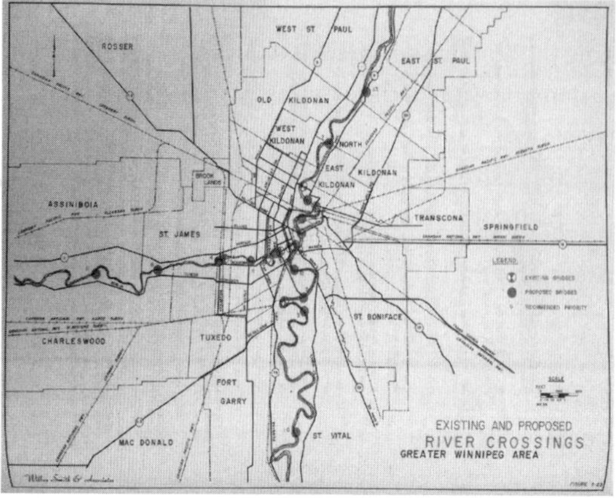

Bridge boom. Greater Winnipeg Area Existing and Proposed River Crossings by Wilbur Smith & Associates, ca. 1957. City of Winnipeg Archives, Smith, Wilbur & Associates. (1957). Report on Traffic, Transit, Parking, Metropolitan Winnipeg. New Haven, Connecticut. (Courtesy of City of Winnipeg Archives)

Roads to nowhere. Waverley Street between Wilkes Avenue and McGillivray Boulevard, Winnipeg, ca. 1963. Photograph by David Portigal & Company. City of Winnipeg archives, Pavement construction Project R, Waverley Street from Wilkes Avenue to McGillivray Boulevard, October 17, 1963. CA COWA C13-P00024-87. (Courtesy of City of Winnipeg Archives)

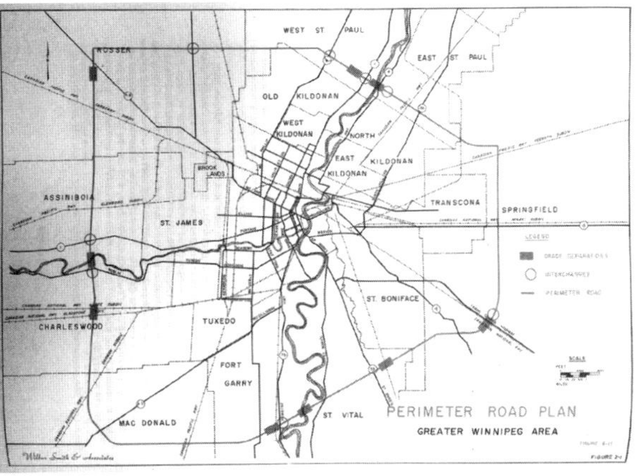

Opening suburbia. Greater Winnipeg Perimeter Road Plan by Wilbur Smith & Associates, ca. 1957. City of Winnipeg Archives, Smith, Wilbur & Associates. (1957). Report on Traffic, Transit, Parking, Metropolitan Winnipeg. New Haven, Connecticut. (Courtesy of City of Winnipeg Archives)

Unicity had another important catalyzing effect on suburbanization. Amalgamation intentionally homogenized development regulations across formerly separate municipalities, making investment far more predictable across the city's various suburban frontiers. Prior to Unicity, "the area municipalities used their power over local improvements and the provision of services to bargain with developers in order to get the best terms for their area," the Metropolitan Corporation explained. "This made Metro's task of overall planning extremely difficult and the situation often led to confusion and delays. Many developers became extremely frustrated with the slow progress made on their plans."[24] In this way, Unicity enabled the dominant bloc to reduce risks and delays posed to its suburban investments by variations in local government, flattening the urban region for capital and accelerating suburbanization.

The Metropolitan Corporation of Greater Winnipeg, the Smith report, Unicity, and the expressways—and myriad other suburban infrastructure they called into being—are clear examples of the crucial and prior role that state power has consistently played in relation to capitalist development and settlement on Turtle Island. The suburban frontier, like the agricultural frontier and the industrial agenda before it, was mapped, promoted, and developed by the state largely in advance of any influx of people or capital acting according to the so-called invisible hand of the market. Capitalist development, in other words, contrary to liberal—and neoliberal—mythology, has always been centrally coordinated by the state. In addition to supplying the material infrastructure necessary for private investment, the history of suburbanization reveals how dominant blocs have used the powerful cultural influence of the state—through the creation of new institutions and the financing and promotion of plans and ideas—in educating populations about the kinds of regional futures that are possible, desirable, and necessary.[25] This was true in the build-up to suburbanization just as it was in the run-up to Canadian expansion in the late 1800s and in the state response to industrial poverty and resistance in the early 1900s.

Bridges create suburbs. St. Vital Bridge, south Winnipeg, ca. 1971. City of Winnipeg Archives, Metropolitan Corporation of Greater Winnipeg. (1971). The End of the Metropolitan. Souvenir Issue December 1971. (Courtesy of City of Winnipeg Archives)

New worlds, new selves. Portage Avenue underpass, Winnipeg, ca. 1971. City of Winnipeg Archives,
Metropolitan Corporation of Greater Winnipeg. (1971). The End of the Metropolitan.
Souvenir Issue December 1971. (Courtesy of City of Winnipeg Archives)

Indeed, manufacturers and other industries followed state investment to the suburbs. As firms' facilities in the old industrial city reached obsolescence by the 1950s and 1960s, those that did not abandon Winnipeg altogether moved to modern industrial parks on the city's fringes. Rail infrastructure was also suburbanized, as Canadian National (CN) abandoned locations at the Forks and Fort Rouge to open new shops, terminals, and marshalling yards near the Winnipeg International Airport and in the suburbs of Transcona, St. Boniface, and Tuxedo. New suburban truck routes, oriented toward the Perimeter Highway and the Winnipeg International Airport, became the new shipping outlets of choice for many firms.[26]

Even more drastic than the suburbanization of industry were the suburbanization of Winnipeg's population, commercial activity, and major centres of civic life. Postwar federal legislation played an important role, as Canada eagerly encouraged suburban home construction and home ownership. The National Housing Act of 1944 and the establishment of the Central Mortgage and Housing Corporation provided capital to developers for new housing construction and generous loans to new homebuyers. The Veterans' Land Act subsidized new housing construction for Second World War veterans, sponsoring entire new suburban subdivisions such as Roblin Park in Winnipeg's South End Charleswood municipality.[27]

The Metropolitan Corporation of Greater Winnipeg devoted itself to providing planning assistance to developers of new suburban subdivisions, mapping out miles upon miles of land on the urban edge on which it encouraged construction of hundreds of thousands of new houses. The planning authority's "subdivision standards" mandated large lot sizes and low densities, encouraging the construction of larger, pricier homes, and therefore the creation of higher income enclaves.[28] This new planning function of the state served a new phase in capitalist housing production.

Winnipeg capitalists at this time, like their cohorts across Turtle Island, were beginning to see housing and even entire communities as commodities—like the automobile—that could be mass-produced and sold for immense profits. New forms of vertical integration combined financiers, engineers, architects, building supply companies, masses of construction workers, realtors, advertisers, and others into a handful of large development firms to build and sell immense suburban subdivisions. "The day when all the average builder needs to know is the use of a saw and hammer is long past," reported the *Free Press* in 1960. "In these times a builder must be an accountant, a purchasing agent, an architect, a salesman, an advertising man and many more things if he is to be successful." Winnipeg's Land Assembly and Development Company—"Ladco" for short—merged 38 firms into the city's first giant house-building corporation to build the 3,000-home Windsor Park, one of Winnipeg's first mass-produced suburbs.[29]

Between 1954 and 1960, developers built over 20,000 new houses[30] in Winnipeg, and housing construction emerged as a key sector in the city's economy, with hundreds of millions in private capital invested in new housing construction.[31] The city's new suburban geography was rounding into form: "Just about every metro municipality has shared in the residential construction boom," noted the *Free Press* as it surveyed the scene. "St. James boasts of its picturesque Silver Heights development while St. Boniface can point proudly to the mammoth 3,000 home Windsor Park project. Other municipalities with substantial housing activity are Assiniboia, site of the new Westwood development, and Transcona (more than 800 new units completed in the past four years)." The *Free Press* dramatized a city ballooning at its edges, using side-by-side aerial photographs showing open prairie morphing into suburban subdivisions from one year to the next.[32]

To make their new subdivisions sell, Winnipeg developers spent millions on advertising, showcasing suburban communities as the height of modern comfort, convenience, and healthfulness—wholesome frontiers where an easier lifestyle and, by extension, a brighter regional future would be found. To finance their promotional activities, Winnipeg developers formed a coalition, the Winnipeg Housebuilders' Association, which, among other things, held an annual "Parade of Homes," a spectacle of display homes featuring live bands and TV celebrities, "fashioned after the car industry which each year presents its new models in the season when sales are normally slack." The Parade of Homes sold "ranch-style bungalows" in "family planned" communities using images of white, car-owning nuclear families, and pastoral place names such as Lindenwoods, Woodhaven, and Garden City.[33]

Building restrictions secured urban apartheid. Ad for Southdale subdivision, south Winnipeg.
University of Manitoba Archives, Winnipeg Tribune fonds, June 11, 1966.
(Courtesy of University of Manitoba Archives)

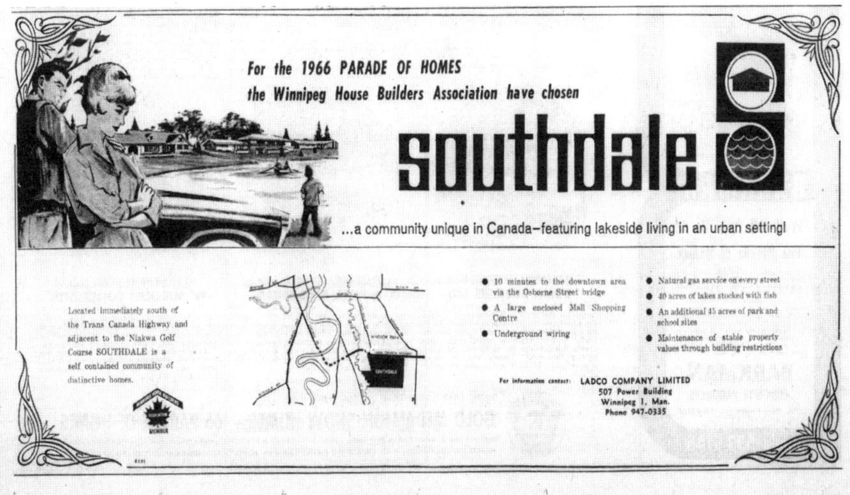

Commercial capital—alongside industrial and residential—provided the third pillar of the suburban vision. Retailers moved from freezing downtown streets into climate-controlled shopping malls, for which the Metropolitan Corporation also provided extensive planning assistance.[34] "Winnipeg's first major shopping centre"—Polo Park—was constructed in 1959 on former polo grounds in the western suburb of St. James, where the city's major sports teams had also recently moved in to new suburban confines. The Winnipeg Blue Bombers' new suburban football field—Winnipeg Stadium—was built in 1953, while the Winnipeg Warriors moved into their own suburban hockey rink—Winnipeg Arena—in 1955.[35] By 1973, 25 suburban shopping malls with at least 2,500 square metres of retail space apiece had been constructed in Winnipeg.[36]

An exciting new concept. Ad for Grant Park plaza in south Winnipeg, by Arnovitch & Leipsic, ca. 1956. City of Winnipeg Archives, City Clerk's Library, A1200/File 6, Doc. #10. (Courtesy of City of Winnipeg Archives)

Suburbs nullius. Illustration of Grant Park Plaza in south Winnipeg, ca. 1956. City of Winnipeg Archives, Greater Winnipeg Industrial Topics, November 1956, page 14. (Courtesy of City of Winnipeg Archives)

STEALING SUBURBIA

Until now, this narrative—like most stories of suburbanization in Winnipeg and across Turtle Island—has tended to cast the postwar urban edge as some version of *terra nullius*: empty space into which civilization advanced more or less unimpeded. However, suburbanization is more accurately understood as the restructuring—rather than mere expansion—of human geographies. More and more scholars and activists now recognize that Winnipeg's postwar edges were home to a longstanding, unsanctioned, yet well-known Indigenous human geography.[37] For Métis families in particular, the outskirts of Winnipeg became one of a severely diminished archipelago of places—including those places known as road allowance communities—where work, shelter, community, and freedom from persecution could be found in the middle of the twentieth century.

A number of geographical processes combined to push the Métis onto Winnipeg's outskirts, the most powerful being the Canadian state's refusal to deliver the 1.4 million acres promised to the Métis in the Manitoba Treaty (as discussed in Chapter 1). As urban development displaced traditional Métis communities along the Red and Assiniboine Rivers, and as anti-Native hostilities barred Métis access to work, housing, and services in white urban and rural areas, land abandoned by speculators on the urban fringes became a valuable space of possibility for Métis life.[38] It was on the urban edge that hundreds, if not thousands, of Métis people created vibrant communities of self-built housing unsanctioned by the Canadian state.

The suburban agenda required the removal of the city's Indigenous suburbs and marshalled both cultural and forcible state power to do so. Métis suburbs across Manitoba came under heightened surveillance in the 1940s and 1950s. In 1956, Manitoba government planners identified 26 Métis "fringe communities" on the edges of white towns and cities.[39] While this was likely the most comprehensive state mapping of Indigenous communities on the urban edge up to this time, government officials had long known about them, tending to portray them as disorderly nuisances—"slums"—to the officially sanctioned city. It was only as the suburban development agenda gained momentum, however, that the state launched a systematic attempt to map and study Métis suburbia. This approach differed significantly from the explorations that preceded late-1800s agricultural expansion—which intentionally ignored the Indigenous communities of the North-West—but it had a similar effect. Descriptions of Native suburbs published by white anthropologists, community development professionals, and journalists in effect construed these communities as *suburbs nullius*: inherently inferior—sad, backwards, unhealthy, immoral—places ripe for removal and replacement.[40] Métis suburbanites, according to this mode of description, became both invisible, as their full humanity and contributions to the city were concealed, and hyper-visible, as they were made out to be threats to the proper white city.[41] The timing of these studies once again demonstrated that while *terra nullius* is an enduring colonial trope, its intensity and character vary according to the convergence of shifting economic cycles, political agendas, and institutional capacities in specific times and places.

In Winnipeg in the 1940s and 1950s, *suburbs nullius* often took the form of an anxious public health discourse that hid the infrastructural determinants of health and instead cast Indigenous suburbanites as both potential contaminants of the settler city and the source of whatever—if anything—ailed them. In 1954, a Winnipeg health officer described the Indigenous outskirts as "a serious menace to the health and welfare of the city."[42] Suburban expansion also coalesced with a revitalized racialism. The local press—in the midst of the eugenics-driven Nazi holocaust—used its own rough version of scientific racism to demonize Métis people living in "hovels on the fringes of little urban centres" who, according to the *Free Press*, possessed "the instincts of the Indian thinly coated over by certain sophistications of the Aryan. He is difficult of assimilation into white culture."[43] In fact, it was the "white" city, dominated by an historically fascist-sympathizing bloc, that took great pains to keep Indigenous communities on the margins, while using racist explanations of inherent marginality to legitimize segregation and organized abandonment.[44]

Despite residents' demands, the state deliberately refused to provide running water, electricity, sewer connections, or improved housing to Métis communities on the urban edge, in the hopes that they would eventually disappear.[45] Neither did the state consider transferring title over surplus state-owned lands to those inhabiting them, despite most inhabitants' status as members of the founding nation of Manitoba that still had not received its treaty-guaranteed lands, and despite their recent history of making homes in a place where no one else appeared willing to do so. Instead, the state carried out an agenda of planned immiseration, keeping these communities poor, cut off from urban infrastructure, and therefore easy to remove. As surplus capital turned its attentions to the urban edge, the state-imposed fragility of such communities would help make suburbanization possible.

To date, the best-known example of this process is the case of Rooster Town, a community of several hundred people established in 1900 in Winnipeg's South End Fort Rouge district.[46] Rooster Town residents lived in self-built homes—often made from old boxcars and other surplus railway materials—on city-owned land near the main line of the Canadian National Railway. Most Rooster Town families were direct descendants of Métis families that had been promised land in the Manitoba Treaty. Yet Rooster Town residents were effectively landless and confined to the lowest rungs of the job market, working as labourers for the railroad and for construction companies, or as haulers, landscapers, trash collectors, or snow shovellers.[47]

In the 1950s, Winnipeg City Council transferred the land under Rooster Town to the developer Arie Realty Ltd., for the construction of a $10 million complex dubbed Grant Park Plaza—advertised as the city's first modern shopping centre—and a new high school to serve the area's growing white population.[48] Rooster Town residents' demands for improved housing and infrastructure—including running water and sewer connections—were denied by City Council, which drew on the popular public health myth to cast them as inherently unsuitable participants in the suburban future of the area. In particular, City Council leveraged complaints by incoming white families that Rooster Town children—due to the supposed shiftlessness of their parents, rather than the City's refusal to extend indoor plumbing to Rooster Town—were exposing their children to infectious diseases at the area elementary school. In 1959, the City of Winnipeg evicted Rooster Town's residents and burned their homes to the ground.[49]

The evisceration of Rooster Town depended on—and reinvigorated—an apartheid tradition established in the late 1800s of construing Canadian cities as non-Native space. Historian David Burley writes that, "In the case of Rooster Town, suburban anxiety was reinforced by a deeply embedded sense that Aboriginal people did not belong in the city and by a history of municipal efforts, from the city's incorporation, to remove their visible presence." Burley correctly positions Rooster Town as an example of how urban restructuring has reiterated colonial dispossession in Canada. "[M]unicipal governance and urban processes generally in Winnipeg remained inextricably connected to the colonizing origins of the city," Burley writes, "and perpetuated the colonialism that, intermittently but relentlessly, dispossessed indigenous [sic] peoples of the land they had occupied historically or that they had been pushed onto."[50] The thefts of Rooster Town, Winnipeg's other Métis suburbs, and road allowance communities throughout the North-West exemplifies the role that subnational regional blocs, development agendas, and state institutions played in orchestrating Indigenous dispossession in the mid-twentieth century.[51] Acknowledging the precipitous role that such thefts played in suburbanization also corrects the dominant Canadian tendency to segregate colonial history from modern urban history. Clearly, settler-colonial dispossession was intimately involved in the making of modern suburbia.

The suburban vision proved immensely profitable for the dominant bloc and wildly popular with much of Winnipeg's working class, who could choose from little else when attempting to secure quality housing. Between 1941 and 1973, Winnipeg's suburban population increased from 80,000 to over 300,000. Sixty-four percent of the metropolitan population called the suburbs home by 1981, up from 26 percent in 1941.[52] Fittingly, in the 1970s, the president of one of Winnipeg's largest suburban developers—McKeag-Harris Realty—was chosen to lead the Independent Citizens Election Committee.[53]

RENOVATING THE RACIAL ORDER

Suburbanization became central to the postwar renovation of the regional racial order. The suburban agenda's dependence on expanded working-class consumption embraced upward mobility for many WASP and non-WASP European-descended workers. In the process—even as WASPs maintained a large degree of political and economic control over the city—industrial-era anti-Slavic racism and other forms of WASP-supremacy became increasingly obsolete to the dominant regional bloc and a new, particularly suburban, pan-European white identity began to emerge.[54]

Well-known signs of this transition include the abolition of restrictions on non-WASPs' entry into professions such as law and medicine in Manitoba in the 1940s, and the election, in 1956, of Winnipeg's first non-Anglo-Saxon mayor, Stephen Juba—a newly wealthy wholesaler originally from the North End—who would become the longest-serving mayor in Winnipeg history, holding on to the seat until retiring in 1977. The new "Ukrainian-Canadian" mayor was both a symbol of non-WASPs' passage into whiteness in Winnipeg and the long-standing political face of the suburban vision, running on a pro-developer, anti-tax platform and spearheading the city's massive suburban investments. Car culture, under the Juba Administration, became an emblem of both racial uplift and the city's suburban destiny. Juba flamboyantly announced his arrival on the city's political scene by driving a brand new yellow Cadillac to City Hall the morning after being elected and, from his Florida retirement home, bragged of having owned over twenty-five Cadillacs in his lifetime.[55] As thousands of would-be Jubas passed through previously locked doors, bought cars, and moved out of ethnic "ghettoes" and into new suburban subdivisions—though WASPS did not entirely welcome non-WASPs into certain subdivisions[56]—they began to share a common white suburban material interest, everyday life, culture, and consciousness with the city's WASPs.[57]

Home ownership was by far the greatest material lure of suburbia for the average worker. The federal subsidies given directly to homebuyers and the massive infrastructural spending of all three levels of government made home ownership newly accessible to people who had long been at the mercy of landlords. Crucially, small-time property ownership sutured workers to landlords and large property owners through a shared material interest in mounting property values and plummeting property taxes, which generally translated into a shared political commitment to liberalism, law and order, and the status quo.

The parallels with late-1800s settlement are striking: once again, a certain slice of the working class was invited to participate in the acquisition of stolen Métis and Anishinabe lands under conditions that encouraged them to align materially, culturally, politically, and racially with the colonizers in the dominant regional bloc. It was, of course, no coincidence that the dominant bloc was able to channel workers' desires for better lives

Culture of property and racism. (R to L) Mayor Juba, Bill Landes, Winnipeg Police Chief Blaw, ca. 1969. University of Manitoba Archives, Winnipeg Tribune fonds, Chief Blaw, Bill Landes, and Steve Juba, October 24, 1969, PC 18721518-6254-020. (Courtesy of University of Manitoba Archives)

in such a direction: the suburban agenda built on groundwork laid during the industrial period, in which much of the city's working class had been successfully encouraged to formulate their visions of freedom in terms that strove for inclusion within the white enfranchised ranks of Canada's settler-colonial order. Suburbanization offered many workers the whiteness they had long aspired to, but under conditions that folded them into the capitalist order rather than challenging it.

Beyond the basic material gains of home ownership, like the classic settler-colonial frontier, the suburban frontier offered workers the opportunity to remake themselves and activate their whiteness by participating in a thrilling, futuristic remaking—and retaking—of a new segment of the region. Suburbia—as promoted by Ladco, the Winnipeg Housebuilders' Association, and the Metropolitan Corporation of Greater Winnipeg—was where the modern, clean, safe, convenient, innovative, healthful, wholesome, peaceful, and pastoral postwar destiny of the region would be found. This image was, in effect, negatively defined against both the existing industrial-era city and the existing urban edge, each profitably derided by the dominant bloc as backwards, dirty, unhealthy, and immoral. Accordingly, a suburban identity, closely tied to the consolidation of pan-European whiteness, began to emerge in which upwardly mobile suburbanites were made to feel superior to those—viewed as unable to prosper in modernity—both left behind in the old city and displaced from the urban edge.[58] The material distinctions of car and home ownership, the new suburb-to-suburb expressway system, the suburban dominance of City Council via Unicity, the suburbanization of work, shopping, recreation, and other daily activities, and participation in new suburban institutions—from property owners' associations to country clubs—all contributed to a cultural distancing of suburbanites from urbanites.

In this way, suburbanization established new racial structures of feeling—on the foundations of apartheid and white supremacy bestowed by export-agricultural and industrial development—that would shape the decades to come. Two dynamics would emerge as particularly influential going forward. First, the victim-blaming way of seeing suburban Indigenous communities—that I have called *suburbs nullius*—updated and reinvigorated white pity and disdain for Native communities within city limits. Second, the feeling of suburban superiority established a new geographical division within the city's working class, encouraging suburban workers to view their urban counterparts as the source of their own misfortunes, and concealing the myriad subsidies making their new suburban lives possible. Both tendencies would come to bear powerfully on the city's next several decades, as Native, Black, and Asian peoples began more and more to inhabit the old city and to fill the lowest tiers of the urban capitalist order.

1   The Winnipeg General Strike is considered by many historians to be "the wellspring of Canadian social legislation." Several strike leaders won elected office at various levels of government. Tommy Douglas, who would become "the father of socialized medicine" in Canada, was a Winnipeg teenager at the time and witnessed the strike. Yet immediate gains were dismally small. For instance, Winnipeg metal workers won a reduced workweek, from 55 to 50 hours, with no wage increase, while building trades workers gained a wage increase of only fifteen cents per hour (Gutkin and Gutkin, *Profiles in Dissent: The Shaping of Radical Thought in the Canadian West*, 2; Bumsted, *Winnipeg General Strike of 1919: An Illustrated History*, 58; The Canadian Encyclopedia, "Tommy Douglas").

2   Artibise, *Winnipeg: An Illustrated History*, 207.

3   "The members of the order have driven the Communists out of factories and restored the plants to their owners...Anyone having difficulty with their labor should apply to the Fiscisti [sic], who will be pleased to furnish them with men," reported the Employers Association of Manitoba's *Special News Bulletin* (Kramer and Mitchell, *When the State Trembled*, 319); "A housing shortage of unprecedented scale was reported in the 1941 housing survey," reported the *Winnipeg Tribune* in 1942. "Housing conditions are so bad in our city that we cannot neglect the situation any longer," said Winnipeg mayor John Queen. "There is a constant violation of health bylaws but we cannot put the people out: they have nowhere to go" (*Winnipeg Tribune*, "Unknown").

4   Artibise, *Winnipeg: An Illustrated History*, 206, 116, 166.

5   Ibid., 199.

6   Harvey, "Consolidating Power."

7   Burley, "Rooster Town: Winnipeg's Lost Métis Suburb, 1900–1960," 9.

8   Metropolitan Planning Committee and Winnipeg Town Planning Commission, "Greater Winnipeg Tax Forfeited Lands."

9   Ibid., 179.

10   File I.7125, Committee on Public Improvements, City of Winnipeg Archives

11   Winnipeg Free Press, "Plan Urged On Highway Approaches: C of C Report Suggests Ways to Relieve Congestion," 7; Bower, "South Bypass Road to Be in Use Next Fall"; Best, "Province Will Build 3 Bridges in City Area."

12   Winnipeg Free Press, "Realism in Traffic."

13   Smith, Wilbur & Associates, *Report on Traffic, Transit, Parking, Metropolitan Winnipeg*.

14   Fletcher, "Winnipeg's Traffic: Blueprint for Action," 29.

15   Fletcher, "Winnipeg's Traffic: Blueprint for Action," 29.

16   Smith, Wilbur & Associates, *Report on Traffic, Transit, Parking, Metropolitan Winnipeg*, 171.

17   Fletcher, "Winnipeg's Traffic: Blueprint for Action," 29.

18   Smith, Wilbur & Associates, *Report on Traffic, Transit, Parking, Metropolitan Winnipeg*, 180.

19   Winnipeg Free Press, "Biggest Yet Road Plan Unveiled By Province."

20   Fletcher, "Council Gets Sweeping Powers Over Planning."

21   Metropolitan Corporation of Greater Winnipeg, *The End of the Metropolitan*.

22   Metropolitan Corporation of Greater Winnipeg, Planning Division, *Draft Development Plan: Metropolitan Winnipeg*; Metropolitan Corporation of Greater Winnipeg, *The End of the Metropolitan*.

23   Artibise, *Winnipeg: An Illustrated History*, 207.

24   Metropolitan Corporation of Greater Winnipeg. 1971. *The End of the Metropolitan*, 21.

25   Antonio Gramsci called this the "educative role of the state" (Gramsci, *Selections from the Prison Notebooks*).

26   Lyon and Fenton, "The Development of Downtown Winnipeg: Historical Perspectives on Decline and Revitalization," 156.

27   Metropolitan Corporation of Greater Winnipeg, *Charleswood Detailed Area Plan*, 5.

28   Metropolitan Planning Committee and Winnipeg Town Planning Commission, *Preliminary Report on Residential Areas*, 58; Metropolitan Corporation of Greater Winnipeg, *Charleswood Detailed Area Plan*, 46.

29   Winnipeg Free Press, "And A Commerce Degree Helps"; Winnipeg Free Press, "38 Builders Set to Work on Big 1,300 Home Project."

30   Winnipeg Free Press, "Residential Construction Ranks As One of Main City Industries."

31   Metropolitan Corporation of Greater Winnipeg. 1971. *The End of the Metropolitan*.

32   Winnipeg Free Press, "Residential Construction Ranks As One of Main City Industries."

33   Winnipeg Free Press, "To Display Latest Homes"; Quality Construction Co., "Parade of Homes" (WFP 9/16/1960).

34   Lyon and Fenton, "The Development of Downtown Winnipeg: Historical Perspectives on Decline and Revitalization," 101.

35   Artibise, *Winnipeg: An Illustrated History*, 178.

36   Lyon and Fenton, "The Development of Downtown Winnipeg: Historical Perspectives on Decline and Revitalization," 101.

37   Urban peripheries across twentieth-century Turtle Island were populated by thousands of self-built, often unsanctioned communities of varied class, race, and ethnic backgrounds (Nicolaides and Weiss, *The Suburb Reader*).

38   Burley, "Rooster Town: Winnipeg's Lost Métis Suburb, 1900–1960," 7, 20.

39   Lagassé, *A Study of the Population of Indian Ancestry Living in Manitoba: Main Report*, 68. Winnipeg's full geography of Métis suburbs is difficult to reconstruct due to their often-covert character, but includes such communities as Dog Patch, Tin Town, Weak City, Camp Hideaway, Stovepipe, Turkey Town, Rooster Town, as well as communities near present-day Garbage Hill, Assiniboia Downs, Grace Hospital, Maple Grove Rugby Park, and Parc Joseph Royal. See Barkwell, "20th Century Metis Displacement and Road Allowance Communities in Manitoba."

40   *"Suburbs nullius"* is a remix of the term *"urbs nullius,"* coined by Glen Coulthard in *Red Skin White Masks*, 176.

41   McKittrick, *Demonic Grounds*.

42   Ibid., 7.

43   Winnipeg Free Press, "A Muskrat Venice."

44   Kramer and Mitchell, *When the State Trembled*, 319.

ENDNOTES

45   Burley, "Rooster Town: Winnipeg's Lost Métis Suburb, 1900–1960," 15.

46   For more on Rooster Town see Peters et al., *Rooster Town: The History of an Urban Métis Community, 1901–1961* (forthcoming in 2018).

47   Burley, "Rooster Town: Winnipeg's Lost Métis Suburb, 1900–1960," 14, 7.

48   Winnipeg Free Press, "Huge Shopping Area to Cost $10 Million."

49   Burley, "Rooster Town: Winnipeg's Lost Métis Suburb, 1900–1960," 19, 3.

50   Ibid., 4, 20.

51   The term "municipal colonialism" has been used to describe this reality. Stanger-Ross, "Municipal Colonialism in Vancouver: City Planning and the Conflict over Indian Reserves, 1928–1950s."

52   Lyon and Fenton, "The Development of Downtown Winnipeg: Historical Perspectives on Decline and Revitalization," 53.

53   Silver, *Thin Ice*, 47.

54   Artibise, *Winnipeg: An Illustrated History*, 174.; Loewen and Friesen, 78.

55   Bumsted, *Dictionary of Manitoba Biography*; Czuboka, *Juba*.

56   Artibise, *Winnipeg: An Illustrated History*, 174.

57   Suburbanization was thus a "racial project" as Omi and Winant define the term in *Racial Formation in the United States*. Harris' concept of the "property of whiteness" in "Whiteness as Property" is also fundamental to understanding suburbanization.

58   For a discussion of the overlap between an emergent "suburban consciousness" and the consolidation of "white identity" across Turtle Island between 1940 and 1970 see Avila, *Popular Culture in the Age of White Flight*.

WAHBUNG

CITY VS. PORTAGE PLACE: THE URBAN POST-INDUSTRIAL VISION

While some may have felt as though life itself—not to mention civilization, modernity, innovation, and progress—was abandoning Winnipeg's city centre in the 1950s and beyond, this was as much a lie as ideas of *terra nullius* or *suburbs nullius* were. In fact, it was only money and its owners, public and private, who were departing. Suburbanization turned Winnipeg's city centre into a place of state and capitalist neglect; in other words, populated more and more by people—full of modern, innovative visions of human progress—who had been similarly abandoned.[1] It was in these years, as suburbia became associated with upward mobility and whiteness, that the city centre became increasingly known, more so than at any time since the conquest of Red River, as Native space.

Winnipeg has always been an Indigenous city, a reality indicated but not exhausted by the 1800s character of Red River and the Indigenous suburbs of the 1900s. The colonial feeling—required for and fostered by apartheid and genocide—that associates modernity with Indigenous disappearance, however, tended to purge long-standing urban Indigenous communities from popular perceptions of twentieth-century Canadian cities. Canadian censuses undercount urban Indigenous populations, perhaps most drastically so in the period between 1870 and 1950. This settler-colonial erasure, as Lunaape historian Mary Jane Logan McCallum calls it, contributes to a "gap in our history that exists after the so-called closing of the frontier" that "makes it appear as if Native people retreated from 'planet earth' only to appear again, angry and tardy, in 1969."[2] The idea that Indigenous peoples somehow first appeared on the urban scene after 1950 is false, and reiterates this colonial erasure.

It is true, however, that thousands and thousands of Indigenous peoples moved back to the area surrounding the confluence of the Red and Assiniboine Rivers after 1950. A mass urbanization of humanity was underway in this moment, as Canada, along with the rest of the world, transitioned to a majority urban society. But as rural white settlers—many of them with wealth linked directly to stolen land gifted to their ancestors by the Dominion Lands Act—moved to Canadian cities in large numbers at this time, the conditions prompting Indigenous peoples' migration to cities were specific to their position within the settler-colonial order.

MAKING CITIES NATIVE AGAIN

Most significantly, First Nations peoples were forced to overcome the systematic exertion of Canadian state power intended to keep them contained within the boundaries of Indian reserves and therefore out of cities. From the outset, Indigenous peoples resisted apartheid on a day-to-day level, and Indian Agents' ability to enforce reserve borders was always partial and incomplete. Throughout the first half of the twentieth century, First Nations peoples also mounted formal campaigns against apartheid. The League of Indians—an early First Nations coalition whose leadership came mostly from west of the Great Lakes—lobbied against the pass system throughout the 1920s and 1930s, until the League dissolved in the 1940s.[3] Cree political leader and author Harold Cardinal argued that the very isolation imposed by apartheid worked against First Nations' attempts to scale-up resistance to it. Totalitarian Indian Agent control, police harassment of political organizers, and inadequate transportation and communications infrastructure, Cardinal argued in his landmark 1969 study, *The Unjust Society,* hampered First Nations' attempts to organize at federal and provincial scales in order to gain freedom from the most authoritarian aspects of the Indian Act.[4]

By the 1940s, however, many First Nations had created successful coalitions at the provincial scale. These "provincial movements," as Cardinal called them, "gradually began to penetrate the isolation of the Indian communities" and generated a growing movement for liberation from Indian Agent control and for the Crown to finally honour its treaties with First Nations. In 1951, through the first significant amendments to the Indian Act in 50 years, this movement won the abolition of the pass system and a significant overall reduction in Canadian state control imposed on First Nations.[5]

Abolitionists. League of Indians, Thunderchild Reserve, Saskatchewan, ca. 1921. Glenbow Archives, NA-928-1, Conference of League of Indians of Western Canada, Thunderchild Reserve, Saskatchewan. (Courtesy of the Glenbow Archives)

Like millions of others around the world in the twentieth century, Indigenous peoples in Canada moved to cities as a result of being dispossessed of their traditional lands. As discussed in Chapter 1, Indigenous peoples' share of the late-1800s land redistribution that inaugurated the Canadian nation-state was minuscule compared to the share taken by the CPR, the HBC, and white settlers. Land bases allocated to First Nations through treaties with the Crown were never designed to provide sufficient livelihoods for *growing* Indigenous populations. Like every action the Canadian state took, land allocations were based on the assumption that Indigenous populations would be decimated.

Even the tiny portion promised to First Nations was never delivered. Canada systematically broke its treaty promises to First Nations and Métis peoples—utilizing police and military force when necessary—leaving Indigenous peoples with even less of an economic base than they initially bargained for.[6] Amendments to the Indian Act gave industrialization and urbanization schemes legal power to dispossess First Nations' lands, often using the language of land "surrender."[7] Through such amendments, the federal government committed itself to dispossessing and displacing any First Nation near to or partly within a town of at least 8,000 people; any First Nation whose lands were said to be required for "roads, railways, or other public purposes"; or any First Nation whose lands were said to be required for agricultural production. The federal government also committed itself to "right-sizing" any First Nation it deemed held more land than its population warranted. The cumulative impact of these attacks was enormous: between 1896 and 1911, 21 percent of First Nations' lands in the Prairie West was taken.[8] Into the 1970s, Canada had not completely fulfilled a single treaty with First Nations peoples.[9]

In addition to straight-up land theft, the gradual industrialization of the country over the course of the twentieth century separated Indigenous peoples from their lands and forced them into capitalist labour markets by wreaking havoc on ecosystems that communities had relied on for generations. In Manitoba, the construction of a provincial railroad network between 1900 and 1930—eventually connecting Winnipeg to northern urban centres such as Churchill and The Pas—"opened up" much of the province to rapid investment in mining, timber cutting, paper milling, and commercial hunting and fishing. Mining companies were especially damaging to the environment—for instance, recklessly setting fire to vast swaths of land to make mineral exploration easier. With feeding grounds levelled for mineral or timber extraction, caribou, fur-bearing animals, and other mainstays of local economies became scarce. New railroads also brought commercial hunters to the region in unprecedented numbers, drastically depleting the numbers of beaver, otter, fox, muskrat, and other fur-bearing animals.[10]

With fur and game animals disappearing, many First Nations peoples relied much more heavily on fishing. But industry—especially pulp and paper mills—ruined many fishing economies by dumping industrial waste into local waterways. Where fishing remained viable, non-Indigenous commercial fishers increasingly began to capture an overwhelming share. The transition from sailboats to gas boats in the 1930s, which non-Indigenous commercial fisheries—predominantly Icelanders on Lake Winnipeg—were able to afford much earlier than Indigenous fishers, rapidly accelerated overfishing.[11]

For a few decades, Indigenous peoples in northern Manitoba were able to forestall the long-term destructive effects of industrialization by participating in the new industrial labour market. Indigenous labour was crucial to early northern industrialization before railways made it easier to import non-Native workers. Much of the labour was seasonal, but the state picked up the costs, through social assistance payments, of maintaining workers' families year round. As a result, between 1900 and 1930 the living standards of many Indigenous peoples improved over the old fur-trade economy. But when the industrial boom ended in the 1930s, as labour-saving technologies were introduced in many industries, and new railways brought workers from the south, Indigenous living conditions steeply declined.[12]

In the 1940s and 1950s, the Canadian state began to officially encourage and finance Indigenous peoples' migration to cities. Dispossessed Native communities that had been a crucial source of labour for northern industry now began to be viewed as liabilities as long as they remained on their traditional lands. As early as the 1940s, Indian Affairs worked with the National Employment Service to place Indigenous women as care workers in urban nursing homes, hospitals, and private residences. In the 1950s, inspired by the US program, the Canadian Department of Indian Affairs created an Indian Placement and Relocation Program to facilitate the relocation of First Nations peoples to cities.[13] One of the program's four placement officers was deployed to Winnipeg in 1956. "By the early 1960s," historical geographer Frank Tough writes, "the surplus Native population of northern Manitoba was being encouraged to move to Winnipeg." More and more, Canadian politicians and bureaucrats began to speak of "integration" as the progressive response to the country's failed history of "racial segregation," positioning urban relocation as the proper means to that end.[14]

By the 1960s and 1970s, a new industry, even more destructive than those of the early twentieth century, took hold in northern Manitoba. Hydroelectric development experienced its "expansionary glory days"[15] in these years, as Manitoba Hydro constructed massive new dams that fractured and displaced many more First Nations communities. In their oral history of Misipawistik Cree Nation (also known as Grand Rapids, Manitoba) on the northwest shores of Lake Winnipeg, political theorists Peter Kulchyski and Ramona Neckoway provide one of the best case studies of the impact of Manitoba Hydro development on a single community. For the construction of the dam at Grand Rapids, homes of Misipawistik residents were bulldozed without consent; fences and other infrastructure were built across inhabited lands without consent; families were forcibly relocated without consent or compensation; graveyards were destroyed, as were vegetable gardens that the community relied on for food; police began to appear regularly in the community for the first time; residents experienced racist harassment from both police and influxes of new Manitoba Hydro workers; and Misipawistik residents were forced into the wage economy and went hungry for the first time in their lives.[16] Despite the radical destruction of economies and ways of life, and decades of organized resistance to Manitoba Hydro, Indigenous communities received little compensation for their lands. By 2007, Misipawistik, for instance, had received only $5.5 million in total compensation while the dam that destroyed their lands produced over $1 billion per year in revenue.[17]

As Indigenous populations began to increase rapidly by the middle of the twentieth century, all of these factors—the abolition of the pass system; ongoing theft of Indigenous land bases; ongoing environmental destruction; faltering labour demand in northern resource industries; and state encouragement of urban migration—combined to make moving to the city the most desirable option for thousands and thousands of Indigenous people. By the 1950s, Indigenous peoples were younger on average, freer, and more alienated from their traditional means of production than at any time in recent memory. As a result, a new generation moved to Canadian cities in search of jobs, education, and an escape from the legacy of apartheid, residential schools, and Indian Agent control.[18]

FEAR OF A NATIVE CITY: URBAN APARTHEID AND THE "URBAN INDIAN" INDUSTRY

But Canadian cities did not welcome Indigenous peoples. Canadian urbanites who had known nothing other than apartheid—and had grown to view it as necessary and proper, if they considered it at all—were troubled to find themselves increasingly sharing space with Indigenous communities.[19] In a reworking of the racial order, at the same time as post-war pan-European whiteness took shape, urban Indigenous peoples emerged— more so, perhaps, than at any time since the turn of the twentieth century—as a conscious target of white violence, exclusion, and management. Soon enough, white Winnipeggers began to take action to control and contain Indigenous peoples moving to cities, in what amounted to a new system of urban apartheid. In postwar Winnipeg, urban apartheid meant that Indigenous peoples were generally unwelcome south of Portage Avenue.[20] "NO INDIANS" signs were posted in storefront windows, and Indigenous peoples were refused service at restaurants and other public spaces.[21] Indigenous peoples moving to cities found themselves largely shut out of urban housing and job markets. Many landlords refused to rent to Indigenous households, pushing them into the worst housing in neighbourhoods with the most deteriorated infrastructure and the fewest amenities— areas hardest hit by the organized abandonment of suburbanization. Clearly, the rhetoric of "integration" deployed by the Department of Indian Affairs was at odds with the actual urban order in cities such as Winnipeg.

As early as the 1950s, Canadian settler society identified growing urban Indigenous populations as one of the country's most serious postwar social problems. Much of the Canadian state remained oriented toward apartheid—First Nations peoples outside reserve boundaries were ineligible for many provincial and federal health, education, and social programs, for instance[22]—and it scrambled to address new post-apartheid realities. Government agencies, churches, and other non-profit citizen's groups organized conferences and drafted reports on the "problem"—as a 1958 Regina, Saskatchewan, conference put it—of "our city Indians."[23] Conferences such as these defined urban Indigenous peoples as a problematic population for which settlers must take ownership and responsibility, framing urban Indigenous communities as urgent objects of white analysis and management.

This dynamic was formalized at the highest levels of the Canadian state. In 1962, the Department of Citizenship and Immigration introduced the concept of the "Urban Indian" as a new category within Canada's de facto typology of Indigenous peoples-to-be-governed. "It is time that the expression 'Urban Indian' began to take its place with others—the Plains Indian, the Woodlands Indian, the Enfranchised Indian, and the Half-breed or Metis [sic]," a department official at the time explained. "From the point of view of the Citizenship Branch, an urban Indian is anyone who is living off the reserve in a setting where there are industrial and commercial job opportunities, and who identifies himself as an Indian."[24] This shorthand entrenched and accelerated the targeted analysis and management of Indigenous communities in Canadian cities.

Following in the footsteps of the white supremacist Kanucks, industrialist moral reformers, and peddlers of *suburbs nullius* who came before them, the "Urban Indian" industry promoted the idea that urban Indigenous peoples themselves were primarily to blame for inhumane living conditions in postwar Canadian cities. This explanation of urban poverty rested on the idea that Indigenous peoples were culturally unfit for, and therefore traumatized by, city life. "Our Indian Canadian is faced or hampered with...his own personality," the organizer of a 1957 conference in Calgary, Alberta, told assembled delegates. "These differences have nothing to do with his blood or heredity but are from his cultural heritage...For instance, his concepts of time, money, social communication, hygiene, usefulness, competition and cooperation are at variance with our own and can prove a stumbling block to successful adjustment."[25]

Through this self-consciously non-biological cultural racism, urban Indigenous peoples—their personalities, customs, and worldviews—rather than settler cities or colonial histories, became the targets of study and adjustment. In effect, this analysis concluded that Indigenous cultures within modern cities were inherently cultures of poverty. This misdirection of analysis and critique away from urban settler power, structures, and attitudes, onto Indigenous peoples themselves, would endure to become one of the most powerful ideological manoeuvres to shape Canadian cities in the twentieth century. In the combination of urban apartheid with the "Urban Indian" industry, we again see the two-sided coin of racial vilification and racial uplift characteristic of settler-colonial capitalism in the North-West; that is, the co-mingling of outright racist violence and dispossession—by landlords, police, employers, banks, shopkeepers, and state institutions—with a gentler approach that seeks to lift Indigenous peoples up to the

level of so-called functional urban settlers through education, training, and the inculca-
tion of capitalist habits and customs, while shielding structural violence from view.

COUNTER-PLAN IV: URBAN INDIGENOUS SELF-DETERMINATION IN THE SPIRIT OF *WAHBUNG*

One of the first targets of grassroots Indigenous organizing in postwar Winnipeg was
the monopoly white settlers held on public explanations of urban Indigenous realities.
The virtually all-white Winnipeg Welfare Council held high-profile "Indian and Métis
conferences" annually throughout the 1950s, showcasing white academics' research
on the "Indian problem."[26] Indigenous peoples were to be seen and not heard at these
conferences; many attended but few were allowed to speak. "We thought this was an
Indian conference and now we find it's a white man's conference," the *Winnipeg Tribune*
quoted an "Indian representative" who had attended the 1959 conference. "Maybe next
year they should leave a few gaps in the agenda in case Indians have something to say."[27]

For Marion Meadmore—a prominent Cree and Ojibwe Winnipeg organizer, originally from Peepeekisis First Nation—attending the white-dominated "Indian and Métis
conferences" was a formative political experience. Meadmore moved to Winnipeg in
1953 to attend the University of Manitoba after graduating from Indian Residential
School in Birtle, Manitoba. "One day I was reading the paper and I found out—this is
how I came downtown [for the first time]—there was a session at the legislative building
at which they were going to be talking about 'Indian problems,' and all the white people
from the churches, from the social agencies, and volunteers, all got around this 'Indian
problem,'" said Meadmore. "What was amazing to me was the fact that the chiefs here
never got together on their own to speak about their own problems, they only got to speak
to the issues that were raised by this white committee as 'Indian problems.' So it didn't
seem right. I said, 'We've just got to have our own organization.'" Meadmore, along with
Jimmy Elk (Dakota), Mary Guilbault (Cree), and Ernie Guilbault (Métis), soon founded
the Urban Indian Association (UIA), one of postwar Winnipeg's first all-Indigenous
organizations.[28]

The UIA organized mutual aid efforts out of members' homes, helping people access
necessities of life—housing, jobs, and health care—and providing much-needed gathering
space for Native people in a city that often refused them entry to meeting places. Funds
were raised by holding dances at local halls. In 1959, with funds from the Winnipeg
Welfare Council and the Manitoba government, the UIA opened the Winnipeg Indian
and Métis Friendship Centre (IMFC) at 376 Donald Street near Ellice Avenue in downtown Winnipeg, the first in what became a national network of Indigenous-run Friendship Centres in Canadian cities.[29]

By starting the UIA and IMFC, Indigenous organizers in Winnipeg were at the
forefront of a national movement to create new Indigenous urban spaces and alliances,
foster strong Indigenous identities and ways of life in settler cities, and reshape those

cities according to Indigenous peoples' priorities, against the settler state's desire to shape Indigenous peoples according to settler cities' priorities. In doing so, urban organizers foreshadowed Cardinal's classic critique of Canada's racial integration agenda: "Curiously, integration seems to be a one-way street with the government," Cardinal wrote in *The Unjust Society*. "Always it is the Indian who must integrate into the white environment, never the other way around."[30] As Leslie Hall, leading historian of the Winnipeg IMFC, puts it, "Aboriginal peoples argued strongly that their cultures were not incompatible with urban living or the modern world and that the 'problem' was actually a series of circumstances that Aboriginal people faced when attempting to access adequate housing, employment, and social services."[31] In other words, urban Indigenous organizers flipped settler scripts of the so-called unprepared urban Indian, imagining a decolonial city that would be prepared for—and by—them instead. As a result, 1960s and 1970s Winnipeg, especially its city centre, became a continental hub of both Indigenous anti-poverty organizing and Indigenous militancy associated with the Red Power movement.

"It really started here," said George Munroe (Anishinabe) — who moved from Camperville, Manitoba, to Winnipeg in 1965—speaking of the rapid postwar rise of urban Indigenous organizing across Canada. Munroe started a 500-member youth group at the IMFC called Club 376 and later became a Winnipeg city councillor, in 1971.[32] Munroe cited the IMFC and Kinew Housing Inc.—the first Native-run urban affordable housing organization in Canada—as made-in-Winnipeg models that quickly spread across the country. Munroe was one of many well-known figures that came up through the Winnipeg IMFC. "The [IMFC] was responsible for a lot of leaders being developed in Winnipeg, Native leaders," said long-time Winnipeg community organizer Louise Chippeway (Anishinabe). "Yvonne Monkman, Allan Chartrand, Tom Jackson, Amy Clemons, Earl Duncan, Phil Fontaine, Ovide Mercredi, Elijah Harper, there were just so many distinguished and creative and unique people that evolved from the [IMFC], it was a movement."[33] The effectiveness of Native organizing in Winnipeg was impossible to ignore. As militant anti-colonial movements overthrew colonial occupiers around the world in the mid-1900s, Canadians worried that Winnipeg would be ground zero for a Native uprising. The *Free Press*, in October 1972, warned of "rumors emanating from eastern Canada that Winnipeg and the Six Nations Reserve area in Ontario are to be the 'testing grounds for Indian militancy' in Canada."[34] A new round of racist vilification emerged in the city at this time, as the city's more militant Native organizers were pathologized in the local press as disturbed troublemakers and settlers resorted to public celebrations of conquest in an attempt to intimidate them.[35]

Urban organizing, for many, was conceived as resistance to the totalitarian control and isolation enforced by Canadian apartheid. "There was a lack of leadership in the Aboriginal community because we weren't allowed to organize, up until the 1960s," said Mary Richard (Métis), a long-time Winnipeg community organizer originally from

Red Power hub. The first Indian Métis Friendship
Centre in Canada, main floor, 376 Donald Street,
Winnipeg, ca. 1960s. (Used with permission of the
Indian & Métis Friendship Centre)

Remaking the city. (L to R) Ernie Guilbault, Mary Richard, and Mary Guilbault at the Winnipeg IMFC,
ca. 1970s. University of Manitoba Archives, Winnipeg Tribune Personalities Collection, UM_pc018_A81-
012_013_0468_007_0001. (Courtesy of University of Manitoba Archives & Special Collections)

Camperville, Manitoba. "We weren't allowed to organize, we weren't allowed to fight for treaty rights and all that, but all of a sudden, all that was available to us. That's when the people really started getting involved."[36] Meadmore critiqued apartheid for preventing Indigenous peoples from maintaining social and political relationships with the rest of the world, and considered urban organizing to be a defiant return to these relationships. "It's a challenge for all of us people to come back into society after we were carefully shelved or put out to pasture, in the old days through boarding schools or reserves," said Meadmore. "We had to fight our way back into society, and guess what? We're doing it."

Solidarity between Indigenous peoples from different nations, Indian reserves, and communities, forcibly isolated from one another by apartheid, therefore became an important goal of postwar urban organizing. For Meadmore and the other founders of Winnipeg's IMFC, building affinities within the city's diverse Indigenous community was a crucial first step. "What we did was, we went and got people together, and we held socials, dances, and we introduced this word 'friendship' as being really important," said Meadmore. "So we got to be a community, and the community started doing things together." According to Hall, the IMFC community was uniquely pan-Native. "Although many different First Nations and Métis cultural groups used the Centre," Hall found, "[Hall's interlocutors] all agreed that in the city there was a shared Aboriginal identity in opposition to the dominant culture of the city."[37] Urbanization and urban organizing, therefore, fostered—and required—alliances within Indigeneity that apartheid had deliberately forestalled.

Work on transnational friendship within the city extended to similar efforts by Winnipeg organizers to build transnational Indigenous unity across Canada and the world. UIA members travelled to Regina, Banff, Edmonton, and other western Canadian cities attending conferences and meeting with fellow urban Indigenous organizers in the lead-up to establishing the IMFC.[38] In 1972, Winnipeg became home to the National Association of Friendship Centres, formalizing its central role in the cross-country network. Early Winnipeg IMFC organizers—including Meadmore, Mary Guilbault (Métis), and Dorothy Betz (Anishinabe)—travelled to places such as New Zealand, Brazil, and the United Nations headquarters in Geneva, Switzerland, attending conferences and building pan-Indigenous alliances across nation-state borders.[39]

The American Indian Movement (AIM), born in the United States, was particularly influential for Winnipeg organizers in the 1960s and 1970s, as Red Power activists from across Turtle Island travelled through Winnipeg.[40] A week into the 1973 occupation at Wounded Knee, South Dakota, a coalition of Winnipeg organizations—including the Committee on Indian Rights, the Committee on Indian Rights for Indian Women, the Canadian Native Justice League, and the Black Action Movement—sent telegrams to US president Richard Nixon, US senator Ted Kennedy, and the US Bureau of Indian Affairs demanding the US meet the occupation's demands and give amnesty to all occupiers. The Winnipeg coalition held a press conference at the Winnipeg Native Club on River

Avenue on the same day, hosting Lakota journalist and former AIM national coordinator Harold Iron Shield.[41] "We are demanding that negotiating sessions be taken seriously by the United States government," said Iron Shield, "so that bloodshed will not occur as it did 83 years ago."[42]

From very early on, Red Power organizers chose Winnipeg as a continental hub. The first six-week Canadian Indian Workshop—inspired by the Workshops on American Indian Affairs that one historian has called "militant activist intellectual training camps"[43]—was held at the University of Manitoba in the summer of 1966. The workshop was organized by the Canadian Indian Youth Council and brought 20 Indigenous student organizers from across Canada—including members of the Cree, Blackfoot, Kwakiutl, Salteaux, Maliseet, Sarcee, Blood, Ojibwe, Montagnais, Odawa, Coast Salish, and Huron nations—together with many young Winnipeggers including Janet Fontaine (Cree), Phil Fontaine (Ojibwe), Marie Annharte Baker (Blackfoot), Agnes Nanowin, and Jackson Beardy (Ojibwe). Workshop activities included "daily work sessions designed to sort out some of the issues of common and central concern," as well as lectures, readings, film screenings, field trips to Lower Fort Garry, Peguis First Nation, and the IMFC (by then relocated to Main Street), and meetings with students from Minneapolis and Mayor Juba.[44] Cardinal, then 21 years old, was President of the Canadian Indian Workshop in 1966 and would later elaborate on many of the workshop's key themes in his writings.

Like the IMFC, the 1966 workshop aspired to pan-Indigenous unity in defiance of Canadian apartheid. "[T]he big problem facing us at the moment is the fact that we cannot accept one another," wrote Carol Wabegijig, editor of *Nish Nawh Be*, the workshop's newsletter. "Are we not Indians? Or, are we a treaty Indian, a non-treaty Indian, an enfranchised Indian or a Metis? When will we wake up to the fact that this is a policy imposed again by the government [?]" "The Indian Reserve is isolated," begins another entry in *Nish Nawh Be*. "There is the overriding power of the government in the everyday life of the Indian living on the reserve," it continues. "There must be more communication among the Indian people—first on the reserve, reserve to reserve in an area, region, on a provincial scale, then on a national scale. In this way, there will be communication of ideas and as a result there will be a broad outlook concerning our own environment."[45]

The 1966 workshop clearly articulated one of the major objectives of Indigenous postwar organizing in Canada: to study white settler modernity not for the purpose of assimilating into it but to effectively survive, critique, and develop alternatives to it. "[T]he Workshop has reversed an historic pattern in which the European studies the Indian," wrote the editors of *Nish Nawh Be*, "and in the course of the Workshop it has been the Indian who has studied the white-man." Workshop participants began from the premise that the prevalence of "poverty, degradation, structural imprisonment, and the sense of rejection" in Canadian society was primarily caused by white settlers, not Indigenous peoples. "If you want to get along," wrote the editors of *Nish Nawh Be*, "Don't say 'Indian problem'…What should you use in your vocabulary??? Well…White-man's problem."[46]

Winnipeg became a laboratory for Indigenous peoples to research white settler modernity. *The Prairie Call*—a newspaper published by the IMFC—circulated reflections on urban life that turned a critical eye to settler society and flipped settler scripts. "Many of us, for instance, find it difficult to cope with the impersonal attitude which is predominant in contemporary society," wrote Tom Stevenson in a 1961 article entitled "The Importance of Defending Our Culture." "Who is sincere and who isn't? Who is genuine? Am I really accepted, or are they just tolerating me? Such questions typify this underlying uncertainty, this vagueness, this craving for that which is real."[47] With articles like this, *The Prairie Call* introduced a new urban type to counter that of the so-called unprepared Indian—namely, the ethically suspect settler.

Winnipeg organizers, activists, and writers conducted rigorous studies of the larger settler-driven postwar urban processes, institutions, and structures that produced urban Indigenous poverty—from deindustrialization and suburbanization to housing and labour markets to policing and government bureaucracy. A 1968 *Prairie Call* article addressed to Indigenous peoples considering a move to the city warns, "Unfortunately, many people think that the city is the land of 'Milk and Honey'; that is jobs and education are here for the asking. Well, what are the facts?" The article goes on to address mounting layoffs in urban industry—citing CPR and McGavin's Bakeries in particular—rising housing costs, the city's housing shortage, and widespread landlord delinquency. "Many unscrupulous landlords offer substandard housing to people in the slum area of the city and people are paying for dilapidated accommodation that isn't worth the price," the article concludes. "Sometimes, it takes two or three weeks to find a place to live because of the housing shortage, many people wind up on the streets."[48] This was definitely not the stance of the wider settler city, which blamed Indigenous peoples' "slum" conditions on their own peculiar lack of capacity for urban living.

The racist function of settler police forces quickly became a priority for urban Native organizers, and critiques of the police often broadened to the entire urban social structure. A thousand people marched from Higgins Avenue and Main Street to the Manitoba Legislature in Winnipeg in the fall of 1972, protesting the recently released Toal Report. Prepared by former Winnipeg police superintendent James Toal, the document exonerated police in Brandon, Manitoba, of "prejudice against Indian and Métis" urbanites that march organizers described as "clearly racist." George Munroe, then a city councillor, spoke at the end of the march, organized by the Urban Native Organizations Coalition. "Our people were and are the most brutally harassed people in the world," said Munroe. "Never has a nation of peoples been ravished so cruelly, so unscrupulously, in the history of man." Standing in front of the Legislature, Munroe cited Winnipeg's built environment as evidence. "Look about you, my brothers and sisters, this legislature, those tall buildings, those fancy stores, and all those other institutions. Are our people housed there? Employed there? And happy there?" asked Munroe. "No, my friends, our people are not in these places. But look further, brothers and sisters, then you will see our people, in ugly ghettos, in slum houses, in flea-bag hotels, in dilapidated apartments, in welfare offices, in stinking, degrading and soul-destroying jails."[49] By pointing to the city's divided geography as an expression of settler power,

Munroe turned rage against racist policing toward the subtler, but just as deadly, workings of urban housing and job markets.

Grassroots organizers—most of them Indigenous women—conducted much of the early postwar research in Winnipeg that proved the racist outcomes of urban institutions. Dorothy Betz helped criminalized Indigenous peoples navigate the settler legal system as the IMFC's court worker. During Betz's years in this role, the IMFC found that Indigenous Winnipeggers were arrested at a much higher rate and for more minor offenses than the general population. Like Munroe, Betz linked the litany of so-called vagrancy and disturbing the peace charges against Indigenous peoples in Winnipeg directly to the structural racism of urban housing markets and the urban apartheid system that kept Indigenous peoples out of most bars, cafés, and other public spaces, forcing them into the streets.[50]

The downtown Winnipeg–based Manitoba Indian Brotherhood (MIB) sponsored one of the earliest formal studies of Indigenous peoples' housing conditions in postwar Winnipeg. "We submit that the Indian has consistently occupied the lowest level of housing in the city, to the extent that one could consider such accommodation the private preserve of the native populace," the MIB concluded. "Upon arrival in the city—usually with the most meager of personal possessions and minimal financial resources, the Indian's primary concern is in locating accommodation…If he is fortunate enough to have friends or relatives residing in the city, he may obtain temporary lodging for his family in an already over-crowded generally substandard dwelling in some deteriorating section of the city's inner core." The MIB went on to add a critique of the modern welfare state:

> If he cannot obtain even temporary lodging and lacks finances, the newly-arrived Indian soon makes the acquaintance of the City Welfare Dept., usually through referral by the Indian Affairs Department. Here he confronts a labyrinth of bureaucratic obfuscation that would boggle the mind of the most sophisticated white and embarks on an extended process of acculturation, the initial exercise of which involves exchanging his name for a number.[51]

Doris Young—a long-time urban organizer originally from Opaskwayak Cree Nation—conducted research for the study. "That was when I started really realizing the services and the lack of services and particularly the bad housing conditions for Aboriginal people in the city," Young recalled. "The housing conditions were really quite bad," especially for elderly people, and "there was overcrowding already."[52]

Marion Meadmore was also involved with housing research and organizing in the 1960s and 1970s. "Housing was the thing that the people wanted," said Meadmore, who studied the Winnipeg housing market primarily while trying to help friends find rental accommodation. "[My friend] would phone up and see if a house was available, and I'd drive her there. When we got there, the house was no longer available," said Meadmore. This was, "A) Because she was Native, B) Because she had a child," said Meadmore. "And this thing kept going on, and I just couldn't believe things like that happened. And then when she finally got a place, and she's allergic to bed bugs, behold, it was bed bugs, and she had to get out." Meadmore and Young were central participants in a wave of 1960s and 1970s Indigenous housing activism that led to the creation of groups such as Kinew Housing Inc. and the Winnipeg Indian Métis Tenants' Association.

Notably, Indigenous critiques of urban modernity extended to the white settler left, including political parties, organized labour, and white feminist groups. Such critiques often stemmed from Indigenous organizers' desires to forge solidarity with white workers against the ruling class. "It is acknowledged that the Labor Movement is also one of the strongest voices in speaking out for and effecting social change and the betterment of our society," the MIB, led by David Courchene (Ojibwe), wrote in its landmark study of Manitoba's postwar political economy, *Wahbung: Our Tomorrows*. "[The Labour Movement] has however, been notably silent on matters related to inequality and injustice as these apply to Indian people," the MIB went on. "Without greater understanding between Labor and Indian we deny both the benefit of productive society."[53] In response, Winnipeg organizers were involved in forming Canada-wide labour organizations specifically for Indigenous workers, such as the Registered Nurses of Canadian Indian Ancestry, in which Winnipeggers Jocelyn Bruyere (Cree) and Ann Callahan (Cree) played major roles.[54]

The silence of so-called progressive whites on issues of freedom and justice for Indigenous peoples became a frequent target. Organizers of the 1972 march from Higgins and Main to the Manitoba Legislature criticized white socialists for not taking the demands and aspirations of Indigenous peoples seriously, using the issue of police brutality as a prime example. The Manitoba New Democratic Party (NDP) Government led by Premier Ed Schreyer was notably silent on the anti-Native racism of the Toal Report. "Mr. Schreyer has only two alternatives," the organizers of the march wrote in a public statement. "1. Reject the Toal report. 2. Or condone and accept it, which will indicate he is satisfied to head a racist government."[55] The Manitoba NDP's failure to heed such criticisms would prove disastrous for many in the 2000s and 2010s, as the party presided over an unprecedented expansion of policing and imprisonment of Indigenous peoples.[56]

Indigenous women organizing against sexual violence also criticized white feminist groups for antagonizing Indigenous women. Indigenous women organized to open a safe house in the late 1970s and early 1980s specifically for Indigenous women escaping male violence in Winnipeg. Osborne House, the city's existing women's shelter, was often a hostile environment for Indigenous women, according to Doris Young. "Native women weren't feeling very welcomed at Osborne House," said Young, "and they didn't stay and sometimes they were told 'there's no room' when they went." Young and her fellow organizers asked the Manitoba government and Osborne House to support the project. "The province said, 'there is a house already for women' and Osborne House didn't want to be helpful to us," said Young. "In fact they were in the way, they weren't supportive, they said, 'We have a house.' We said, 'Yeah we know that, but Aboriginal women need one.'" Winnipeg became a hub of Indigenous feminist organizing in the 1980s—in part, it would seem, because of white feminists' hostility to the specific concerns of Indigenous women—as Winnipeggers created groups such as the Committee on Indian Rights for Indian Women, the Indigenous Women's Collective, the 400-member Original Women's Network, and "Not Vanishing," the first Native women's call-in radio show in Canada.

Urban Indigenous organizing in postwar Winnipeg, heavily influenced by and interwoven with the Red Power movement, emerged as a struggle for Indigenous self-determination over urban communities. *Wahbung: Our Tomorrows*, which many grassroots Winnipeg organizers worked on, outlined three "fundamental facts" of modern Indigenous organizing:

> First, we are determined to remain a strong and proud and identifiable group of people. Second, we refuse to have our lives directed by others who do not and who can not know our ways. Third, we are a 20ᵗʰ-century people, not a colourful folkloric remnant. We are capable and competent and perfectly able to assess today's conditions and develop ways of adjusting positively and successfully to them.[57]

Grassroots Winnipeg organizers took to heart that the second of these "fundamental facts"—the call for self-determination and autonomy—ought to apply to all Indigenous communities, including those in the city. Over the course of the 1970s, 1980s, and beyond, Indigenous communities in Winnipeg took over urban housing, schools, grocery stores, daycares, child-welfare agencies, employment agencies, and other institutions that greatly affected their lives. Children of the Earth High School, Payuk Cooperative Housing, Neechi Foods, and Ma Mawi Wi Chi Itata Centre are just a few examples from this era that remain fixtures in Winnipeg to this day.

Grassroots Indigenous organizers in Winnipeg viewed the fight for urban community control and the fight for national self-determination as two sides of the same struggle. Many fights over Indigenous self-determination in the city—such as those over education and child welfare—were conceived as logical next steps after winning self-determination. "All of this is self-determination you know, you can't really escape from that," Young said, reflecting on the gendered yet mostly supportive relationship between urban and national struggles. "Where the men were being involved was in another political process...they would have been running for chiefs and maybe the MMF as well," said Young. Meanwhile, Indigenous women took direct action to transform the city into a place where Indigenous peoples could survive and thrive. "That's where we shone," said Young, "in what we saw as a need in the city."

Achieving Indigenous self-determination over settler cities was not easily done, of course, as those in power resisted losing it at nearly every turn. In Winnipeg, direct action was often necessary to win Indigenous community control. In the early 1980s, the Winnipeg Native Child Welfare Coalition (WNCWC)—co-chaired by long-time Winnipeg activists Louise Champagne (Métis) and Kathy Mallett—was organized to take control of child welfare from the non-Native Children's Aid Society (CAS). "[The CAS] was shipping these kids right out of the province," said Champagne. "They were sending them south to U.S. farmers, you know, as farm labour." "We were aware that a lot of the Aboriginal organizations outside of the city were moving towards trying to take control of the members that are taken out of their communities," said Champagne, "and nothing was happening in the city...so we organized." One year, the WNCWC sent busloads of people to disrupt the CAS annual general meeting by sitting on the floor eating bag-lunches while CAS members ate hot food during an official luncheon. Actions such as this one finally led to the creation in 1984 of Ma Mawi Wi Chi Itata, Winnipeg's first Native-run child welfare agency.[58]

Four years later, in 1988, Indigenous students organized to establish Winnipeg's first Native-run high school. "How powerful those young people were," recalled long-time Winnipeg organizer Vern Morrissette. "They were saying, 'we're tired of this'...'we want a school of our own, we want a place where we can go be with our own people and learn in our own way,' and that was young people, like sixteen, seventeen, eighteen, who were just tired, tired of going to schools and feeling racism, discrimination, all the stuff that I've gone through, that they were still going through at the time." The students used similar tactics as the WNCWC had. "What we started to do was we organized, we organized and we started lobbying Winnipeg School Division," said Morrissette. "We went to their board meetings, and we filled up the galleries, and we spoke...and they resisted us, they resisted, they resisted, and we lobbied them for years and we kept taking up the podium and taking up their time, and we forced them to finally listen to us."[59] These direct actions led to the opening of Children of the Earth high school in 1991.

Postwar Indigenous organizing in Winnipeg took the form of building new Indigenous urban spaces free from settler oppression—in other words, of decolonial urban planning and development. As the previous examples show, urban organizers directed their efforts toward the imagination and realization of Indigenous-controlled institutions that would replace, rather than reform, existing settler institutions. This mode of organizing was the result of both careful studies of modern settler cities' structural inadequacies as well as a strong emphasis on meeting people's basic needs in their immediate environments, regardless of whether Indigenous sovereignty was recognized by settlers within those spaces. "Freedom is a place," geographer Ruth Wilson Gilmore has said, and Indigenous peoples in postwar Winnipeg acted in this spirit as they sought to create an urban landscape made to the measure of their radical aspirations.[60] "We're building a world here," Louise Champagne said of Winnipeg's Indigenous-run housing and worker co-ops. "We want to be a model for a sharing and caring culture, we have to make it up as we go along because we've been indoctrinated in a different direction and to me that's revolutionary work."

Survival School Demanded

Native people seek control of education

Demands by Winnipeg's native community for an aboriginal survival school—a native-controlled school where education and native culture come together—are getting louder.

Last month, a group of native people took their demand for a native survival school right to the offices of Winnipeg School Division No. 1.

With the pounding of a drum reverberating through the building, about 40 native adults and students occupied a board room for several hours in the afternoon to demand that the division set up a survival school, run by native people, by next September.

Big change

The group also called for the division to quickly hire 600 or 700 aboriginal teachers, and to expand childcare for the children of students in the school division.

The division's Task Force on Race Relations last summer made a recommendation for the formation of an Urban Aboriginal Education Advisory Committee to study the idea of a survival school. But protest organizer Larry Morrissette said that is not good enough.

"As native people, we've been studied too much," he told a press conference that afternoon.

organizer, said a survival school would strengthen native people's identity.

"It will be based on our culture and values, and teach them in an environment that students feel safe in," he said.

Community involved

Vern Morrissette said a survival school would stress involvement of the native community, such as the use of parents and elders in teaching. This does not happen in schools now, he said.

"A lot of native people are afraid to approach the schools because of the historical damage they have done," he said.

The subject of an aboriginal survival school was also discussed at a conference on education sponsored by the Ma Mawi Youth Program.

Howard Green is an employee of the Native Education Centre, an adult training centre in Vancouver. He told the young people at the assembly that concerns by some non-natives that a survival school represents "segregation and separation" are unfounded.

"It isn't separation in the negative sense, like when native people were forced to go to school in residential schools. A survival school is one choice, a good choice if the community wants it," Green said.

He conceded there are "some dimensions of multiculturalism that are lost" in a native-only school. "But native people know a lot more about mainstream culture than the other way round."

Different teaching

Green, who was involved in establishing survival schools in Vancouver and Calgary, said he sees the teaching process among native people as different than among non-native Canadian educators.

Native teaching emphasizes immediate rather than long-term goals, experiential learning (learning by doing rather than reading, for instance), group rather than individual work, and co-operative rather than competitive relationships.

Teachers can be trained to use this method, he added.

Green said Winnipeg was ready for a survival school. "The question is what it is going to look like, rather than do we need it."

Students speak out on education

Direct action for community control. Indigenous students occupy the offices of Winnipeg School Division No.1, demanding Indigenous-controlled schools. Inner City Voice, [1989]. Manitoba Legislative Library.

Revolutionary work. Dennis Champagne (left) working at Neechi Foods, Winnipeg, ca. 1989. Inner City Voice, [1989]. Manitoba Legislative Library.

The idea that urban and community planning was critical revolutionary activity prevailed in early 1970s Winnipeg. *Wahbung: Our Tomorrows* was a militant document: "Without justice there can be no freedom, and without freedom there can be no peace," its introduction affirmed. Indigenous Winnipeggers wrote a decolonial world into being by demanding land reform for the construction of new Indigenous-controlled schools, hospitals, housing, transportation infrastructure, and economic development projects.[61] Written in response to the Liberal federal government's White Paper, *Wahbung* positioned its grand vision as the necessary outcome of a radical historical-materialist understanding of the roots of the Canadian nation-state. The preface states:

> The increasing encroachment of white settlers into the historic lands of the Indian people imposed more and more restrictions upon the freedom of movement and freedom of access of Indian people until a hundred years later, all that was left were essentially small areas set aside as reserves for Indian people, areas totally incapable of offering even minimal support or subsistence to those who once possessed the entire country...Notwithstanding the fact that most of the lands assigned to Indian people proved to be literally worthless, the major deplorable aspect was the parsimonious attitude on the part of the Crown in settling a mere 400,000 acres upon the Indian people, while at the same time, giving 1.4 million acres to the Metis; 1.9 million acres to the railroads, and .45 million acres (eventually 7 million) of the 'Fertile Belt' to the Hudson's Bay Co.[62]

The authors of *Wahbung* go on to point out that First Nations peoples at the time controlled only 0.38 percent of Manitoba's land base, while even Richard Nixon had promised 11 percent of Alaska's land base to that region's Indigenous peoples.

As a consequence of such extensive inequality in land distribution, *Wahbung* called for massive land reform via the radical "restructuring of the treaties," the contents of which were described as "unconscionable" and based on a foundation of settler deceit. "It is essential to our future independence and indeed our future participation in the larger society that we collectively review this whole question of land," wrote the authors, "and bring about an adjustment in land allocation that provides for Indian people an opportunity for self-support consistent with our needs and requirements and compatible with that extended to white society." *Wahbung* called for "compensation for losses incurred by the treaties...compensation in land, money, programs, etc. for the assignment of uncultivable land," compensation for broken treaty promises, and "confirmation of the principle that land assignment be adjusted to population growth and economic realities."[63] In keeping with the original Anishinabe insistence that relations with Canada be "constantly fostered, re-defined, re-examined, and re-negotiated,"[64] this was a powerful call for a new deal — with redistribution of land at its core—between Indigenous peoples and Canada based on modern social, economic, and geographical realities, rather than those of the late 1800s.

The thousand people who marched from Higgins and Main to the Manitoba Legislature in the fall of 1972 marched not only for an end to police brutality but for a radical new urban development vision in the spirit of *Wahbung*. Marchers, according to the *Free Press*, called for "an economic development program designed for Indian peoples moving into large urban centres, with management and control by native people," as well as "a community town centre on the former site of the Royal Alexandra Hotel at Main Street and Higgins Avenue so that all services required by native people are under one roof." Marchers also called for "adequate housing accommodation for all" and "a full employment program operated by Indians," to be funded through nothing less than a complete renegotiation of all treaties applying to western Canada.[65] Much of this agenda—particularly the "town centre" at Higgins and Main—was part of an extensive urban redevelopment plan called "Neeginan" (this will be discussed further in Chapter 6).

As Champagne's comments indicated, urban development visions such as the above circulated intimately with visions of revolution. "No man has the right to oppress people," Iron Shield told the crowd in 1972, "and all oppressed people have the right to revolution." Howard Adams, the renowned Métis Marxist scholar-activist, was in Winnipeg that day as well. "Build your own political power bases and own local governments in the ghettos and on reserves," Adams urged Indigenous Winnipeggers, noting the structural impossibility of winning freedom through settler elections.[66] Part of the revolutionary spirit of the time—and an ethic that would persist beyond the Red Power 1970s—was a commitment to anti-capitalist planning and development.

Indigenous organizers in Winnipeg articulated anti-capitalist development visions largely oriented around revitalizing customary Indigenous modes of relating to the land, in the spirit of Anishinabe writer Winona LaDuke's famous phrasing: "We're not talking about getting a bigger piece of the pie, we're talking about a different pie."[67] Lands taken back by Indigenous peoples would be held collectively, according to *Wahbung*, which described individual private property as an irredeemable settler institution. "Indians believe that individual ownership of land is a European concept," the authors wrote. "Therefore, Indians should be allowed to control land in a way that respects both their historical and legal rights."[68] Prominent Oji-Cree leader Elijah Harper—who studied at the University of Manitoba in the early 1970s and worked as a community development worker and with the MIB before becoming a Manitoba MLA from 1981 to 1988—placed an ethic of collective land ownership at the core of his political vision:

> I have a vision for this country called Canada. It is not a new vision, nor is it only mine. It is a vision of my people, the First Nations, the vision of my forefathers...Land is very sacred to us. It is essential to our existence, our philosophy, our way of life. We live on the land, we belong to it, and we return to it when we die. Our forefathers had difficulty understanding the concept of owning land. It is alien, like the concept of owning air. But we understand the need to use the land for the benefit of everybody, not for greed.[69]

The eagle in the MIB logo represents, "A vision that is founded on the spirit of love," while the white part of the head, with red eye and mouth, represents, "The leadership of the Red People in helping our white brothers and sisters see and feel a love for the land as we do." *Wahbung: Our Tomorrows*, Manitoba Indian Brotherhood, Winnipeg, ca. 1971. (Courtesy of the Assembly of Manitoba Chiefs)

The Indigenous worker and housing co-op movement in 1980s Winnipeg converged with Harper's vision by aiming to build a new post-capitalist city according to customary Indigenous principles. "There's a difference here between use values and community values and commercial values," Louise Champagne explained, "and we have a commercial economy here that is so different from the values of a communal band society where we're from, and it's not that long ago that we're from there." Champagne went on, "And unless we take charge and build a local economy that is about sharing and caring and producing for the community, we're going to lose all that." Champagne, her fellow organizers, and a broad cross-section of Winnipeg's Indigenous leaders forcefully explained that they did not want to hold the reins of the capitalist status quo but to radically transform it.

From Neeginan to Payuk to Neechi and beyond, Indigenous urban planning and development in postwar Winnipeg has largely—but not exclusively—been a project of transforming the city centre. Indigenous organizing in postwar Winnipeg has therefore been inseparable from, though not reducible to, the unequal power relation between city centre and suburbia that emerged during the same period. Winnipeg's city centre was systematically abandoned by the state, by capital, and by moneyed white settlers at the precise historical moment that its Indigenous population began to spike. As a result, social relations between Indigenous peoples and white settlers in postwar Winnipeg have regularly been coded, overdetermined, and lived as geographical relations between city centre and suburbia.

COUNTER-PLAN V: "INNER-CITY" PEOPLE FOR RAIL RELOCATION

By the 1970s and 1980s, the uneven development wrought by the suburban vision—deteriorating old housing and infrastructure in the centre and a gleaming new built environment on the edge—became an intense focus of struggle. As the unintended consequences of the suburban development vision became impossible to ignore, opposing groups promoted different explanations of how things had gone wrong. Predictably, the dominant regional bloc dusted off its well-worn mode of social explanation—forged in nineteenth-century settler colonialism and sharpened through twentieth-century strike breaking, *suburbs nullius*, and the "Urban Indian" industry—by blaming those who suffered the most and possessed the least power to shape social conditions. In doing so, they sought to hide the many ways their members had planned, carried out, and profited from urban neglect.

To distract attention from the organized abandonment of the city centre it had carried out since the end of the Second World War, and to therefore avoid taking fiscal responsibility for it, the dominant bloc renovated the concept of the unfit "Urban Indian." Specifically, the racial category of the supposedly unfit "Urban Indian" was transformed into the spatial category of the supposedly unfit "inner-city" person. The cunning of this turn was that it blamed Indigenous peoples not only for their own circumstances but also for the circumstances of an entire geographical area. The so-called inner city was a place with "problems," according to this explanation—popular by the late 1970s—and these were understood to be, though not necessarily stated to be, Indian problems.

In 1978, the IMFC, MIB, and Greater Winnipeg Indian Council (GWIC) organized a press conference to repudiate the growing tendency for local urban planners and politicians to recite this explanation. "Winnipeg's Indian community has reacted with anger and indignation at the Winnipeg Development Plan Review which spokesmen say unjustly blames native people for all the problems in the inner city," reported the *Free Press*. IMFC President Greg Murdoch instead pointed to "discrimination in housing, social services and a complete lack of concern by government officials about their problems." GWIC leaders criticized the city's plan for "ignoring such problems as absentee landlords, absence of adequate housing inspections and unwillingness of banks to support much-needed renovation and construction." Victor Pierre of the MIB "said the Indian people have drawn up their own proposals, such as the three-year-old Neeginan Report, which recommend solutions to the problem. Rather than conducting more studies…it is essential to provide decent housing immediately for all those in need." With this critique, the IMFC, MIB, and

GWIC reframed city-centre living conditions as the product of decisions made by landlords, banks, and state agencies to abandon the area. This process of organized abandonment, the coalition pointed out, was a function of anti-Native racism. "Native people just aren't a priority in city planning," said Murdoch.[70] Even rare state-led attempts to build affordable urban housing were met with skepticism by Native organizers. "We often hear of public housing projects, urban renewal," said Amy Clemons, Anishinabe community organizer and great-great-granddaughter of Chief Peguis, at a 1968 city council meeting where she represented the Indian and Métis Women of Greater Winnipeg. "Will our Indian and Metis residents benefit? Or will they be moved into the old houses deserted by white families transferred to new housing?"[71] Even when the state proposed to invest in the basic needs of people in Winnipeg's city centre, Indigenous peoples were forced to fight to ensure they would benefit alongside non-Native residents.

The growing understanding that the suburban development agenda was a significant cause of unacceptable living conditions for Indigenous peoples in the city opened up the potential for alliances between Indigenous and non-Indigenous city-centre residents who shared, albeit unevenly, the burden of organized abandonment. In the 1970s, a strong place-based identity and consciousness of injustice emerged among city-centre residents—Native and non-Native—in opposition to the dominant bloc's mythic figure of the unfit inner-city person. Instead, Indigenous and non-Indigenous city-centre residents increasingly advanced the idea of the toxically lopsided development agenda that sacrificed them and their children in order to subsidize the profits of suburban land developers and the comforts of well-to-do suburbanites.

Struggles against state-sponsored urban redevelopment plans that threatened to destroy city-centre neighbourhoods were particularly generative. Federally funded urban renewal programs in the 1950s and 1960s had bulldozed many city-centre Winnipeg neighbourhoods, forcibly displacing many and leading to a strong sense of resentment against the unilateral imposition of state-led development programs. The Metropolitan Corporation of Greater Winnipeg estimated that Winnipeg required 45,000 additional units of affordable low-income housing and completed plans for nine new large public housing projects to be built in the city centre.[72] While these programs built much-needed affordable housing—including Winnipeg's first two large public housing projects, Lord Selkirk Park and Gilbert Park—much of the federal funding was captured by the city's political and cultural elite for the construction of stylish modernist headquarters including a new opera house, museum, city hall, and civic government complex. The "Citizens' Advisory Committees" for federally funded urban renewal in Winnipeg were not representative of city-centre residents, and instead were filled exclusively with "experts," "prominent businessmen," and members of the professional classes.[73]

City-centre residents' place-based political consciousness blossomed between 1977 and 1979, when Winnipeg City Council approved $22 million for a freeway—dubbed the Sherbrook-McGregor overpass—to span the CPR yards. Houses, apartment buildings,

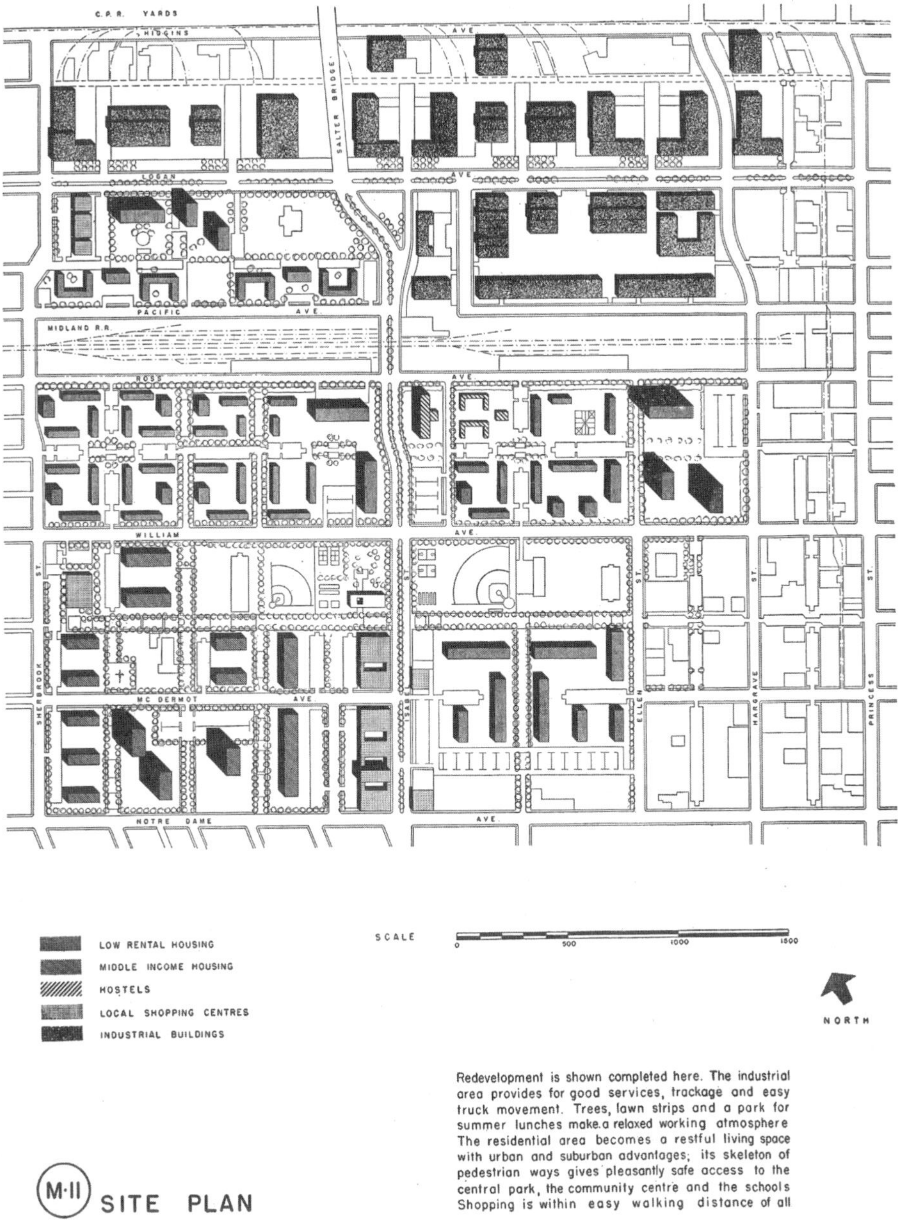

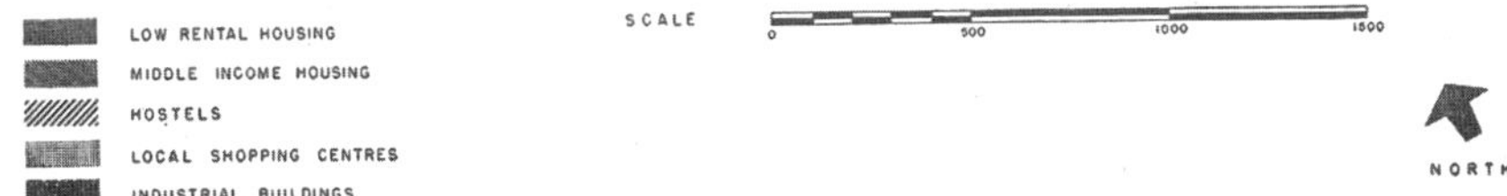

Some of the 45,000 units of public housing planned but not built in mid-20th century Winnipeg. City of Winnipeg urban renewal study for the Centennial neighbourhood, ca. 1957. City of Winnipeg Archives, Gerson, W. (1957). *An Urban Renewal Study for the City of Winnipeg: The CPR-Notre Dame Area*. Winnipeg: City of Winnipeg. (Courtesy of City of Winnipeg Archives)

and other amenities in Winnipeg's Centennial, West Alexander, and Logan neighbourhoods were to be sacrificed in order to speed up suburbanites' commutes through the
city centre. As a necessary infrastructural requirement of the suburban development
agenda, the dominant bloc's Independent Citizen's Election Committee (ICEC) and the
Chamber of Commerce supported the project without so much as asking the opinion of
Centennial, West Alexander, and Logan residents.

On October 11, 1978, 150 city-centre residents attended a mass meeting to formalize
solidarity with Centennial, West Alexander, and Logan residents in their resistance to
the freeway under the banner of the Inner City Committee for Rail Relocation (ICCRR).
"There's been a total lack of concern for people in the area, the little people who can't
afford the lawyers to fight City Hall," said Shirley Green, a lifelong resident of Maryland
Street who stood to be displaced by the freeway. "If this was River Heights [a wealthy
South End neighbourhood] there would have been environmental impact studies and
the whole thing would have been thrown out," said Green. "It's being done to us because
we're in a low income area." Over the next year, the ICCRR forged a broad coalition
of city-centre community organizations—including Native organizations, churches,
schools, residents associations, parents groups, "handicapped organizations," and
small businesses—to act in unison against the "disregard and neglect" of the city centre
represented by the proposed freeway.[74] In the process, the ICCRR took back the term
"inner city" from those who used it disparagingly, instead using it as a marker of solidarity between the various neighbourhoods and social groups who bore the brunt of the
suburban development agenda's organized abandonment.

The principle of community-controlled urban planning was a crucial aspect of the
ICCRR's organizing, as indicated by the second half of the group's name. *Rail relocation*
was shorthand for the coalition's alternative plan to relocate the CPR yards entirely—
and make the CPR pay for it—while redirecting public infrastructural investments into
new affordable housing and other community services for the city centre using former
rail yard lands. The ICCRR's rail relocation plan was intended to benefit city-centre
residents in four ways: it would remove pollution and hazards posed by the CPR to
neighbourhoods along the rail yards; it would prevent freeways from destroying valuable existing housing and amenities; it would free up land and public funding to meet
the basic needs of city-centre residents; and it would remove a barrier many felt segregated the North End from the rest of the city.[75] The ICCRR packed city council hearings
and meetings, published newsletters, issued press releases, gave media interviews, and
arranged meetings with politicians and planners in its struggle to shift support from
the Sherbrook-McGregor overpass to its rail relocation plan. In the process, city-centre
organizers struggled to redefine the definitions of development and infrastructure. In
particular, they advanced the idea that development agendas should invest directly in
the infrastructure necessary for human beings to thrive—housing, childcare, health care,
education, clean air, and safe neighbourhoods—rather than for capital to accumulate.

The ICCRR was eventually able to put rail relocation on City Council's agenda, but the CPR—and the ruling bloc's inclination to side with the billion-dollar firm over the people of the city centre—became its biggest obstacle. The decision came down to who would pay for rail relocation. The CPR agreed to relocate on the condition it received generous state subsidies to do so. The ICCRR rejected the notion and demanded the federal and local governments force the CPR to pay for relocation itself. The ICCRR based their position on knowledge of the environmental hazards posed by the CPR to the surrounding community and on a clear-eyed understanding of the history of public subsidies to the CPR that made the firm, in the eyes of the ICCRR, "the largest government welfare recipient in Canada." "[The CPR] has received over $11 billion in subsidies since 1916," ICCRR organizer Sister Geraldine MacNamara told City Council, "and that was after they got all that tax-free land to build a railroad. It's about time they took on their share of the load." The ICCRR's research found that rail relocation would cost the CPR only $1 million and that title to the land would revert to the federal government. The ICCRR later discovered internal CPR memos in which the firm described the yards as inefficient and reported "that relocation would be economical even without government funds."[76]

At its core, the struggle for rail relocation opposed endless state subsidies for capitalist firms and connected these subsidies directly to the lack of public money available for city-centre residents' own plans and unmet basic needs. This was the anti-capitalist position of the ICCRR's broad coalition, which included many of the city's trade unions and communist elected representatives from the city centre such as Joe Zuken and Bill Kardash. "Anything that is physically possible is financially possible," said Kardash in response to the ICEC's argument that the city could not afford rail relocation.[77]

Lining up with the CPR and the subsidies-to-capital status quo against the ICCRR were the ICEC and the Chamber of Commerce. ICCRR organizers highlighted the openly undemocratic alliance between ICEC city councillors and the CPR. "They seem to adopt the position that C.P. Rail is the most favoured citizen in the City," said Sister MacNamara.[78] In response, the ICEC attempted once again to divert blame for city-centre disinvestment to city-centre residents themselves. At a 1979 city council meeting where city-centre residents packed the galleries in support of rail relocation, ICEC Councillor and future Conservative Manitoba premier Gary Filmon argued that urban planning did not cause "blight" and did not "destroy neighbourhoods," to which Cree-Métis city-centre councillor Cyril Keeper replied, "I am not surprised at the insensitivity of this Council to the inner city, a Council dominated by the interests of land developers."[79] Keeper's words exposed the ICEC's alliance with capitalists as one that directly oppressed city-centre residents, an important achievement of the ICCRR's organizing.

The ICCRR's rail relocation campaign accomplished many such key political manoeuvres. It enabled city-centre organizers to map the dominant regional bloc—described as an ICEC-CPR-Chamber of Commerce-land developer alliance—that stood in the way of residents' own plans for achieving justice and freedom through urban redevelopment.

Looking the dominant bloc in the eye. Cyril Keeper speaks out for rail relocation, addressing city council at a public meeting, Winnipeg, ca. 1981. Manitoba Legislative Library, Masenayegun fonds, February 1981. (Used with permission of the Indian & Métis Frienship Centre)

MP Cyril Keeper addresses City Council at a public meeting at the Convention Centre.

It associated that alliance's position with more than 100 years and $11 billion of state subsidies to the CPR, thereby exposing the immense accumulation of public resources by capitalist firms and the contemporary endurance of a bloc aimed at guaranteeing such accumulation into the future. It held this bloc responsible for organizing the abandonment of the city centre through its suburban development agenda—of which it identified the Sherbrook-McGregor overpass as a typical component—that required the city centre to be sacrificed in multiple ways: through the destruction of homes and neighbourhoods, but, perhaps more importantly, through the redirection of public resources away from the infrastructure necessary to meet city-centre residents' basic needs.

CO-OPTING THE PEOPLE'S CITY: THE DOMINANT BLOC'S GENTRIFICATION AGENDA

Another key political intervention made by the ICCRR—although, in light of later events, it was perhaps not articulated forcefully enough—was to emphasize the fact that the survival of city-centre residents had nothing to do with the profitability of large firms in the city centre but with direct public investment in housing and other social goods. The dominant bloc, however, deliberately dismantled this distinction in the decades to come—a tactic that has become one of the most effective weapons used against the people of Winnipeg's city centre over the past 50 years.

The modern movement to blur the distinction between private corporate profits and the public good—key to the rise of neoliberalism—can be traced within the context of Manitoba politics to 1958. While the massive subsidies offered to the CPR by the Citizen's Railway Committee demonstrate that public gifts to attract footloose capital were at the heart of Winnipeg's industrial development vision, historians have argued that this so-called entrepreneurial logic of governance became entrenched at the provincial level after the election of Conservative Premier Duff Roblin.

In 1958 Roblin created the Manitoba Development Fund (MDF) to provide loans, land, tax abatement, and infrastructure to foreign firms. By 1966, the lending power of the MDF was $100 million. "We are going flat-out to attract U.S. capital," said the head of the MDF in 1967. "The provincial government is willing to use its influence where appropriate to create a profit opportunity where none might otherwise exist." Its proponents described the MDF as the latest advance in state capitalism: "It's the opposite of socialist," said the Minister of Industry and Commerce in the face of criticism from opponents of state-spending, "it's strongly anti-socialist, to help the small business to be successful." Much of the capital provided by the MDF to foreign firms as loans—for instance, $92 million to an Austrian pulp and paper company—was never paid back.[80]

The idea that the economic strength of a given area depends on the availability of subsidies to investors there would soon be adopted and redirected toward Winnipeg's city centre by a small but growing faction of the dominant bloc. By the 1970s, the power balance within Winnipeg's dominant bloc had shifted from manufacturing to finance capital—with insurance company Great West Life as the largest firm—but it remained as "closely knit" as ever.[81] A clear geographical divide would soon emerge, however, as a coalition of property owners, merchants, and real estate capitalists whose profits were tied most closely to Winnipeg's city centre began to push against the long-standing suburban development agenda. The birth of this "urban wing" can be traced to 1974, when two ICEC councillors split from the party over its continued preference for suburban over city-centre infrastructural investment.[82] The urban wing's first major victory came in 1979, when Winnipeg City Council gifted $20 million ($67 million in 2017) to Montreal-based Trizec Corporation for the construction of a new office tower and shopping mall at the intersection of Portage Avenue and Main Street.

The original political and intellectual leader of the urban wing was Lloyd Axworthy, a Princeton PhD graduate and Liberal Party politician who established the largely technocratic Institute of Urban Studies (IUS) in Winnipeg in 1969. The IUS published a litany of reports that documented the so-called decline of the city centre and called for a variety of urban policy innovations. Deindustrialization and the abandonment of land and buildings were a key concern of IUS literature: a 1979 report identified an "abandonment phenomenon within Winnipeg's inner city" and counted over 200 abandoned buildings there.[83] "The key factor is to find a successor land use," a typical IUS report warned. "To leave the land idle or underutilized leads to the precipitation of decay and decline."[84] Descriptions of the city centre as a place of idleness and underutilization—evoking 1800s colonial descriptions of the North-West that set the stage for the dispossession of the Anishinabe and Métis peoples—positioned the city centre as ripe for outside intervention while erasing existing residents' own claims to the area and visions for its future. The urban wing would turn to this technique time and again for decades to come (as the rest of this book will show). In addition, by calling for public intervention to make city-centre land and buildings attractive to investors, the IUS deftly re-characterized the problem of suburbanization as state abandonment of capital, rather than state abandonment of people. With its expanding portfolio of reports, the IUS built an intellectual foundation for the urban wing's "back to the city" vision.

When the grassroots struggle for rail relocation, housing, and social services gained momentum in the winter of 1979, Axworthy and the urban wing latched on to the movement as a vehicle for its own agenda. Axworthy—a Liberal MLA at the time—built his federal political career directly on the back of city-centre residents' years of organizing. Axworthy presented his federal political ambitions as nothing more than a requirement of the rail relocation movement. "Continuing debate between the federal government and Winnipeg City Hall about building a Sherbook-McGregor Overpass or removing the Canadian Pacific railyards," wrote the *Winnipeg Tribune,* "convinced [Axworthy that] Manitoba needs a strong voice in the federal government." After meeting with Prime Minister Pierre Trudeau at the 1979 Canada Winter Games in Brandon, Manitoba, Axworthy arranged an impromptu press conference where Trudeau himself endorsed the ICCRR's vision and announced, "The Liberal way is not to destroy neighbourhoods."[85] The Liberal Federal Government officially jettisoned the Sherbook-McGregor overpass plan in April 1980, citing its support for the ICCRR, but dragged its heels on finding money for the ICCRR's plan for rail relocation, housing, and social services.

The ICCRR pressed the Liberal Government to fund the broad vision around which it had organized. On May 4, 1980, 200 people attended a public meeting at Rossbrook House—a youth drop-in in the Centennial neighbourhood—to demand rail relocation. "They have promised rail relocation, they have stopped the Sherbrook-McGregor overpass," said Joe Zuken, the communist city councillor from the North End. "Now it's time for action. Let Mr. Trudeau, Mr. Axworthy, and Mr. Pepin [federal transport minister] implement their promises."[86] The Liberal government, however, did not wish to challenge the CPR any more than Winnipeg's ICEC City Council did, and cited prohibitive costs and "political barriers" as impediments to rail relocation.[87] Nor, it would later be revealed, were real estate capitalists in Winnipeg interested in redeveloping the CPR yards, a key stumbling block for the Liberals.[88]

In fact, Axworthy had already begun to organize federal, provincial, and municipal officials around a different, investor-friendly vision for Winnipeg's city centre.[89] On May 30, 1980, Axworthy announced that he had secured federal funds of $32 million—condi-

Ma-se-na-ye-gun, August 1980, page 2

FIGHT GOES ON FOR RAIL RE LOCATION

"The Rail Relocation issue is not dead," says Sister MacNamara, spokesperson for the Inner-City Steering Committee.

The fight to block construction of the Sherbrook-McGregor overpass still continues in spite of City Council's unanimous approval in June for the construction of the six-lane expressway.

In order to re-establish their position and to make Federal politicans in power aware, the steering committee and supporters, including members of the Indian & Metis Friendship Centre staff, distributed 2,600 leaflets at the Liberal convention last month. The leaflets argued for rail relocation and stated their position to continue to fight against the construction of the overpass.

The leaflet called the "Rail Relocator," stated that "the removal of the CPR yards represents the last opportunity on any scale to renew and revitalize the old core of the City," a view that is not shared by the city council, even though the City got $50 - $60 million from the federal government in May to "revitalize the city core area." According to the Free Press, the opposite view was made clear when Mayor Bill Norrie said that "the construction of an overpass above the CP railyard is almost a certainty," after receiving the federal money.

To further complicate matters, with contradictions, Immigration Minister Lloyd Axworthy made a press statement at the Liberal convention in response to the leaflets handed out, stating "The federal government has put the money up that's available for rail relocation and there's nothing more we can do...these people are fighting an issue that in part has already been won." However, just two weeks earlier the federal government gave the city permission to build the overpass.

The steering committee and concerned citizens of the Inner-City feel the construction of the overpass will destroy neighborhoods of the Inner-City creating an "expanding ghetto". To nave the CP railyard and mainline removed instead would create land for housing, parks and light industry, and would eliminate the threat of a major disaster through a chemical spill in the Inner-City area.

While the city planners have begun a 10 - 12 month job creating a design for the overpass project, the steering committee is designing an action plan to convince the residents, private sector, city council and all levels of government that the Sherbrook-McGregor overpass proposal is not good for the Inner City.

One part of the action plan involves building a case against the danger of chemical spills to Inner-City residents such as the accident that took place last April in Winnipeg's CP railyard where about 13,000 gallons of highly inflammable methanol leaked into the air.

* * *

Fighting for a people's city. Ma-se-na-ye-gun [Winnipeg IMFC newsletter], ca. 1980.
Manitoba Legislative Library, Masenayegun fonds, August 1980, page 2.
(Used with permission of the Indian & Métis Frienship Centre)

tional on matching contributions from the provincial and municipal governments—for a five-year, $96 million plan ($274 million in 2017) to redevelop Winnipeg's city centre. Axworthy claimed that the new plan—dubbed the Core Area Initiative (CAI)—was a direct result of the grassroots rail relocation movement. "In the summer of 1980, a crowd of inner city residents packed Rossbrook House to demand of representatives of the three levels of government that some action be taken to arrest the serious deterioration of the core area of Winnipeg," Axworthy told the *Free Press.* "Out of this Rossbrook town hall meeting, the CAI was born."[90] In fact, the high-level meetings to create the CAI took place before the Rossbrook House meeting, and Axworthy cut his ties with the ICCRR shortly after the CAI announcement.[91] The CAI's self-proclaimed grassroots origin story was a myth—and a typical piece of Liberal Party statecraft—intended to disguise the transfer of public resources to large firms as an authentic expression of poor people's struggles and aspirations.

The scale of state investment channelled into Winnipeg's city centre by the CAI was unprecedented in modern urban planning on Turtle Island. Based on a model of regional economic development that had previously been applied in Canada only to very large, so-called underdeveloped rural areas, the CAI was described as "an experiment in urban policy-making which was arguably the most ambitious and comprehensive ever undertaken in North America."[92] Three more five-year plans followed the original CAI: CAI I ($96 million from 1981–86) was followed by CAI II ($100 million from 1986–91), then the Winnipeg Development Agreement ($75 million from 1995–2001), and finally the Winnipeg Partnership Agreement ($75 million from 2004–8). In the end, a total of $346 million ($1 billion in 2017) in state spending was poured into Winnipeg's city centre over 20 years.

From the outset, it was clear that the CAI was not a grassroots, community-controlled development program to meet city-centre residents' basic needs for affordable housing, food, clothing, health care, childcare, education, and other social services. The CAI's decision-making structure was rigidly hierarchical, with three politicians—one federal minister, one MLA, and the mayor of Winnipeg—at the top and an administrative staff of non-resident professionals. The CAI administration took most of its direction from the real estate industry, maintaining close connections to groups such as the Manitoba Real Estate Association, Winnipeg REALTORS, and the Manitoba Home Builder's Association.[93] Indeed, just one year into the CAI era, city-centre residents found themselves up against the CAI in all-too familiar ways.

One of the CAI's first proposed projects sought to expropriate and bulldoze housing and amenities—including a school—in the Logan neighbourhood, the same community that the Sherbook-McGregor overpass had threatened. Residents formed the Logan Community Committee (LCC) in 1982 to stop the CAI from replacing them with a modern industrial park. The LCC critiqued the CAI for demonstrating the same disregard for city-centre residents as the suburban development agenda had. "Don't you think that we as a people should have some input into what is happening to our lives?" asked LCC Chairperson Helen Shultes. "Someone should have recognized that we are people, not just a bunch of old houses."[94] The LCC sued the CAI and won $39,500 to create an alternative resident-driven neighbourhood plan.

The LCC—now incorporated as a non-profit under the name Logan Community Development Corporation (LCDC)—teamed with Kinew Housing Inc. to research and write the new plan. The LCDC's plan critiqued the CAI's "pejorative" assessment of the Logan area—the latter characterized Logan as dysfunctional and lacking a significant residential presence—for being "subjective, superficial, and biased." The LCDC's plan documented the value of neighbourhood housing and amenities the CAI planned to bulldoze. It also highlighted the importance of the area to the people who called it home, as well as a large community, one-third of whom had lived in Logan for over ten years and four-fifths of whom wanted to stay in the neighbourhood long term. Whatever physical deterioration had occurred, the LCDC pointed out, was due to the suburban development agenda's divestment from the city-centre; the CAI's logic, therefore, amounted to blaming the victim. The LCDC eventually won the support of City Council for the alternative plan, thwarting the CAI.[95] Through their alternative planning process, the LCDC emphasized how the urban wing's city-centre redevelopment vision rested on the same disregard for existing poor and working-class city-centre residents as the suburban development agenda had.

Counter planning against organized abandonment. Save North Logan! Composite Neighbourhood Plan, Logan Community Committee Inc., Save North Logan! Alternative Plans for the North Logan Neighbourhood, Winnipeg, ca. 1982. (Used with permission of Prairie Architects Inc.)

Taking back the land. CPR Rail Relocation, Logan Community Committee Inc., Save North Logan! Alternative Plans for the North Logan Neighbourhood, Winnipeg, ca. 1982. (Used with permission of Prairie Architects Inc.)

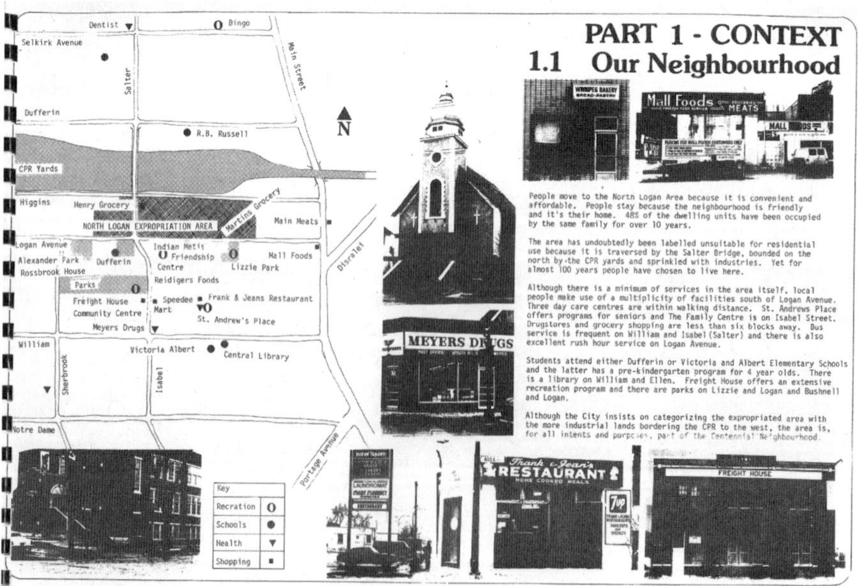

Insisting on a human geography. Our Neighbourhood, Logan Community Committee Inc., Save North Logan! Alternative Plans for the North Logan Neighbourhood, Winnipeg, ca. 1982. (Used with permission of Prairie Architects Inc.)

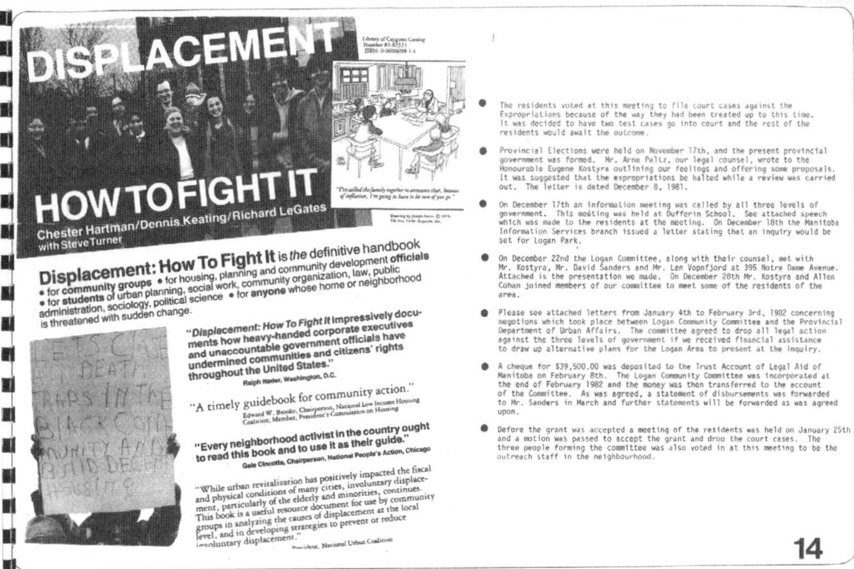

The residents voted at this meeting to file court cases against the Expropriations because of the way they had been treated up to this time. It was decided to have two test cases go into court and the rest of the residents would await the outcome.

Provincial Elections were held on November 17th, and the present provincial government was formed. Mr. Arne Peltz, our legal counsel, wrote to the Honourable Eugene Kostyra outlining our feelings and offering some proposals. It was suggested that the expropriations be halted while a review was carried out. The letter is dated December 8, 1981.

On December 17th an information meeting was called by all three levels of government. This meeting was held at Dufferin School. See attached speech which was made to the residents at the meeting. On December 18th the Manitoba Information Services branch issued a letter stating that an inquiry would be set for Logan Park.

On December 22nd the Logan Committee, along with their counsel, met with Mr. Kostyra, Mr. David Sanders and Mr. Len Vopnfjord at 395 Notre Dame Avenue. Attached is the presentation we made. On December 28th Mr. Kostyra and Allen Cohan joined members of our committee to meet some of the residents of the area.

Please see attached letters from January 4th to February 3rd, 1982 concerning negotions which took place between Logan Community Committee and the Provincial Department of Urban Affairs. The committee agreed to drop all legal action against the three levels of government if we received financial assistance to draw up alternative plans for the Logan Area to present at the inquiry.

A cheque for $39,500.00 was deposited to the Trust Account of Legal Aid of Manitoba on February 8th. The Logan Community Committee was incorporated at the end of February 1982 and the money was then transferred to the account of the Committee. As was agreed, a statement of disbursements was forwarded to Mr. Sanders in March and further statements will be forwarded as was agreed upon.

Before the grant was accepted a meeting of the residents was held on January 25th and a motion was passed to accept the grant and drop the court cases. The three people forming the committee was also voted in at this meeting to be the outreach staff in the neighbourhood.

14

Fighting to stay. Displacement, how to fight it, Logan Community Committee Inc., Save North Logan! Alternative Plans for the North Logan Neighbourhood, Winnipeg, ca. 1982. (Used with permission of Prairie Architects Inc.)

Fighting to stay. Logan Community Committee headquarters, Winnipeg, ca. 1982. Photo by Andy Blicq. Winnipeg Free Press, November 27, 1982. (Courtesy Winnipeg Free Press)

Fighting to stay. Logan Community Committee event, Winnipeg, ca. 1983. Inner City Voice, [1983]. Manitoba Legislative Library.

The CAI expressed this disregard in the new urban landscape it produced. When federal funds for urban renewal in Winnipeg were cut in the 1960s, Winnipeg's Metropolitan Planning Commission estimated the city required 45,000 additional units of affordable low-income housing and had completed plans for seven more public housing projects in addition to Gilbert Park and Lord Selkirk Park.[96] But when major federal funds for urban redevelopment returned to Winnipeg just twelve years later, these plans were jettisoned. Instead of improving housing for city-centre residents, the CAI prioritized spectacular commercial megaprojects aimed at bringing upwardly mobile white consumers from the suburbs back to the city centre to shop, dine, and drink. Two privately owned shopping centre developments received the bulk of CAI money from 1981 to 1991: Portage Place, a shopping mall built over three blocks of Portage Avenue owned by Cadillac-Fairview, and The Forks, a festival marketplace built on abandoned Canadian National Railway rail yards and immigration sheds at the confluence of the Red and Assiniboine Rivers. These two shopping malls received over three times what the first CAI invested in affordable housing, while the CAI spent more on The Forks alone than on all the housing it built from 1981 to 1991.[97] Neither did city-centre residents significantly benefit from jobs created by these projects. One study found that "fewer than 50 percent of the jobs created in the cost-shared programs went to core area residents," while another found that "fewer than one-third of non-construction projects honoured the CAI's affirmative action hiring policies for inner-city residents."[98] At the close of the 1980s, it became evident that the urban wing—under Lloyd Axworthy's leadership—was stealing public resources won by poor, working-class, Indigenous and non-Indigenous city-centre communities in the 1970s to meet basic needs and giving them over to large capitalist firms to build shopping malls. Three sprawling 1980s city-centre shopping complexes—Portage Place, Winnipeg Square, and The Forks— materialize the theft of affordable housing, childcare, education, and an economic base from the people of Winnipeg's city centre. These places materialize, as well, a reiteration of racist notions—inherited from 1800s settler colonialism and 1900s industrialism—of the inability of Indigenous peoples, peoples of colour, and poor whites to govern themselves or to carry out development agendas for the good of the region as a whole.

COUNTER-PLAN VI: COMMUNITY INQUIRY INTO INNER-CITY REVITALIZATION

Furious at the CAI, city-centre organizers doubled down on their people-first vision for the city. At a time of especially powerful Indigenous resurgence in Winnipeg—marked by round dances, demonstrations, and occupations in response to the murder of Oji-Cree leader J.J. Harper by the WPS and the deployment of Canadian troops against Mohawk land defenders in Oka—Winnipeggers' urban visions drew on and contributed to wider political currents.[99] The spirit of a people-first inner city and the inter-racial alliances it would require was kept alive by 1980s community organizers, many of whom published incisive criticisms of the CAI—as well as articles promoting expropriation of landlords, prison abolition, and Native control over urban education—in the CAI-funded *Inner City Voice*. In early 1990, a coalition of Indigenous and non-Indigenous city-centre organizers—including Dorothy Betz and Kathy Mallett—convened a Community Inquiry into Inner City Revitalization with the twin goals of critiquing the dominant agenda and demanding state funding for a new community-driven five-year plan that would actually address the basic needs of city-centre residents. The Inquiry held nine public meetings at various city-centre community halls— including Rossbrook House, Freight House, and the Indian Family Centre—and received 90 verbal and written presentations from a broad coalition that included tenants' associations, neighbourhood community councils, teen councils, residents' committees, parent councils, labour unions, daycare centres, community theatre groups, the IMFC, Ma Mawi Wi Chi Itata Centre, Native Women's Transition Centre, North End Women's Centre, Prostitutes and Other Women for Equal Rights (POWER), and the Social Assistance Coalition of Manitoba. The community organizers who made verbal presentations—the majority of whom were women, most of them Indigenous—outlined a highly imaginative, highly detailed alternative urban development vision inspired by decades of urban organizing and based in radical opposition to the past ten years and $200 million of CAI spending done in their name but not in their interests. City-centre residents showed up in droves to hear organizers' critiques of the CAI and to support their alternative visions for the city.[100]

Planning a world without violence against Indigenous women. Aboriginal Women's Unity Coalition meeting, (from L) Dorothy Betz, Marilyn Fontaine Brightstar, Kathy Mallett, Bev Chippeway, Josie Hill, Yvonne Armstrong, Bev Jones, Winnipeg, ca. 1990. Inner City Voice, November 1990, Manitoba Legislative Library.

Oka everywhere. Oka solidarity night demonstration, Peace Village, Winnipeg, ca. 1990.
Inner City Voice, [1990]. Manitoba Legislative Library.

Community control over the resources the urban wing had leveraged in their name became one of the biggest demands of city-centre residents in 1990. The Inquiry and later evaluations of the CAI found that "direct community participation in the day-to-day functioning of the initiative was minimal or nonexistent," that "community input was sought on an after-the-fact basis,"[101] and that CAI advisory committees had "inadequate inner city/Aboriginal representation" and were "insufficiently sensitive to inner city needs."[102] As such, Inquiry organizers observed, the CAI had "been dominated by narrow interests reflecting a one-sided, largely commercial or corporate vision of what Winnipeg should be." To remedy this, Inquiry organizers called for the CAI administration to be dismantled and replaced with elected citizen councils. The solution to the CAI's problems was "to open up planning processes to public participation, thus acknowledging the legitimacy of alternative visions." Indigenous self-determination over urban planning processes was central to demands for community control and to the alternative visions that city-centre residents proposed. Inquiry organizers demanded that, "The next phase of inner city revitalization must recognize the resource needs of aboriginal communities and [align with]...the strengthening network of expertise and organizations dedicated to self-help, self-determination and alternative services/ programs delivered in holistic and culturally-appropriate ways."

Jokes. Inner City Voice, [1989]. Manitoba Legislative Library.

Once again, unmet basic needs for housing, health care, education, and jobs were at
the heart of city-centre residents' proposed development vision. Since the inception of
the CAI, Inquiry organizers observed, "little change has occurred with regard to the
economic and social development of the city's inner-city areas." In fact, some conditions
had seriously worsened, organizers pointed out, citing an "escalating mortality rate
among aboriginal infants and children." Inquiry participants crafted a detailed vision of
what the city centre would look like should the CAI meet their primary demand: "Focus
on the real needs of the residents."

Affordable quality housing, again, was at the top of residents' minds. The Inquiry's housing plan called for: "Worker cooperatives to build and renovate housing"; "application of the Logan Community Committee model for administering housing services and providing community groups with a financial base"; "tougher enforcement of rental regulations and building standards"; home maintenance programs for elders and single parents; and emergency shelters for women and youth. The focus on housing exemplified a broader commitment to quality of life for poor and Indigenous women, children, and elders—people who were evidently not at the top the CAI agenda.

The Inquiry prioritized women's health and their children's education as crucial components of urban redevelopment. Organizers imagined an urban revitalization agenda that prioritized building Native women's resource centres, immigrant women's resource centres, childcare facilities—especially "more aboriginal-controlled child care facilities"—preschools, parent-child centres, adult literacy and GED-prep facilities, neighbourhood-based health services, post-natal programs, shelters and other supports to address violence against Indigenous women, "measures to deal with escalating mortality rate among aboriginal infants and children," and "long term funding for aboriginal social services, umbrella groups, and women's organizations." The Inquiry's insistence on these concerns revealed how out of touch the CAI agenda was with city-centre residents. When planning processes were led—as the Inquiry demonstrated—by people who actually lived and organized in the city centre, issues such as violence against Indigenous women and deaths of Indigenous babies rose to the top of the urban revitalization agenda. In the spirit of Ruth Wilson Gilmore's definition of racism as "group-differentiated vulnerability to premature death," the 1990 Inquiry was truly anti-racist city planning.[103]

Up against the co-opting, regressive economic logic that justified immense gifts to already immense capitalist firms, Inquiry organizers articulated a clear commitment to economic justice and a rejection of the CAI's implicit trickle-down theory. "The physical 'megaprojects' stimulated or sponsored under the CAI umbrella stand as constant reminders of where priorities for the revitalization of the heart of the city were found over the last ten years," organizers told the Inquiry, demanding that CAI resources be redistributed primarily on the basis of need. "Several concerns were voiced about the extent of public-sector investment in North Portage, the Forks, commercial streetscaping and up-scale housing," the report found. "The kinds of projects noted above have not met the basic shelter, employment and other needs of many inner city residents, nor have they provided significant 'trickle-down' benefits to core area people." "These expenditures are perceived to represent an inequitable distribution of public resources," the report continued, "and an inappropriate balance between the objectives of improving the quality of life for existing residents and attracting non-residents to work, visit and/or live in the inner city." Underneath measured summaries such as these, residents' rage against the large firms and affluent suburbanites who benefitted on the backs of their movements is palpable.

Behind the face of Portage Place

By ALAN LADYKA

For many inner city people, the name Portage Place bring to mind unpleasant images — overpriced goods sold in chain stores, harassment of youth and natives by security guards, destruction of housing between Portage and Ellice Avenues.

But the North Portage development, including the Portage Place shopping mall along with housing units, accomplished what it set out to do.

Unfortunately, its goal was not the revitalization of a part of the inner city to benefit the residents, using their input and participation, but rather a business development to attract Winnipeggers from outside the core area.

Lori Bell sat on the board of the North Portage Development Corporation for five years. Appointed to the nine-member body by the provincial government, she says she was intended to be the "community" representative among the business people and developers.

Dollars wanted

But people and dollars from outside the core area, not community input, was what the NPDC wanted, she says.

"I felt there was a social impact (by the project) in the downtown area. But I saw it

soon that it was very much a business venture. There was never any talk about the social impact except to say we had to expropriate these tenants," she says.

Bell says she tried to push the board to recognize the social implications of the North Portage development. The provision of money and resources to help relocate residents forced from their homes around Ellice Ave. by the development was one successful result of her participation, she says.

But many other goals for the project — affirmative action in hiring by businesses there, housing, safety issues — were never completed, she says.

Allies needed

Bell feels that community influence in projects such as North Portage still depends on residents having elected representatives on their side.

"Governments can want citizen participation, or they can create vehicles that don't allow citizen participation," she says.

While North Portage was an instance of the latter, Bell cites the help of a sympathetic NDP provincial government in helping residents save the Logan neighbourhood.

Inside Portage Place: chain stores for suburban shoppers.

Sharpening the people-first vision. "Behind the Face of Portage Place" by Alan Ladyka, Inner City Voice, June 1989. Manitoba Legislative Library.

Resistance to the CAI generated a radical grassroots economic vision based on the view that urban redevelopment initiatives could be powerful vehicles for transforming, rather than entrenching, economic structures that required poverty and inequality. Throughout the 1980s, the CAI had "not been sufficiently pro-active in pursuing systemic reforms," noted the Inquiry's final report. "The CAI has not met its potential to be a catalyst for addressing structural issues affecting social and economic conditions in the inner city." Indigenous organizers in particular fought for structural transformations: "A clear message was conveyed that the focus of [Indigenous communities participating in the inquiry] is on systemic change, not on minor tinkering with structures and processes that have ineffectively responded to aboriginal peoples in the past."

The Inquiry's economic plan—echoing almost exactly the demands of those who marched against the Toal Report eighteen years earlier—had four major planks: tax the rich; guarantee jobs for all; transfer ownership of city-centre land and buildings to city-centre residents; and promote collective ownership by co-operatives and non-profits. Organizers reminded the CAI administration that if the CAI was a product of the grassroots rail relocation movement, the economic goals of that movement—"reclamation of the land for residential/community purposes," for instance—ought to be the goals of the CAI.

Finally, Inquiry organizers critiqued the belaboured, precarious, and competitive non-profit funding structure the CAI had invented to channel a fraction of the CAI budget to city-centre organizations. By establishing a competitive, short-term, grant-based funding structure—the sort that elsewhere has been referred to as a non-profit industrial complex (NPIC)—the CAI had turned the energies of city-centre organizers away from the militant community organizing and coalition building of the 1970s and toward the perpetual competition and kowtowing of grant applications and funding reports.[104] Inquiry organizers noted that not only had most of the public funds won by 1970s organizing not gone toward city-centre residents' own development visions, but the little that had was used strategically to control, pacify, and pit city-centre communities against each other. "The observation was made that other sectors of society would not stand for, or long survive under, the 'fiscal run-around' and divisive funding processes that now confront social services and community development," the Inqui-

Serious anti-racist city planning. Public meeting of the Community Inquiry into Inner City Revitalization, Winnipeg, ca. 1990. Inner City Voice, May 1990, Manitoba Legislative Library.

ry's final report noted. To protect their organizations against defunding and to promote cooperation rather than competition among city-centre communities, Inquiry organizers called for sustained, guaranteed funding through the transfer of "property or another type of equity base" to the community. This demand echoed *Wahbung*, which had called for a similar community-controlled economic base in 1971.

The 1990 Community Inquiry into Inner City Revitalization revealed the dominant bloc's post-industrial redevelopment vision for the establishment-driven, capital-centric accumulation strategy it was, and proposed a radical urban development alternative in the people-centric tradition of the Manitoba Treaty, Treaty 1, the Winnipeg General Strike, and *Wahbung*. The CAI's attempt to co-opt the struggles of city-centre residents inadvertently pushed those communities to deepen their critique of dominant bloc planning and elaborate their own development vision even further. While the CAI facilitated the literal ascension—in steel, concrete, and glass—of the dominant bloc's dream shopping-mall city, it unintentionally stoked dreams of a radically different city and generated one of the most extensive, detailed, and systemic plans ever for a just, decolonial city.

RACIAL CAPITALISM INTO THE 1990S: HUNGER, HOMELESSNESS, POLICE, PRISONS

The dominant bloc's co-optation of the people's vision for city-centre redevelopment contributed to the drastic expansion of poverty in Winnipeg's city centre into the 1990s. In 1971, 33 percent of city-centre households lived in poverty; by 1996, it was 50 percent. Sixty-seven percent of Indigenous city-centre households lived in poverty in 1971; this rose to a staggering 80 percent in 1996.[105] It was during this period that Winnipeg Centre became known as Canada's poorest federal electoral district, alongside Vancouver's Downtown East Side. The gap between Winnipeg's poor and wealthy neighbourhoods widened even further during this time. Between 1980 and 2010, nearly all neighbourhoods with average household incomes below the city average fell even further below, while nearly all above-average income neighbourhoods rose even further above the average.[106]

The decline in living conditions in Winnipeg's city centre occurred at the same time as the area became home, more and more, to Indigenous peoples and to other people of colour. By 2016, Indigenous peoples comprised 20 percent of the city-centre's 130,000 residents, while non-Indigenous people of colour represented 40 percent. Whereas two out of five residents of the Winnipeg metropolitan area were Indigenous or people of colour in 2016, in the city centre that number was three out of five.[107]

Regional development visions alone were not responsible for the collapse of living conditions in Winnipeg's city centre. Global economic restructuring played a role in the proliferation of poverty nationwide in this period as many companies dispensed with the relatively stable, well-paying jobs won by labour in the first half of the twentieth century and replaced them with part-time, temporary, poorly paid positions. Shifts in federal governance—in step with the global rise of neoliberalism and austerity—also significantly deepened poverty across Canada by abandoning efforts to address human need and transferring ever-larger shares of the country's wealth to big corporations and those with incomes in the top 1 percent.

This shift was particularly pronounced in Canada beginning in the 1990s. One example is the case of federal divestment from affordable non-market social housing. In 1982, social housing accounted for over 15 percent of all new housing construction in Canada. But on December 31, 1993, the Liberal Federal Government divested from social housing construction entirely, sending the social housing number plummeting to 1 percent of all new housing construction, where it has remained ever since.[108]

The federal government transferred this wealth to large capitalist firms in the form of massive corporate tax cuts. By 2012, the World Bank and PricewaterhouseCoopers ranked Canada the eighth "most advantageous place to pay corporate taxes" out of 185 countries studied (the US ranked 69th). In 2011, *Forbes* magazine named Canada "*the best country in the world to do business*," referencing its "dropping tax rate, sound banks, investor protection and relative lack of red tape."[109] Between 1982 and 2010, the incomes of Canada's richest 0.01 percent grew by 160 percent while the incomes of the bottom 90 percent grew by less than 5 percent. The share of Canada's economic growth captured by the top 1 percent during this period, according to one economist, "surpassed anything seen in Canadian history."[110] The immense gains of the wealthiest people and the largest capitalist firms in Canada during the 1990s and 2000s came at great—and sometimes deadly—cost to poor and working-class people.

Poverty, homelessness, and hunger increased significantly across Canada after 1980. The number of poor people in Canada jumped by 50 percent from just under 3 million in 1979 to nearly 4.5 million in 2000.[111] Whereas homelessness and emergency food banks were extremely rare in Canada in the 1970s, by 2016 nearly 250,000 people in Canada found themselves without a home, and almost 1 million turned to emergency food banks for survival.[112]

The Canadian state invested heavily in policing and prisons in the 1990s and 2000s to punish and control the communities abandoned by its neoliberal agenda. The number of police officers per capita in Canada steadily increased starting in the 1990s, and by 2011 national annual spending on police totalled $13 billion. In 2012, annual federal spending on prisons rose to $4 billion as the federal government, under the Conservative leadership of Stephen Harper, aimed to increase both the number of Canadians being sent to prison and the length of their sentences.[113] In only nine years, from 2006 to 2015, federal and provincial Canadian governments built 10,000 new jail and prison cells and added 2,600 double bunks.[114]

The Manitoba government pursued its own one-two punch of divestment from social spending and investment in corporate tax-cuts, prisons, and policing. From 1999 to 2016, the Manitoba NDP maintained and deepened corporate tax cuts introduced by the Manitoba Conservative Party—in power from 1988 to 1999 under the leadership of Tuxedo MLA and former ICEC member Gary Filmon—while expanding prisons and police at an unprecedented rate. The Manitoba NDP increased provincial jail capacity by 50 percent, adding 651 new beds during its time in office, as Manitoba's prison population doubled between 2000 and 2014. By 2011, the NDP had doubled provincial spending on police, a $126 million investment that funded 150 new Winnipeg police officers, most of whom were deployed to the city centre. Provincial spending allowed the budget of the WPS to increase by 80 percent between 2005 and 2015. This drastic expansion of Manitoba's police and prison capacities was not a response to increased crime or interpersonal violence. In fact, it occurred during a period of declining crime rates.[115]

Winnipeg's dominant bloc remained a well-organized force in both provincial and municipal policy making in the 1990s and 2000s. While usually preferring to keep a low profile—organizing in private clubs and using the Chamber of Commerce as a public face—moments of crisis have forced them, like any loose coalition, to intensify their level of cohesion, create new organizations, and mount public campaigns. Such a moment arrived in the mid-1990s, as anxiety over Winnipeg's competitive position in national and transnational economies mounted. In particular, the National Hockey League's (NHL) impending divestment from Winnipeg—the Winnipeg Jets left the city in 1996—prompted the dominant bloc to launch a public campaign to "Save the Jets," and in doing so salvage Winnipeg's reputation as a profitable place for large corporations to do business.

To coordinate its campaign, the dominant bloc went into formation as the Group of 58—a clear homage to their strikebreaking, fascist-sympathizing great-grandfathers' fondness for numeral-based names—and attempted to capture substantial new public subsidies for the privately owned hockey team.[116] In doing so, as is typical of such crises, the membership of the bloc became far more identifiable. Virtually all of the most active members of the Group of 58—mostly senior corporate executives in their thirties and forties—it was revealed, were the grandsons and great-grandsons of prominent dominant bloc families, including the Richardsons, Rileys, and Oslers.[117]

While the Group of 58's "Save the Jets" campaign failed, the dominant bloc maintained its grasp on municipal state power through the 1990s. After controlling Winnipeg City Council into the 1980s, the ICEC morphed—as formal political parties were removed from Winnipeg municipal politics—into the so-called Gang of 18, a group of city councillors who held a majority on City Council and met regularly before Council meetings to determine Council's agenda.[118] By 2012, Winnipeg achieved the lowest tax rates and the lowest public spending levels of nearly any major Canadian city and boasted the most police officers per capita of any city in the country.[119]

This combination of economic restructuring, neoliberal economics, and expansion of prisons and police—deployed at global, national, provincial, and regional levels—had devastating effects on Manitoba and Winnipeg, as it did on nearly the entire world at this time. By 2016, 62,000 Manitobans used emergency food banks.[120] By 2013, a stunning 10,000 Winnipeggers were homeless—70 percent of whom were estimated to be Indigenous—while 135,000 Winnipeggers were considered "at risk" of being homeless.[121] In a sign of the times, the carriageway where Louis Riel's body was brought into a Winnipeg funeral home in 1885—where the nineteenth-century people-first development vision was prepared for burial—in 2015 had become an impromptu shelter for homeless young people.

By 1990, the landscape of the North-West had been disfigured by the succession of thefts that began in 1870 into tremendous towers of wealth surrounded by deep valleys of poverty. At the place demarcated by the Red and Assiniboine Rivers, two opposing streams of thought and feeling flowed simultaneously. The first stream—disfiguring hearts, minds, and selves to match the new geography—made these thefts and the landscape they produced seem natural, normal, and proper, or hid them from view altogether. The fiction of race—the idea that certain groups were unfit to prosper within modernity—remained central to this tradition. As the architects of each new round of accumulation drew from, and added to, a reservoir of such beliefs, they built an infrastructure that underlay their capacity to remake the world.[122]

The second stream—attempting to restore the spiritual and intellectual humanity of the region—resisted these thefts at every turn. Despite repeated silencing, the people of the North-West built up their own reservoir of thought and feeling, a counter-planning tradition that recognized and rejected the human sacrifice required by the dominant development tradition and proposed radically different combinations of land, labour, and collective capacity. Indeed, over the course of the 1950s, 1960s, 1970s, and 1980s, the working people of Winnipeg's city centre—many but not all of them Indigenous peoples—contributed immensely to this tradition. They accumulated a wealth of knowledge about the forces dictating urban life and amassed an array of extensive, detailed, revolutionary plans for transforming those conditions. By the 1990s, residents of Winnipeg's city centre were perhaps more conscious of their interests, more organized, and more united around a concrete people-first vision for Winnipeg's city centre than ever before. As the CAI gave way to a new era, Indigenous and grassroots movements seemed well-positioned to take control over the city's post-industrial future.

1   Winnipeg's post-suburbanization city centre fits Greenberg and Schneider's descriptor, "marginal people on marginal lands" as well as Gilmore's "forgotten places" (Greenberg and Schneider, "Violence in American Cities"; Gilmore, "Forgotten Places and the Seeds of Grassroots Planning").

2   McCallum, *Indigenous Women, Work, and History, 1940–1980*, 10.

3   Dickason, *A Concise History of Canada's First Nations*, 222.

4   Cardinal, *The Unjust Society*, 82–84.

5   Cardinal, *The Unjust Society*, 84; Hall, "The Early History of the Winnipeg Indian and Métis Friendship Centre, 1951–1968," 224.

6   Carter, *Aboriginal People and Colonizers of Western Canada*, 133.

7   Perry, *Aqueduct*, 26.

8   Dickason, *A Concise History of Canada's First Nations*, 217–21.

9   Cardinal, *The Unjust Society*, 14.

10   Tough, *As Their Natural Resources Fail*, 291–92.

11   Tough, *As Their Natural Resources Fail*, 289, 295.

12   Tough, *As Their Natural Resources Fail*, 309; Hall "The Early History of the Winnipeg Indian and Métis Friendship Centre, 1951–1968," 224; Mochoruk, *Formidable Heritage*, 191; Fernandez and Silver, "Indigenous People, Wage Labour, and Trade Unions," 6.

13   McCallum, *Indigenous Women, Work, and History, 1940–1980*, 65; Peters and Anderson, *Indigenous in the City: Contemporary Identities and Cultural Innovation*, 24

14   Tough, *As Their Natural Resources Fail*, 309; Miller, *Shingwauk's Vision: A History of Native Residential Schools*, 382.

15   Kulchyski and Neckoway, "The Town That Lost Its Name," 24.

16   Kulchyski and Neckoway, "The Town That Lost Its Name"; Ballantyne "We Had A Good Life."

17   Kulchyski and Neckoway, "The Town That Lost Its Name," 28.

18   Hall, "The Early History of the Winnipeg Indian and Métis Friendship Centre, 1951–1968," 224.

19   Peters, "'Our City Indians': Negotiating the Meaning of First Nations Urbanization in Canada, 1945–1975," 75.

20   Personal interview, January 13, 2014.

21   Greyeyes, *Mary Richard*; personal interview, January 23, 2014.

22   Hall, "A Place of Awakening," 224.

23   Peters, "Our City Indians."

24   Sim, as quoted in Peters, "'Our City Indians': Negotiating the Meaning of First Nations Urbanization in Canada, 1945–1975," 81.

25   Renaud, as quoted in Peters, "'Our City Indians': Negotiating the Meaning of First Nations Urbanization in Canada, 1945–1975," 80.

26   Meadmore, research interview for *Preserving the History of Institutional Development in Winnipeg*. All other quotations from Meadmore in this chapter are taken from the same source, unless otherwise noted.

27   Hall, "A Place of Awakening," 55, 57.

28   Hall, "A Place of Awakening," 58. Individuals' national affiliations are listed whenever possible out of respect for the specificity of Indigenous nations, recognizing that the term "Indigenous" represents a political identity sutured together from hundreds of distinct groups. See Vowel, *Indigenous Writes*, 10.

29   Hall, "A Place of Awakening," 58–59.

30   Cardinal, *The Unjust Society*, 48.

31   Hall, "The Early History of the Winnipeg Indian and Métis Friendship Centre, 1951–1968," 225.

32   Munroe, research interview for *Preserving the History of Institutional Development in Winnipeg*. All other quotations from Munroe in this chapter are taken from the same source, unless otherwise noted.

33   Chippeway, research interview for *Preserving the History of Institutional Development in Winnipeg*. All other quotations from Chippeway in this chapter are taken from the same source, unless otherwise noted.

34   Dennison, "Native Peoples Will Hold Protest March on Legislature"; Herron, "There is No Way Back."

35   Herron, "There is No Way Back"; Winnipeg Free Press, "Native Policy Outlined"

36   Richard, "Interview with Kurt Sargent, re: History of Urban Aboriginal Organizations." All other quotations from Richard in this chapter are taken from the same source, unless otherwise noted.

37   Hall, "A Place of Awakening," 75.

38   Hall, "A Place of Awakening," 59.

39   Guilbault, Research interview for *Preserving the History of Institutional Development in Winnipeg*; Meadmore, Research interview for *Preserving the History of Institutional Development in Winnipeg*; Winnipeg Free Press, "Faces of the aboriginal community."

40   Fontaine, Research interview for *Preserving the History of Institutional Development in Winnipeg*. All other quotations from Fontaine in this chapter are taken from the same source, unless otherwise noted.

41   Not to be confused with Second World War veteran Harold Iron Shield, also known as Harold Crowchild, of the Tsuu T'ina nation.

42   Dennison, "Native Groups Support Occupation Demands."

43   McKenzie-Jones, "Removing Imagined Borders," 2.

44   Canadian Indian Workshop, *Nish Nawh Be*, 1.

45   Canadian Indian Workshop, *Nish Nawh Be*, 28, 15.

46   Canadian Indian Workshop, *Nish Nawh Be*, 23, 6, 21.

47   Stevenson, "The Importance of Defending Our Culture"; for more on *The Prairie Call* see Sinclair & Cariou (Eds), *Manitowapow*, 155.

48   Jones, "Outlook in City—Bleak."

49   Dennison, "Indians March in Protest."

50   Hall, "The Early History of the Winnipeg Indian and Métis Friendship Centre, 1951–1968," 234.

51   Manitoba Indian Brotherhood, *Wahbung*.

52   Young, research interview for *Preserving the History of Institutional Development in Winnipeg*. All other quotations from Young in this chapter are taken from the same source, unless otherwise noted.

53   Manitoba Indian Brotherhood, *Wahbung*, 184.

54   McCallum, *Indigenous Women, Work, and History, 1940–1980*, 225.

55   Winnipeg Free Press, "Indian Party Possible."

56   Dobchuk-Land, "'Tough on Crime, Tough on the Causes of Crime'."

57   Manitoba Indian Brotherhood, *Wahbung*.

58   Champagne, research interview for *Preserving the History of Institutional Development in Winnipeg*.

59   Morrissette, research interview for *Preserving the History of Institutional Development in Winnipeg*.

60   Gilmore, Paper presented at the *Annual Meeting of the American Studies Association*.

61   Manitoba Indian Brotherhood, *Wahbung*.

62   Manitoba Indian Brotherhood, *Wahbung*, xii, xiii.

63   Manitoba Indian Brotherhood, *Wahbung*, 13.

64   Craft, *Breathing Life into the Stone Fort Treaty*, 113; Borrows, Negotiating Treaties and Land Claims, 191.

65   Dennison, "Indians March in Protest"; Winnipeg Free Press, "Native Policy Outlined."

66   Dennison, "Indians March in Protest."

67   As quoted in Simpson and Klein, "Dancing the World into Being."

68   As quoted in Kirkness, et al, *Women of Wahbung*, 6.

69   Harper, "What Canada Means to Me."

70   Rosner, "Indians Angered by Inner City Report."

71   Winnipeg Free Press, "Indians Here Have to Live in Slums, City Council Told."

72   Metropolitan Corporation of Greater Winnipeg, *Downtown Winnipeg*.

73   Gerson, *An Urban Renewal Study for the City of Winnipeg: The CPR-Notre Dame Area*, 6.

74   Selinger, "Viable Policy and Plan Making," 25, 103.

75   Selinger, "Viable Policy and Plan Making."

76   Selinger "Viable Policy and Plan Making," 64, 78, 28, and 49.

77   Selinger "Viable Policy and Plan Making," 103.

78   Selinger "Viable Policy and Plan Making," 39.

79   Selinger "Viable Policy and Plan Making," 41.

80   Gonick, "The Manitoba Economy Since World War II," 29–30.

81   Silver, *Thin Ice*.

82   Axworthy, *A Test Case for Institutional Innovation*.

83   Benell et al., *The Building Abandonment Study: Winnipeg's Inner City*.

84   Lyon and Fenton, "The Development of Downtown Winnipeg: Historical Perspectives on Decline and Revitalization," 156.

85   Selinger "Viable Policy and Plan Making," 43.

86   Selinger "Viable Policy and Plan Making," 63.

87   Silver and Toews, "Combating Poverty in Winnipeg's Inner City, 1960s–1990s: Thirty Years of Hard-Earned Lessons."

88   Selinger "Viable Policy and Plan Making," 119.

89   Mungai "Citizen Participation and the Renewal of a Declining Inner City Neighbourhood," 56.

90   Winnipeg Free Press, "Why Kill it Now?", 7.

91   Selinger "Viable Policy and Plan Making," 118.

92   Kiernan, "Intergovernmental Innovation: Winnipeg's Core Area Initiative," 25.

93   Tom Carter (Chair of the Community Inquiry into Inner City Revitalization) personal communication, November 12, 2015.

94   Mungai, "Citizen Participation and the Renewal of a Declining Inner City Neighbourhood," 56–57.

95   Mungai "Citizen Participation and the Renewal of a Declining Inner City Neighbourhood," 64–78.

96   Metropolitan Corporation of Greater Winnipeg, *Downtown Winnipeg*.

97   Silver and Toews, "Combating Poverty in Winnipeg's Inner City, 1960s–1990s: Thirty Years of Hard-Earned Lessons."

98   Decter and Kowall, *The Winnipeg Core Area Initiative: A Case Study*, 42; Silver and Toews, "Combating Poverty in Winnipeg's Inner City, 1960s–1990s."

99   McLeod, research interview for *Preserving the History of Institutional Development in Winnipeg*.

100   Tom Carter (Chair of the Community Inquiry into Inner City Revitalization) personal communication, November 12, 2015.

101   Stewart, "A Critique of the Winnipeg Core Area Initiative: A Case Study in Urban Revitalization," 159; Layne, "Marked for Success??? The Winnipeg Core Area Initiative's Approach to Urban Regeneration," 266.

102   Unless otherwise noted, all quotations from the Community Inquiry in the following pages are taken from Urban Futures Group *Community Inquiry into Inner City Revitalization*.

103   Gilmore, *Golden Gulag*, 28.

104   INCITE! Women of Color Against Violence, *The Revolution Will Not Be Funded*.

105   Lezubski et al, "High and Rising, " 39–40.

106   Distasio & Kaufman (Eds.), *The Divided Prairie City*, 22.

107   Manitoba Collaborative Data Portal, "Community Data Map, Winnipeg Health Region."

108   Brandon, "Winnipeg and Manitoba Housing Data."

109   Canadian Press, "Canadian Business Tax Rate among World's Lowest," emphasis added.

110   Lemieux and Riddell, *Top Incomes in Canada: Evidence from the Census*; Yalnizyan, "The Rise of Canada's Richest 1%," 3.

111   Silver, *About Canada*, 15.

112   Gaetz, *The State of Homelessness in Canada 2016*; Food Banks Canada, *Hungercount 2016*.

113   Statistics Canada, *Police Resources in Canada*; Piché et al., "The Front and Back Stages of Carceral Expansion Marketing in Canada."

114   Piché et al., "The Front and Back Stages of Carceral Expansion Marketing in Canada."

115   Dobchuk-Land, "'Tough on Crime, Tough on the Causes of Crime'."

116   Silver, *Thin Ice*, 89; Kramer and Mitchell, *When the State Trembled*, 319.

117   Silver, *Thin Ice*, 84–85.

118   Winnipeg Into the Nineties, "Winnipeg Into the Nineties Fonds."

119   Lett, "Day of Reckoning on the Horizon"; Statistics Canada, *Police Resources in Canada*.

120   Food Banks Canada, *Hungercount 2016*.

121   Mental Health Commission of Canada, "Initiatives"; Cooper, "Excuse Me, Canada, Your Homelessness Is Showing."

122   This insight is indebted to Gilmore's concept of "infrastructures of feeling," elaborated in "Abolition Geography and the Problem of Innocence."

NEW FRONTIER

CASTLES: NEW CAPACITIES FOR AN OLD AGENDA

"All these condos around here," William[1] says, doing a breaststroke in the air, "they should be putting all that money for condos into housing for the homeless and towards fixing up the housing around here." It's late December 2013, and William and I are sitting in a hamburger restaurant on the western edge of Winnipeg's downtown. William is a member of Tataskweyak Cree Nation, in Northern Manitoba, but he's spent all of his 40 years in Winnipeg. He grew up on Main Street in the city's North End but has been without a home for much of his life, sleeping in shelters, on the streets, and occasionally locked in prisons. We're in the back of the restaurant, where an ad-hoc group—mostly elders, a mix of white and Native men and women in jeans, toques, and parkas—have commandeered the red vinyl bench that spans the room. We sip our coffees, chat, laugh, and watch snow fall against the low winter sun. William is talking about how bad homelessness has gotten in Winnipeg. It's been an exceptionally cold winter so far, and William mentions a man who froze to death on Main Street a few weeks previous. "I wish I could open my door to everybody," he says, "but there's only so much you can do."

William's perspective, common among residents of Winnipeg's city centre since at least the 1990 Community Inquiry, offers a radical critique—rooted in a lived experience of homelessness and an ancestral history of dispossession—of a dominant urban redevelopment vision that prioritizes luxury condos for the wealthy over the basic human rights of the poor, such as those of the homeless to shelter. It is a swift and powerful rejection of both right-wing theories of poverty and homelessness in Canada (that view access to housing as an outcome of personal rather than social failings) and liberal spins on those theories—such as the "housing first" model—that view lack of access to housing and other basic needs as a matter of poor health or educational attainment. To William it is clear: homelessness is the result of a political decision not to house people.

William's critique also points to the ways that contemporary inequalities—such as Indigenous peoples' experiences of homelessness—that are often chalked up to colonial "legacies" are in fact reproduced by powerful interests in the present. As Haitian historian Michel-Rolph Trouillot observes, "The historicity of the human condition also requires that practices of power and domination be renewed…The so-called legacies of past horrors—slavery, colonialism, or the Holocaust—are possible only because of that renewal. And that renewal occurs only in the present."[2] People in Winnipeg, according to William's analysis, are not made homeless primarily by the regional history of settler-colonial dispossession, but by the renewal of this history's effects by development decisions made in the present.

In fact, William is one of an astounding 10,000 people who experience homelessness in Winnipeg.[3] Yet the voices, experiences, and analyses of homeless or precariously housed people like William are nearly always excluded from mainstream imaginings of urban progress and redevelopment. William's perspective highlights the social and political narrowness of a dominant urban "revitalization" agenda that falsely claims to possess no ties to any particular social group or political agenda.

KEYS

William and I spoke at length about Winnipeg, its enormous shortcomings, and the different tactics he uses for surviving them. William has had various jobs over the years: he's worked on and off as a bouncer and put in a stint as a radio repairman for the military; he's also a skilled craftsman, illustrator, and powwow dancer. In the winter of 2013, he was working as a panhandler. William explained that, to him, panhandling is a good, peaceful way to make a living; it doesn't harm other people, and the income gives him some freedom from the city's authoritarian shelter system. Plus, he's good at it. He told me how to spot undercover bylaw officers on the bus (Winnipeg passed anti-panhandling bylaws in 2005), and he has a favourite spot, a grocery store parking garage where he returns people's shopping carts for them. Whenever the manager confronts him, William told me, he smiles wide and says, "Don't I have the right to ask people for their carts?" He has a line for customers, too. "Hey, Dave," William said at one point, calling his friend over. "You know what I say at the Big Foods?" William lifted his head high with a goofy, polite smile: "Excuse me, ma'am. I'm homeless and starving, may I please take your shopping cart to return it for a dollar? I'm not trying to take the money out of your purse, I'm just trying to work my way up." William grinned ironically.

"That really works?" Dave asked.

"Yeah!" William replied. "I was saying stuff like that when I was 10," said Dave, as they both cracked up laughing.

William often infiltrates downtown buildings when other options for obtaining shelter don't work out. "I can look at any building and see the weakness in it," he said, "like how it's constructed and where the cracks are." He went on, gripping the arm of his sunglasses like a tool, telling me how he can use something like that to manipulate a door and get inside any building to keep warm. "On Broadway, anywhere downtown," he says, "multi-million dollar buildings, corporate buildings, I just make sure there aren't any cameras on me, and I look up in the corner for those white things with the little lights on them." William waved his hand in the air like he was warding off a mosquito.

William's tactics for making money and finding shelter—while maintaining whatever dignity and independence he can—are among a whole set of techniques he's been forced to perfect in order to survive in the city, from forging bus passes to hacking prison computers to connect with friends to negotiating diplomatically with nurses, shelter workers, and police. His critique of urban redevelopment is crafted in the context of the proliferation—all in the name of civic progress—of even more places he is locked out of, policed and surveilled in.

One of the warm places in Winnipeg that people in William's position sometimes manage to secure shelter is The Warbler, a luxury condo building in CentreVenture's marquee development, Waterfront Drive.[4] I rented a condo in The Warbler in the summer of 2013 from Albinka, a retired professor.[5] Albinka owns two suites here—one is a revenue property—and she and her partner, between the two of them, own four homes, the other two located in Manitoba's lake country. In some sense, Albinka is the prototypical new urbanite that CentreVenture seeks to entice to the centre of the city. She is of a social class, and of a place—Winnipeg's wealthy South End—that has benefitted directly from CentreVenture's activities. Juxtaposing Albinka's story with William's draws out the specific historical and geographical situatedness of those people who are and who are not cared for by the dominant development vision—those who are given keys, and those who are left out in the cold. This includes the way that categories like race and ancestry are structured—in effect, if not by intention—into contemporary remakings of urban space. Indeed, it reveals one way that regional racial capitalisms—whether we are conscious of them or not—continue to structure the arcs of our lives and the intimacies of everyday encounters.

Albinka's grandparents emigrated from Poland to Canada in 1922, when her father was a baby. Both of her parents were Jewish, of Eastern European heritage. One afternoon, Albinka and I had coffee in her condo—a light, open-concept corner suite outfitted with colourful, modern furniture and fixtures. She looked down over the city's warehouse district through her large west-facing window and told me about her grandfather. "[He settled] on Jarvis Avenue with his family, which is probably the poorest street in the city," Albinka told me, pointing north. "And he had a horse and cart, and he would go around in the mornings and collect old bottles and rags—he would have been called a rag-and-bone man, in London." By the end of his life, Albinka's grandfather had turned rag picking into a booming business. His main innovation was to have the rags come to him: people would mail him their torn clothes and in return he would send new towels, blankets, and other merchandise. He named the company Abotinam—Manitoba spelled backwards.[6]

A few doors down from The Warbler is the Enterprise Building, a former factory originally financed in 1898 by E.F. Hutchings, the leather baron who once celebrated the presence of "Indian graves" as a symbol of the city's progress.[7] Albinka's family acquired the Enterprise Building in the 1950s when her father, who eventually became a physics professor, inherited Abotinam and needed somewhere to store his newfound rag collection. Albinka coveted the place. "I used to go into that building," she told me, "and dream of converting the top two floors to condos and living there." Her dream was deferred. In 1990, the steam plant supplying heat to the building closed forever, and Albinka's father sold the building, refusing to sell it to Albinka because he feared it would become a financial liability. "So when buildings started going up on Waterfront," Albinka told me, "and one of them was actually right beside the building I had always dreamed about, I was the first buyer." Albinka moved from River Heights to The Warbler shortly after it opened in 2007.

Albinka is warm, funny, unassuming, and—like many condo owners on Waterfront Drive—takes care to come across as sophisticated, cosmopolitan, and, especially, urban. She called the suite I rented—a small apartment among many others on the top floor of the building—a "penthouse," and she loves that she can walk from The Warbler to the opera, the symphony, and the theatre. I asked her why she hadn't lived downtown prior to moving to The Warbler, so late in life. "Even when I was looking for the house in River Heights," she told me, "I actually wanted to live here, in downtown, I could see potential in downtown." Living in the South End, she said, her eye was always trained north, on the city centre: "I watched as the city very slowly started to do what many European cities that I knew had already done. I mean, you could live downtown in London, you could live downtown in Paris, you could live downtown in Toronto, but you couldn't live downtown in Winnipeg. There was some weird perception, of one, it being dangerous, and two, it not having any infrastructure to support family life."

Albinka's perspective was shared by many of the condo owners I talked to on Waterfront Drive. It is nearly impossible, when speaking to people who live in city-centre Winnipeg condos about their choice of residence, not to encounter a tone of defiance in response to the city's prevailing anti-urban culture. To Albinka and others, the stigma ascribed to Winnipeg's downtown is a kind of backwater tendency: "I thought [the perception of danger] was a misperception. So I had no fear, and I really loved watching what was happening here, and it was very slow, really, really slow [laughs]. But a few things started happening, the building just behind you converted, and it was the first, as far as I remember, the first place that you could actually rent or buy into."

Very often, talk of anti-urban attitudes turns to talk of race, especially outside perceptions of the city's "Aboriginal community." I asked Albinka if her feelings had borne out, if she felt safe living downtown, so close to some of the most stigmatized places in the city—the Main Street strip and the North End. "The worst scenario is that I've been approached by someone who was too drunk to talk," she replied, "or I get approached for money, often, but that's no different from any other city I've ever visited or lived in, and I don't find that frightening. And the Aboriginal community that people are concerned about, they're human beings, I don't find them frightening either. So, I'm always surprised when my River Heights friends say, 'Oh my God, you're living downtown, aren't you scared?' I don't take it. I don't buy it."

Albinka's comments reveal how closely a certain strain of wealthy urban sophistication in Winnipeg is tied to a liberal tolerance of urban Indigenous peoples and urban Indigenous poverty. Condo owners' fearlessness on the urban frontier, grounded in the desire to include Indigenous peoples within the category of the human, is genuine and well-intentioned. Its profound limits, however, show just how much the urban wing's doctrine of *urbs nullius* continues to shape everyday consciousness.[8] Most importantly, newly arrived condo owners are seemingly unaware of the contest over the city centre that has taken place since the 1970s. Nor do they identify as beneficiaries of a process that has displaced and dispossessed the land's prior owners and inhabitants and silenced those communities' plans for the area.

Indeed, condo owners relate to the area's prior residents—Indigenous peoples, in particular—as nuisances, rather than full participants in the area's future. Albinka and most of her condo-owning neighbours take great pains to keep the rest of the neighbourhood at bay, through a variety of moves that seem intended to minimize encounters with the neighbourhood's long-time inhabitants as much as possible. Elaine, my neighbour in The Warbler, told me that she does not walk down Main Street north of the opera house, an area that has long been known as a major hub of Indigenous social and cultural life, and where most of the city's temporary shelter infrastructure is now located. Albinka made a point of praising the multiplicity of locked doors one must pass through to enter The Warbler, and on the day I moved in, lowering her voice, she warned me about people who sneak in through the parking garage door to sleep in the building unpermitted. In the early days of The Warbler, Albinka said, the building's lobby used to be open to the public, until homeless people began to sleep in the lobby, a situation Albinka described as "not so nice." The Warbler's front door is now locked to outsiders.

REVIVING THE URBAN WING FOR THE TWENTY-FIRST CENTURY

The history of the land under Waterfront Drive—a luxury enclave carved into the edge of Winnipeg's North End—contains much of the regional history of dominant development visions detailed in Part 1. After Wolseley's invasion, Anishinabe and Métis land on the west bank of the Red River was given to railway capitalists. A spur line connecting Winnipeg's two massive rail yards was installed on the land, and thousands of people worked in factories along the line.[9] (A public space adjacent to the rail line, Victoria Park, became a hub of worker organizing and the "spiritual centre" of Winnipeg's 1919 General Strike; following the Committee of 1,000's military defeat of the strike, City Council quickly sold the land and a steam-heating plant was built over the park grounds.[10]) In the 1960s, a large new rail yard was built on Winnipeg's southeastern suburban edge, and the old spur line was soon abandoned. Title to the land reverted to the City of Winnipeg through tax foreclosures in the

1990s, by which time most of the area's industrial firms had long departed for the suburbs. City Council established a public park along the riverbank, named for former mayor Stephen Juba, and the rest of the land was used as dirt parking lots.

The land on the west bank of the Red River was a small, if significant, portion of the "surplus" lands—former industrial sites, hotels, theatres, and vacant lots—begrudgingly owned by the City of Winnipeg as a result of its organized abandonment of the area. While the University of Winnipeg's Institute of Urban Studies (IUS) construed abandonment of city-centre land and buildings as a regional crisis as early as the 1970s, the situation sank to new depths in the 1990s. By the time of Winnipeg's 1998 civic election, "surplus" land and buildings had become a high-profile political issue.

I spoke with Eliza, a middle-aged professional who worked closely with Glen Murray's successful 1998 mayoral campaign.[11] "Especially the late nineties and Portage Avenue, almost every second window was totally abandoned," Eliza told me. "There were empty storefronts all over the place; it was big." The issue was amplified in part by a moral panic around child "firebugs" who were understood to be torching abandoned properties for sport. The Toronto-based *Globe and Mail* declared Winnipeg Canada's "Arson Capital,"[12] while the *Winnipeg Free Press* ran the headline, "POLITICIANS TALK AS WINNIPEG BURNS."[13]

Apart from moral panics around the city's growing Indigenous and immigrant youth populations, the late 1990s were an exciting, progressive political moment in Winnipeg when the urban vision elaborated by the 1990 Community Inquiry and kept alive by city-centre residents like William could well have ascended to dominance. It was an historical moment, in other words, when the character of "urban revitalization" was particularly up for grabs. Young, left-leaning leaders were elected to Winnipeg's City Hall and Manitoba's Provincial Legislature in 1998 and 1999, respectively, after years of far-right regimes at both levels. The social-democratic NDP—originally known as the Co-operative Commonwealth Federation (CCF), founded in 1932 by Winnipeg General Strike leader J.S. Woodsworth, Tommy Douglas, and others—embarked on what would become an unprecedented seventeen-year mandate. During the campaign, the NDP positioned a remade Winnipeg city centre as one of its key priorities. More importantly, city-centre community organizers had a ready-made redevelopment plan to meet the actual needs and aspirations of their communities.

With a growing archipelago of "surplus" urban land now owned by a left-leaning municipal government, and with social democrats committed to urban improvement in control of the more substantial provincial budget, a state development vision that would work in partnership with increasingly organized city-centre communities would seem to have been more possible than ever. Such a vision did not come to pass. Instead, the development vision that came to dominate overwhelmingly abandoned existing residents, catering instead to a set of people—suburbanites, tourists, and wealthy investors—with little attachment to, or even interest in, the area. How did things turn out this way, despite indications that a different future might have taken hold?

By the 1990s, the Core Area Initiative had failed to achieve the full breadth of the urban wing's vision, and grassroots community groups had taken control of a significant degree of CAI resources. Faced with these circumstances, the urban wing attempted to stabilize its leadership over city-centre redevelopment and silence the Indigenous-led grassroots vision by establishing a new model of institutional power. The spirit of the urban wing's frustrations at the time were captured by a 1995 City of Winnipeg planning document, through which its members instructed state policy-makers: "A healthy downtown requires a long-term commitment to a vision and a plan. Isolated projects and short-term programs do not meet that requirement. The foundation of a long-term commitment must be a coherent concept, both to protect existing investment and to direct growth."[14] These words convey the urban wing's twin desire for institutional durability—organizational power that could stretch over time—and a coordinated "vision," a master plan that all members of the urban wing could put their energies behind.

Letters to the Editor

Politicians talk as Winnipeg burns

OUR CITY IS BURNING. We are losing our city's heritage. Politicians, where have you been? We have not seen you doing any cleanup at any of these fires. We have not seen you consoling the business owners and neighbours of these tragedies. We have not seen you put on a pair of gloves and apron and try to salvage what you can of someone's life.

Have any of you once thought of coming down and helping, instead of sitting behind closed doors? Offering more money for these crimes is not the answer. Having bigger headlines and photographs of these tragedies only spurs the arsonists on. I dare any of the politicians to shed their suits and help the next business or home that goes up in flames.

Please don't talk your politics. You don't know how this affects people until it happens to you or you have gotten dirty doing cleanup.

So get dirty.

MICELLE CHRETIEN
Winnipeg

Firefighters cut at worst time

I find it very interesting to hear Mayor Murray and Coun. Dan Vandal vow that they will do everything they can to control the arson epidemic in our city. Their suggestion about forming a joint task force to combat the recent increase in deliberately set fires could be a positive initiative.

However, the police department with help from the Fire Commissioner's Office last year, arrested and convicted numerous people for arson. These convictions did little to stop the problem. Many of those convicted were young offenders and it seems that the current group of arsonists also come from that age bracket.

When Mayor Murray campaigned for election, he promised a more open forum for the citizens of Winnipeg. What I find incredulous is that in front of the camera he says that he will "do anything to stop arson," while in the back rooms of city hall he cut 52 active firefighting positions last year and has stated he will cut more this year.

When our city is the "Arson Capital of Canada" would it not make more sense to keep our firefighting force at a level that can respond to emergencies rather than maintaining skeleton crews and in some cases temporarily taking halts off duty due to a lack of manpower?

How to reach us

The Free Press welcomes letters from readers. Letters must be signed and should include a clearly printed name, address and telephone number. Names will be published but not addresses. All letters may be edited for style and length. Short letters are less likely to be condensed. Please address letters to: Letters to the Editor, Winnipeg Free Press, 1355 Mountain Avenue, Winnipeg R2X 3B6. Letters can be sent to our Fax number: 697-7412. Letters may be submitted through the Internet at Letters@FreePress.Mb.Ca. Letters sent via the Internet obviously cannot be signed, but must include home address and telephone number.

cials, book deals, etc. The last few months have been the all-time worst for this. Just try and open a newspaper (you are not the only ones) or flyers, and not come across an ad with Gretzky's picture on it. He's on cereal, tires, clothing, hockey equipment, hockey cards, hockey training videos, etc. During his hockey career, I always felt it was just too much commercialism on his part, and now that he's retired its beyond overdrive. How many millions does he need to make already?

Enough Gretzky! Find religion or hit the showers for awhile. You are over-exposed!

ELEANOR DORST
Winnipeg

Medical students need contracts

It is quite obvious from articles and letters to the *Free Press* the University of Manitoba medical faculty has some very serious admission problems. It is also obvious that getting young graduating physicians to where they are really needed, Northern and rural Manitoba, is a huge problem.

This is a ongoing situation that the Tory government could not solve, though it tried a variety of solutions. It remains a challenge for the present NDP government.

One solution that may have been proposed in the past, but is certainly worth looking at, is that a medical school candidate in the admission process — besides having very good scholastic ability, goal scores on the MCAT, interview, etc. — must be sponsored by a northern or rural community reserve

A William Avenue house is among the many burned by arsonists.

Asper letter not whole story

As Leonard Asper states in his recent letter to the editor, private broadcasters like Global in Canada want CBC television out of local news. They promise to "fill the void." Respectfully, we offer the viewpoint that this so-called void may be larger than they think.

Public opinion polls indicate that CBC's identity and value is meshed in the depth and quality of our journalism. At the local level, we are the only broadcaster to provide in-depth investigative journalism, consumer investigative journalism, long-form contextual journalism dedicated to daily major issues, documentaries featuring Manitoba artists, daily political journalism, a forum for public feedback and commentary. All of our journalism is governed by a journalistic standards policy, unique in broadcast in Canada, to ensure the highest possible standards. Thiscode of ethics and conduct is a public document, one that governs our daily journalistic programs on both the local and national level.

As a former network journalist who has worked exclusively in Western Canada, I can tell you that national journalism does not exist without strong local roots and a commitment to producing daily local journalism. The ability to break stories happens at the local level with a strong connection in the community. Last year, 24 Hours delivered approximately 500 affairs pieces (I-team, consumer, documentary and arts) to network programs such as the Fifth Estate, Marketplace, Venture, and Undercurrents. These programs offer unique opportunities for Manitoba stories to appear on popular network current affairs programs for a substantial Canadian audience. These programs do not exist on the private networks.

Every night, a sizable audience chooses 24 Hours at 6 p.m. A sizable number of Canadians chose CBC news and current affairs programs on the network — Canadian programs that occupy prominent blocks of the prime-time schedule. Mr. Asper states that CBC should not produce shows that the "private sector is willing to do." As a public broadcaster, we agree. That's why we approach our journalism and set our priorities the way that we do. In that context, suggesting that program genres such as "local news" should become the domain of private broadcasters does not tell the complete story.

JANE CHALMERS
Regional Director
CBC Manitoba

Heritage buildings lost to skyscrapers

I have been a citizen in Winnipeg for over 30 years. I am writing because it saddens me to see our historical buildings get demolished to make way for the modern skyscrapers this city sees so much of. It enrages me that the government is doing absolutely nothing in its power to prevent our precious architecture from being destroyed. These buildings should have never been removed in the first place. They were an important reminder to us of our richly beautiful heritage and history.

SANDRA MAY COOK
Winnipeg

Manufacturing a crisis. "Politicians Talk as Winnipeg Burns", Winnipeg Free Press, November 2, 1999. (Courtesy Winnipeg Free Press)

The urban wing's search for both durability and vision gained political traction with the 1998 election of Glen Murray—a young, ambitious, openly gay liberal of Irish and Ukrainian ancestry—as Winnipeg's 41st mayor. Murray made the creation of a new urban redevelopment model a cornerstone of both his campaign and his time in office. Despite an avowed commitment to "fiscal conservatism," Murray sold himself as a progressive visionary who represented a totally new kind of urban future. "The [Murray] campaign was mostly about just giving the people of Winnipeg an opportunity to dream and dream big," Eliza recalled, "and to have a really, really great vision for their city, and to have a really progressive type of person that would lead them in that direction." Murray was an avid supporter of the urban wing's doctrine, and an effective salesman. "He was just a really big thinker, and he always thought outside the regular box," Eliza said. She remembered a State of the City speech Murray gave to almost a thousand people in 1999, a year in which Winnipeg hosted the Pan American Games. "People were so fired up and people were so excited, and then he started doing stuff, you know, he did CentreVenture, he initiated Waterfront Drive, and the condos, and everything happening down there," Eliza reflected. "It was a time of great hope." In a cunning move, Murray put the urban wing's decades-old quest for downtown profitability at the top of his agenda and sold it to Winnipeggers as a radical departure.

While Murray did not dream up CentreVenture by himself, it is true that he seems to have been left to draw up the city's new redevelopment plan with minimal assistance or interference from other levels of government. The federal government showed little interest in committing additional funding or technical assistance for the restructuring of Winnipeg's city centre beyond the CAI. And the new provincial government, though openly touting its support for the redevelopment of Winnipeg's city centre, appeared content to follow Murray's planning lead.

To give political clout to the plan for CentreVenture, Murray picked up on the long-time urban-wing assertion that renewed investment in downtown Winnipeg would be crucial to any broader regional economic future. "The health and vitality of downtown Winnipeg is important for those who live and work there, but also for the entire city and province," Murray wrote in what amounted to CentreVenture's founding document, his *CentreVenture Working Draft*. The idea that Winnipeg's city centre actually functioned as the economic "heart" of the region would become a go-to, if entirely unfounded, analogy in the years to come. "Winnipeg's downtown is its heart," Murray quoted a 1995 City report, "And, like a heart, it must be healthy if the city as a whole is to be fit and strong." "The renewal of the downtown produces a domino effect on the city and the provincial economy," he went on, quoting a 1990 City of Winnipeg planning report, which stated: "Our image, and therefore our competitive position, will undoubtedly be influenced by the impressions created within ten blocks of Portage and Main. Planning and coordination are essential."[15] In this sense, the urban wing positioned the city center as an avatar for the entire region's future.

Indeed, this doctrine achieved a new degree of hegemony across Manitoba's political spectrum following Murray's election. Candidates jostled to position themselves as the face of urban redevelopment during the 1999 Manitoba provincial election. Even arch-conservative incumbent Gary Filmon, whose base lay far from downtown Winnipeg, told the *Winnipeg Free Press*, "It's vitally important that Winnipeg—which is the capital city, which is what people internationally see about us—become vital, become exciting, and become seen as a great place to invest." Gary Doer, the eventual premier-elect, was equally enthusiastic, telling the *Free Press*, "We have to bring back the 'can-do' attitude that led to The Forks and business improvement zones...With a new mayor and council that are ready for downtown renewal, it's time to get the job done."[16] Doer's words were telling: this was a time of renewal for the urban wing's nearly 30-year-old agenda.

In fact, despite his reputation for thinking outside the box, Murray drew heavily from plans that had been drafted by the urban wing long before he came to power. The *Centre-Venture Working Draft* Murray submitted to City Council references downtown plans dating from a 1969 report entitled *Downtown Winnipeg*, which identified downtown disinvestment as a general civic crisis and laid the groundwork for, among other things, the construction of the Winnipeg Convention Centre.[17] The general concept of making downtown attractive to investors through grants, tax breaks, free land, and technical assistance had been in place since at least the late 1970s when the City gave $20 million to Trizec Corporation. But Murray provided political leadership for several important new innovations the urban wing had begun to call for after reflecting on 30-plus years of untransformative organizing.

Responding to what it viewed as a fragmented organizational landscape—since the 1970s the urban wing had established a litany of business improvement districts, tourism and economic development offices, property-owners' associations, and an authority to manage the two shopping malls constructed under the CAI—a 1997 planning committee urged City Council to, "Explore the possibility of creating a downtown planning and development corporation...a downtown development corporation with a broader geographical mandate would be in a better position to make decisions which would likely benefit all of downtown." Murray, in his *CentreVenture Working Draft*, built on the committee's view. "There are a myriad of organizations currently working on the different aspects of improving the downtown," he wrote. "They have said that what is missing is something that will bring them together, coordinate activities, focus all of the efforts to revitalize downtown. We agree. We believe that a new development corporation which takes on this leadership role is the best way of achieving this goal."[18]

Murray made clear that a cornerstone of the new authority would be its access to the city's wealth of "surplus" land and buildings. "CentreVenture must have access to City assets in order to do business," he wrote. "City Council will have to make critical decisions about transferring City-owned assets or other options. This could involve transferring property assets related to heritage buildings. Or, the City could provide access through options to purchase, right of first refusal, leases, air rights parcels or other vehicles." Murray concluded, "Upon approval from Council, the administration will immediately begin work on the feasibility of transferring assets."[19] Instead of privatizing public lands piece by piece—and subjecting every decision to potential neighbourhood claims—creating CentreVenture would allow the dominant bloc to privatize all the land it wanted to in a single move.

City Council welcomed the plan. While two city-centre councillors unsuccessfully objected to transferring funds from an affordable housing program to CentreVenture, the transfer of "surplus" City-owned land and buildings to the authority received little resistance. "CentreVenture, the city's newly minted development corporation," the *Winnipeg Free Press* reported less than seven months after Murray introduced the idea, "just became the busiest real estate agent in the downtown. City council approved an asset agreement yesterday that gives the agency an option on 44 city-owned downtown buildings and parcels of land. CentreVenture's job is to find buyers and developers for the properties." The properties in the original "bundle" were given to CentreVenture for $1 apiece, according to the asset agreement between CentreVenture and the City. "Properties that the city acquires in the future under tax sales," the *Free Press* also reported, "will be turned over to CentreVenture for the value of the outstanding taxes."[20]

By design, the new authority turned City-owned resources over to private developers with an unprecedented absence of democratic or "political" oversight. "We believe that for CentreVenture to be effective, it will have to be able to expedite decisions," Murray wrote in the *CentreVenture Working Draft*. The local state would continue to make policy and provide infrastructure, he wrote, "However, we believe that attracting and finalizing business deals should be handled through an entrepreneurial group. ...What is needed is a pro-active group to support private sector investment and partnerships—a development corporation to work with the private sector and with government to spur the revitalization of downtown." "The agency will report to council twice a year," the *Free Press* announced five months later, "but it will not need political approval for any of its deals." The president of the Chamber of Commerce, according to the *Free Press*, "said the agency needs to operate independently in order to establish credibility with the private sector." "It has to transcend the political agenda of the day," the *Free Press* quoted the Chamber president, "and operate untouched through successive administrations."[21] With the creation of CentreVenture, the urban wing established a new institutional form to orchestrate settler-colonial dispossession at the regional scale for years to come.

"OPEN FOR BUSINESS," CLOSED FOR JUSTICE: THE CENTREVENTURE DOCTRINE

The plans cited in the creation of CentreVenture and the newspaper accounts that introduced the authority to the public were imbued with a powerful set of values and ideas that are now physically manifested—and thus naturalized—throughout Winnipeg's city centre. Through these publications, the dominant bloc promoted established colonial conceptions about human geography—above all, the doctrine of *urbs nullius*[22]—that ensured the burial of alternative development visions, including those of the predominantly poor, working-class, Indigenous, and people-of-colour communities in the centre of Winnipeg. These conceptions were not entirely new, nor entirely old. Instead, they represented new spins on traditional geographical ideas that have dominated—however invisibly—the development of the North-West for 150 years.

This time around, the urban wing's first achievement was to depoliticize the planning process, allowing its members to monopolize decision making. It did so by narrowing the field of qualified participants from the diverse array of communities with a stake in the city centre to a small cadre of "experts," technocrats, politicians, "business people," and property owners who would serve the interests of capital. The primary discursive tactic used to depoliticize the process was to describe the city centre as a place that "belongs to everyone," in effect silencing any "special" claims made by communities who actually lived there, and hiding the specific class and race makeup of the urban wing. This was done in close connection with a trickle-down economic analysis that asserted universal benefits would follow from profitable capitalist investment downtown. The City's 1995 *CentrePlan: Working Together for Winnipeg's Downtown* was the first plan to call for a single urban development authority in Winnipeg. After rehearsing the "heart" analogy that Murray would echo in his 1999 *CentreVenture Working Draft*, the document introduces the city centre as "a special place with a responsibility to all Winnipeggers" and asserts the need for a plan that will "benefit the city as a whole by creating a predictable investment climate" through "consensus" and the creation of a "shared vision." *CentrePlan* reiterates the longstanding assertion of the urban wing that city-centre profits will create an economic "domino effect" benefitting the entire region. "[Downtown] determines Winnipeg's competitive position within the country," the plan claims. "The future of the whole Winnipeg region hinges to a very great degree on what is going to become of the city's downtown in the future."[23] The similarities between the urban wing's position and that of the mid-1800s western expansionists—who boldly claimed the fate of the whole Dominion of Canada depended on occupation and redevelopment of the Prairie West—are striking. When the fate of an entire city or country is said to be located in one relatively small segment, the stakes become too high to listen to the aspirations of those who actually live there.

With the claim that "a predictable investment climate" is universally beneficial, the task of improving one of the poorest, most Indigenous places on the continent was transformed into the task of maximizing profitability and reducing risks to capital investment. In turn, this framing made logical the appointment of members of the dominant bloc to positions of power within CentreVenture. The authority's first board consisted of eight people: an heir to a national newspaper and television empire who was the chair of the board; the owner of the oldest luxury hotel in the city; a former president of the Winnipeg Chamber of Commerce; a business consultant with ties to the Aboriginal Chamber of Commerce; an editor of a magazine for tourists; the executive director of the National Screen Institute; and an architect.

I spoke with Angela, a city-centre community organizer of Cree, Métis, Irish, and Scottish ancestry, about the lack of Indigenous participation in CentreVenture.[24] Angela has long been active in Indigenous struggles in Winnipeg, including organizing in response to missing and murdered Indigenous women and establishing an organization to support the everyday needs of Indigenous women and their families in the downtown and surrounding neighbourhoods. "Hey," Angela asked me, "does CentreVenture have any Indigenous people on the board?" At that point, almost fifteen years after its creation, CentreVenture's board consisted of the president of a multi-billion-dollar agriculture and food processing firm; the vice president of a multi-billion-dollar insurance company; the regional president of a multinational bank; a real estate developer and owner of the city's NHL hockey team; a broker in a multinational real estate firm; the president of a shipping company; a partner in a law firm; a public relations strategist; and an architect. I told Angela that none of them were Indigenous. "That's a problem right there," she said. Angela told me it reminded her of a summit that had been convened recently about the future of Manitoba, attended by high-level politicians, including former Manitoba premiers Gary Filmon and Gary Doer. One of the main topics of conversation, Angela had noticed, was the importance of Indigenous peoples to the future of the province. The problem was, "not a single Indigenous person was at the table," Angela said, shaking her head. "White people just want to manage us," she told me, adding that, to her, authorities like CentreVenture and events like the summit indicate that instead of reflecting on "whiteness," "centuries of colonialism," and "structural" factors, white people continue to speak as if there's some "inherent" problem with Indigenous peoples and the places they inhabit.

Despite the homogeneity of CentreVenture's board—the absence of downtown residents, tenants, homeless people, youth, seniors, wage workers, people on social assistance, people of colour, and Indigenous peoples—there is a tendency for those involved to emphasize its diversity. Eliza told me a story about drinking with Murray one evening, as the mayor brainstormed the first CentreVenture board by writing names on a coaster. "He looked for people he thought had a real passion for downtown," she said. "He tried to be as inclusive as possible." Annitta Stenning, the first CEO of CentreVenture, described the authority's first board to me as "a wonderful mix of entrepreneurs and professionals" with "just a wonderful, rich mix of perspectives, but with a deep passion, and all of them very much committed to Winnipeg and the value of downtown."[25] These comments point to just how narrow the social world of the dominant bloc is. Only from within its limited world can a collection of wealthy white professionals and capitalists—jotted down on a coaster off the top of the mayor's head—be imagined as "diverse."

The "passion for downtown" that Eliza and Stenning speak of is another popular concept within this world, and it is closely related to a second powerful geographical feeling advanced by the urban wing. That is, the feeling of the city centre as a place that has been lost but that is now an object of righteous desire and repossession. This way of relating to lost territory and to those who are perceived to have taken it is usefully encapsulated by the term "revanchism." A typically liberal, non-confrontational way of doing this is to present the area as sadly dead, sick, or empty. Stenning told me that CentreVenture prioritized residential developments in particular—"those kinds of things that would breathe some life into it"—"because the work day, there's 60,000 people that work in the downtown, but at the end of the day it really was vacant." Characterizations like this enable the urban wing—like the western expansionists of the 1800s—to present the retaking of Indigenous space as an innocent, beneficial, vital, even thrilling move-ment of people into uninhabited terrain. Murray and others relied on a common set of floating signifiers to erase the existing human geography of the downtown within the plans that set the stage for CentreVenture. "Everyone wants to do something to improve the downtown and make it a vibrant, active place," Murray wrote in the *CentreVen-ture Working Draft*, making sure to reiterate that the area's lack of "health and vitality" threatened the entire province's future. "However, everyone agrees that the goal of a revitalized downtown has not been realized."[26] In these renderings, the city centre is simply unhealthy, lethargic, and empty—a geographical mythology that completely erases the actual active, vital human geography that takes place downtown but that does not exhibit the class and race markers of Winnipeg's affluent suburbs.

Existing occupants of the downtown, however, were not entirely erased by the plans that created the basis for CentreVenture. The authors of the 1995 *CentrePlan: Working Together for Winnipeg's Downtown* actually went to some effort to include them. "The downtown has a population of 14,000 and increasingly is home for recent immigrants and aboriginal people," its authors acknowledge. Indigenous claims to the area are hinted at in *CentrePlan*. "In our vision of the future," the report asserts, "the downtown exhibits a strong sense of community and belonging…It respects and honours its aborig-inal ancestry recognizing their pivotal role in the success of the downtown."[27]

Even the "boundary neighbourhoods" that *CentrePlan*'s geographical boundary excludes come into view for a moment. "Downtown Winnipeg is framed by a number of older residential neighbourhoods all of which have a significant impact on the down-town," the plan states, and in a section entitled "Promoting Social Harmony," the plan-ners elaborate their views. "By far the most rapidly growing sector of the downtown and boundary neighbourhoods population is the aboriginal community," they write, going silent on the history of Indigenous plans for the city centre and pivoting instead to racial uplift. "It faces challenges related to poverty, unemployment, and low education attain-ment as well as the need to strengthen traditional cultural and spiritual values."[28]

Under a second subheading, "New Immigrants," the planners go on: "The downtown continues to be the most significant location in the city and the province for migrants. Since the mid-1980s international migration has been on the increase. However the countries of origin for immigrants, have shifted from those in Europe to those in South-East and East Asia." The authors conclude the section with a discussion of "Street Youth": "The existence of street youth in Winnipeg is both well documented and plainly visible. These youth are either extremely vulnerable to, or are already enmeshed in, a lifestyle of unmet basic needs, high risk activities, and alienation. In order to meet basic needs for food, clothing, and shelter, street youth often resort to illegal activities." [29]

Instead of aiming to meet the needs of these groups, however, *CentrePlan* distances them from the heart of its development vision, which consistently remains the attraction and protection of capital investment. Downtown neighbourhoods are treated as problems that, if left unmanaged, could negatively affect the attraction of investment. A special section on "Community and Belonging" instructs the City to, "Implement a long-term neighborhood management approach for dealing with boundary communities" and recommends separate "programs designed to address the multitude of issues manifest in these communities." In so doing, *CentrePlan* construes lack of access to the necessities of life for people already living downtown as a side issue related to "social deterioration" rather than a result of the sustained exclusion of those communities from dominant development visions over decades and centuries.

In the *CentreVenture Working Draft* Murray wrote based on *CentrePlan*, he fails to mention existing residents and the presence of Indigenous, migrant, or "street youth" communities. Those groups were also subsequently written out of media depictions of the city centre after Murray's plan was released. Planners, politicians, and reporters were able to present the city centre as a space devoid of inhabitants, and thus ripe for the introduction of humanity in general. "PEOPLE AT HEART OF CITY PLAN," the *Free Press* proclaimed on the front page of its April 27, 1999, edition. "PEOPLE, PEOPLE, PEOPLE" ran a May 9, 1999, headline. "CentrePlan's vision is more people downtown—more people living downtown, more people working downtown, and more people playing downtown," CentrePlan committee chairman Brad Hughes told the *Free Press*. Media coverage hid the social engineering practised by CentreVenture, which tended to divide the city's population into "dead" and "vital" subjects. Existing Indigenous, migrant, and "street youth" residents signalled the death of the city, while the majority white, suburban, white-collar workforce represented its salvation. [30]

Stenning revealed more of the substance of the authority's revanchist approach than did official plans and newspaper coverage. In a 2013 interview, Stenning spoke at length about Stephen Juba Park, on the former railway land on the west bank of the Red River, adjacent to the "surplus" lands where CentreVenture intended to build its Waterfront Drive luxury condominium development. An existing public park next door to the planned condominium development could have been a valuable built-in amenity, but remaking the park soon became one of CentreVenture's top priorities. "Well, as it turns out, it was a very unsafe park, very untoward people were using it, lots of drug deals," Stenning told me. "We actually cut in to the park, to create private space, so we

Downtown Winnipeg

City centre with Indigenous neighbourhoods. "CentrePlan Action Plan, 1997-99", Winnipeg, ca. 1997.

could create development, so we could create condominiums, so we could create residential opportunities." It was initially an unpopular move. "People said, 'You're crazy, you're cutting into a park, you're cutting down trees.' And we said, 'Mmhmm, we are, because nobody uses it, it's unsafe, and there's no place for development.'" Much of the $10 million redevelopment of the park, as Stenning recalled, was intended to expose its "untoward" inhabitants to the gaze of presumably more "toward" people. "So, we're actually going to use the road to facilitate residential development, we're going to change the park, we're going to cut some of those berms, we're going to cut the trees up, so there's beautiful sight lines right down to the river, it's open, so people will go there during the day and at night and feel safe, we're going to put lights in." Today, Stenning continued,

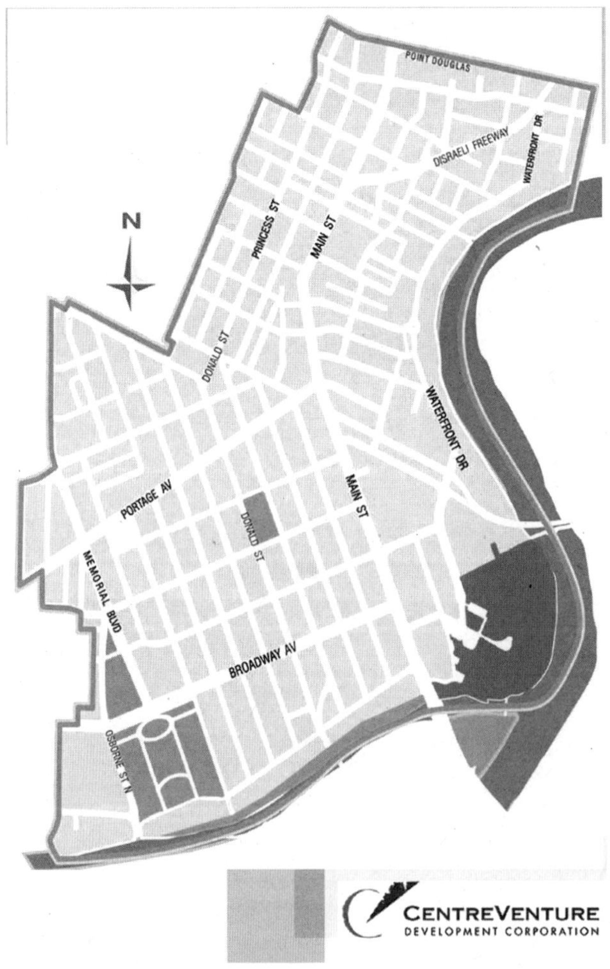

194   CentreVenture's dominion, with Indigenous neighbourhoods erased. CentreVenture, 2006 Annual Report.

"You look out on the park, and when people know there's lots of activity and eyes on the park, that's not where bad people want to hang out." Stenning's description of Stephen Juba Park provides an excellent example of CentreVenture's revanchist project: in the same breath, the CEO describes Stephen Juba Park as both empty ("nobody uses it") and full of "bad" and "untoward" people engaged in activities the authority disapproves of. For CentreVenture, places like Stephen Juba Park must be wrested away from their existing inhabitants on behalf of a more desirable—and profitable—class of people.

Indeed, the retaking of Stephen Juba Park signalled the "reopening" of the area not only to respectable populations but also to moneymaking in general. "As a result, it facilitated millions and millions and millions of dollars of development," said Stenning, sounding like a modern-day Walter Begg (the prominent Winnipeg merchant who penned a popular history of the city that saw war as a means of ushering in profit). "It facilitated residential [development], the park is used, and I still have conversations with people to this day, over ten years later, saying, 'Annitta, the best thing they ever did in the downtown was create Waterfront Drive.'" For CentreVenture, Waterfront Drive became an important early foothold in the broader effort to retake the city centre. As if to confirm this symbolism, City Council erected a monument to the Selkirk Settlers— widely known as the first Europeans to attempt a year-round agricultural colony in the Canadian Prairie West—in Stephen Juba Park in 2010.

An important part of CentreVenture's function is to coax other arms of the state into supporting the urban wing's vision (as the Crown Lands Department did for the 1800s western expansionists). This means convincing suburbanites in general, and suburban politicians in particular, of the righteousness of retaking the city centre. "I think people knew that [building Waterfront Drive] was the right thing to do," Stenning told me, "and the big piece that we had to convince council and others of, is…that it would take twenty years to get it back, and it would take discipline, it would take courage, it would take leadership, it would take investment on all fronts." The urban wing's desire for a state courageous enough to go downtown contains a crucial if implicit assertion about the proper role of state power in the project of retaking the city.

In another striking parallel to the 1800s export-agricultural vision, the urban wing's activities indicate that their revanchist vision requires significant application of state power before real estate capitalists—and finally the "toward" people who buy condos— can be expected to enter a given area. Stenning confirmed the magnitude of this dynamic in her explanation of how Waterfront Drive came to be. "The first part was the public investment [in road and park redevelopment for Waterfront Drive] had to happen," said Stenning, "because without that, absolutely not, there wouldn't have been the private investment, because it would have had nowhere to work, right?" Urban wing capital, as Stenning's statements reveal, depends fundamentally on public investment to create the ground it walks on.

A third, related geographical achievement of the urban wing involved the visual representation of Winnipeg's city centre as an abstract two-dimensional space, devoid of human, social, cultural, or political life. The repeated use of maps, charts, and graphs in *CentrePlan*, the *CentreVenture Working Draft*, and other planning documents depicted an emptied-out world of zoning designations, legal titles, and the occasional "important site"—such as business improvement districts, shopping malls, and universities. This provided an easily digestible, supposedly objective representation of the city that clearly supported the urban wing's plans to rid the city of its existing social character.

Similar to the "imperial panorama"[31] of the Dominion Lands Survey, urban wing maps made the city centre visible to outside investors—and intending settlers—at a glance, flattening and partitioning a complex community so it could be easily known, divided up, and possessed. The privileging of the property grid above all else reinforced and made visible the neoliberal orientation of the urban wing's agenda, naturalizing the market as the proper, desirable, even inevitable mode of conceiving and redistributing land. Meanwhile, most maps created for CentreVenture's purposes depicted the most residential city-centre neighbourhoods in a darker shade than the rest of city, and also usually devoid of any features whatsoever—even property outlines. This omission clearly erases the way that residential communities just outside CentreVenture's jurisdiction possess long-standing lived, day-to-day attachments, claims, and aspirations for places CentreVenture aims to control. By erasing such realities, the urban wing sought to reassure investors of the absence of democratic, social, cultural, or political factors that might impede their ability to gain swift and easy access to land for development.

Finally, in order to sell their new vision for the city's future, Murray and the urban wing pushed the idea that publicly held "surplus" wealth—in the form of land and buildings—as well as government grants, infrastructural spending, loan guarantees, and technical assistance, was best redistributed upwards, to wealthy developers, and indirectly to the wealthy suburbanites who would populate new condo, office, and retail developments. This idea was ushered in and made appealing through the assertion that the value of public "investment" could be measured by the value of the private investment it attracted. The true task of public spending, according to Murray and the urban wing, was not to meet people's needs but to meet the needs of investors, who in turn would decide what the new "revitalized" city looked like. Because of the tricky, potentially risky (to capital) nature of democratic institutions such as City Hall, Murray stressed that a publicly funded institution with the "flexibility" of a private firm would be necessary to achieve such an upward distribution.

Murray thus used as a model for CentreVenture the Lowertown Redevelopment Corporation in St. Paul, Minnesota, which according to Murray, "levered over $428 million in investments with seed money of approximately $10 million." "Leveraging" or "levering" private investment—in this case providing handouts to wealthy businessmen in order to lure their money to a given jurisdiction—would become the ultimate rubric through which the new authority was graded. "In the long-term, we would like to see every public dollar lever significant private sector investment," Murray concluded. Through this turn of phrase, the broad and inclusive potential of "the economic, physical, and social revitalization of downtown Winnipeg" was sacrificed and transformed into a "predictable investment climate" measured in hard cash.[32] As such, the only claims to public land and wealth earmarked for urban improvement with any legitimacy in the eyes of CentreVenture would be those claims backed by large sums of money. Land claims backed by a spirit of social or economic justice, reconciliation, or Indigenous self-determination would be systematically cast as without value.

Fittingly, on September 30, 1999, the front page of the *Winnipeg Free Press*, quoting Mayor Murray—now also the first chair of CentreVenture's board—declared Winnipeg "open for business."[33] As a result of Murray's strategy, virtually the entire archipelago of "surplus" city-owned land in the centre of Winnipeg was handed over to the private sector through CentreVenture in the years following 1999. Most of the land was given over to millionaire developers for the creation of for-profit condo, office, and retail developments.

"WATERFRONT DRIVE IS THE FUTURE"

The former spur line on the west bank of the Red River was the largest single concentration of such land during this phase. In its first years, CentreVenture turned nearly all its energies towards the transformation of this site: it drafted a plan for the area; won $10 million in new infrastructure from the three levels of government; and courted developers by offering cheap land, special financing arrangements, and stipulating strict land-use guidelines—the area would become an exclusive enclave for luxury condos. As developers signed up in the mid-2000s, CentreVenture sold its new luxury district to the local media as an early model of a retaken city. "Waterfront Drive is the future," the *Free Press* editorialized in the summer of 2004, days after CentreVenture unveiled architectural drawings of condos intended for the area. "Waterfront Drive is the symbol of what the downtown and Winnipeg can become," the *Free Press* editor in chief wrote, in an article replete with references to "the frontier spirit," urban "pioneers," and their "castles."[34] Between 2005 and 2008, 200 luxury condos in four complexes were constructed along this segment of the west bank of the Red River, each originally priced from $200,000 to $700,000 (many are now valued at over $1 million).

In 2011, the *Free Press* checked in on the now-completed district in a piece entitled "Its Ship Has Come in: Waterfront Drive Transformed into a Beacon of Success." "Today, Waterfront Drive is a sight to behold," wrote the *Free Press*, citing as its main evidence "all the magnificent condominium developments that line the street." Reiterating the passive aggressive revanchism of CentreVenture's founding documents, and mixing in a bit of nostalgia for the area's sweatshop days, the piece continued: "Once a run-down, listless area, it has regained the vibrancy that once characterized the area in the early

Searching for suitable settlers. Avenue Building with CentreVenture banner, Winnipeg, ca. 2000s.
(Photo by Ken Gigliotti/Courtesy Winnipeg Free Press)

1900s." "An area that was once a beacon of failure," the *Free Press* quoted then-CentreVenture CEO Ross McGowan, "[has been made] into an area that's now a beacon of success."[35] Simply by attracting investment in the built environment, Waterfront Drive was a success, according to the rubric of the urban wing. Official documents and mass media representations, however, provide little to no understanding of the actual lived reality of officially "vibrant" and "successful" space.

The people I met in The Warbler—and in the other officially "vibrant" parts of Waterfront Drive—were outgoing, friendly, and very much alive. But the area itself is much colder and more "dead"—to use the parlance of the urban wing—than the official story makes it out to be. Cars far outnumber pedestrians on the street. There is little to no sign of life in The Warbler itself; not a casual human trace in the lobby, hallways, or elevator; no notes, posters, shoes, decorations, or children's toys. Virtually no one hangs around outside the building, or in its shared areas. The building's private parking garage is its main hub of social interaction, if it could be said to have one. A few neighbourly touches accompany the Audis and BMWs, including a novelty sign reading "NO PARKING—ICELANDERS ONLY." It is only in the garage that people in The Warbler visit momentarily while getting out of the car. This is for the simple reason that almost everybody—even in Winnipeg's few warm summer months—drives in and out of the building for just about every purpose, from buying toilet paper to visiting friends. In this sense, the *Free Press*'s use of the word "castles" to describe Waterfront Drive condos, even before they had been constructed, was prescient. Condo owners in this "beacon of success" live largely sealed away from their surroundings in Winnipeg's city centre, entering and exiting luxury complexes through underground parkades.

Commerce, a typical measure of "vibrancy" by dominant bloc standards, was barely in evidence during my stay on Waterfront Drive. Three of the four condo complexes have ground-floor commercial space built into them, but only about half of the storefronts were active. The shops that had been set up—a few nail, massage, and skin-care parlours, for the most part—were closed on evenings and weekends. A $50 per plate Brazilian restaurant had recently opened in the condo complex next door and seemed to be doing well; many of the people I spoke to mentioned it as an example of the area's improving fortunes. But all of them agreed that Waterfront Drive was a disappointment when it came to commercial life.

The condos and storefronts of Waterfront Drive face onto Stephen Juba Park, now a strip of well-manicured lawns, bright flowers, old elms, and shaded benches running along the west bank of the Red River—the place Stenning takes such pride in. It is a popular path for spandex-clad joggers and cyclists, as well as the odd dog walker and young professional with a briefcase. But these people—people whose physical appearance indicates their membership in the class for whom the area is being retaken—are not the main inhabitants of the park. CentreVenture may have "opened up" sightlines on the area's pre-existing human geography, but it has not eliminated or even overtaken it.

The west bank of the Red River adjacent to Waterfront Drive remains home to an extensive, if unsanctioned, residential community. Near the water's edge, Waterfront Drive slopes steeply down to a muddier, less manicured, mostly tree-covered terrain. In spring, summer, and fall there is a tent city here, formed by many separate camps lining the riverbank along and beyond Waterfront Drive. Couches, armchairs, and folding chairs encircle fire pits; clothes hang from lines attached to trees; handwritten notes are left in front of tents. It is this much older, unsanctioned city that arguably gives Waterfront Drive and Stephen Juba Park most of their urban "vitality": teenagers ride dirt bikes at the river's edge; couples share a bench in the early morning; people dumpster dive in front of the new condo buildings; big groups climb up from the riverbank in the morning, heading west to Main Street; people scrawl long messages in Cree syllabics on the benches in Stephen Juba Park. This is still the prevailing form of public social life in the area now dubbed "Waterfront Drive," a reality the urban wing dismisses and erases at every turn.

State-orchestrated luxury housing. Waterfront Drive, Winnipeg, ca. 2018.

Settler spirit on the gentrification frontier. Selkirk Settlers statue, Waterfront Drive, Winnipeg, ca. 2018.

In the summer I spent on Waterfront Drive, I learned of only one community event intended for the district's official, condo-owning residents. A public consultation was being held for a new condo complex that an unknown developer was proposing for Waterfront Drive. It was to be built on one of the final parcels of land that CentreVenture still owned in the area. The event hadn't been advertised publicly, but I received a last-minute invitation from my neighbour, Elaine. Inside an old brick-clad industrial building, a uniformed guard welcomed us into a small room of freshly painted white drywall, where people in dresses, suits, khakis, and polo shirts milled around. A scale model of a 25-story condo tower stood on a table in the centre of the room. The walls were filled with computer-generated illustrations of the tower—displaying its height and the shadow it would cast at different times of day—and various graphs and maps, including one that divided the city into four categories: "residential," "cultural," "parking," and "greenspace."

The scene that day perfectly encapsulated the formula the urban wing has mastered under CentreVenture. A public consultation on the fate of publicly owned land was advertised exclusively through private networks, while neither the developer (who remained anonymous) nor CentreVenture (which owned the land in question) identified themselves as proponents of the project, craftily shielding themselves from public attention. Not that it likely would have mattered, since the "public" in attendance was held—with guards at the door—to precisely those catered to by the urban wing: financiers, developers, design professionals, and condo owners, almost entirely white and affluent. A charming, abandoned industrial building was opened for this group, dressed as if for an art opening, as the setting for a leisurely consideration of the neighbourhood's future. Finally, the show itself—while appearing at first glance to be a rigorous, extensive representation of the neighbourhood and the potential effects of the new tower—actually said very little. There was no mention, of course, of the various Indigenous and working-class attachments to and aspirations for the area; no mention of the existing, unsanctioned human geography of the west bank of the Red River; no mention of the social and economic characteristics of the surrounding neighbourhoods; and no mention of the vast range of unmet basic human needs here in the country's second-poorest constituency.

As is often the case, however, actual conversations with urban wing adherents reveal a far more tangible feeling of frontier occupation, entitlement, and hostility towards those being supplanted. As I was looking at one of the maps in the display, a short man in a polo shirt sidled up to me, and we said hello. His name was Guy, and he lived in the condo complex next to mine. After talking about the proposed tower for a minute, Guy's wife, Val, joined us, wearing a stylish red leather jacket. They said they'd moved to Waterfront Drive from St. Boniface several years earlier, and I asked them what they would most like to see in the neighbourhood. "Parking," Guy said, as Val nodded. Guy said he thought he should be able to permanently buy a parking space on Waterfront Drive, "for twenty thousand dollars or something." He went on, "If they can put a man on the moon they could do that." "What about safety?" I asked Guy, a bit surprised he didn't mention it first. "That's the one thing that everybody asks us, but it hasn't been a problem," Guy replied. "But," he added, "there are some Natives." Guy went on talking about the "Natives" in the neighbourhood. "It doesn't look good for the area," he said. "Panhandlers," Val specified, nodding. "I don't know what it is," Guy went on, "but there are more and more Natives these days."

Guy and Val's perspective is indicative of the way that anti-Native racism often coalesces with the righteous feeling wealthy suburbanites have of retaking Winnipeg's city centre. As the dominant redevelopment agenda renews the legacies of a colonial past—by silencing and excluding existing inhabitants and their alternative visions for the city—Indigeneity is recoded by the urban wing as something ranging from a threat to an eyesore (which, in the real estate business, can amount to the same thing). Beyond this, the fact that the Indigenous human geography of Canada's most Indigenous city is inscrutable to Guy reveals just how powerful the urban wing's renderings—of a city scrubbed clean and ready for "people, people, people"—can be.

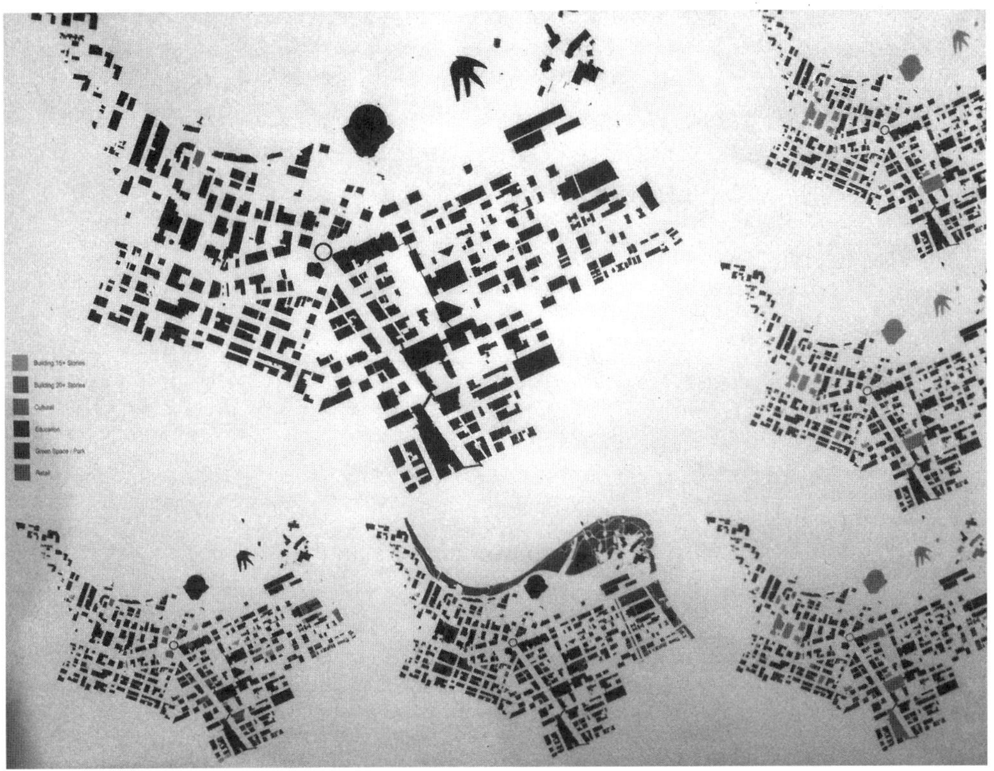

Abstract space. CentreVenture community consultation, Waterfront Drive, ca. 2013.

1   William, interview with author, Winnipeg, MB, December 24, 2013. Throughout the book, all interlocutors' names have been changed except those who indicated they preferred to be identified by their real name and those of public figures.

2   Trouillot, *Silencing the Past*, 151.

3   Cooper, "Excuse Me, Canada, Your Homelessness Is Showing."

4   The name of the condo building has been changed.

5   Albinka, interview with author, Winnipeg, MB, July 25, 2013. Details of Albinka's story have been changed to protect her privacy.

6   The name of the company has been changed.

7   The name of the building has been changed.

8   Coulthard, *Red Skin White Masks*, 176.

9   Manitoba Historical Society, "Walking Tour of North Point Douglas."

10   Lewycky, "1919 Strike Tour"; Lewycky, "Property and Public Access."

11   Eliza, interview with author, Winnipeg, MB, July 10, 2013.

12   Friesen, "Winnipeg's Culture of Fire Lighting"

13   Winnipeg Free Press, "Politicians Talk as Winnipeg Burns."

14   City of Winnipeg, "Plan Winnipeg...Toward 2010."

15   Murray and Stephens, *CentreVenture Working Draft*, 2, 3.

16   Anonymous, "Politicians on Downtown."

17   Klos and Douchant, "'Development at the Core' A Brief Outline of Downtown Winnipeg Development Over the Last 35 Years."

18   CentrePlan Committee, *CentrePlan Action Plan, 1997–99*; Murray and Stephens, *CentreVenture Working Draft*, 2.

19   Ibid., 9–10.

20   O'Brien, "CentreVenture Becomes Busy Player"; Goeres and Buchwald Pitblado Asper Barristers and Solicitors, "Asset Agreement between the City of Winnipeg and CentreVenture Development Corporation."

21   Murray and Stephens, *CentreVenture Working Draft*, 3; O'Brien, "City 'Open for Business.'"

22   Coulthard, *Red Skin White Masks*, 176.

23   City of Winnipeg, *CentrePlan: Working Together for Winnipeg's Downtown*, 2, 3.

24   Angela, interview with author, Winnipeg, MB, July 23, 2013.

25   Annitta Stenning, interview with author, Winnipeg, MB, July 17, 2013.

26   Murray and Stephens, *CentreVenture Working Draft*, 2.

27   City of Winnipeg, *CentrePlan: Working Together for Winnipeg's Downtown*, 3, 7.

28   Ibid., 17, 21.

29   City of Winnipeg, *CentrePlan: Working Together for Winnipeg's Downtown*, 21, 22.

30   McArthur, "People at Heart of City Plan"; Winnipeg Free Press, "People, People, People."

31	Bantjes, *Improved Earth.*

32	The increased mobility of firms in the age of "globalization" has intensified inter-urban competition, allowing capital to hold local places hostage all over the world by requiring payment in the form of money, land, infrastructure, "site preparation," or loosened regulations. The problem with the idea that public investment "leverages" private investment is that firms cannot just sit on their surplus capital, they must reinvest it *somewhere*. At best, public spending to "leverage" private investment merely shifts investment from one place to another, which has zero benefit for, and in fact steals immense resources away from, the working people of the world as a whole. At worst, it simply lines the pockets of millionaires who would have invested regardless. In reality, it creates new state-guaranteed outlets for surplus capital investment, which can be very attractive in contexts, such as recessions, when such outlets are rare (Hilderman, Thomas, Frank, Cram Landscape Architecture, Planning and Property & Services Department, Planning & Land-Use Division, *CentrePlan Development Framework*).

33	O'Brien, "City 'Open for Business.'"

34	Hirst, "Waterfront Drive Is the Future."

35	Lewys, "Its Ship Has Come in."

CHAPTER 6

"THIS CITY IS RED": THE MAIN STREET STRIP

we gave our permission
to live side by side
watching our side lose
and places were removed
piece by piece
and invisible walls rose
to the sky

—Duncan Mercredi, *The Duke of Windsor: Wolf Sings the Blues*

The Nazis of Main, in my opinion, were the economic ones.

—Marvin Francis, "Voices from Dark Rooms"[1]

Winnipeg poets, musicians, and other artists, in addition to community organizers and activists, have produced a rich world of Indigenous urban analysis, a sense of place, and visions of urban decolonial futures. These demand to be reckoned with, and yet they are systematically dodged by dominant redevelopment visions. Indigenous "city poetry"[2]—that is, texts by poets writing *as* Indigenous poets about the city—expresses a powerful Indigenous connection and claim to Winnipeg, not merely as a setting for Indigenous life, but as a source of identity itself, as a social relation, as the basis of a new politics, and as a place that will be crucial to the future of life itself on Turtle Island. More than any corner of the city, Winnipeg's Main Street strip—its past, present, and future—is the soul of this world.

CITY TREATY

In 1989, a circle of poets came together under the banner of the Aboriginal Writers Collective of Manitoba, now known as the Manitoba Indigenous Writers Collective (MIWC), holding its meetings in Winnipeg's warehouse district. It was a time of resurgent Indigenous radicalism and cultural production—one year after the death of J.J. Harper at the hands of the WPS; one year before Oka; one year before the historic Native American/First Nations gay and lesbian conference in Winnipeg, at which the term

"Two-Spirit" would originate; and three years before the 500th anniversary of Christopher Columbus' invasion of Turtle Island. Within this circle, the Cree poet, playwright, printmaker, actor, and theatre director Marvin Francis—a long-time Winnipegger originally from Heart Lake First Nation—became a central figure. Francis passed away in 2005, three years after the publication of his best-known work, the epic poem *City Treaty*.

In *City Treaty*, Francis crafts a dense, anarchic vision of life in Winnipeg that ranges across centuries and landscapes but repeatedly comes back to the contemporary city's centre, the space and time from which a new relationship between inhabitants of Turtle Island will be forged. Francis, in this sense, writes in the tradition of the Anishinabe negotiators of Treaty 1, who understood the necessity of updating past agreements to address shifting circumstances.[3] Francis' attention to new conditions drives *City Treaty*, as it traces the litany of present-day relationships through which, as literary scholar Warren Cariou writes, "Native people are sold short, or sold out, by the economic and political bosses who manipulate the situation for their own advantage."[4] *City Treaty* is told loosely from the point of view of JOE TB, member of "the city band." TB stands for "treaty buster," and JOE sets out to replace an old "truce" with a new "city treaty" based on current conditions.

Before he can get down to work, though, JOE is side-tracked by questions, memories, and hallucinations most often inspired by Winnipeg street scenes. At one point, Francis imagines Christopher Columbus walking down the Main Street strip:

> just think what if columbus had discovered himself instead
> so to drink
> to drink
> there's the rubbie walking down Main
> doing that santa maria shuffle[5]

Neither can JOE escape the specific challenges posed by the city's liberal capitalist order; he needs to hire a lawyer to get the city treaty going—"lawyer = life"—so he comes up with a money-making scheme called "mcPemmican:"

> let the poor intake their money take their health
> sound familiar[6]

In the end, JOE is overtaken by a group of Indigenous writers Francis lists using code names:

> here come the leaders the mavericks who cannot shut up
> word drummers

"[T]he landscape now has city," Francis instructs, on the poem's final page, leaving us with only this list of urban authors from which to move forward. "follow the word drummers to the city treaty."[7]

Word drummers. Poster for an event by the Aboriginal Writers Collective of Manitoba (now known as the Manitoba Indigenous Writers Collective), Winnipeg, ca. 2003. University of Manitoba Archives, Marvin Francis fonds, A.06-51, Box 1, Folder 11. (With permission of Duncan Mercredi)

One of the writers Francis refers readers to at the end of *City Treaty* is Duncan Mercredi, a Winnipeg-based Cree and Métis poet originally from Misipawistik (Grand Rapids, Manitoba). Mercredi is a legendary Winnipeg poet, a senior member of the MIWC, and a mentor to many. His books are populated by images of smoke-filled bars, endless concrete, deafening city traffic, white bigots, the blues, and visions of destroying the colonial world. Mercredi often writes about "the Wolf," which—in so far as wolves have been driven out of their long-time habitats and forced to find new places to live—he refers to as a symbol of urban Indigenous experience.[8] In 1997's *The Duke of Windsor: Wolf Sings the Blues* (named for a downtown Winnipeg blues bar), Mercredi includes a poem called "Mistress," which hinges on the city's apartheid geography:

> locked inside their fortress in the suburb
> they neatly side step out stretched hands
> cursing under their breath
> I see them sometimes circling the red light
> drawn into its hypnotizing gaze
> long legs beckon and they forget their hate
> for a quick few seconds of forbidden fruit
> sampled under the blanket of the night[9]

In "Mistress," the divide between the suburbs and the city centre is dramatized through the image of suburbanites coming down from their "fortress" to visit the city centre's red light district. For this purpose, the suburbanites are willing to navigate panhandler-esque figures—"out stretched hands"—who irritate them, and to overcome their hostility toward the area's inhabitants—"they forget their hate"—to get what they need. The poem brings out a theme that runs through much of the work produced by the MIWC; that is, the dynamics that exist between Indigenous and non-Indigenous urbanites, the way urban life puts them into relation, and the tendency for encounters between the two groups to be fuelled by a complex, power-laden mixture of fear, desire, pleasure, and pain.

At the 2014 Manitoba Indigenous Writers Festival, in a café on the Main Street strip, Mercredi debuted a new poem, entitled "this city is red."[10] It is perhaps the most overt take on urban dynamics of any of Mercredi's—or perhaps any MIWC members'—poems. It opens:

> built on the bones of a thousand generations
> this city is main street each generation with its own stories
> told in the back alleys and city core

Early on, Mercredi gives the reader a glimpse of the city's apartheid mentality:

> a promise followed down from a northern road
> seeking a dream armed only with hope
> walking down portage to wolseley to st. james
> then north again
> with the same answer, no room, no job
> don't bother me, I'll call the cops

"A colour divided only by imaginary borders," another line begins, "afraid to cross":

> this city hides its hate
> but we have felt it for so long
> we know it's there
> buried beneath the manicured lawns
> behind the drapes
> inside your gates

Later in the poem, Mercredi's voice becomes more defiant:

> this city is red
> a blood red history you have chosen to ignore
> and when you become dust
> i will dance on your ashes
> and when the seed of a new flower blossoms
> where your ashes have settled
> becoming one with the soil
> i will dance again

As in "Mistress," Mercredi is interested in the partitions—"imaginary boundaries"—that govern urban life and structure encounters between urban dwellers differently situated in the country's colonial geography. But Mercredi is even more forceful here, as he confronts his non-Indigenous neighbours directly, calling out the fear, hatred, and wilful ignorance that in his analysis rule their engagements.[11]

THE HEYDAY OF THE MAIN STREET STRIP

Of all the urban locations written about by MIWC poets, Winnipeg's Main Street strip is the most mythologized. "All the Aboriginal writers live on Main Street," Francis joked while teaching at a local university. According to the story, Francis' students had inquired whether Trevor Greyeyes, author of the poem "The Strip," actually lived on the Main Street strip.[12] "Natives and the strip are synonymous," Francis once wrote—while pointing out that several other groups have established strong connections to the strip, including "The Chinese," who "have always had a strong presence on Main Street." "A white person who lives on the strip is more of an outcast than is a Native person who lives there." Like Mercredi, Francis viewed Main Street as an important site of encounter between Indigenous and non-Indigenous peoples. The large Indigenous presence on Main Street, according to Francis, "leads to the only interaction that many non-Native Winnipeg citizens have with Native peoples."[13]

For Mercredi, the story of the Main Street strip is a crucial but largely buried chapter in Winnipeg's history.[14] "It all started after the 1940s," he said, "when the Aboriginal people began to move into the city." Prior to the 1950s, Mercredi told me, there were only five Indigenous families in the city, but in the 1950s and 1960s, more and more people began to move from First Nations and Métis communities near Winnipeg—places like Roseau River and Sagkeeng—into the city. In Mercredi's recollection, many if not most were high school graduates heading to Winnipeg to attend university.

By the 1970s, families from more distant, mostly northern First Nations and Métis communities—not merely those within a short drive of the city—began moving to Winnipeg in greater and greater numbers. Something changed in Winnipeg at that point, Mercredi said. In the 1940s and 1950s, Winnipeg's few Aboriginal families were more or less tolerated by the city's white majority. But when "the invasion," as Mercredi put it, began, white hostility towards Indigenous peoples increased, and the city's de facto system of urban apartheid began to take hold.

Mercredi mapped the emerging geography of urban apartheid in Winnipeg. The first Indigenous families to move to Winnipeg in the 1940s and 1950s settled on a few specific West End blocks—Young, Spence, and Furby Streets, north of Portage Avenue. "That was our territory," Mercredi said. "We didn't go south of Portage [Avenue] because we weren't welcome there." A city planning study commissioned by urban Indigenous organizers in 1975 summarized the tactics used by landlords to maintain apartheid, including "refusal to sell or rent, anonymous threats, acts of extreme nuisance, and so on."[15] Mercredi pointed out that so-called public spaces—hotels, bars, theatres, cafés, and restaurants—south of Portage Avenue were bitterly inhospitable to Native people in those days.[16]

"Let me tell you a story," Mercredi said. "I was a little boy, and we were staying at the Mac, the McLaren Hotel [on the Main Street strip], because my father was a war veteran, and the McLaren gave discounts to veterans in those days. And my mother loved going to Eaton's [the famous Canadian department store on Portage Avenue just south of the Main Street strip, where the city's corporate hockey arena stands now]." Mercredi continued: "So one day she got all dressed up and dressed all of us little kids up, and took us to dine at the fancy restaurant that used to be in Eaton's. So we sat down, and we waited two hours without being served." His mother had been so set on dining at Eaton's with her children that she refused to move, Mercredi said. "Eventually that waitress ended her shift, and a new waitress took over, who served us," said Mercredi. "But my mom never went back."

In typical Canadian settler-colonial fashion, white Winnipeggers combined silence and terse lips with overt violence to keep Indigenous peoples in their place. The WPS regularly enforced the city's de facto apartheid system. Jack, an elder involved in the early days of the Main Street strip, moved to Winnipeg from Ebb and Flow, Manitoba, in the 1950s. The WPS frequently took Native people on "floaters," also known as Starlight Tours, according to Jack, throughout the 1950s, 1960s, and beyond. "You were taken out of town, dropped there, no charges, but you were left there," said Jack. "'Don't come back here or you're going to go to jail,' and that's what happened."[17]

In an attempt to reduce their exposure to degrading encounters at the hands of white landlords, businesses, and police, Indigenous Winnipeggers—including Mercredi's family—headed to the housing, restaurants, cafés, bars, and theatres of the North End, and the Main Street strip in particular. Although there were some lively Indigenous social spaces at the time in and around Young, Spence, and Furby Streets—for example, a now-demolished hotel and bar near the old Greyhound bus station—Mercredi said, the scene shifted north as more and more Indigenous people moved. IMFC organizer George Munroe moved to Winnipeg from Camperville, Manitoba, in 1965. As he put it: "The racism was very, very pronounced, I mean, you could see it. We were kind of confined to one area of the city, which was the North End, as the place that welcomed us better than any other place so that's where we ended up, our hang out was Main Street."[18]

By the late 1960s—a period Francis describes as "the heyday of the strip"[19]—the hotels, bars, restaurants, theatres, and cafés of Main Street had become a booming cultural and political scene where Indigenous peoples from nations and communities across the North-West and Turtle Island came together to create new movements of all kinds. Of any place in Winnipeg, the Main Street strip of the 1960s and 1970s was the concrete manifestation of Indigenous resistance to apartheid's attempt to divide and isolate. Mercredi emphasized the diverse, exciting mix of people who frequented the strip in those days. University students, musicians, artists, and activists hung out with blue-collar workers—including Mercredi, one of the younger children in a family that could not afford to send every child to university, who worked in highway crews and other manual labour jobs—as well as elders and more "hardcore" people who tended to live in the hotels on the strip. As young people piled into cars, sometimes eight or nine

The Main Street strip at Logan Avenue. Winnipeg, date unknown. University of Manitoba Archives & Special Collections, RAHM-55a. (Courtesy University of Manitoba Archives & Special Collections)

On the brink of its heyday. Main Street strip, Winnipeg, ca. 1956. Archives of Manitoba, Winnipeg – Streets – Main, 1956, 1, South from Higgins. (Courtesy of Archives of Manitoba)

at a time, and headed for Winnipeg, Main Street was the first stop.[20] If you didn't know somebody's address or phone number, said Mercredi, you went to Main Street to look for them. More often than not, you would find them.

At the time, the Main Street strip gave voice to postwar Indigenous realities, analyses, and struggles most famously through music. Indigenous blues, country, rock and roll, and folk music scenes took root and flourished on the strip beginning in the 1960s.[21] Line-ups stretched down Main Street to see the "forefathers of Indigenous rock and blues"—musicians such as Billy Joe Green (Ojibway), Percy Tuesday (Ojibway), and Errol Ranville (Métis)—play the Occidental, the Savoy, and the Brunswick hotels, the latter of which Billy Joe Green called the "Grand Ole Opry of Indian country."[22] Musicians, many of whom were residential school survivors, articulated a bold sense of Indigenous identity and community in resistance to colonialism and apartheid. "One of the universal themes...was the articulation of resistance through music," documentary filmmaker Vanda Fleury-Green (Métis) told the CBC. "That was both in the music and the expressions of lyrics but also the people who were frequenting and participating in the Main Street scene."[23]

The Main Street music scene overlapped significantly with Indigenous student radicalism and the political scene at the IMFC, a hub of Red Power organizing and other Indigenous radical politics in the 1960s and 1970s. Anti-Native racism was so rampant in Canadian universities during the strip's heyday, Mercredi recalled, that many Winnipeg students involved in the early days of the American Indian Movement (AIM) convened on the strip rather than on campus. Munroe first learned of the IMFC and its political activities by frequenting the strip, an encounter that sparked a lifetime of political organizing. With friends he met on Main Street, Munroe formed Club 376, which eventually became a 500-member Indigenous youth group inspired in part by the US civil rights and Red Power movements. Organizers planned Red Power marches—including the 1,000-person march against the Toal Report—to start on the Main Street strip, and newspaper photographs from the 1970s show the strip covered in posters calling to "FREE LEONARD PELTIER," the Anishinabe, Dakota, and Lakota AIM activist imprisoned by the US since the 1975 uprising at Pine Ridge, South Dakota.[24] In its heyday, Winnipeg's Main Street strip was a crucial hub of what Glen Coulthard describes as an "unprecedented" period of "pan-Indian assertiveness and political mobilization."[25]

Memories and cultural representations of the strip can, however, be deeply ambivalent. In his poem "Main Street," the late Salteaux poet and MIWC member Douglas Nepinak described the strip as both "beautiful" and "ugly," a "refuge" and a "rip-off," "the only mother some of us have ever known" and "all the hell most people will ever need."[26] Main Street hotel owners exploited Indigenous peoples' subjection to urban apartheid—specifically their lack of employment and housing options, and the fatigue of colonialism—for immense profits. "The Nazis of Main," as Francis put it, "were the economic ones."[27] Day-labour offices set up shop on Main Street to prey on unem-

Political hub. Free Leonard Peltier posters, Main Street strip, Winnipeg, ca. 1977. Photo by Frank Prazak. Winnipeg Free Press, April 2, 1977. (Courtesy of Winnipeg Free Press)

ployed Indigenous workers, paying starvation wages for the city's most dangerous and back-breaking work. Hotel owners charged exorbitant rates—described by an anthropologist in the 1980s as "usurious"[28]—for run-down rooms and made millions selling booze on the strip. Jack, who recalled Main Street fondly, also criticized the hotels along the strip as "a contributor to the problems people had," particularly addictions.

COUNTER-PLAN VII: NEEGINAN

Indigenous community organizers responded to this ambivalence by attempting to take control over the strip in order to expand its usefulness as a social, cultural, and political hub while simultaneously transforming its uneven, exploitative social relations. Neeginan, an Indigenous development vision for turning the strip into a Native "village," was drafted by the IMFC in 1969.[29] The plan's name translated from Cree to English as "Our Place" and conveyed a clear pan-Indigenous claim to the strip. "Let's work together on this opportunity to build a place for ourselves and our children," a newsletter published by Neeginan organizers urged, "a place that we can truly call 'Our Place.'"[30] Coming on the heels of settler suburbanization and its requisite destruction of the Indigenous suburbs, the choice of Main Street as the location for Neeginan's work was a decision to define Winnipeg's entire city centre as a place of special significance to Indigenous peoples. When Neeginan organizers posed the question at a gathering of 60 Indigenous community organizers in 1974, "Where would you like to see this take place—in the city or in the suburbs?" 93 percent responded in favour of the city.[31]

Neeginan was conceived, in part, as a single concrete project that diverse Indigenous communities in Winnipeg could unify around and into which they could channel the general feeling of decolonial desire in the city. "If you are among those who are fed up with such empty talk that passes for concern, and want something really meaningful to take place," a Neeginan newsletter implored, "then join us in our crusade to bring about positive action."[32] When 1,000 people marched against the Toal Report—ostensibly a march against anti-Native police brutality—their list of demands included Neeginan.[33] Using the slogan "UNITY IS STRENGTH," Neeginan organizers built an impressive coalition of urban Indigenous peoples to shape the plan.

In 1972, 21 Indigenous organizations united under the banner of the Winnipeg Native Coalition (WNC) to unanimously pass a resolution supporting Neeginan and appoint a smaller group, dubbed the Winnipeg Indian Council (WIC), to negotiate with settler governments to support its implementation. Two years later, 50 community organizers—representing organizations such as the MIB, IMFC, the Native Women's Group, Kinew Housing, Winnipeg Ehnakumiguk, Youth Action Project, Dufferin Action Centre, Winnipeg Centre Project, MMF, and the Winnipeg Native Club—convened to further develop the Neeginan plan.[34] Prominent organizers from this period included people such as Bev McCorrister, Celestin Guiboche, Linda Bennett, and Darlene Tomasson.

Neeginan organizers came from the same political milieu that published *Wahbung* a year earlier, and Neeginan pursued the same fundamental goals. Primarily, this meant restoring land and self-determination to Indigenous peoples according to present-day social, economic, and geographical—in this case urban—conditions. Organizers summarized the Neeginan vision in the following five-point program:[35]

WHAT IS NEEGINAN?

NEEGINAN...is native peoples working together to accomplish a common goal in a community which will promote, produce, and preserve an urban cultural and economic base for all Indian and Métis people!

NEEGINAN...means proper housing, good schools, and business enterprises—owned, operated, and controlled by you!

> NEEGINAN...means native people, themselves and in their own
> way, solving the real problems of everyday city life!
>
> NEEGINAN...means building a future for your children – a future
> in which they can control their own destiny and not have to face
> the frustrations we now feel and fight every day!
>
> NEEGINAN...means "OUR PLACE"!

Organizers' first step was to build grassroots support for this vision and involve residents in shaping it. A team of Neeginan "fieldworkers" visited people in their homes, spoke with people on the strip, and held picnics on land intended for Neeginan, where people discussed their visions for how the new community could be laid out. A "comprehensive mailing list of all Indian and Métis people in the city" was compiled and regular newsletters sent out. Organizers urged fellow Indigenous Winnipeggers to join them in creating a place "about which we can honestly say 'This is Our Place and I helped build it'...NEEGINAN workers are always available for consultation, just call 943-1501. They will come and see you at your home if you so request, so feel free to contact them." Elaborate maps, slideshows, and displays showing what Main Street could look like according to the Neeginan vision were created—including contributions by renowned artists Daphne Odjig (Potawatomi/Odawa) and Jackson Beardy—and exhibited in the community, including in the storefront windows of the IMFC.[36] Organizers were extremely successful in generating widespread grassroots support for an Indigenous village on the strip. More than half of Indigenous Winnipeggers consulted said they would be interested in living on the strip when Neeginan was built.

Drafted over a year of consultation with the area's Indigenous residents, the plan for the Main Street strip was a bold, comprehensive vision for an urban district owned, built, and operated by and for Indigenous peoples to address the basic needs that the settler city systematically deprived them of. The Neeginan plan envisioned Main Street as a residential village consisting of a mix of quality, affordable low-rise and high-rise housing for Indigenous families, elders, and single people. The plan included a special proposal for short-term "hostel" housing for people living in the city temporarily, including students and those visiting to access healthcare. Non-residential components of the plan included new schools, health care facilities, childcare facilities, meeting space, youth recreation infrastructure, a "reception and orientation" centre for people new to the city, "centrally delivered social services," and worker co-operatives. To find enough land for this sweeping vision, the plan called for parts of the Neeginan village to expand onto and replace the CPR tracks.[37] Neeginan, in this sense, was a forerunner to, and one of the desired outcomes of, the rail relocation movement.

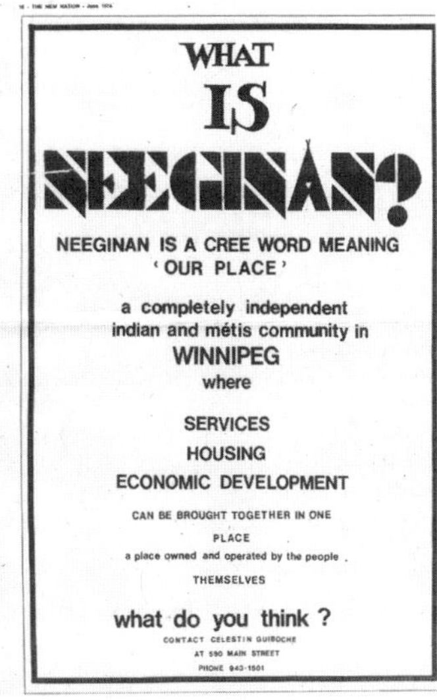

Neeginan invitation placed in Winnipeg Free Press, Winnipeg, ca.1974. (Used with permission of George Munroe)

Neeginan invitation placed in The New Nation, Winnipeg, ca.1974. University of Manitoba Archives, IMFC fonds, A13-70, MSS 395, IMFC Programs, Neeginan, 1974, Box 1. (Used with permission of George Munroe)

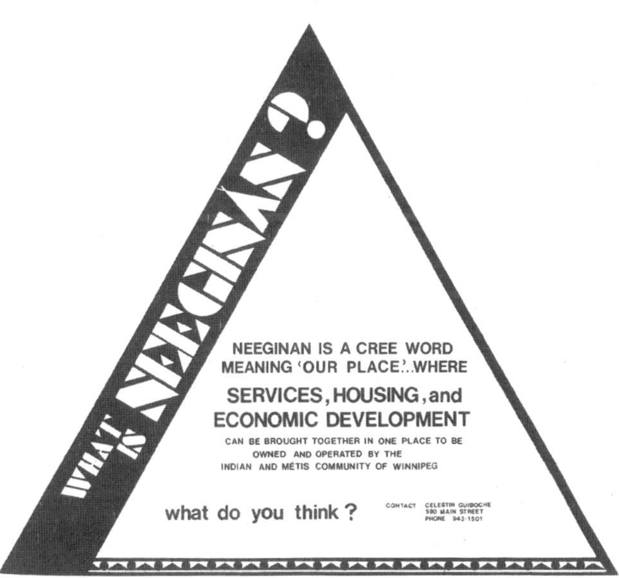

Neeginan invitation, Winnipeg, ca. 1974. Damas and Smith Limited. (1975). *Neeginan: A Feasibility Report Prepared for Neeginan (Manitoba) Incorporated.* (Used with permission of George Munroe)

Taking back Main Street. Neeginan newsletter, Winnipeg, ca. 1974. Damas and Smith Limited. (1975). *Neeginan: A Feasibility Report Prepared for Neeginan (Manitoba) Incorporated.* (Used with permission of George Munroe)

But the City of Winnipeg—flush with federal urban renewal cash and looking to transform Main Street—was not interested in Indigenous peoples' plans for the strip. White city councillors derided Neeginan as a plan for a "ghetto," conveniently ignoring the fact that it was they—and the city's landlords, businesses, and police—who had segregated Indigenous peoples on the strip in the first place. "I don't want to see a reserve in the middle of Winnipeg," said ICEC councillor Bill McGarva. "Indian people have a tough time making their way in the city," Councillor Munroe responded. "There is also strong objection to Indians moving into other areas of the city, so we plan to work in this area."[38] If settlers refused to tolerate urban Indigenous peoples anywhere but Main Street, as Munroe's response implied, how could they deny what they themselves had established: Main Street was Native space.

Instead of embracing the vibrant, highly organized Indigenous community that had established itself on Main Street and made serious plans to improve the area, the settler city derided it as a pathological danger that—like Rooster Town two decades earlier—ought to be policed, contained, and eventually eliminated. Among other things, in the age of Red Power, this was a counter-revolutionary tactic. Settler journalists went out

Taking back Main Street. Neeginan plan cover, Winnipeg, ca. 1975. Damas and Smith Limited. (1975). *Neeginan: A Feasibility Report Prepared for Neeginan (Manitoba) Incorporated.* (Used with permission of George Munroe)

of their way to portray Red Power marches and posters on the strip as, paradoxically, signs of the area's supposed pathology, destitution, and powerlessness.[39] The lengths settler journalists went to in order to depict Main Street as "down and out" were often comical. In more than one case, newspapers literally fabricated images of the strip to

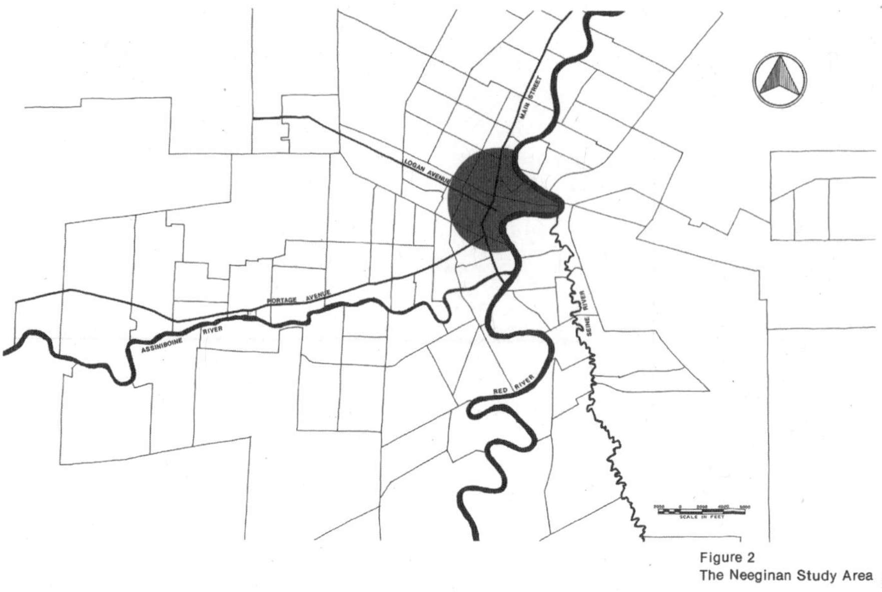

Figure 2
The Neeginan Study Area

Claiming the city centre. Neeginan study area, Winnipeg, ca. 1975. Damas and Smith Limited. (1975). *Neeginan: A Feasibility Report Prepared for Neeginan (Manitoba) Incorporated.* (Used with permission of George Munroe)

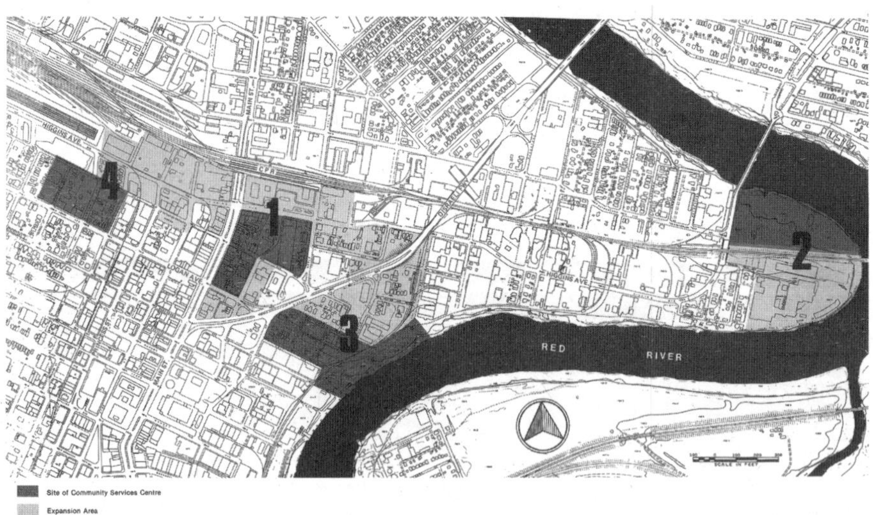

Figure 4A
Alternative Sites for Neeginan

Places of special importance. Alternative sites for Neeginan, Winnipeg, ca. 1975. Damas and Smith Limited. (1975). *Neeginan: A Feasibility Report Prepared for Neeginan (Manitoba) Incorporated.*

   (Used with permission of George Munroe)

fit their narrative. "On two occasions the author observed reporters photograph each other," noted Christopher Hauch, an anthropologist who conducted fieldwork on the strip during the 1970s and 1980s, "in staged supine and disheveled poses, when efforts to locate an unconscious 'drunken derelict' had failed."[40] The image of the strip generated by settler media is far from the image provided by people who actually spent time there, a point made repeatedly by the musicians and music fans interviewed by Jesse Green (Ojibway) and Fleury-Green in *Brown Town Muddy Water*. The strip could get lively, Mercredi said, and—like anywhere else—there were sometimes fist fights in front of the bars, but none of the hotels on the strip were nearly as unruly as settlers made them out to be.

Settlers who deemed the Main Street strip a blight on the city—like Canadian expansionists who had never travelled west of Ontario yet cast the mid-1800s North-West as a wasteland—had no first-hand knowledge of its actual, vibrant Indigenous geography. Their image of the strip conformed much less to lived reality than to racist fantasy. MIWC poets have long critiqued the knowledge-gathering methods of white Winnipeggers who attempt to make claims about urban Native space. It was Mercredi's impression that City officials and journalists, like most of the rest of the city, obtained almost all of their knowledge of the strip by driving past and gazing at Native people hanging out in front of the hotels. This dynamic of detached encounter is a theme in Mercredi's poetry and in the work of many other MIWC poets and writers; it is the trope of a white city gawking at Native people and places through the windshields of cars, and thinking they've learned everything there is to know.

The mass destruction of a beloved and historic district was initiated from nothing more than this tepid form of geographical knowledge. Winnipeg's white-dominated City Council deliberately dismantled one of the country's most important hubs of Indigenous social, cultural, and political life in the 1970s while totally ignoring the Indigenous redevelopment plan for the area. This fact has never been officially acknowledged at City Hall, not even in 2016, its official Year of Reconciliation. At the top of City Council's hit list was the "Grand Ole Opry of Indian country"—the Brunswick Hotel—which the City demolished and replaced with a European-style opera house. For years, according to Mercredi, the Main Street scene danced in step with the City's wrecking ball, as the centre of the scene moved from the Brunswick to the Savoy and the Manor, and finally to the Leland Hotel, as each was demolished in turn. When the Leland closed, the scene moved farther north, past the tracks, as well as west, to places like Brooklands. The demolition of the Leland Hotel, for Mercredi, was the blow that signalled the end of the strip's heyday.

In the post-heyday 1980s, Main Street became less diverse and increasingly populated by only the most "hardcore" people, Mercredi said. Most of Main Street's hotels, bars, theatres, and cafés were replaced—if they were replaced at all—with a sterile, authoritarian infrastructure of shelters, food banks, and the city's "drunk tank," a bunker of

The Grand Ole Opry of Indian country. Brunswick Hotel, Main Street strip, Winnipeg, ca. 1970.
University of Manitoba Archives, Winnipeg Tribune fonds, May 13, 1970, Thordarson, PC 1884718-847-001_preview. (Courtesy University of Manitoba Archives & Special Collections)

short-term cages for people arrested for public intoxication.[41] "They started to patrol it more," said Mercredi, and many university-educated Indigenous people moved away from the strip, sometimes leaving the North End entirely. Much of the remaining bar scene moved south of Portage Avenue, into places like the St. Regis Hotel and the Garrick Hotel. Today, Mercredi pointed out, CentreVenture is targeting these places for closure and demolition.

I asked Mercredi about the significance of city council's lust for demolishing Native urban space. "I think we're losing a lot of our history," he said. Mercredi said that he thought the "older generation" didn't like to talk about the worst days of urban apartheid and settler demonization of urban Native people and places. They prefer to keep silent, hoping that it will go away if they don't talk about it. "Kind of like residential schools," Mercredi said. "But I think the opposite is true," he continued, saying that he makes a point of telling the story of Main Street to his children and grandchildren. Mercredi listed a few other examples that he thought compared to the loss of Main Street, including three Indigenous burial mounds and an informal settlement that had all been built over and erased by development projects dating as far back as the construction of the railway. Mercredi's telling communicated a sense of the cultural importance of Indigenous spaces in the city and the pain of losing them. His history of the Main Street strip—as well as the immense labours of the early-1970s Neeginan organizers—has been doggedly erased from the city's official memory.

Last stand of the heyday. Leland Hotel, Main Street strip at William Avenue, Winnipeg, ca. 1990s. University of Manitoba Archives & Special Collections, Leland Hotel, LHBB-53. (Courtesy University of Manitoba Archives & Special Collections)

The story of Neeginan, however, does not end in the 1980s. Indigenous planners and activists nurtured Neeginan over the years, continuing to insist on the special significance of Main Street to Indigenous peoples. The 1990 Community Inquiry into Inner City Revitalization (discussed in Chapter 4) was instrumental in reviving the Neeginan vision. The Inquiry "urged that a long-term, multi-faceted commitment be made to the future development of Main Street and that significant representation from aboriginal communities...be included in decision-making and implementation."[42] In 1990, a coalition of Indigenous organizations came together under the name Aboriginal Centre of Winnipeg Incorporated (ACWI) to purchase the CPR depot on the strip—a large, ornate turn-of-the-twentieth-century railway station, staffed by 1,500 CPR workers before being decommissioned in 1978— and transform it into offices for their organizations.[43]

In 1997, as a result of the Inquiry's criticism of the CAI, the Winnipeg Development Agreement (WDA) sponsored a more grassroots planning process for the Main Street strip aimed at building on the momentum of the Aboriginal Centre.[44] Mary Richard—a Métis community organizer and restaurant owner originally from Camperville, Manitoba—was appointed by Winnipeg Mayor Susan Thompson as co-chair of the WDA's North Main Street Task Force. Richard took the opportunity to install Neeginan as the official vision for Main Street. "We had to redo Main Street from City Hall," Richard recalled, "so then I just pulled out the Neeginan plan...We were the only ones that already had a plan since 1972...We had community meetings and reviewed the original plan of

Neeginan."[45] The final plan of the WDA's North Main Street Task Force—drafted by a predominantly Indigenous sub-committee chaired by Richard—was a slightly reworked version of the 1970s Neeginan plan.

"We, the aboriginal people of the City of Winnipeg, have joined together to make a commitment to the future of our children," the 1997 Neeginan vision statement begins. "We have joined together to carve our future into the heart of Winnipeg, and by doing so, save our children and heal our tragic past. Neeginan and North Main Street will be our contribution not only to ourselves but to the City of Winnipeg." The plan included a mix of not-for-profit infrastructure and for-profit commercial initiatives that would complement the Aboriginal Centre. It called for 160 units of "housing for Aboriginal students who are in Winnipeg for educational and technical training, and housing for Aboriginal families who are here for relatively short periods for medical treatment or visiting friends and relatives who are hospitalized or receiving specialized treatment"; a Centre of Excellence for Children's Well-Being; a Hall of Justice to facilitate Indigenous restorative justice models; an art gallery and youth recreation and athletic facilities; and a Round House to function as the "spiritual and cultural focus" of the Neeginan village. To centre the needs of existing residents, the plan included a well-funded "Relocation Assistance Program" to ensure that any residents displaced from the strip would "have the opportunity to relocate to comparable accommodation within their community."[46]

Beyond the official plan published by the task force, organizers envisioned much more for the Neeginan village. Richard imagined Neeginan as the potential concretization of a new Indigenous territorial and political model that she summarized, in a 2002 interview, as a Native version of Vatican City. Indigenous peoples would obtain a degree of sovereign jurisdiction over the Main Street strip according to Richard's plan. "I was thinking of the Vatican because it's a central area and it has its own small geographic area that it governs," said Richard. "It has its own laws, up to a certain level." Extending the Vatican City model, Neeginan would operate as a political capital of Indigenous Turtle Island, formalizing its role as a pan-Native hub. "We're so scattered across the country," Richard said:

> We could still have a central location of government and then
> you have all these little arms. Then you've got to make sure each
> community is self-reliant. So you have to develop that capacity.
> That was why I was interested in the Vatican model.[47]

Richard envisioned Indigenous communities across Turtle Island uniting on the Main Street strip to pursue collective goals while retaining their autonomy in a similar way that self-sufficient Catholic dioceses relate to the Vatican. The Neeginan village, according to Richard's plan, would be the seat of a central Indigenous government that would support Indigenous communities across Turtle Island to achieve their plans for the future.

The WDA and the three levels of government accepted the Neeginan plan in principle—minus the Vatican City model—but did not provide the land and money necessary to build it. Some money for the Round House—which would become known as Thunderbird House—was provided initially, but this funding soon dried up. "[The mayor] just stopped funding, that's it, we couldn't go any further," Jack recalled. Organizers were forced to scramble to find money just to complete Thunderbird House. "I think that [the larger Neeginan plan] wasn't completely developed before [Thunderbird House] was built and then it just became like an all-consuming priority to get that house up there and then special money had to be found," recalled Neeginan organizer Janet Fontaine. "There had to be this huge fundraising campaign to put the roof on that house...so there were some financial challenges there."[48] The feeling that Thunderbird House and the Aboriginal Centre represent only a fraction of the full Neeginan vision persists. "I think there should be twenty Thunderbird Houses in this city," said Albert McLeod, a Cree and Métis Two-Spirit Winnipegger and long-time community organizer.[49] In the midst of the push to build Neeginan in the 1990s, City Council established its new urban redevelopment authority and tasked it with facilitating an alternate future for the Main Street strip.

Neeginan in action. Event hosted by the Aboriginal Council of Winnipeg, (from L) Linda Bloom, Mary Richard, Anita Flett, Wayne Helgason, Trevor Greyeyes, George Munroe, Main Street strip at Higgins, Winnipeg, ca. early 2000s. (With permission from the Aboriginal Council of Winnipeg)

NEGLECTING NEEGINAN: HEART OF GOLD

CentreVenture took control of a large swath of land on the Main Street strip just two years after the 1997 Neeginan plan was drafted. While the authority focused most of its energies in the early 2000s on convincing the local and provincial governments to build Waterfront Drive and luring capital to invest there, it also went to work destroying what remained from the heyday of the Main Street strip. CentreVenture demolished several of the strip's remaining hotels and theatres in these years, sodding over dirt lots and erecting signage aimed at potential buyers. "We've been talking to a couple of interested developers," said CentreVenture CEO Annitta Stenning at the time. "But the first stage is to clear the land and do some greening up."[50] The authority hoped that by paying for demolition and other costly preparations for development, it could subsidize developers' costs and convince them to take the land. CentreVenture replaced the old structures with billboards advertising the number of cars that regularly pass through the area, and featuring slogans aimed at motorists, such as "PUT ASIDE YOUR PRECON-CIEVED IDEAS ABOUT MAIN STREET AND BECOME PART OF THE DOWNTOWN REBOUND." "Forget the squalor," the *Free Press* joined in, "bring on the lawyers and office workers."[51]

By 2006, with construction underway on Waterfront Drive, CentreVenture cast about for a new geographical focus. Despite the advertising and site-preparation subsidies, the authority had had little success luring new investment to Main Street during the previous years. A consensus seemed to emerge between CentreVenture and its urban-wing allies that Waterfront Drive was an isolated success that had not done enough to transform the city's appearance to the outside eye. To the dominant regional bloc, it seemed that CentreVenture had sorely neglected far more "visible" parts of the downtown—the city's busiest thoroughfares, Portage Avenue and Main Street.

"[CentreVenture] has properly recognized that something needs to be done urgently to repair the pitiful state of Portage Avenue and Main Street," the *Free Press* editorialized in a 2007 piece entitled "It's Our Downtown." City Council's decision to destroy Indigenous Main Street had left it with a new problem: a landscape of destruction unpleasing to the eye. "As it stands now, visitors to Winnipeg are left with the impression of a city in decline," continued the *Free Press*. "It tells out-of-town investors that Winnipeg is not a good place to do business and it tells tourists there's nothing here worth seeing."

The editorial concluded by urging local and provincial governments to eliminate taxes for developers on Main Street, rather than, say, taxing developers and funding Neeginan. "A healthy downtown is somewhat intangible," the *Free Press* wrote, utterly ignoring Neeginan's very specific definition of a healthy downtown, "but at a minimum, downtown Winnipeg must be seen by investors as a place where money can be made."[52] This spirit of neoliberal urbanism—the exclusive definition of the city as a money-making tool—so pithily espoused by the *Free Press*, was a basic logic through which public

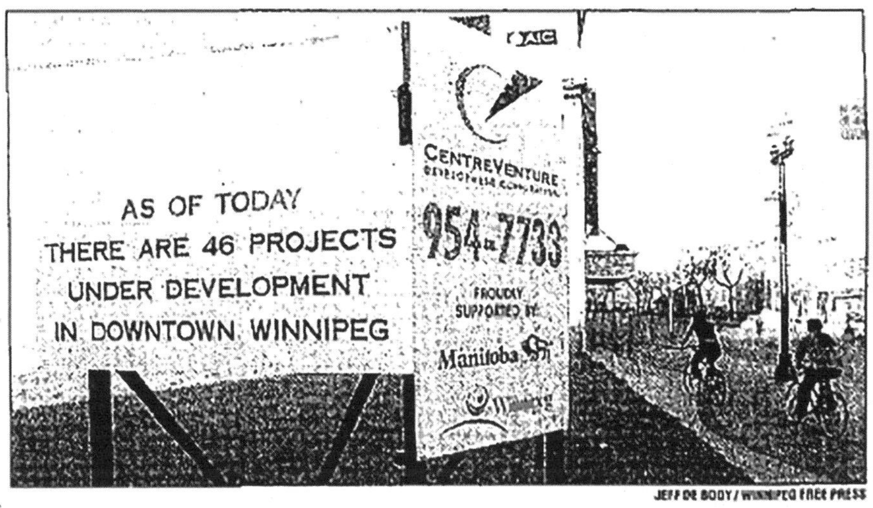

A billboard on the corner of Main St. and Logan Ave. lures developers.

Planting the flag. CentreVenture billboard, Main Street strip, Winnipeg, ca. 2001. Photo by Jeff De Booy. Winnipeg Free Press. (Courtesy of Winnipeg Free Press)

land and money for Neeginan became unthinkable. This free-market orthodoxy would come to dominate CentreVenture's approach to a much greater extent in the coming years. Whereas the authority enforced very narrow land-use and architectural regulations on Waterfront Drive in order to produce its specific vision of a luxury condo district, when it came to Main Street—a place for which Indigenous peoples had clear plans—the authority stubbornly refused to endorse any particular vision for the strip's future outside of what the market would dictate. The ascendance of neoliberalism, in this way, reinvigorated the colonial impulse to see Main Street as *urbs nullius*. On the flipside, CentreVenture drew on the regional tradition of *urbs nullius* to make a neoliberal future for Main Street feel reasonable or even obvious.

The *Free Press* editorial came on the heels of CentreVenture's second comprehensive plan, its *Heart of Gold Strategic Business Plan 2007–2009*, which it presented to City Council for approval in January 2007. The *Heart of Gold* plan was an aggressive—if coded—expression of racial-capitalist engagement with Native urban space. "Arguably, the private marketplace is performing adequately in many parts of CV's mandate area," *Heart of Gold* begins. However, "it is CentreVenture's contention that the market is not yet functioning adequately with respect to the properties in two related areas," namely Main Street and Portage Avenue. These areas were "plagued by an exodus of businesses and residents," according to CentreVenture, which ignored the fact that City Council itself had manufactured the exodus. Somewhat more ominously, "civil society," according to CentreVenture, was "not functioning adequately" in the area. At the time, an estimated 1,000 people still lived in hotels on the Main Street strip.[53]

In *Heart of Gold*, CentreVenture refers to Main Street and Portage Avenue as the "Focus Area." "The Focus Area is an embarrassment," CentreVenture writes, citing "unsightly entire blocks," "unattractive" empty lots, and a "skid row collection of hotels, restaurants, and pawn shops." By way of explaining why City Council should fund its plan, CentreVenture rehearses the self-evident truth of the urban wing—"The downtown of any city is a snapshot of the real health, even the real *meaning* of a city."[54] But this time, CentreVenture forwards a new claim: downtown may be crucial to the region's future, but Portage Avenue and Main Street are the downtown's most crucial segments:

> For better or (mostly) worse, the most visible and vital section of
> Winnipeg's downtown is the Focus Area. If suburban Winnipeggers
> "see" (with their eyes and their minds) the Focus Area as an embar-
> rassment, then they will "see" the entire downtown as an embar-
> rassment—a place they do not wish to be, or even to think about.[55]

CentreVenture claimed that once the area's fortunes are reversed, Main Street and Portage Avenue could act as a nearly literal "Heart of Gold," driving the entire regional economy and lifting all boats. "[T]he Heart of Gold will act as the pump of economic power, and of vitality to the suburbs and beyond," CentreVenture explains. "The word 'Gold' in this context, connotes the commercial success that will flow to participants (building owners, merchants, employees, local residents, and the tax collectors) in the new, invigorated economy in the area." But first the existing neighbourhood—that old "disgrace"—must be eliminated. "Everything must be done to remove this disgrace," CentreVenture concludes, "there is no time to lose."[56] The future of capital accumulation—not merely in the city centre but in the entire urban region—the authority contended, depended on the swift removal of the existing human geography of the strip.

The Main Street strip became CentreVenture's almost exclusive focus in the years following the release of *Heart of Gold*. While its framing of the situation was extremely dire, CentreVenture's actual "prescriptions" for Main Street were surprisingly modest. This was an outcome of the authority's even bolder commitment to free-market ideology. "CentreVenture does not take a position as to what a resurrected Winnipeg downtown would or should look like," the authority explained, "only the market can determine that. CentreVenture and others can only create conditions that allow the market to function efficiently."[57] CentreVenture proposed three related strategies to create conditions for capital accumulation in the Heart of Gold.

First, it would "secure" the area by working with the WPS to increase its police presence there. CentreVenture's new emphasis on policing came at a time of renewed geographic targeting of city-centre residents by the WPS. Two years prior, in 2005, Winnipeg Mayor

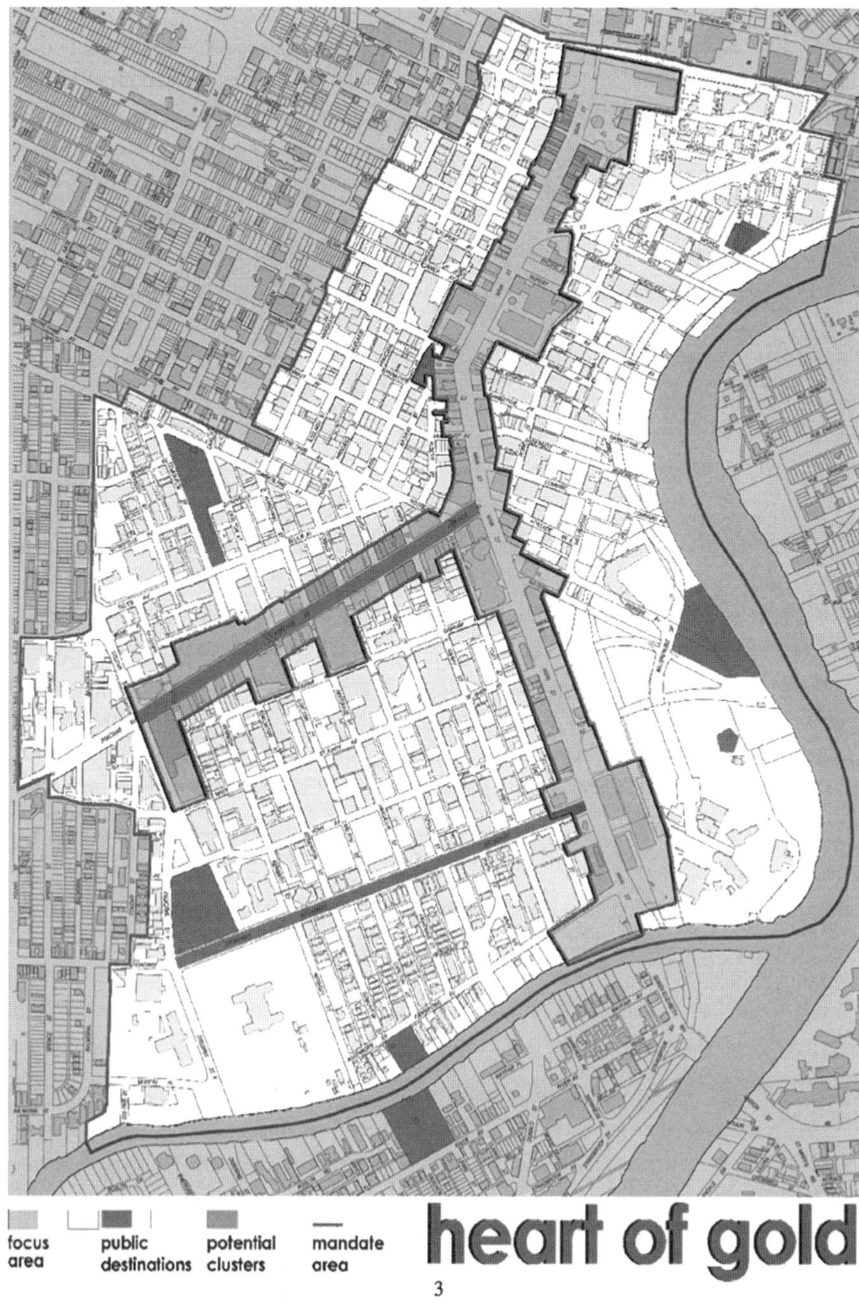

Jettisoning Neeginan. CentreVenture, Heart of Gold Strategic Business Plan 2007-2009, Winnipeg, ca. 2007.

Sam Katz announced an unprecedented round of broken-windows-style policing in the city's West End, which the mayor dubbed "Operation Clean Sweep." Pioneered most notoriously by former New York City Mayor Rudolph Giuliani—whom Katz brought to Winnipeg in 2006 for a keynote address on the topic—broken-windows-style policing, also known as quality-of-life policing, involves aggressive enforcement of minor legal violations such as vandalism or public intoxication, based on the false premise that more serious crimes proliferate where minor acts of disorder go unpunished. In the same year as Giuliani's visit, with the help of the Manitoba NDP Government, Operation Clean Sweep was expanded to target the entire city centre.[58] In *Heart of Gold,* CentreVenture promises to "continue to support strongly all existing security initiatives"—including already prevalent private police forces sponsored by multiple business improvement districts—but also proposes to deploy a team of "Special Safety Wardens" to the area: "[T]he knowledge that a figure of authority can always be found in a specific spot, during specific times, would come to be an important component in creating the reality, and the perception, of security in the Heart of Gold."[59]

Second, moving beyond its role as mere inheritor of surplus City-owned properties, CentreVenture vowed to continue doing what city council had been doing on its own for decades: purchasing outright and eliminating privately owned properties—usually residential hotels—that it viewed as troublesome. CentreVenture categorized its purchase of such properties as "profile investments." "In this category," it wrote, "is the outright, unconditional purchase of a troubled property whose rehabilitation will anchor the resurrection of a Cluster." CentreVenture continued, "This type of investment is intended to create high visibility and interest, to raise the flag—in circumstances where it is difficult for the private marketplace to appreciate the potential for profitable investment."[60]

The final method proposed by CentreVenture to "unleash the power of the market" along the Main Street strip was, predictably, the removal of existing taxes and regulations on investment. "[A] long history of difficulty and disappointment, surrounding the development and ownership of property in the Heart of Gold, has left a legacy, amongst many members of the local, national, and even international development community, of cynicism at best," it wrote. "At worst, the notion of development in downtown Winnipeg, particularly in the Heart of Gold, has simply disappeared from their thoughts."[61]

To perk up the development community, CentreVenture suggested a general clear-cutting of local and provincial property taxes in the area. Failing this, it proposed a litany of "special incentives" for capitalists willing to invest on the strip, from low-interest loans to "outright grants." CentreVenture proposed that a few tax breaks already in place—most for the private redevelopment of heritage-designated buildings—be expanded into a general "Urban Tax Credit" for any investment in the downtown built environment. "The intent," CentreVenture wrote of its proposed interventions, "is to tilt the playing field back in favor of the smooth working of market forces." Of course, the very existence of CentreVenture and its new plan indicated the impossibility of capitalist markets functioning without police and a litany of other state supports. In making its case for the new plan, CentreVenture aggressively discouraged criticisms of its prescribed mix of police, eviction of the poor, and gifts to capital. "It is not socially acceptable to stand in the way of this project," CentreVenture told City Council, which quickly approved the plan.[62]

THE BELL HOTEL

The Bell Hotel—constructed in 1904 to house settlers arriving on the CPR—was one of the most famous residential hotels and bars remaining on the strip by the 2000s. As one of the last hotels standing after decades of city council's onslaught, the Bell was an emblem of the strip's long-standing Native community. Cree writer Tomson Highway perfectly captured Native writers' ambivalence about this in his take on the Bell in 1998's *Kiss of the Fur Queen*: "Cree? In Winnipeg? Why not? He was, after all, in the Hell Hotel."[63] The Bell became the first high-profile battleground of the CentreVenture era on Main Street. CentreVenture's way of relating to the Bell's residents and its attempts at guiding the building's future encapsulated the authority's broader colonial mode of engaging the strip. This included the authority's overriding tendency to pathologize the people of Main Street—casting them as subjects of social control rather than participants in planning the area's future—that enabled it to bury the Neeginan plan.

CentreVenture's first order of business was to purchase, close, and evict the Bell's 75 residents, some of whom had lived there for upwards of 25 years.[64] CentreVenture described the Bell as the last stand on the modern Main Street frontier, and its residents—especially those who patronized its bar—as the final remaining threats to the strip's golden future. Shutting down the Bell "could well be the catalyst that would kick-start a grand redevelopment of an entire neighborhood," said CentreVenture's new CEO Ross McGowan, a condo developer who had received land on Waterfront Drive from CentreVenture a few years previous. "In recent years," added Jim Ludlow, President and CEO of the city's professional hockey team and Chair of the CentreVenture Board, "CentreVenture has received numerous complaints from area businesses regarding the negative effect the activities related to the liquor sales in the beverage room and beer vendor was having on their ability to conduct business." "CentreVenture's mandate is to attract business and residential development to the downtown, not to sit idly by while negative activity causes an exodus," the authority stated, once again profoundly confusing the source of depopulation on the strip.[65]

CentreVenture's elimination of the Bell and displacement of its residents was swift and, in some eyes, cruel. I spoke with Simon, a University of Manitoba urban planning graduate who—interested in the progressive potential of reversing suburban sprawl—took a job at CentreVenture during the mid-2000s.[66] Simon was assigned to oversee the evictions of the Bell's residents. "My boss basically said, 'Make sure it's empty by the end of the day.'" CentreVenture offered no relocation assistance program, as had been called for in the 1997 Neeginan plan. "People were moving with shopping carts," Simon recalled, raising his eyebrows. He remembered hearing residents sneer at the "big, evil developer" as he oversaw their evictions. Winnipeg Mayor Sam Katz appeared oblivious to the reality of the situation. In a video statement, Katz appeared to be under the impression that Bell Hotel residents enjoyed their own evictions. "Although that was their home," said Katz, "I can assure you they would not have been very proud to tell you that was their home."[67] The mayor's statement only makes sense, of course, if the Bell's residents are understood to have no aspirations of their own for the strip's future. Simon eventually quit his job at CentreVenture, in part because he had not realized how "conservative" the authority was. Within processes of gentrification—Simon's experience indicated—as within processes of imperial conquest, the inhumane requirements of racial capitalism are generally hidden in order to convey a progressive, cutting-edge, adventuresome image.

Seventy-five units of affordable housing were lost in the closure of the Bell, adding to the city's booming homeless population.[68] The CBC interviewed the director of one of the largest homeless shelters on the strip, writing that the director "expects many former Bell residents will end up sleeping in his shelter."[69] But in its editorial, "Last Call at the Bell," the *Free Press* ignored this significant loss of affordable housing, focusing strictly on the wholesomeness of eliminating the hotel's bar and the removal of its clientele from the strip. "The Bell Hotel will serve its last drink on Friday," the *Free Press* wrote. "That may make some people cry in their beer as they remember the good old days of brawling, boozing and bar-hopping, but it's welcome news for those working to revitalize Main Street."[70]

The Bell remained vacant and boarded up for years, as CentreVenture waited for the market to decide its fate. "We know there is interest by various private-sector developers in this property," McGowan said in 2007, but none emerged. Jessica, a CentreVenture employee, later told me that there had been virtually no private market interest in the Bell.[71] Compared to Waterfront Drive, Main Street was still seen as a "rough area" with little to no potential for profitable condo or even rental housing development. The lack of market interest in the Bell and the Main Street strip in general highlighted the perversity of evicting its residents and ignoring the Neeginan plan. Capital in general—as represented by CentreVenture—wanted the strip's existing, largely Indigenous, community gone without a trace as part of its larger vision for the city centre, but not a single developer actually wanted the land on the strip itself. This was the imperative to which 75 people were sacrificed into homelessness.

As a last resort, CentreVenture agreed to bring a reduced number of neighbourhood residents back to the Bell—although none of the hotel's previous residents were given homes in the new Bell[72]—forestalling the invasion of "lawyers and office workers" envisioned by the *Free Press*. In a moment of capitulation, CentreVenture, which retained ownership of the Bell, accepted a proposal by the Winnipeg Regional Health Authority

Pre-CentreVenture takeover. Bell Hotel, Main Street strip, Winnipeg, date unknown. University of Manitoba Archives, Bell Hotel, BELLHB-50. (Courtesy University of Manitoba Archives & Special Collections)

(WRHA) and a large area homeless shelter—Main Street Project (MSP)[73]—which had secured provincial funding to convert the Bell into 42 tiny bachelor suites as part of the "housing first" public health trend the WRHA was pursuing at the time. CentreVenture echoed the "housing first" ethos, giving more credence to the insulting idea that the strip's residents—rather than the region's long history of immiserating dominant development visions—were the source of the area's "problems": "The philosophy behind the project," CentreVenture explained, is that "before an individual's problems can be addressed, they first need a roof over their heads."[74]

Almost immediately, CentreVenture looked for ways to cease its involvement with the new Bell. I spoke with Will, a manager there, who told me that CentreVenture would likely sell as soon as it could. He told me that the provincial government and the WRHA had made their investment in the Bell conditional on the building being part of the government's "housing-first" strategy. "It wasn't their cup of tea," Will said of the plan to use the Bell as affordable housing, adding that he didn't think CentreVenture knew what it was getting into. This view is confirmed by a 2011 report on the Bell authored by CentreVenture, in which the authority writes, "Ultimately, a separate organization, dedicated to addressing the issue of homelessness in Winnipeg may be established who might incorporate the Bell Hotel into their portfolio."[75]

In the meantime, CentreVenture parlayed the new Bell into a significant public relations tool, using its involvement with the "housing-first" trend to soften its image and portray itself as compassionate towards existing city-centre residents. "It's just the right thing to do," McGowan told the *Free Press* in 2009, in a total reversal. "I think it's important when we talk about community building to...help the people within the neighbourhood. And we see this as an opportunity to do that."[76] In fact, CentreVenture handled the Bell in such a way as to serve the two hostile intentions—eviction and policing—that ruled its engagements with the strip's residents. Through its restructuring of the Bell, CentreVenture achieved a net displacement of low-income residents—which resulted in an overall loss of 33 affordable housing units. And by shutting down the Bell's bar, it eliminated one of the few remaining unsupervised gathering places for neighbourhood residents.

The design of the new Bell extended the authoritarian, paternalistic restructuring of the Main Street strip from the vibrant 1970s social, cultural, and political hub that it was to the sterile, heavily policed, tightly managed shelter infrastructure—where residents are treated as pathological charity cases—it has become today. This is true despite the fact that many aspects of the new Bell appear earnestly tailored to meet the needs of the strip's residents in a dignified, humane way. Will took me—past two police officers loitering at the front desk—to have our conversation in the Bell's Culture Room, where a circle of chairs sat on a carpet with a Navajo design, beside a flip chart with "SHARING" and "HEALING" written on it. Bernice, a Métis woman in her fifties who lives in one of the Bell's new apartments, said she prefers the Bell to the Main Street Salvation Army, which she described as "just like prison." "I have my own place here," Bernice told me.

She has friends in the building, and she likes volunteering in the kitchen.[77]

But Bernice felt that she lived under the control of Bell staff who impose unreasonable rules and don't understand Native culture. To illustrate, Bernice told me a story about her boyfriend, Richard, visiting her at the Bell. Richard was asked by staff to leave the building, but he declined, saying he had come to visit Bernice. Instead of contacting Bernice, the front desk staff called the WPS. Richard spent the weekend in jail, Bernice told me, and she was furious at the front desk staff. "She said she cancelled the call," Bernice said of the front desk worker, "but how naïve can you get? You can't cancel a call to the cops once you make it—once you call, they're coming." Part of the reason Bernice was so upset was that Richard had recently been locked in Stony Mountain Penitentiary—a federal prison just outside Winnipeg—for eight and a half years. Through their ignorance and insensitivity, according to Bernice, not only had the Bell's staff forbidden her from seeing her significant other, they had also put his entire future in jeopardy.

This heavy-handed approach appeared to be the rule, rather than the exception, during my visit. A sign in the lobby warned tenants, "VISITORS CAN ONLY STAY OVERNIGHT 5 TIMES in 3 MONTHS," a draconian rule that, as Bernice's experience demonstrates, prevents residents from seeing their loved ones. Will told me that he does not hesitate to evict tenants if they behave in a disorderly manner, and the Bell has strict visitation rules. "We can't even have *any* guests on Wednesdays," Bernice complained. Another sign in the lobby announced that Wednesday was "TENANT/STAFF DAY," dedicated to tenants and staff doing "some important work together." The rigorous control exercised over tenants by Bell staff reminds one of CentreVenture's ominous assertions, in *Heart of Gold*, that "civil society" was not functioning adequately on Main Street. In failing to remove the old community entirely, CentreVenture settled for placing a reduced number of residents in a "controlled environment"—essentially the City's approach to the strip since the 1980s. By positioning residents as "problems" in need of fixing, supervision, and policing, the housing-first model fit CentreVenture's colonial approach to the strip's residents; and it was a far cry from the affordable housing, based on restoring land and self-determination to Indigenous peoples, envisioned by Neeginan.

MAKING MAIN STREET WHITE COLLAR

CentreVenture capped an extensive round of destruction on the strip that involved shutting down the Bell and demolishing six other buildings—among them the Club Hotel, Epic Theatre, and Starland Theatre—by transforming a large segment of the area into a new white-collar district of massive office-space developments. To do so, the authority mobilized new techniques to transfer state resources to capital. Among the various financial innovations proposed by CentreVenture for the *Heart of Gold* initiative, the recommendation that gathered the most momentum was its call for a widened application of tax increment financing (TIF) grants for developers—essentially, large upfront grants in the amount of tax breaks promised over the coming years. Combined with new federal "economic stimulus" grants rolled out in response to the 2008 global economic crisis, TIF grants made the area newly profitable for developers. Rather than "stimulating" Indigenous economic development on the strip, CentreVenture maneuvered the new federal funding into supporting a vision for the area reminiscent of Macdonald's 1870s "swamping" strategy. While city council had been destroying Main Street for decades, developments in the late 2000s constituted the first successful creation of a more affluent, non-Indigenous human geography on the strip since the replacement of the "Grand Ole Opry of Indian Country" with an opera house in the 1960s.

In 2008, CentreVenture transferred an entire city block in the heart of the strip to Re Solve Group Inc. "The biggest commercial development on North Main Street in nearly a century was to be unveiled today," the *Free Press* announced on March 18, 2008, "as part of a multimillion-dollar plan to breathe new life into one of the most desolate sections of downtown."[78] The deal called for Re Solve Group Inc. to construct a four-storey, 74,000-square-foot office building and a four-storey 300-car parking garage to house the WRHA's corporate and administrative headquarters. CentreVenture gifted $500,000 to Re Solve Group Inc. in the form of a TIF grant.

CentreVenture soon brokered a second large white-collar development on the strip, immediately next door to the WRHA building. In 2010, the United Way began construction on a new $10 million three-storey, 20,000-square-foot headquarters on the site. The federal and provincial governments paid $7 million of the total cost, with matching "economic stimulus" grants of $3.14 million. Winnipeg City Council and CentreVenture together contributed $700,000 in land and TIF grants. With its United Way and WRHA developments, CentreVenture replaced most of Main Street's remaining single-room occupancy hotels with a landscape of gleaming glass and steel office buildings. The hotels' low-income residents were replaced with 300 white-collar office workers.

The arrival of hundreds of white-collar workers to the strip prompted a renewed police sweep of the area. Will told me that the opening of the WRHA headquarters coincided with a steep increase in broken-windows-style policing on Main Street. Since then, Will said, the WPS increasingly descend on the strip to do "shake-downs," ticket people, crack down on public drinking and drug use, check if people have prior convictions or are breaking conditions of their parole, and order people to leave the area. Jessica, the CentreVenture employee I spoke with, confirmed that CentreVenture works closely with the WPS to maintain an expanded police presence in the Heart of Gold district. These events clearly demonstrate a racial capitalist approach to policing. Capital, expanding into Native space, requires police to harass and jail existing inhabitants in order to ensure the profitability of its investments. CentreVenture, responsible for guaranteeing the profitability of urban space, intensified this dynamic by nudging the WPS towards an area of importance to developers.

The local media broadly embraced CentreVenture's transformation of the Main Street strip, but the authority did not escape at least some perfunctory criticism. "Respect the Locals When It Comes to Main Street," read the headline of a 2008 *Free Press* editorial. "What is going to happen to people and institutions already in the neighbourhood?" the author asks, citing the WRHA development, the closure of the Bell, and the "trendy condos" popping up on Waterfront Drive. "If you are going to redevelop an inner-city area, treat the people who are already there with dignity." "[I]n the continuing effort to gentrify the area for our civil servants," a 2009 *Free Press* editorial went on, "six of the worst hotels were torn down to improve the neighbourhood's climate with no one, apparently, ever giving a single serious thought to where the people who lived in them...might go when they were gone."[79] A louder line of criticism, however, rather than critiquing CentreVenture's colonial vision, lamented its lack of success.

Urban wing–aligned commentators blamed Winnipeg suburbanites for not being courageous enough on the new frontier. "The bunker mentality demonstrated in WRHA design," wrote the *Free Press*, "seems typical of the mentality of most Winnipeggers when it comes to Main Street—keep your head down and you might get through it."[80] In another piece, the paper interviewed a Main Street business owner about the strip's new office workers. "Main Street now looks great from the car," the man told the *Free Press*. "No one driving by would think there were any problems." But he criticized the strip's new white-collar inhabitants for not livening things up enough. "The people here make big salaries, eat lunch at their desks and drive home to Lindenwoods at 5," the business owner lamented. The newspaper responded by blaming and insulting the strip's remaining long-time residents. "Nobody wants to sip a latte or browse an art gallery while somebody who just crawled out from under a bridge walks by."[81]

Exchanges such as this conjured a new urban settler–colonial culture, defining suitable settlers as those who embraced urban life by purchasing lunch at local restaurants, drinking expensive coffee, and supporting the local art scene. On the other hand, the embers of the area's longstanding Indigenous community—coded as homeless and therefore ineligible to participate in the district's white-collar future—were defined as threats that frightened away desirable settlers and therefore posed an obstacle to civic progress. CentreVenture continued to pursue a corresponding policy of Indian removal on Main Street into the 2010s, attempting, for instance, to make the biggest park on the strip—the former site of the Royal Alexandra Hotel, now owned by the Aboriginal Centre—its next "profile investment." "CentreVenture wants to get the park off us real bad," explained Wayne Helgason, a founder of the Aboriginal Centre. "But no, those people there still need a place to hang out...those people are important...so we're going to leave it green until such time that others have a plan that is respectful of what goes on around here."

YOUTH FOR CHRIST

CentreVenture's total rejection of Indigenous Main Street and Indigenous urban planning histories soon materialized into a far more incredible symbol of settler colonialism's resilience. In a startling twist, in 2010, CentreVenture directed the city's post-industrial redevelopment agenda towards the construction of an institution on the Main Street strip that paid uncanny tribute to a key genocidal institution of an earlier phase of Canadian settler colonialism. The depth of the dominant bloc's historical amnesia and the severity of its disregard for Indigenous Main Street and the Indigenous city centre generated irrepressible grassroots resistance to CentreVenture's agenda. This resistance revealed more clearly than ever the colonial relationship of capital and the dominant bloc to Winnipeg's Indigenous city centre.

Events began in early 2010, when the multinational evangelical Christian organization Youth for Christ (YFC) requested funding from the City of Winnipeg to build a $10 million youth recreation complex somewhere in the city—a project for which YFC had already gained a federal stimulus grant of $3.2 million. YFC needed to find another funder quickly, as the federal stimulus money was time-sensitive and would soon expire. The City directed YFC to CentreVenture, which proposed the former site of the Savoy Hotel, a plot of land long envisioned as part of Neeginan, located at the same intersection as Thunderbird House and a stone's throw from the Aboriginal Centre. Simon, the former CentreVenture employee, told me that the parcel of land—formerly surplus City-owned land then owned by CentreVenture—was CentreVenture's "last big obstacle" on the Main Street strip, and that in order to sign on to the project, "the City's condition was that this is the piece of land it's on." It was the City—taking cues from CentreVenture—and not YFC that insisted on locating the evangelical Christian youth centre on the Main Street strip.

While CentreVenture itself was able to finance developments without city council oversight, the large TIF grants it brokered for developers still required city council approval. This requirement— the kind CentreVenture was originally designed to side step—made the deal public and provided a formal opening for grassroots resistance. On February 17, 2010, the Executive Policy Committee of Winnipeg's City Council passed a motion to provide a TIF grant of $3.375 million to YFC. Less than a week later, Diane Roussin (Anishinaabe) and Tammy Christensen, Executive Directors of Ma Mawi Wi Chi Itata Centre, Inc. and Ndinawemaaganag Endaawaad Inc. respectively, published a scathing critique of the proposal, highlighting the racial hierarchy and genocidal logic implicit in attempts to Christianize youth in an Indigenous neighbourhood. "Aboriginal youth represent the majority of youth in the neighbourhoods near the proposed Christian centre," Roussin and Christensen wrote, noting that YFC's guiding purpose is the "Christianization" of children, and that the organization explicitly targets "the aboriginal youth community as a prime area for development." "While the Youth for Christ approach is more subtle than that used in residential schools," Roussin and Christensen continued, "it is in essence based on the same model—Christianity is viewed as superior and missionaries from outside the community will teach people a better way." Roussin and Christensen emphasized the long history of Indigenous organizing in Winnipeg, and then critiqued the state's lack of support for it. "Existing organizations working with youth in the inner city—Aboriginal as well as many non-Aboriginal—have been working for years to reverse the great harm caused by assimilationist policies and attempts to 'Christianize' a people with a strong culture and spirituality of their own," the authors went on. Taking millions of dollars for YFC, they explained, "out of a budget that is supposedly so strained that it cannot support existing public recreation programs and more culturally appropriate community-based initiatives, is extremely troubling for those who know first hand the damage that 'well meaning' Christians have caused."[82]

A grassroots coalition of Indigenous and non-Indigenous city-centre organizers—most of them youth service providers—filled the city council chambers on February 24, 2010, to speak against CentreVenture's plan. Speakers positioned the plan within the context of more than a century of Indigenous resistance to Canadian colonialism, tracing the impact of residential schools through present-day efforts to establish Indigenous-run education and youth programming in Winnipeg with a decolonizing mandate. Activists positioned a publicly funded YFC Centre on the strip as a betrayal of the hard-won 2008 Canadian apology for Indian Residential Schools and Canada's new high-profile mandate to "reconcile" with Indigenous peoples.[83] Nahanni Fontaine, Director of Justice for the Southern Chiefs' Organization, attempted to educate Winnipeg's City Council about the Indian Residential Schools apology and their responsibility to honour it:

> As a result of this apology, Aboriginal peoples were assured that these sort of strategic and infringing policies and practices would never occur again, and despite this assurance, we're gathered here today debating the construction of a Youth for Christ Recreational Facility which is entirely founded on Christian world views and practices...[if the project is approved] this council will be doing nothing short of reinstituting and state sanctifying another more contemporary, altered form of the Residential School experience, mentality and practice all under the guise of helping at-risk Aboriginal youth...To suggest that the same institution who on the one hand is complicit in the total destruction of Aboriginal peoples' culture, traditions, lands, economies and language, can on the other hand, be the ones to offer change and healing is absolutely ridiculous and insulting.[84]

Indigenous activists who spoke against the project invoked the five-decades-long tradition of community control over the Main Street strip and broader North End, and described this tradition as a plan to reverse Canada's colonial destruction through the creation of urban space by and for Indigenous peoples. The street corner in question—Main Street at Higgins Avenue—was positioned as the geographic heart of the still only partially realized Neeginan plan. "Now we are at the corner of Main and Higgins," Damon Johnston, former director of the Aboriginal Centre, told City Council. "They're going to be across the street from the Thunderbird House, which is our spiritual, the first spiritual house of the Aboriginal people, the First Nations in this city." "[O]ne of the things about that corner lot that we've all agreed on," said Marileen Bartlett, director of an Aboriginal economic development organization based at the Aboriginal Centre, "is that we wanted it to be something that would reflect our culture, our heritage and a promise to our people that we are developing and we are moving forward."[85] In this way, Indigenous organizers attempted to remind Winnipeg's wilfully ignorant white-dominated City Council about the long history of Indigenous plans for the Main Street strip. Presenting this history—including settler governments' history of refusing to fund the Neeginan plan—as the backdrop for the City's eagerness to fund YFC clearly revealed the settler city's profound hostility toward Indigenous Main Street and Indigenous urban planning.

In order to defend the YFC plan, CentreVenture erased the reality—eloquently established by Johnston, Bartlett, and others—of a well-organized Indigenous community with a rich history of planning and redeveloping Main Street and replaced it with an updated story of *urbs nullius*, recasting the Main Street strip as an unwanted, underdeveloped territory inhabited by inferior people with no idea how to use the land properly. This story erased city council's previous four decades of systematically attacking the strip and refusing to support the full Neeginan plan, making the area appear naturally empty, unstable, and in need of intervention. "Yes, Higgins and Main, who would have thought we'd be here arguing over Higgins and Main a few years ago?" said CentreVenture CEO Ross McGowan, transmitting CentreVenture's fundamental obliviousness to local people's histories and claims to space. "Stabilizing the area and providing a framework for further private and public investment is of paramount importance," McGowan continued, making the capitalist case for an updated Indian Residential School. "The proposed Centre for Youth Excellence meets this objective and fills a major void on North Main." City councillors assisted CentreVenture by mobilizing the geographical knowledge of their suburban constituents—CentreVenture's target audience—to describe an area in desperate need of a saviour. "I know for a fact, Higgins and Main is a bad place," said one city councillor. "People will not venture from Tuxedo, from Transcona, [they] say; 'Don't go there because it's a bad place.'...You've got transients hanging out, it's a place that should not be visited."[86] With Neeginan removed from the equation, YFC was positioned as the only possible healthy future for the strip. "If it's that [YFC] or crack, I'd rather have somebody have that," said one councillor.[87] Replacing Neeginan with crack cocaine as the image of Main Street's Indigenous future perfectly captured the anti-Native racism of the dominant bloc's geographical imagination. In fact, the "void" YFC proponents conjured—as well as the idea of the "at-risk" Indigenous young person critiqued by Fontaine—were produced by the settler state's attacks on Indigenous communities and its refusal to fully support Indigenous development agendas. The YFC plan only reiterated and deepened both of these patterns. Rigorously ignoring this, Winnipeg's entirely non-Indigenous City Council voted ten to four in favour of funding the project. The YFC centre held its official opening at Main Street and Higgins Avenue on December 9, 2011, polluting the North End with perhaps Winnipeg's single most noxious example, to date, of contemporary urban settler colonialism.

Indigenous organizers who resisted CentreVenture's YFC plan made clear, again and again, how CentreVenture's actions infuriatingly recreated the colonial dynamics of Indian Residential Schools. The sense of déjà vu—of colonialism repeating itself in the contemporary city—generated by state funding for the YFC centre, of course, is not limited to the comparison between state funding for YFC and the Indian Residential Schools system. The colonial dynamic extends, fundamentally, to the contest over land. CentreVenture's support for YFC reiterated colonial dispossession of Indigenous lands as much as it reiterated the construction of Indian Residential Schools. While CentreVenture's

CentreVenture's residential school. Youth For Christ Centre for Youth Excellence,
Main Street strip at Higgins Avenue, Winnipeg, ca. 2013. (Photo by Bryan Scott, used with permission)

other, lower-profile projects did not attract the same fierce, open opposition, they were equally rooted in the same racial capitalist project: the removal of land from the reach of Indigenous peoples. Ultimately, wealthy developers, evangelicals, and foundations were the most immediate beneficiaries of this round of Indigenous dispossession, while the entire urban wing of the dominant regional bloc—who approved the plan but opted not to invest—profited indirectly.

Trevor Greyeyes—poet, long-time MIWC member, and publisher of *First Nations Voice*—has produced some of the MIWC's best writing about the strip. I asked Greyeyes what he made of the particular geographic logic that seems to motivate CentreVenture, whereby the authority explains that spaces inhabited predominantly by Indigenous peoples are not intolerable in and of themselves but are intolerable in particular locations. "Well, you know," Greyeyes responded, "it's been done for years—why do you think most First Nations are located where they are?"[88] For Greyeyes, in order to understand Main Street—and gentrification in Winnipeg in general—it is necessary to understand it as part of the much longer regional history of serial Indigenous dispossession.

Greyeyes, who is a member of Peguis First Nation and has spent most of his life in Winnipeg, compared Main Street to the history of Peguis First Nation itself, which—when it was still known as St. Peter's First Nation—was forcibly relocated from its original location near the city of Selkirk, Manitoba. Greyeyes compared the stories used to dispossess St. Peter's to those used to dispossess Indigenous Main Street. "I remember part of the reason they gave for having St. Peter's relocate," Greyeyes said, "was because of the 'rampant poverty' and 'drunkenness' and that sort of thing" so close to the largely white city of Selkirk. Greyeyes went on, outlining the economic motivations for the relocation and the fraudulent means used to carry it out:

> Because if you look north of Selkirk, that's prime farming land
> here in Manitoba, so they had a huge swath of it, they were dealing
> with it in their own ways, and they did have private property, and
> people had their own farms, and there were little settlements here
> and there and that sort of thing, but there were also people, say,
> like my great-grandparents who lived the way that they had lived
> for untold generations. They didn't permanently live anywhere,
> you know, they worked out in the bush. In fact, they lived so far
> out in the bush that the RCMP [Royal Canadian Mounted Police]
> didn't even care to go there to get my grandfather to go to residen-
> tial school. But they wanted that land, so they tried on a number
> of occasions to get them to sign a surrender, but they weren't able
> to do it, until one time, a number of people had gone off hunting
> in the fall for the gathering of the season, you know, so I imagine
> they did ducks and geese and that sort of thing. Then, with the
> people they had in the local parish, they called them down for a

> meeting, and most of them spoke either Cree or Ojibway, it was
> a mixed reserve. And then they, the guy, the judge who was in
> charge, knew a little bit, so he said to them, "Anybody who wants
> $50 line up over here, anyone who doesn't want $50 line up over
> there." Then the guy who was the local deacon of the church, you
> know, he could actually speak English well, and he could speak
> the other languages, so he was trying to warn the people, "No, no,
> no, no, this isn't just for money." They kind of cut him off, and they
> didn't even have a vote, but these people took the money.

Members of the Peguis First Nation immediately contested the so-called surrender, but it took 90 years for Canada to recognize that the relocation had been fraudulent and therefore illegitimate. "The exodus happened over, like, a 20-to-30-year span," Greyeyes said, "to what is now known as Peguis." The relocation was a serious economic blow to Peguis. "It basically was like a swamp area, you know," Greyeyes said of the relocation area. "So it floods everywhere." The original lands were never returned. Instead, in 1998 Peguis received a one-time cash settlement.

"So it's the same thing," Greyeyes reflected, "that's happened over and over and over again." "You know," he went on, "Canadians have a certain image of themselves, a mythology, and so they would rather embrace the mythology than actually confront the reality of historical foundations." This mythology amounts to a kind of wilful amnesia, Greyeyes said, that sustains present-day agendas—including but not limited to urban gentrification agendas—to fracture and displace Indigenous communities. The human consequences of these agendas are never genuinely addressed, only moved around—evicted, policed, imprisoned—in perpetuity. "They just want to sweep us under the carpet," said Angela, the community organizer who runs an Indigenous women's organization in Winnipeg's city centre. Angela positioned CentreVenture's activities as part of a larger, ongoing dynamic of "racial cleansing." Greyeyes' and Angela's analyses recall Mercredi's poem "This City is Red," in which the non-Indigenous city suppresses the ghosts, bones, voices, and heartbeats—the "blood red history you have chosen to ignore"—that form its historical foundations. They also advance a truth that grows from listening to Francis when he writes, "the landscape now has city."[89]

The power to reactivate colonial mythology into a determining force in the remaking of the world—in the face of decades of powerful opposition—comes, as the story of Main Street teaches, in part from the creation of new institutional arrangements and capacities such as CentreVenture's "entrepreneurial" power to dispose of public land and money with little to no opening for community input. The theory of colonial amnesia—the idea that what happened in the 2000s and 2010s is "the same thing that has happened over and over and over again"—is not necessarily an insistence that the present is identical to the past, but an observation that capitalist solutions to the fall-out of dispossession, new as they may be, fail over and over again to redress dispossession itself.

1   Francis was referring to Main Street strip hotel owners, who extracted wealth from the community and ignored its struggles.

2   Francis, "Duncan's Worlds," 8.

3   Craft, *Breathing Life into the Stone Fort Treaty*, 113; Borrows, "Negotiating Treaties and Land Claims," 191.

4   Cariou, "Introduction." One of the important effects of *City Treaty*, according to Cariou, is that it "reminds us that colonization was, and remains, even more an economic system of inequity than a political one."

5   Francis, *City Treaty*, 36.

6   Ibid., 6.

7   Ibid., 69.

8   Green and Fleury-Green, *Brown Town Muddy Water*.

9   Mercredi, *The Duke of Windsor: Wolf Sings the Blues*.

10 Published in 2017 by *Prairie Fire*.

11 Mercredi, "This City is Red."

12 Greyeyes, "The Strip."

13 Francis, "Voices From Dark Rooms: Winnipeg's New Occidental Hotel and the Spectre of Main Street," 7–10, 4.

14 Duncan Mercredi, interview with author, Winnipeg, MB, January 13, 2014.

15 Damas and Smith Ltd, *Neeginan*, 22.

16 Francis also wrote about being turned away from Portage Avenue restaurants in the 1970s ("Duncan's Worlds," 9).

17 Jack, interview with author, Winnipeg, MB, October 1, 2015.

18 Munroe, Research interview for *Preserving the History of Institutional Development in Winnipeg*. All other quotations from Munroe in this chapter are taken from the same source, unless otherwise noted.

19 Francis "Voices From Dark Rooms: Winnipeg's New Occidental Hotel and the Spectre of Main Street," 1.

20 Green and Fleury-Green, *Brown Town Muddy Water*.

21 Ibid.

22 Canadian Broadcasting Corporation, "Brown Town Muddy Water Documents Winnipeg's Early Indigenous Music Scene."

23 Green and Fleury-Green, "Interview."

24 Krotz, "Down and Out on Main Street."

25 Coulthard, *Red Skin White Masks*, 4–6.

26 Nepinak, "Main Street."

27 Francis, "Voices From Dark Rooms: Winnipeg's New Occidental Hotel and the Spectre of Main Street."

28 Hauch, "Coping Strategies and Street Life," 27.

29   Winnipeg Free Press, "City Contributes $7,500 for Study."

30   Neeginan Newsletter, June 1974, see Damas and Smith Ltd, *Neeginan*.

31   Damas and Smith Ltd, *Neeginan*.

32   Neeginan Newsletter, June 1974, see Damas and Smith Ltd, *Neeginan*.

33   Dennison, "Indians March in Protest."

34   Damas and Smith Limited, *Neeginan*.

35   Damas and Smith Limited, *Neeginan*.

36   Damas and Smith Limited, *Neeginan*.

37   Damas and Smith Limited, *Neeginan*.

38   Winnipeg Free Press, "Opposes Indian Village In City."

39   Krotz, "Down and Out on Main Street."

40   Hauch, "Coping Strategies and Street Life," 6.

41   Winnipeg's "drunk tank" continues to operate despite being ruled unconstitutional by a Manitoba judge who called it a form of "arbitrary detention" that enables racist policing practices (Bertrand, "Judge Claims Police Can't Lock Up Drunks").

42   Urban Futures Group, *Community Inquiry into Inner City Revitalization*, 27.

43   Helgason, Research interview for *Preserving the History of Institutional Development in Winnipeg*. All other quotations from Helgason in this chapter are taken from the same source, unless otherwise noted. The Aboriginal Centre has gradually expanded over the years—inspired by the original Neeginan plan—to include job training facilities and just under 100 units of housing on four acres.

44   Urban Futures Group, *Community Inquiry into Inner City Revitalization*.

45   Richard, "Interview with Kurt Sargent, re: History of Urban Aboriginal Organizations," 12.

46   North Main Task Force, *Our Place: North Main Task Force*, 38, 19.

47   Richard, "Interview with Kurt Sargent, re: History of Urban Aboriginal Organizations," 12.

48   Fontaine, Research interview for Preserving the History of Institutional Development in Winnipeg.

49   McLeod, Research interview for Preserving the History of Institutional Development in Winnipeg.

50   Janzen, "Committee Pulls Plug on Historic Savoy Hotel."

51   Hendry, "Main Street Hot Spot for Growth."

52   Winnipeg Free Press, "It's Our Downtown."

53   CentreVenture, *Heart of Gold*, 6, 11; Distasio and Mulligan, *Beyond a Front Desk: The Residential Hotel as Home*.

54   CentreVenture, *Heart of Gold*, 13, 6.

55   CentreVenture, *Heart of Gold*, 13.

56   CentreVenture, *Heart of Gold*, 14, 13.

57   CentreVenture, *Heart of Gold*, 13–14.

58   Province of Manitoba, "Sustainable Funding of Operation Clean Sweep Announced by Macintosh and Katz."

59   CentreVenture, *Heart of Gold*, 7.

60   CentreVenture, *Heart of Gold*, 8.

61   CentreVenture, *Heart of Gold*, 16.

62   CentreVenture, *Heart of Gold*, 20, 13.

63   Highway, *Kiss of the Fur Queen*, 215.

64   Giroday, "Bell Hotel Gave Them a Home."

65   CentreVenture, "Revitalization of Main Street Expected with CentreVenture's Strategic Purchase of Bell Hotel Properties."

66   Simon, interview with author, Winnipeg, MB, July 11, 2013.

67   CentreVenture, "Ringing the Bell."

68   CentreVenture, "Bell Hotel Supportive Housing RE: IDA Downtown Achievement Awards."

69   Canadian Broadcasting Corporation, "Bell Tolls for Downtown Winnipeg Hotel."

70   Winnipeg Free Press, "Last Call at the Bell."

71   Jessica, interview with author, Winnipeg, MB, July 17, 2013.

72   Will, interview with author, Winnipeg, MB, August 2, 2013.

73   The Main Street Project originated as a street patrol organized by the IMFC in 1972.

74   CentreVenture, "Bell Hotel Supportive Housing RE: IDA Downtown Achievement Awards."

75   Ibid.

76   McNeill, "Full Steam Ahead for Main Street."

77   Bernice, interview with author, Winnipeg, MB, August 2, 2013.

78   McNeill, "North Main Getting Major Facelift."

79   Ford, "Respect the Locals When It Comes to Main Street"; Oleson, "Walking Down Main."

80   Ibid.

81   Connors, "'They Killed It Man.'"

82   Roussin and Christensen, "Public Funds for Youth For Christ: Have Our Politicians Learned Nothing from Past Mistakes?"

83   Harper, "Statements by Ministers: Apology to Former Students of Indian Residential Schools, House of Commons Debates."

84   City of Winnipeg, "Hansard of the Council of the City of Winnipeg Wednesday, February 24, 2010."

85   City of Winnipeg, "Hansard of the Council of the City of Winnipeg Wednesday, February 24, 2010."

86   City of Winnipeg, "Hansard of the Council of the City of Winnipeg Wednesday, February 24, 2010."

87   Hugill and Toews, "Born Again Urbanism: New Missionary Incursions, Aboriginal Resistance and Barriers to Rebuilding Relationships in Winnipeg's North End."

88   Trevor Greyeyes, interview with author, Winnipeg, MB, January 23, 2014.

89   Francis, "City Treaty," 69.

ENDNOTES

CAPITALIST FRAGILITY, COLONIAL DURABILITY: REDRAWING URBAN APARTHEID

The gentrification frontier absorbs and retransmits the distilled optimism of a new city, the promise of economic opportunity, the twin thrills of romance and rapacity; it is the place where the future will be made. …Behind the line, civilization and profit-making are taking their toll; in front of the line, savagery, promise and opportunity still stalk the landscape.

—Neil Smith, *The New Urban Frontier: Gentrification and the Revanchist City.*

After years of remaking the Main Street strip, the urban wing of the dominant bloc reorganized in the early 2010s to delineate a new zone of intervention—the city's next gentrification frontier—where they would focus the energies of the city's urban redevelopment authority for the next decade. The human geography of the area selected, chosen for its proximity to the city's downtown hockey arena, had been produced in part by the destruction of the Main Street strip, as the strip's predominantly Indigenous community was pushed south and west. CentreVenture continued to stalk this community and destroy the urban spaces it produced into the 2010s. In order to do so, the authority stretched its TIF capacities significantly over time and space, further closed openings for grassroots resistance, and reinvigorated the regional tradition of blaming city-centre residents themselves, rather than the dominant bloc's suburban development agenda, for city-centre disinvestment. CentreVenture transported myths about the Main Street strip to a new segment of the city centre in this period, continuing to deny both the full geographical humanity of existing inhabitants and the full humanness of the existing city-centre geography.[1] This approach became the authority's go-to method for pursuing a new mandate of "investment protection," whereby capital investment in Winnipeg's city centre, defined by its supposed fragility, would be protected via the renewal of colonial geographies both material and imagined.

CENTREVENTURE'S NEXT FRONTIER

In the years following the 2008 global economic crisis, Canadian capitalists—wary of overdeveloped markets in Vancouver and Toronto—expressed a budding interest in Winnipeg real estate, particularly in its underdeveloped city centre. Compared to the country's so-called global cities, Winnipeg had long been considered a stable, low-risk, low-return market for investors and an ideal outlet during economic bust times. In an effort not to squander the opportunity, the urban wing of Winnipeg's dominant bloc leapt into action to coordinate a new round of regional planning. CentreVenture remained the redevelopment vehicle of choice for the urban wing in this phase, but its capacities were redirected. Rather than attempting to lure capital in general to an area of its choosing, as it had done on Main Street, CentreVenture followed specific capitalists to an area of *their* choosing, and then acted on their behalf to secure the area against financial risk.

The new planning phase was made public in a 2010 City Council meeting, where the city's Director of Planning, Property, and Development, Barry Thorgrimson, informed City Council that an unnamed real estate developer had requested a meeting with CentreVenture in autumn 2009, to discuss the developer's trepidations about a new Portage Avenue development he was plotting. "The developer's main concern with developing on Portage Avenue was related to protecting their significant investment," Thorgrimson continued. "In January 2010, CentreVenture assembled the Downtown Council to discuss issues surrounding our downtown and what needs to be done to protect private and public investment."[2]

This small "Downtown Council," acting in solidarity with the anonymous developer, would chart CentreVenture's course into the next decade. Unsurprisingly, the group consisted exclusively of long-time urban-wing members of the dominant regional bloc, including representatives of the Winnipeg Chamber of Commerce; Economic Development Winnipeg Inc.; Destination Winnipeg; two city-centre business improvement districts (BIDs); the Winnipeg Convention Center; and the WPS.

Meetings with the Downtown Council redirected CentreVenture's geographical focus away from the Main Street strip. "From those sessions," CentreVenture CEO Ross McGowan wrote in a 2010 report, "our vision and action plan will direct us as we 'Turn the Corner' to focus our revitalization efforts on another important artery—Portage Avenue." McGowan's report, entitled "Turning the Corner," included photographs of the new "revitalized" white-collar Main Street appearing in rear-view mirrors, while photographs of Portage Avenue—now referred to by CentreVenture as "Winnipeg's most significant street"—appeared through front windshields.

The Downtown Council's plan, it would later become evident, was not to attract capital in general to Portage Avenue, but to remake the area for a wealthier, more lucrative consumer. Like the old Main Street strip, Portage Avenue in the 2000s was not unprofitable; capital was accumulating and many people were getting rich from the existing landscape of low-income hotels, fast-food restaurants, bars, dollar stores, and payday loans outlets. But the largely poor, largely Indigenous human geography of this capitalist landscape was perceived as a threat. Existing inhabitants were considered incompatible with a new, more profitable city dependent on the consumption of people who were understood to desire the kind of socially homogenous, sanitized, and controlled environments they'd grown accustomed to through various apartheid regimes.

McGowan presented CentreVenture's new *Portage Avenue Action Strategy*—later renamed the *Portage Avenue Development Strategy*—to City Council in the summer of 2010. It was another moment in which CentreVenture needed to justify ongoing operating funding and continued political support. Central to McGowan's presentation was the recognition that much if not most recent investment in the city centre had come from the state, rather than private capital. "While public investment is often the necessary catalyst of development, our real objective should be to attract and support private investment, the true indicator of economic success and community well-being," McGowan argued.[3] "In order to achieve this objective it is essential that a comprehensive plan be in place—one that articulates a vision, that encourages and supports such investment and most importantly protects that investment." McGowan was emphatic: "This fundamental principle of investment attraction and protection is the cornerstone of the *Portage Avenue Action Strategy*." "To attract public and private capital," McGowan explained in that document, "an Investment Protection Strategy, that is predictable and vigorously defended, is required."

Coming on the heels of the global financial crisis, the *Portage Avenue Action Strategy* dwelled on the fundamental fragility of capital accumulation. As Karl Marx explained in Volume One of *Capital*, capital accumulation is the perpetual cycling of value between the money form and the commodity form, whereby money is turned into commodities that are turned into even more money—also known as surplus value—in perpetuity. A key moment within this cycle is the time between capital investment and return on investment, the moment after money has been turned into commodities but before it has been turned back into surplus value. This moment is infused with uncertainty and anxiety for capitalists, since there is always a risk of not turning commodities back into even more money. In this case, the risk was that condominiums, hotel rooms, and banquet halls built in Winnipeg's city centre would not sell, or not sell fast enough. The speed with which this cycle moves—also known as turnover time—is extremely important to capital, for every day that value remains in the commodity form the investor effectively loses money.[4]

This "commodity phase," then, is a moment of tremendous fragility, and it can prompt capitalists to engage in heightened levels of social, political, and geographical intervention, which often takes the form of colonial violence. The same dynamic, for instance, characterizes the struggle over oil pipeline construction (which several of the millionaires and billionaires invested in Winnipeg's city-centre real estate also have a hand in). Oil producers can extract all the oil in the world, but if they can't get the oil to market, it's effectively worthless. Many things threaten capital's ability to turn commodities into money, but when the commodity is a segment of the built environment—because it cannot be picked up and moved—the character of the space surrounding the commodity takes on special importance. Thus, CentreVenture's role—the essence of "protecting" and "defending" real estate investment—was to shape the urban space around new real estate investments in such a way that would guarantee the speedy sale of condos and hotel rooms.

CentreVenture proposed two "key elements" for doing so. The first "key element" of the Investment Protection Strategy would be for CentreVenture to "adopt a 'mall management' approach to Portage Avenue, providing for visitor expectations and social responsibilities similar to what one would experience at a regional shopping centre." In doing so, CentreVenture renewed the urban wing's four-decades-old tradition—established by the CAI and the BIDs—of attempting to transform Winnipeg's city centre into a hyper-controlled suburban subdivision–style environment. In attempting to turn the city centre into a new growth area, capitalists deployed techniques they had learned in the suburbs; that is, they tapped CentreVenture to produce a total community, a totally planned, totally controlled area surrounding the commodities—the units of residential and commercial real estate—they needed to sell.

The most specific method for doing this—in addition to increased lighting, expanded parking infrastructure, and a new "comprehensive safety strategy"—would be to "increase public comfort by working closely with adjoining hotels and vendor owners...to address and resolve the impact of offsite [alcohol] sales within and adjacent to Portage Avenue." The urban wing's six-decades-long war against the Main Street strip had long established the tradition of invoking city-centre hotels and beer vendors as code for Native people. CentreVenture's latest proposed attacks on such spaces were clearly viewed as a response to the unintended geographical effects of its Main Street conquest. In a piece entitled "Hotel Buyouts in Core for Fewer Drunks?" the *Free Press* explained, "After the city closed down a series of skid-row hotels on Main Street, some of the clientele moved to Portage Avenue."[5] "We have some problems on Portage Avenue," McGowan told the *Free Press*. "We sure don't have them on Main Street anymore."[6] CentreVenture's new round of planning, in other words, was largely an agenda for stalking the Indigenous human geography of the Main Street strip—coded as "hotels," "drunks," or simply "problems"—it had displaced to Portage Avenue, now that capital was interested in the latter.

In fact, CentreVenture's vision for the elimination of low-income and Indigenous spaces in the district was much more expansive, including an agenda for the abortion of affordable spaces already in the early stages of development. In the same year as it drafted its *Portage Avenue Development Strategy*, CentreVenture secretly thwarted a deal that would have installed a large "discount retailer" on Portage Avenue. "I went to my board," McGowan later recalled, "and said we are either going to let Portage Avenue become a discount mall or we are going to make Portage Avenue into the great Winnipeg street it is."[7] "It was our position that this was the last straw in the decline of our iconic avenue," McGowan told the *Free Press*. "And if action was not taken, our fear was that we would lose Portage Avenue for decades to come."[8] McGowan's comments betrayed CentreVenture's attachment to the city's long-standing apartheid geography, whereby Portage Avenue was imagined as a bastion of whiteness where—in contrast to Main Street—Indigeneity was not to be tolerated. In order to boost the profits of a particular segment of real estate capital—the segment that sought to profit through white luxury rather than Indigenous discount consumption—CentreVenture rolled out a fear-based, revanchist story wherein "losing" Portage Avenue to poor, working-class, and Indigenous peoples would spell disaster for the city. In order to make Portage Avenue "great" again, CentreVenture purchased the building in question, demolished it, and made the land a centrepiece of its luxury Portage Avenue vision. While the authority had similar designs on other properties in the district, it first needed more money to fund its plans.

CentreVenture turned to an unprecedented expansion of TIF to fund its new mission. The second "key element" of its *Portage Avenue Development Strategy*, CentreVenture proposed, would be to designate an entire eleven-block TIF zone around the Portage Avenue hockey arena—the Manitoba Telecom Services (MTS) Centre—built in 2005 by the Chipmans, one of Winnipeg's richest families, with the help of $40 million in public money. Rather than propose TIF for individual projects in a piecemeal fashion as it had done on Main Street—and as the Government of Manitoba had stipulated in its 2009 TIF Act[9]—CentreVenture proposed that every cent of "incremental" property tax revenues from all properties in the zone be automatically taken out of general state revenue streams and placed in a special fund controlled by CentreVenture for spending on its "mall management" strategy. Among other things, this would close the opening for resistance—the requirement that every TIF-based spending decision be approved by city council—that communities had used to mount resistance to Youth For Christ on Main Street. CentreVenture suggested that the new TIF zone—which it dubbed its Sports, Hospitality and Entertainment District (SHED)—would become "the focal point of the new Portage Avenue."[10] CentreVenture vowed to lobby the municipal and provincial governments to make the zone a reality—noting that the cooperation of the provincial government, in particular, which controls half of all property tax revenue in Manitoba—would be "crucial." City Council unanimously endorsed the plan, but waited for the provincial government to commit to the TIF zone before committing itself.

Both the *Free Press* and the *Winnipeg Sun*, the city's far-right tabloid, lauded the *Portage Avenue Development Strategy*, amplifying the idea that the area's existing human geography was a "problem" and a "stain," while implying that city-centre residents themselves—and not the dominant bloc's suburban development agenda—had caused capital's abandonment of the area. Both newspapers valorized the upward distribution of public resources represented by TIF as essential to the "greater good." "Portage Avenue," a *Free Press* editorial commented, "remains a challenge, and a problem." "The city and province can get the ball rolling immediately by declaring the area a TIF (tax increment financing) zone that would use the new taxes raised by the developments to fund other improvements in the area." "It can be done," the *Free Press* continued. "All it takes is an agreement to act decisively for the greater good of the community."[11] The *Sun* pushed CentreVenture to go even further with its "mall management" strategy. "[C]onsider making the area a 'zero-tolerance' zone for public intoxication, panhandling and vagrancy," the *Sun* wrote. "Until these crime-related issues are addressed first, no amount of boutique hotels or TIF zones will make people go downtown and stay downtown—especially after 5:30 or 6 p.m." "These beverage rooms and hotels," the *Sun* went on, "are simply feeder zones that fuel the downtown's demise."[12]

Less than a year later—in what many Winnipeggers consider a miraculous advancement for the city—Winnipeg's city centre received an investment that gave CentreVenture's SHED plans a new, high-profile context. On May 20, 2011, the Chipman family, in partnership with billionaire David Thomson—chairman of Thomson Reuters and Canada's richest person[13]—announced that they had purchased the NHL's Atlanta Thrashers and were in the process of relocating the team to Winnipeg for the upcoming 2011–12 NHL season. The new NHL franchise—which would bring back the old "Winnipeg Jets" name (the original Winnipeg Jets departed for Phoenix, Arizona, in 1995)—would play in the MTS Centre. A month after the NHL announcement, the formerly anonymous developer who had originally prompted CentreVenture to draft its *Portage Avenue Development Strategy* was revealed to be the Chipman family themselves, under their Longboat Development Corporation banner.

CentreVenture announced that the Chipmans would construct the first major development in the new district—a 20-storey, $75 million hotel, restaurant, retail, and office tower complex called "CentrePoint"—on the land CentreVenture had purchased in order to thwart the arrival of the "discount retailer." McGowan had reportedly travelled to Montreal to convince the Germaine family, described by the Manitoba media as "the Chipmans of Quebec," to build a hotel on the site in partnership with the Chipmans. It was reported that the tower would include a 150-room hotel owned by the Germaine family; office space for the Winnipeg headquarters of Alberta-based resource extraction consultants Stantec Consulting; a 450-stall parking garage; and restaurant and retail space.[14] City Council, through its Winnipeg Parking Authority, provided $5 million for the project.

Politicians of all stripes hailed the publicly funded boutique hotel as evidence of a revanchist victory. "Downtown Winnipeg's historic comeback as an exciting destination for Manitoba families and visitors alike is in full swing," Manitoba's NDP premier Greg Selinger enthused. "This major private investment next to the home of the reborn Winnipeg Jets," Selinger continued, advancing a vision of Manitoba state-capitalism reminiscent of the 1960s Manitoba Development Fund, "demonstrates the kind of private-sector confidence that results when governments, agencies and community partners work together toward a shared vision of renewal."[15] Formerly "one of the most active members"[16] in the grassroots resistance to the CAI, who fought to privilege affordable housing and education over the dominant regional bloc's vision of corporate redevelopment in the 1980s, Selinger now chose to educate the public on the importance of public funding for large capitalist development projects aimed at tourists. The reversal of Selinger's opinion, after gaining state power, indicates the hegemonic power of the urban wing's subsidies-for-capital agenda.

The next day, it was announced that local hotelier Leo Ledohowski—owner of the multinational Canad Inns chain—would receive $3 million in state funding to turn a theatre formerly owned by CentreVenture into a "state of the art conference, banquet and meeting facility." CentreVenture had sold the 90-year-old Metropolitan Theatre (or the MET) to Ledohowski four years earlier for a mere $100,000. The $20 million development would add two new bars and a large banquet space to the SHED. "I think many high school graduations will be held here," Ledohowski told the *Free Press*. Winnipeg City Council and the Province of Manitoba each gave Ledohowski $1.5 million for the project. "The province is demonstrating its confidence in the future of downtown Winnipeg," said NDP MLA Ron Lemieux. "The MET renovation project will create another star attraction for the city centre."[17]

Despite the urban wing's open excitement, and the announcement of almost $100 million in new real estate investment in two days, the arrival of the NHL—which brought with it three consecutive sold-out seasons to the 15,000-seat (and 57-luxury box) MTS Centre—cast an anxious light on the still disinvested, heavily poor, working-class, and Indigenous downtown. McGowan attempted to foment such anxieties in order to garner support for the SHED TIF zone, for which CentreVenture had yet to receive provincial support. "Think of television broadcasts on Portage Avenue," he told the *Free Press* soon after the NHL's return. "What's the backdrop to our international media exposure? Is it a surface parking lot or is it a vibrant district?"[18] McGowan's take was accurate in some ways; the arrival of the NHL to Portage Avenue brought national, if not international, attention to the area.

The new spotlight amplified the anxieties of the urban wing. "The Winnipeg Jets are packing in the fans and sold out for years to come," Toronto-based The Canadian Press wrote in a nationally syndicated piece. "But does the return of the NHL hold the benefits for the city's troubled downtown boosters have always insisted would materialize?" It did not, according to The Canadian Press. "Boarded up windows, payday loans storefronts and dollar stores aren't going to draw tourists or suburb dwellers, who complain about panhandlers, drunks, litter and crime," continued the article, which was almost entirely framed around comments from McGowan. "The real challenge is changing the demographic of the people who frequent the area, a loaded issue but something that has to happen if new development is to work, says McGowan." The piece concluded with comments from an unnamed "activist working on homelessness issues" who critiqued the dominant development vision. "It detracts from the work we're doing here," the activist told The Canadian Press. "Low income people need housing. They should be

CHAPTER 7 | CAPITALIST FRAGILITY, COLONIAL DURABILITY: REDRAWING URBAN APARTHEID housed downtown…They should not be displaced. But we're a million miles away from having governments ready to do that kind of thing."[19] The casualties of CentreVenture's revanchist agenda, as pointed out by the unnamed activist, were not simply isolated low-income and Indigenous spaces, but the people's city-centre development tradition as a whole.

In the spring of 2012, the Province of Manitoba announced that it would make the SHED TIF zone a reality. The two levels of government would transfer $25 million to CentreVenture over two years to pursue its SHED restructuring strategy. The provincial funds, in keeping with 2008 TIF legislation, would come entirely out of Manitoba's education budget. These funds were guaranteed no matter how little investment actually occurred in the SHED; if incremental taxes from the SHED TIF zone over fifteen years did not amount to the full $25 million, then the rest of the provincial and municipal property tax base would subsidize the shortfall. The governments seem to have been encouraged by the Chipman and Ledohowski developments—Winnipeg City Council cited "two primary private development opportunities within the TIF zone" as the existing initial sources of TIF (despite both developments receiving large government subsidies).[20]

Politicians again framed the return of capital to Winnipeg's city centre as the harbinger of a regional revival that would take back the city for its respectable classes. "Downtown Winnipeg is undergoing a truly remarkable renaissance," Selinger announced. "By supporting the development of a sports, hospitality and entertainment district," Mayor Katz added, "we can help turn downtown into a destination all on its own—a place where students, professionals, and families want to hang out in their free time." The announcement signalled a landmark achievement for CentreVenture, the Downtown Council, the Chipmans, and other TIF beneficiaries. Rather than pay taxes to fund public education, affordable housing, and other social services, Chipman, Thomson, Ledohowski, and their fellow millionaire and billionaire investors would contribute only to a special fund—controlled by CentreVenture—dedicated solely to the protection of their investments through the "mall management" of the city. Notably, the political justification for this extreme instance of neoliberal statecraft was—via coded language of a "renaissance" for "students," "professionals," and "families"—anti-Native revanchism. To capture significant public resources for themselves, in other words, capitalists appealed to white fears of a Native city.

In the spirit of the people's city-centre development tradition, anti-poverty organizers voiced frustration that an NDP government with social-democratic roots would so heartily embrace public gifts to millionaire and billionaire developers in the name of "community revitalization," while food and housing shortages among city-centre residents remained at crisis levels. These critiques specifically resisted the legislation's revanchist logic, arguing that area residents' needs should be built in to TIF eligibility requirements. The provincial legislation made eligible any developer who could promise

CentreVenture's *Lebensraum*. The Sports, Hospitality, and Entertainment District, as stipulated by the City of Winnipeg's SHED TIF Zone By-law No. 98/2012.

"significant improvements" deemed "in the public interest." "This criteria says nothing about financial or community need," the Canadian Centre for Policy Alternatives (CCPA) Manitoba office noted. "Projects that qualify for TIF should have to demonstrate, beyond just the generating of revenue, how they will benefit the surrounding community and the residents that live there." The CCPA criticized the process through which developers were granted TIF: "It leaves community residents out of the process...Stronger public consultation mechanisms would give community residents a voice in determining how TIF funds could be best used to address the needs of the surrounding community, such as by investing it in affordable housing for the area's lower-income residents." The CCPA also noted that the Manitoba School Board Association opposed the taking of revenue from public education for private developers in the name of "community revitalization," arguing that "schools themselves are important players in building stronger communities, particularly in marginalized areas such as Winnipeg's inner city."[21] Premier Selinger and the NDP Government did not acknowledge such criticisms, sticking steadfastly to the urban-wing ideology that downtown capital investment of any sort held universal benefits for the region.

By late 2012, CentreVenture had put in place everything it needed to take action on behalf of the Chipmans, Thomsons, Germaines, Ledohowskis, and the rest of their class. The authority had taken on the task of reorganizing the urban wing into a new coalition (the "Downtown Council"); drafted a plan of action (the *Portage Avenue Development Strategy*); drummed up renewed support from media and politicians; and secured a new source of financing to carry out its plan (the province's first TIF zone). This was community organizing—in the politically neutral sense of the term—at its finest.

In the course of doing so, CentreVenture reframed an eleven-block area around the MTS Centre as a place of exceptional importance to the city's future, where usual levels of tolerating difference would no longer be exercised, and existing inhabitants would no longer be welcome. In essence, this was a redrawing of the city's apartheid geography. This idea, which rolled easily off the tongues of politicians, journalists, and CentreVenture officials, demonized existing residents (widely understood to be Native but rarely acknowledged as such) as "drunks," "panhandlers," and "vagrants," and celebrated future inhabitants (widely understood to be white but rarely acknowledged as such) as "families," "professionals," "students," and "tourists." Existing inhabitants were charged with taking the city away from its proper occupants, who—with the help of strong-willed and visionary leadership—would soon regain it. Popularizing this feeling about the city's past, present, and future would remain a key way of justifying endless public transfers—of land and money—into the pockets of billionaires.

REDRAWING THE LINE

Newly flush with cash, CentreVenture embarked on its "mall management" vision, which soon revealed itself as a direct attack on existing inhabitants of the area. On November 15, 2012, CentreVenture announced the first major expenditure of its new $25 million SHED fund: it had purchased the St. Regis, one of the hotels near Portage Avenue that in recent years had come to host more and more of the "clientele" displaced from the Main Street strip. The St. Regis's 101 rooms predominantly hosted families from First Nations communities visiting the city for medical care, according to media accounts and CentreVenture's own press release. The St. Regis's bar had also been a long-time hub of the Winnipeg Two-Spirit community.[22] The St. Regis happened to sit two blocks from the Chipmans' under-construction CentrePoint boutique hotel, office, and luxury condo development, which McGowan would soon describe as "the iconic face of the SHED, ground zero for the redevelopment...the spark that lights the fire throughout the district."[23]

CentreVenture announced that it would immediately shut down the St. Regis's bar and lease the hotel back to its previous owner—prominent Winnipeg developer Karampaul Sandhu—until a redevelopment deal could be brokered. "The purchase of this downtown hotel and parking lots is a major achievement for CentreVenture and the City of Winnipeg," Mayor Katz said of the deal. "In order to attract public and private investment, an Investment Protection Strategy became the backbone of our Portage Avenue Development Strategy," said McGowan in a prepared statement about the purchase. In a speech to local realtors days after purchasing the St. Regis, McGowan spoke about CentreVenture's recent activities in the SHED: "This has sent a clear message to the private sector that a new era has emerged, that we want a great downtown, and that if you choose to invest here, our standards have been raised and your investment will be supported and protected."[24] While CentreVenture's purchase did not lead to the immediate removal of the existing community, it essentially put the future of First Nations families in the area at risk—a harbinger of greatness and high standards in the eyes of the Chipmans and their class.

CentreVenture and Mayor Katz were initially careful not to articulate this dynamic in public explanations of the St. Regis buyout, but local newspaper editors were not. The *Free Press* lauded CentreVenture for facilitating the removal of the St. Regis—in effect renewing the spirit of urban apartheid that treated Native people south of Portage Avenue with extreme hostility—and described its inhabitants in virulently derogatory terms. "The troublemakers, addicts and aggressive panhandlers may try to move to nearby upscale hotels," the *Free Press* warned, casting CentreVenture in the role of pest-control, "but McGowan says a strategy is being developed in co-operation with hotel owners, police and several agencies to prevent that from happening." The editorial admitted CentreVenture's St. Regis purchase was only the most recent in Winnipeg's long march of forced hotel closures, and went on to call for "real solutions...to lift the homeless, addicted and mentally ill out of their misery." "Otherwise," the newspaper concluded, "they will remain a permanent stain on the conscience of the community."[25] What the *Free Press* failed to acknowledge, of course, was that a century and a half of racial capitalist development—in the lineage of the agenda it celebrated—had produced the misery it bemoaned and systematically prevented the realization of proposals that would have alleviated it.

McGowan later confirmed that a war-like mentality was indeed at the root of CentreVenture's actions. "Part of the rationale for buying the St. Regis was that when we were working with the [Germaine family's] Alt Group to come to Winnipeg to build their hotel on Portage Avenue," he told the *Free Press*, "one of their questions to us was that if we make our investment on the north side of Portage Avenue, which has some challenges to it, what is it that you're going to do to help protect that investment?" McGowan continued, "One of the issues that was constantly being expressed to us was the excessive drunkenness and the aggressive panhandling that was going on in the area—the Winnipeg Police Service helped us identify that one of the primary center points of that was in fact the St. Regis Hotel."[26] CentreVenture continued to work closely with the WPS in the following years, collaborating most successfully to establish operation "Centreline" in 2016, through which 200 specially trained foot patrols were deployed within a one-kilometre radius of the MTS Centre primarily to police "social disorder."[27] The sequence leading to the purchase of the St. Regis summed up CentreVenture's activities well. Acting on direct orders from investors, in consultation with police intelligence, the authority moved to destroy a key stronghold of health care-seeking Indigenous families.

Policing is real estate policing. Centreline press conference, (L to R) WPS Division 11 Commander Inspector Jim Anderson, CentreVenture CEO Angela Mathieson, and Downtown Winnipeg BIZ Executive Director Stefano Grande, Winnipeg, ca. 2016. Photo by Boris Minkevich. Winnipeg Free Press December 15, 2016. (Courtesy of Winnipeg Free Press)

CentreVenture sought to demolish the St. Regis immediately after purchasing it. McGowan publicly promoted the fact that the structure was not an officially designated heritage building and could therefore be bulldozed easily by any prospective developer.[28] There is also evidence that CentreVenture was not waiting for the market to determine the St. Regis's future—as it so often stated—but instead sought a specific land use deemed compatible with the new accumulation agenda. Brian, an employee of the University of Winnipeg Community Renewal Corporation (UWCRC), told me that CentreVenture approached the UWCRC with the prospect of turning the St. Regis into university student housing. The UWCRC declined the opportunity, but Brian offered a different suggestion. He has a close working relationship with Peguis First Nation and Brokenhead First Nation, he told me, and he knew they had significant funds for development as a result of Treaty Land Entitlement (TLE) payments—money received as compensation for broken treaties and fraudulent negotiations. Brian suggested that CentreVenture get in touch with these First Nations since, he reasoned, the St. Regis already predominantly housed people from these and other First Nations. Brian thought it would be an obvious fit, but CentreVenture was not interested. "He kind of didn't say anything," Brian said of the CentreVenture representative to whom he made the suggestion. "That's what made me think, oh, this is a brown faces outside smoking thing."[29] In 2015, CentreVenture sold the St. Regis to Toronto-based Fortress Real Developments Inc., who closed the hotel's doors for good in 2017, with plans to clear the land for a $200 million luxury condo tower, for which it received a $6.5 million grant from the City.[30] As this and so many other examples indicate, CentreVenture's institutional capacity was used as a tool by a specific bloc of real estate capitalists to remove Native people from the area around their properties. This can be determined not only by examining CentreVenture's destruction of existing spaces but through considering its thwarting of future ones.

CentreVenture announced a second hotel buyout in the SHED less than a month later. In early December 2012, City Council increased CentreVenture's SHED funds by $6.6 million to allow the authority to purchase the Carlton Inn, located just feet from the MTS Centre and the expanding Winnipeg Convention Centre. The Convention Centre had recently embarked on a $200 million expansion in the southwest corner of the SHED, a project CentreVenture had lobbied for—or simply saw coming—in its *Portage Avenue Development Strategy*. CentreVenture's request to City Council for additional funds noted the proximity of the Carlton Inn to the expanding Convention Centre. Like the St. Regis, the 108-room Carlton predominantly housed First Nations families visiting Winnipeg for health care.

McGowan said CentreVenture had identified "the Carlton and the St. Regis as the two properties which most affect development in the SHED." "Quite often there are things going on there that are not what you and I would call lawful to say the least," Mayor Katz said—ironically, in light of a subsequent RCMP investigation of Katz on corruption allegations, which focused on Katz's activities in the same year—by way of explaining City Council's almost $7 million commitment. CentreVenture demolished the Carlton in the summer of 2013 and offered no relocation program for residents of either the Carlton or the St. Regis, emphasizing that both had provided "short term" to "medium term" housing. "There are sufficient spaces in the other hotels nearby to handle the (two) losses," McGowan told reporters when pressed to explain CentreVenture's responsibility for the loss of over 200 low-income housing units in the downtown.[31] CentreVenture would later transfer the lands under the Carlton to the Chipman family, who in partnership with the billionaire Richardson family and the billionaire Gagliardi family (the Vancouver-based owners of the NHL's Dallas Stars) would replace the Carlton with a $400 million luxury condo, hotel, retail, and office complex—dubbed "True North Square"—for which they received over $20 million in public subsidies, including millions of dollars over and above their SHED TIF subsidies.[32]

Although CentreVenture handled the St. Regis and Carlton shutdowns less than sensitively, it was not until February 2013 that public criticism of CentreVenture's scorched-earth approach to the SHED seemed to galvanize. On February 22, 2013, McGowan appeared on CBC radio to announce that CentreVenture was in negotiations— which would ultimately fail—with the Manitoba Liquor Control Commission (MLCC)

Clearing the city. The St. Regis Hotel after being shut down by CentreVenture and Fortress Real Developments Inc., Smith Street at Portage Avenue, Winnipeg, ca. 2018.

Destruction in advance of the Chipmans' CentrePoint complex, Portage Avenue at Donald Street, Winnipeg, ca. 2012. Photo by Joe Bryska. Winnipeg Free Press, September 15, 2012. (Courtesy of Winnipeg Free Press)

CentreVenture demolishes the Carlton Inn, Carlton Street at St. Mary Avenue, Winnipeg, ca. 2014. Photo by Wayne Glowacki. Winnipeg Free Press, April 21, 2014. (Courtesy of Winnipeg Free Press)

to shut down a government-operated liquor store one block north of Portage Avenue, across the street from CentrePoint. A few days later, an editorial published in the *Free Press*—under the headline "New Doubts About CentreVenture"—provided a summary of McGowan's comments. In announcing CentreVenture's intentions to relocate the liquor store, the paper reported, "McGowan likened drunks and aggressive panhandlers downtown to ill-mannered children who were not welcome to sit around the dining room table with the adults." "If you're too poor to afford a beer at Tavern United"—an expensive bar in the SHED owned by Ledohowski—"then you're not responsible enough to purchase alcohol downtown," the *Free Press* theorized, summing up McGowan's remarks. "The social rebirth that McGowan seems to have in mind for the downtown has nothing to do with actually addressing the issues of poverty, addiction or racism in our city," the editorial concluded. "Rather, [McGowan] is openly advocating for the simple removal of undesirable elements from our downtown so that we can all feel safe and happy flooding in and out of the MTS Centre before-and-after Jets games."[33]

The next day, in a response to the *Free Press* piece, McGowan doubled down on his statement: "In a recent interview," said McGowan the next day, "I did make reference to the SHED being compared to the 'living room' in one's house where the kids are sent to the basement until they can abide by the rules of the living room...Regrettably, my comments were taken out of context." McGowan, in full patriarch mode, went on:

> The "kids" are always welcome in the living room; however, there
> are rules, boundaries and expectations of individual behavior.
> Actions such as excessive public intoxication and aggressive
> panhandling that make downtown residents, employees, and
> visitors uneasy, fearful, or unsafe should not be acceptable.[34]

McGowan's comments were an unusually open articulation of the fascistic tendencies underlying the dominant bloc's social engineering of the city centre, from their assertion of an authoritarian parent-child relationship between the state and the people, to advocating arbitrary punishments beyond the letter of the law, to the concept of the "living room," which has the ring of the Nazi's Aryan *lebensraum* or "living space." The "living room" comments also expressed very clearly the persistence of an apartheid mentality according to which colonized peoples must be spatially segregated until they can be trained to abide by the rules and expectations of the conquering society. According to this logic, Indigenous peoples must be compelled to reconcile to—in the sense of coming to peace with rather than disrupting—not only past continental-scale dispossession but present-day urban dispossession.

Despite failing to send the liquor store's patrons "to the basement," by early 2013 CentreVenture began to claim that its interventions had attracted real estate capital to the SHED at unprecedented levels. "In the last five years," Mayor Katz wrote in CentreVenture's 2012 annual report, "we've seen over $1.3 billion invested in [the SHED]." "What is clear is that we are seeing a renaissance that will change the city forever," McGowan told an audience of realtors while echoing the billion-dollar figure. "Who would have thought this possible ten, even five years ago?"[35] The "billion dollars" line—which soon became "two billion dollars"—would become a touchstone in CentreVenture reports and media accounts in the months and years to come. In this way, the authority absorbed and retransmitted not only the idea of the SHED as the next frontier of profitability, but the long-standing tenet of racial capitalism in the North-West that the disappearance of Indigenous peoples foretold capitalist prosperity.[36] Taken as a whole, in other words, CentreVenture's activities in the SHED emboldened a lethal set of feelings in which the disappearance of Native life accrues tangible economic value. This form of value—the currency of Indigenous disappearance—flows not only to individual billionaires, according to the dominant bloc's propaganda, but to the entire enfranchised population, who are encouraged to identify as fellow beneficiaries.

While CentreVenture's numbers were padded significantly by the Convention Centre expansion and the recently constructed headquarters for Manitoba Hydro, the SHED did attract a level of high-profile capital investment unseen in previous years—much of it in previously rare condo development. Three large projects were announced for the SHED in 2013, including a new $55 million 195-condo tower—"Glasshouse Skylofts"— developed by the Chipmans next door to the CentrePoint complex, in partnership with Toronto-based Urban Capital; a $200 million 200-condo tower on the St. Regis Hotel lands; and the $400 million 130-condo, 275-hotel room, office, and retail "True North Square" on the former Carlton lands.[37] Celebratory headlines and computer-generated images of the towers filled the pages of the *Free Press* and the *Sun* in 2013, adding to a popular sense of regional revival.

Led by the Chipmans, with CentreVenture at their side, Canada's real estate capitalists did seem to be taking a more serious interest in Winnipeg's centre than they had in a very long time. When I spoke with her in 2013, former CentreVenture CEO Annitta Stenning was seriously impressed by the investors McGowan had been able to lure to Winnipeg's downtown. It seemed to Stenning that it was not simply the return of the NHL to the city but global economic events that had capitalists looking at Winnipeg in a new light. Stenning told me that in her opinion, Winnipeg—long a city of marginal but steady growth—became viewed as a safe bet for risk-averse capitalists in the wake of the 2009 economic crisis. "I think the crisis shook people up around the world, and they do start looking for places like a Winnipeg...we're unique in a lot of the larger cities in Canada, in that we have a solid, stable economy," Stenning said. "We're kind of like that bonds, slow, sure environment." In March 2013, Toronto's *Globe and Mail* ran a feature on Winnipeg's improving fortunes, again based largely around comments from McGowan. "The NHL's return has sparked a commercial real estate boom downtown," the *Globe* wrote. "New development—an unfamiliar sight in the city's downtown since the 1980s—is becoming commonplace, says the head of the city's arm's-length develop-ment agency." The *Globe*'s business section heralded CentreVenture for "helping to drive up property values" and noted "Winnipeg was the third-fastest growing commercial real estate market in the country, posting a 16.8 percent return for 2012."[38] "We're now seeing national and international developers coming to town," McGowan told the *Free Press* a few months later, "and they're game-changers."[39]

ON THE NEW FRONTIER

As CentreVenture deployed its "mall management" operation against specific people and places in Winnipeg, it demonstrated the way in which abstract capitalist processes such as turnover time can come to depend heavily on the specific cultural, and espe-cially racial, histories, customs, and dynamics of different places. In its attempt to manage a risky commodity phase—in addition to hotel shutdowns, increased policing, and even a proposal to give a $10,000 public subsidy to anyone purchasing a city-cen-tre condo—CentreVenture offered weekly "downtown urban living tours" to drum up interest among real estate agents and prospective condo buyers. The tours confronted urban-wing representatives with the actually existing people and places of the city centre, revealing how they are troubled or comforted by particular material intersec-tions of race, class, and physical appearance, and exposing—more concretely than any press release or newspaper article—the rubric against which the dominant bloc judged various parts of the city.

One afternoon in the summer of 2013, eight people—five real estate agents and three CentreVenture employees—took a tour led by Jon, a CentreVenture employee in his thir-ties who dutifully guided the group west down Portage Avenue from a business plaza at Portage and Main.[40] Portage Avenue bustled with people, including lanyard-marked office workers, bus stop crowds in dirty sneakers, and small groups sitting on concrete planters panhandling. After guiding the tour past a group of the latter, Jon stopped in front of the MTS Centre and turned the tour's gaze across the street to the construc-tion site where a crane towered over a turn-of-the-twentieth-century bank's columned facade. This was where the new "Bargain World" would have opened several years ago, Jon told the tour, if McGowan had not flown to Toronto to tell the "Bargain World" executives to forget the idea. "How would you like it if you had a dollar store right in the middle of your downtown," said Jon, imitating McGowan's plea to the developer. Having barely escaped that fate, Jon went on, the land was now the future home of the Chipmans' CentrePoint complex, the "impetus," said Jon, for CentreVenture's TIF zone. "It represents everything we're trying to do," Jon explained, saying that CentrePoint would be "mixed-use" and exemplify quality design. The realtors nodded in agreement.

Before moving on, Jon pointed to a boarded-up storefront two doors down from the CentrePoint construction site, the former "4-Play" bar and restaurant—"a horrible name for a bar," Jon pointed out—and said there were plans for a "microbrewery" there. One of the realtors asked about a store, O'Calcutta, that sat immediately next door to CentrePoint and looked a little rough around the edges. "That's where you can get a John Lennon t-shirt and a bong," Jon said with a kind of light-hearted contempt. The realtors giggled. "John Lennon t-shirt and a bong," they repeated nervously. Jon tried to reassure them by saying that the owners of the O'Calcutta building "would get a great price" when they sold.

Jon guided the tour a few steps farther and pointed to an abandoned building across the street. He said that a "major financial institution" had recently committed to the space. "They've told us it's definitely not the Dollar Store, or," he corrected himself, "the Cash Store" (a Canadian payday-loans chain). Jon turned down Donald Street, past the Bargain Store, one of the many large dollar stores already doing business in the area. "It's not really what you want to see across from your NHL arena," said Bethany, a CentreVenture employee carrying a sign that read "TIME TO LIVE HERE" and featured a picture of a suited white man superimposed on to Waterfront Drive. CentreVenture, Bethany said, is "trying to work with the building's owner to get something in there that we want to see."

The tour turned south off Portage Avenue, behind the MTS Centre. Stopping in front of a huge parking lot, Jon spoke about the towers planned for the site. "This is going to be the keystone development," he said, pointing at the parking lot. He talked about "linkages" and "connections" between the future towers and CentrePoint, the Glasshouse Skylofts, and the MTS Centre. Jon told the tour that there would be a large outdoor public space incorporated into the development, for people to gather in "when the Jets win the Stanley Cup." "We've also purchased the Carlton Hotel," Jon added, the Carlton visible across the parking lot. Jon said that the Carlton would be replaced with a larger, much more luxurious hotel. "The church, too, can you buy that?" asked one of the realtors, pointing toward an old church at the end of the parking lot. "No," Jon explained, "it's a national historic site." "Is there a shortage of hotel space, or just too many crappy old hotels?" asked another realtor. Since the purpose of the convention centre expansion is to attract bigger conventions, John replied, the area will also need bigger hotels. "We need the hotels to get the conventions." The realtors nodded. "Is this where the screens are going to be?" one of the realtors asked Jon, who nodded. The realtor—who was then selling the Chipmans' Glasshouse Skyloft condos—enthusiastically explained that huge outdoor TV screens would show hockey games there one day. "Just Google SoPo." "We've sold sixty units already," another Glasshouse realtor chimed in, adding that young professionals were extremely interested in SHED condos.

The tour headed into a nearby shopping mall where an elaborate simulated Glasshouse Skylofts condominium—complete with stylish clothes in the closet and big photography books on the coffee table—had been set up. Jon announced that this was the end of the tour. Realtors eagerly guided prospective buyers through the suite, distributing maps of the condo tower's future location—its entrance half a block from the liquor store CentreVenture tried to shut down—and describing the rooftop patio where "all owners" will have access to a full bar, yoga area, and "resort-style" cabanas. "This whole mall will be revamped," one of the realtors said, pointing toward the Chipmans' slick new bar and casino—Shark Club—that had recently opened on the second floor of the mall. "That's a good template for what you're going to see," said the realtor, adding that while the area may not seem like much at the moment, the Glasshouse Skylofts will "get life back on the streets."

The performance put on by CentreVenture employees, realtors, and the developers they work for is over the top, but not surprising—they are economically invested in it. Far from being exclusive to the real estate industry, however, these perspectives have been popularized through various efforts to integrate the concerns and logics of real estate capital into people's imagination of the city. One way that these ideas—which make otherwise questionable ways of relating to other human beings feel reasonable and necessary—achieve the ring of common sense is through repetitive speech, as people construct shared meanings of complex places and lived experiences by drawing on prefabricated narratives. The dominant bloc has been so successful at this that even left-leaning, politically correct Winnipeggers often erase and even casually stigmatize the existing poor, working-class, and Indigenous city centre.

This came across especially strongly one day in a conversation with Andrea, a white woman who held top positions in both the Doer and Selinger Manitoba NDP governments in the 2000s. "We always measured our success based on how well downtown Winnipeg was doing," Andrea said, recalling how much criticism the Manitoba government faced in the mid-2000s for its role in locating the MTS Centre downtown.[41] Andrea recalled people who said there was too much "crime" and too many "panhandlers" and "Aboriginals" in the area for an arena to be successful. "You know," Andrea went on, "there's just so much inherent, endemic racism in people's views of downtown." It seemed like Andrea was about to tell a familiar white liberal story about her—or the NDP government's—passion for downtown, disgust with anti-Native racism, and fearless encounters with Indigeneity. But when our conversation turned to Portage Place—one of the two shopping malls built by the CAI in the 1980s—Andrea's tone changed. "Of all things," she said, shaking her head, "that should have brought people downtown." Andrea's eyes narrowed. "But it's become a hangout," she continued. "It's a wasteland, you know, like a cancer on the downtown." Andrea's casual vitriol surprised me at the time, but only because of the aggressiveness of her tone. At its root, this is the dominant racial capitalist vision of Winnipeg's city centre, a mental map that spans the full spectrum of mainstream politics in the region.

As Winnipeg's dominant bloc tried to redraw urban apartheid, it needed to rearrange common-sense feelings about who belonged where.[42] Part of its success in doing so was that it drew on a pre-existing tradition, dominant in the North-West since 1869, to render existing inhabitants of the SHED at once invisible and hyper-visible. This dynamic was illustrated by the increasing tendency to call the existing landscape both "dead" and "dangerous." Invisibility and hyper-visibility worked together, in accordance with this tradition, as unknown terrain set the stage for hyper-visibility, whereby what was unknown, unseen, or two-dimensional was easily mythologized into a source of fear and disdain in need of vanquishing. There was an important temporality to this narrative, whereby panhandlers, dollar stores, and job banks—and the people associated with them—were highlighted in the story of the city's supposedly degraded present and erased in the story of its revitalized future. This was, to quote geographer Katherine McKittrick, the "profitable erasure and objectification" of city-centre people through which millionaires and billionaires renewed their accumulation of Indigenous lands.[43]

A BROADER SENSE OF PLACE

The current dominance of racial capitalist narratives makes it necessary to insist on alternative ways of seeing that are rich enough to honour the full geographical humanity of people and places that capitalists allege do not matter.[44] In fact, hidden from view by the dominant mappings is the fact that Winnipeg's city centre—including the so-called wastelands—constitutes an extensive, highly productive urban infrastructure produced by the area's existing community to meet a variety of basic needs, from food to shelter to raising children and taking care of elders.

The St. Regis Hotel, for example—viewed by the Chipmans as the primary threat to their CentrePoint investment—provided crucial accommodation to First Nations families visiting Winnipeg to access health care. Prior to being shut down in 2017, the St. Regis offered rooms with multiple double beds and bunk beds to accommodate large families, starting at $78 per night, about half the price of a room at the Ledohowski-owned Radisson Hotel across the street. The dining room—decorated with a mural depicting Turtle Island from sea to sea, with tipi-dotted plains in the centre—offered breakfast for $4.99, less than half the price of most other downtown restaurants. The former bar room had by 2014 been turned into a play area for kids, complete with a toy castle, slide, and children's books. The St. Regis's lobby included a colour-coded map of the numbered treaties published by the Assembly of Manitoba Chiefs, a pile of *First Nations Voice* newspapers, and a gift shop that sold shirts and hats featuring medicine wheels, dream catchers, and wolves.

The cluster of dollar stores around the MTS Centre—which CentreVenture would prefer "not to see"—continues, as of 2018, to provide a range of everyday necessities including groceries, clothing, shoes, diapers, toiletries, bedding, luggage, and children's toys. These stores primarily serve the people who live in the city centre, who raise children and take care of elders there, rather than the suburbanites who work in offices and attend NHL games. On weekends, the dollar stores—bustling with children, parents, teenagers, and elders picking through racks of shirts, jackets, and boots, and browsing aisles of fruit, bread, and canned goods—are by far the busiest places on Portage Avenue.

One of the liveliest corners of the SHED is Ellice Avenue and Hargrave Street, home to a large medical clinic and to the Quest Hotel, which bills itself as an "independent living facility providing accommodations for senior and/or tenants with special needs as well as First Nations medical access." The lobby of the Quest buzzes with people of all ages—children run around, elders chat on couches—and the dining room offers a popular hot buffet. Posters in the lobby speak to a northern First Nations audience, advertising weekly buses departing the Quest for places such as Easterville Junction (450 kilometres north of Winnipeg, near Chemawawin Cree Nation), and upcoming membership meetings for northern First Nations. Angela, the community organizer I spoke with, pointed out that CentreVenture systematically targets the most visible clusters of Indigenous peoples on city streets, and predicted that once CentreVenture shut down the St. Regis and the Carlton Hotels, the Quest would, sooner or later, be the next target.

Spaces of sustenance. Sports, Hospitality, and Entertainment District, Winnipeg, ca. 2018.

Across the street from the Quest is Portage Place, the shopping mall—formerly owned by multinational corporation Cadillac Fairview and now owned by Vancouver-based Peterson Group—built by Lloyd Axworthy and the CAI after co-opting the people's development vision articulated by the rail relocation movement in the 1970s and 1980s. Above all else, Portage Place is a bricks-and-mortar manifestation of public funding stolen—out of day cares, affordable housing, and community health clinics—from the people of Winnipeg's city centre. In a fitting twist, however, high-end retailers and restaurants catering to suburbanites have largely abandoned the mall since the 1980s, and it has increasingly come to serve the requirements of the city-centre community as it actually exists. Among other things, Portage Place now offers several dollar stores, a youth break-dancing non-profit, and a welfare office.

Portage Place is a modern-day successor to the Main Street strip in certain geographical imaginings of the city. "I saw you one last time in Portage Place," Trevor Greyeyes writes in his poem "The Strip," about a woman the protagonist met years earlier on Main Street.

CHAPTER 7 | CAPITALIST FRAGILITY, COLONIAL DURABILITY: REDRAWING URBAN APARTHEID

Spaces of sustenance. Sports, Hospitality, and Entertainment District, Winnipeg, ca. 2014.

In Greyeyes's poem, the Portage Place encounter comes at a time when "The strip was dying off / And only those who knew nothing else / Clung to the bones."[45] In Marvin Francis's poem "New Crossing," Portage Place gives rise to complex, hazardous encounters: "Last nite on that late nite crowded sidewalk I saw this kid get jacked for his stainless steel colored Walkman," the poem begins, "right up against the windows of the portage place bus shack." "I call this the madhattan bus transfer," Francis continues:

> there were about six of them, all hood young, all part of this downtown
> mall culture, the great economic hope of the last millennium, I know,
> let's build a mall and put a fountain in it, a mall of portages from street
> to jail to mall to street to long walk home in the hood late at nite.[46]

Portage Place was built across multiple city blocks in the 1980s and literally functions as a portal—or portage—connecting Portage Avenue and the city's central business district to Ellice Avenue and the more working-class West End and Central Park neighbourhoods. A four-storey-high atrium surrounds the Ellice Avenue entrance on the north side of the mall. The atrium—bright with lush gardens—is an obvious place to hang out, especially in the depths of winter, and mall-goers easily mount what dominant bloc–aligned urbanists might recognize as a "sidewalk ballet" if they cared to look. Kids in snowsuits sprint down ramps through the gardens; mothers chat and rock babies in strollers; elders and people in wheelchairs sip coffees, waiting for Handi-Transit to pick them up; Francis's "mall culture" teenagers socialize in big groups, laughing, teasing each other, going for smokes.

Around the corner from the atrium is the mall's food court—the busiest social space in the mall and perhaps the entire city centre. At least this seems to be the case for teenagers, elderly people, young parents, people with disabilities, low-wage workers, Indigenous peoples, and people of colour—actual residents of the city centre, in other words, rather than the white, able-bodied professionals from the suburbs for whom most of the downtown is designed. Offering pizza slices, subs, burgers, seafood, fried chicken, sushi, coffee, and Thai, Vietnamese, Chinese, and Indian dishes, with seating for 200, the Portage Place food court is practically the only place downtown to purchase hot, affordable food seven days a week from morning to night. A hundred people or more can be found at any given time dining, sipping coffee, chatting, checking their phones, sharing newspapers, or selling small household items, sketches, home remedies, and other things. The food court is busy every day of the week, for every meal, as lively for breakfast on Sunday as it is for lunch on Wednesday.

The atrium and food court are popular sites for political rallies and other community activities. Since 2012, many Idle No More actions have occurred at Portage Place, and the regular food court crowd is sprinkled with "NATIVE PRIDE" hats, AIM hoodies, jackets featuring emblems from various First Nations, and t-shirts promoting Indigenous radio stations. In addition to the Idle No More actions, the largest and most common rallies held at Portage Place have been organized in resistance to the mall's racist, abusive team of security guards.

As Francis pointed out, one of the portages at Portage Place—especially for young Indigenous peoples—is the mall-to-prison portage. The mall's corporate owners aspire to serve suburban office workers and are openly hostile to the city-centre community that actually uses the mall and whose movement for social justice was co-opted to build it. In 2008, mall management installed a small white box— dubbed "The Mosquito"—in front of the mall to deter young people from spending time there. The Mosquito emits a piercing high-frequency tone apparently audible only to youth, as adults' ears are supposed to have deteriorated sufficiently not to pick up the tone. Metal ribbons jut from the concrete planters outside the mall, making sitting impossible, and large signs announce "24 HOUR SURVEILLANCE...WPS CCTV IN EFFECT." The atrium near the mall's Ellice Avenue entrance is lined with knee-high planters—perfect for sitting and especially necessary for elderly mall-goers—but mall security has covered them with bold red and black signs that read "PLEASE DO NOT SIT ON THE PLANTERS" and threaten "CHARGES UNDER THE TRESPASS TO PROPERTY ACT." Each year since Idle No More, grassroots rallies have been held in the mall denouncing mall security's treatment of Indigenous peoples. Carrying signs, waving flags, and beating drums, people deliberately sit on the planters.

For Julie, a community organizer in the neighbourhoods north of Ellice Avenue—an area sometimes known as the Central Neighbourhoods, which includes Central Park, Centennial, and West Alexander—Portage Place is a major flash point in the battle over Winnipeg's city centre that pits poor, working-class, Indigenous, and people-of-colour residents against capital bent on catering to affluent white suburbanites. Julie, who is in her forties, has worked for a number of community organizations in the Central Neighbourhoods, including an immigrant and refugee social service organization; an advocacy group for incarcerated women; and, most recently, a grassroots community development corporation. More and more, Julie said, city-centre residents rely on Portage Place and downtown dollar stores to obtain the basic necessities of life, especially now that neighbourhood grocery stores have largely abandoned the city centre. "Where do people shop in Centennial?" said Julie. "There's no place for people to shop in Centennial, with the closing of Riediger's, and the closing of Extra Foods that was on Cumberland, there's really no place, and so people now are shopping at Dollarama, they're shopping at Giant Tiger, people go to Portage Place to shop."[47] Julie dismissed the imaginary dividing line—often invoked by CentreVenture—between the supposedly commercial downtown and the residential inner city as concealing this reality. "I think a lot of the people that are living in Central Park, they don't register for a lot of these [pro-business] organizations," said Julie. "I think they're invisible for a lot of people." As Julie's comments show, those who assume the existing city-centre community is present, human, and valuable—rather than disdainful and disposable—tend to perceive the dominant bloc's intense policing and displacement as an inscrutable, aggressive affront, neither a necessary nor a reasonable way to improve the city for anyone.

———————————

Winnipeg's city centre, as this brief sketch indicates, is already a place where the lives of thousands of families, children, elders, and parents take place. It is a territory that is crucial to the sustenance of life itself, where children and elders are cared for, where basic necessities—affordable groceries, hot food, children's toys, diapers, furniture, health care—are procured, and where people meet to socialize with one another. In this way, it is a crucial site of social reproduction, the whole set of mundane activities necessary to maintaining human life. Mapping this geography—however fleetingly—exposes the racism of CentreVenture's common sense hierarchy of people and places that matter. It also, perhaps, indicates the possible contours of a radical development vision aimed at maintaining and expanding space for life itself—rather than for capital accumulation— through which infrastructure for giving birth, educating children, feeding families, and housing the elderly becomes the measure of urban progress.

1	McKittrick, *Demonic Grounds*.

2	Winnipeg City Council Executive Policy Committee, "Item No. 8 Portage Avenue Action Strategy." Unless otherwise noted, all quotations dealing with the "Portage Avenue Action Strategy" are taken from this source.

3	City of Winnipeg, "Hansard of the Council of the City of Winnipeg Wednesday, July 21, 2010."

4	Marx, *Grundrisse*.

5	Kives, "Hotel Buyouts in Core for Fewer Drunks?"

6	Kives, "More Feet on Street Best Core Fix: Poll."

7	Cash, "Good To Grow. Winnipeg Is an Investor's Dream: Stable, Diversified and Growing."

8	Cash, "North Portage Gets Makeover."

9	Province of Manitoba, *The Community Revitalization Tax Increment Financing Act*.

10	CentreVenture, *2010 Annual Report*.

11	Winnipeg Free Press, "Let's Make It Happen."

12	Turner, "Licensing Mayhem"; Kives, "New Plan to Save Downtown."

13	The Thomsons are Canada's wealthiest billionaire family by far, with a net worth of $41 billion. Canadian Business, "Canada's Richest People 2018."

14	Cash, "North Portage Gets Makeover."

15	CentreVenture, "CentreVenture Development Corporation Announces Major Development in the Sports Hospitality and Entertainment District (SHED)."

16	Mungai, "Citizen Participation and the Renewal of a Declining Inner City Neighbourhood," 80.

17	Canad Inns Corporate Office, "Canad Inns to Rejuvinate MET as Vibrant Downtown Destination Funding Assists with Costs Unique to Historical Building."

18	Kirbyson, "Downtown Soaring with the Jets."

19	Edmonds, "Downtown Development Gets Kickstarted by Return of the NHL to Winnipeg; NHL Renews Interest in Downtown Winnipeg."

20	City of Winnipeg Executive Policy Committee, "Minute No.218 Establishment of a Tax Increment Financing Zone to Support Strategic Public Investments Consistent with the Portage Avenue Development Strategy and Sports Hospitality and Entertainment District."

21	Knight, "Tax Increment Financing and Social Enterprise: Promoting Equitable Community Revitalization in Winnipeg."

22	CentreVenture, "Revitalization Efforts of Portage Avenue Continue with CentreVenture's Strategic Purchase of St. Regis Hotel and Surface Parking Lots"; McLeod, Research interview for *Preserving the History of Institutional Development in Winnipeg*. This bar had been a hub for Two-Spirit people particularly in the 1970s and 1980s, along with the Silver Slipper Saloon across the street (on the lands of the present-day Radisson Hotel).

23	McGowan, "Speech to Winnipeg Realtors."

24	CentreVenture, "Revitalization Efforts of Portage Avenue Continue with CentreVenture's Strategic Purchase of St. Regis Hotel and Surface Parking Lots"; McGowan, "Speech to Winnipeg Realtors."

25	Winnipeg Free Press, "The Hotel Domino Effect."

26   McGowan, "McGowan to Talk Downtown Development at News Cafe. "

27   Winnipeg Police Service, "Winnipeg Police Service Announces Downtown Safety Strategy."

28   Ibid.

29   Brian, interview with author, Winnipeg, MB, July 11, 2013.

30   In 2018, the RCMP raided Fortress Real Developments headquarters on suspicion of mortgage fraud. CentreVenture remained effectively silent on the matter, once more highlighting the hypocrisy and racism of the urban wing's law-and-order approach. CBC, "CentreVenture Sells St. Regis Hotel, Plans for Parkade and Retail"; Kives, "St. Regis Hotel Plans to Lay Off Staff, Close as Prelude to Redevelopment"; Levasseur, "Future of Winnipeg's SkyCity Condos Questioned after RCMP Raid."

31   Hammond, "Carlton Inn Finds Itself on CentreVenture Buyout Chopping Block."

32   McNeill, "True North Square Towers to Rise in Spring"; Kives, "Winnipeg City Council Approves True North Square Tax Rebates." Gagliardi invested via his Vancouver-based Northland Properties Corp.

33   Sharpe, "New Doubts About CentreVenture."

34   McGowan, "CentreVenture Door Always Open."

35   CentreVenture, *2012 Annual Report*; McGowan, "Speech to Winnipeg Realtors."

36   Smith, *The New Urban Frontier: Gentrification and the Revanchist City*, 186.

37   Kirbyson, "City to Get a Touch of Glass"; Cash, "New Structure to Be King of Downtown?"; Schlesinger, "Jets Effect Heats up Winnipeg's Commercial Real Estate Market."

38   Schlesinger, "Jets Effect Heats up Winnipeg's Commercial Real Estate Market."

39   McGowan, "McGowan to Talk Downtown Development at News Café."

40   I attended the tour as a researcher.

41   Andrea, interview with author, Winnipeg, MB, July 6, 2013.

42   McKittrick, *Demonic Grounds*, xiv. Documenting dominant spatial narratives, geographer Katherine McKittrick writes, reveals dominant groups' predilection for "repetitively spatializing where nondominant groups 'naturally' belong...accomplished through economic, ideological, social, and political processes that see and position the racial-sexual body within what seem like pre-determined, or appropriate, places and assume that this arrangement is commonsensical." McKittrick, *Demonic Grounds*, xv.

43   McKittrick *Demonic Grounds*, x.

44   McKittrick *Demonic Grounds*, x; Césaire, *Discourse on Colonialism*; Hall, *A Casualty of Colonialism*; Gregory, *Black Corona*. This formulation is indebted to Césaire's concept of "a true humanism—a humanism made to the measure of the world," and by critiques of both colonial histories and sociological accounts of the "inner city" that exoticize and pathologize. Indigenous peoples "are seldom represented as wholly 'normal'...Rather they continue to be seen/presented as exotic and as outsiders to colonial and imperial projects," in most colonial histories, Norma Jean Hall writes. Hall, 'Settler': Upsetting the Semantics of Superiority, footnote 2.

45   Greyeyes, "The Strip."

46   Francis, *Bush Camp*, 36.

47   Julie, interview with author, Winnipeg, MB, August 2, 2013.

CHAPTER 8

FEELING FUTURISTIC: SETTLER-COLONIAL SPIRIT AND GRASSROOTS CRITIQUE

If we take to heart the fact that we make places, things, and selves, but not under conditions of our own choosing, then it is easier to take the risk of conceiving change as something both short of and longer than a single cataclysmic event. Indeed, the chronicles of revolutions all show how persistent small changes, and altogether unexpected consolidations, added up to enough weight, over time and space, to cause a break with the old order.

—Ruth Wilson Gilmore, *Golden Gulag*

Visions for radically different regional futures abound in Winnipeg's present-day city centre, where various future cities struggle to emerge through small changes and unexpected consolidations from the old city. In a landscape disfigured by 150 years of racial capitalism and settler colonialism, the images that dominate the streetscape—on large billboards and in the towers where power is concentrated—propose radical breaks from the past that are in fact innovative schemes for conserving longstanding relations of deadly inequality. Meanwhile, truly radical counter-development agendas—responding to the past century and a half of destruction, and motivated by non-capitalist and non-colonial visions of relating to each other and to the world—persist in the words and actions of the ordinary people who make places, things, and selves in Winnipeg's city centre.

"OWN THE FUTURE"

Winnipeg's city centre is littered with wooden billboards, vinyl banners, glassy street advertisements, and metal signs announcing the imminent arrival of a new city, and with it, a new lifestyle for the city's comfortable classes. The advertisements seek to lure moneyed suburbanites to the area, and in doing so, function as placeholders or simulations of the city envisioned, but not yet achieved, by the urban wing of the dominant regional bloc. Within the existing economically depressed, largely poor, working class, people-of-colour, and Indigenous present, a new, more profitable, luxurious, largely white and professional future is depicted at every turn. Images and slogans foment suburbanites' desires for a city centre they can finally call their own—a dreamy setting for an exceptional, sexy new urban life oriented around conspicuous consumption. "LIVE THE HIGH LIFE," commands a three-storey-high banner on Portage Avenue across from the MTS Centre. Around the corner, another enormous banner offers, "BE PART OF THE EXTRAORDINARY: GET CENTRED." "GLASSHOUSE IS A WHOLE NEW STYLE OF URBAN LIVING," proclaim the exterior walls of the Glasshouse simulation condo, where "TWENTY-ONE STOREYS OF CHIC DESIGN WELCOME YOU HOME." On Waterfront Drive, a new boutique hotel is under construction behind a banner reading "SUNSTONE GROUP: CREATING A NEW URBAN LIFESTYLE."

Sex, alcohol, and gambling—particularly as they figure in the desires of straight Canadian men—feature prominently in the new "family friendly" city, despite claims by the mayor, premier, and others that the old city is being vanquished in the name of safety and morality. The Chipmans' Shark Club casino is a celebrated outpost of the coming downtown. In the skywalk system near the MTS Centre, in the middle of the walkway, is mounted a sign—featuring a thin white woman in a glittering cocktail dress holding a martini, fist raised in celebration—notifying passersby that "SLOT MACHINES, BLACKJACK, AND ROULETTE ARE JUST STEPS AWAY." Other Shark Club promotional material features a blonde waitress—"Jenny from Red Deer"—in a little hockey jersey, handing you a beer: "GET TOGETHER WITH YOUR FRIENDS FOR A NIGHT YOU WON'T SOON FORGET." A sandwich board in front of the Shark Club advertises the Chipmans' other nearby investment: "WHEN YOU LIVE AT GLASSHOUSE, YOU CAN PRE-GAME IN YOUR LIVING ROOM."

In 2013, CentreVenture mounted a print and internet campaign called "Time to Live Here"—"condos & rentals for your new life downtown"—featuring a series of yuppie vignettes. It's "8:14 a.m. on Waterfront Drive," one begins, as a white man in an expensive suit strolls past The Warbler, holding a coffee. In the text, the man obsesses over the sexy artist who made his coffee, an opportunity his downtown condo affords him:

> I watch her hands tamp the grinds as she tells me about her new
> gallery showing. Her eyes tell me I should probably check it out.
> We both know I will. I step back into the warm morning, and in
> the shade of the city's most historic buildings, I walk the last few
> blocks to work.

Reminiscent of Mercredi's poem, "Mistress," the advertisement attempted to sell city-centre real estate to suburban men by promising them an opportunity to rub shoulders with, and possibly fuck, poor people. "Time to Live Here," in this limited way, actually made the existing city-centre community a selling point. But the dominant bloc's future city does not belong to minimum-wage workers; it simply features them as remnants who—for those ready to "forget their hate"—add decoration to the lives of luxury condo owners.

The physical juxtaposition between the officially wished-for city and the actually existing city can be jarring. Outside the Chipmans' Glasshouse simulation condo one day, a velvet rope divided intending condo buyers from the downtown mall crowd. Behind the rope, waiters served hors d'oeuvres to prospective settlers in suits, as the area's existing inhabitants—mothers with babies, resting elders, workers in hi-viz jackets—looked on from the other side. The Shark Club is another excellent example of urban-wing capital navigating an existing downtown that does not yet conform to its fantasy. In contrast to its sexy, youthful promo material, décor that features artificial exposed concrete, and a top-40 sound track, the social scene in the Shark Club—at least in the daytime—in fact more closely resembles a seniors' bingo hall than anything else. On any given day, the casino's roulette and blackjack tables can be found vacant and unstaffed, its rows of VLTs surrounded by the walkers, wheelchairs, and oxygen tanks of area elders playing the slots. As these contradictions accumulate, the top-down, manufactured essence of the "new urban lifestyle" becomes evident.

CentreVenture's "Time to Live Here" campaign compares uncannily to the Department of the Interior's "Letters from Satisfied Settlers" campaign in the 1900s, with the important exception that the former narratives are fictional. This is because the dominant bloc's twenty-first-century advertisements depict a city that is yet to come—it's up to "you" to make it happen. And if you don't get in now, you might be left behind. There is a particular alchemy at work here, where the future of capital accumulation, regional survival, and whiteness are brewed into a single post-industrial urban vision. Just like the nineteenth-century settler-colonial propaganda, the twenty-first-century version promises that intending settlers will get in on a regional future that is larger than any single one of them; and just as in the nineteenth-century scripts, the spectre of an historical break is deliberately circulated to drum up interest in real estate. "WATCH THE FUTURE UNFOLD," a CentrePoint advertisement urges. "OWN THE FUTURE," an ad for condos near Waterfront Drive commands. But this idea of a break with the past is, in fact, deployed to sell a development vision that deliberately *conserves* the regional balance of power, serving as it does real estate capital, merchant capital, and white desires for a modern lifestyle free from the contaminating influence of those who have been left out for the past century and a half. Just like the wholesome twentieth-century suburb and the rugged nineteenth-century frontier that came before it, the sexy twenty-first-century city is the space through which whiteness and capital accumulation—and therefore the entire region—will find new life.

While the benefits of such a scheme for urban capital and a segment of the city's professional classes is obvious, what is striking is how thoroughly this often violent and openly revanchist agenda has been cast as progressive and universally beneficial. In particular, the unwavering support for the scheme on the part of social-democratic planners, economists, and others in the left-leaning Manitoba NDP government that oversaw CentreVenture's first seventeen years is a strikingly impressive achievement.

New epoch for sale. James Avenue at Waterfront Drive, Winnipeg, ca. 2013.

The perceived importance of Winnipeg's city centre to the entire provincial economy—a perception that, as we have seen, has been formulated and circulated again and again by the urban wing of the dominant bloc—is a central factor in explaining this. But what is perhaps most interesting is the way that the urban wing has positioned its agenda as a progressive, even left-wing project, despite the fact that it conserves unequal power relations and only deepens the overwhelming level of unmet human need that exists in Winnipeg's city centre. CentreVenture—and the urban wing's agenda more broadly— was embedded within the workings of Manitoba's NDP government between 1999 and 2016, as the government justified upward state redistribution of resources to wealthy developers and luxury condo buyers as well as the elimination of poor, working-class, and Indigenous spaces, all in the name of regional progress.

Waterfront Drive, Winnipeg, ca. 2013.

White-supremacist slogan. Downtown Winnipeg, US presidential election night, ca. 2016. (Photo by Joel Ferguson, used with permission)

THE FUTURE THE NDP WANTS

Provincial government planners were not at all surprised when I approached them to talk about Winnipeg's urban development authority. "[CentreVenture is] a very important conduit, if you will, for the province to sort of achieve its downtown objectives," said Mike, a senior project manager in the Finance, Priorities and Planning Secretariat.[1] "We work hand in hand with CentreVenture all the time," Sandra, an assistant deputy minister, said in a separate interview. "Almost everything that they've done, we have contributed to."[2] The Manitoba government's "downtown objectives" seem culled straight from condo advertisements, insofar as they are aimed primarily at luring suburbanites and tourists to Winnipeg's city centre beyond the nine-to-five workday. Mike, who has a master's degree in economics, explained: "I guess it's often thought that to renew the downtown, to have a vibrant downtown, you have to have some people living in the downtown, not just working in the downtown." "The biggest challenge that I think developers face," he added, "is just sort of changing folks' mentality about thinking, considering downtown as a place to live." Mike's tendency to view the city centre through the eyes of a private land developer—rather than those actually living in the city centre—is indicative of the NDP's allegiances.

Mike told me that the NDP government works closely with luxury condo developers to make sure they can turn a sizable profit in Winnipeg's city centre. "We talked with some developers about what the gap is, if you will, in terms of what they needed to generate a reasonable rate of return," said Mike. "At the time, it was in the neighbourhood of 6 to 10 percent." "What we did was we partnered with one developer, we came up with sort of a model building…[to] get a sense as to what the gap was," he continued, "and it was thought to be fifteen to twenty thousand dollars a door, for example, a subsidy, in the form of a tax break would be sufficient." This planning process led to the creation of the Downtown Residential Development Grant Program, a pool of money the provincial government gave to CentreVenture to dole out to condo developers.

Sandra, on the other hand, had been closely involved with CentreVenture's hotel shutdowns. She told me that the NDP government commissioned a confidential report that recommended the elimination of no fewer than seven low-income city-centre hotels, and that this report contributed to CentreVenture's purchase of the St. Regis. "We did a study with [a consulting firm] on the St. Regis, the Garrick, and I can't remember the name of the other, but three, specifically," said Sandra, "and in the report they also named another four that they recommended be purchased." "And so what CentreVenture did was they made an offer to purchase the St. Regis Hotel. We contributed to the cost of the purchase, they closed the beverage room and the VLTs," Sandra continued, "and then they recently put out an RFP [request for proposals] for redevelopment of the site. …So, the idea is to try to do this with several of those downtown hotels."

The same fears and prejudices that motivate CentreVenture's desire to enforce urban apartheid also seem to motivate the NDP. "Crime," "safety," and "comfort" were very often at the fore of provincial officials' explanations about the importance of CentreVenture. "CentreVenture is always involved to some extent when we're talking about crime and safety initiatives," Mike told me. "Every year we fund, we've been funding more and more police," he continued. "Recent commitments have focused on what we call beat cops, to patrol the downtown, you know, to give people a feeling of safety." I asked Mike why policing was so integral to city-centre redevelopment. "A lot of it stems from the fact that even though the downtown's made strides in terms of getting, you know, higher income people living there," Mike replied, "there's still a segment of the population downtown that is lower income. Not to stereotype, but you know, where you have lower income people, crime is generally prevalent in that area."

The NDP has orchestrated both the "swamping"—to recycle John A. Macdonald's phrasing—of the city centre, sometimes referred to as "densification," and the removal of existing city-centre people. Mike told me the provincial government hopes initiatives like CentreVenture's SHED will spearhead a demographic shift in the area, which itself could reduce crime levels. "With crime, one of the best ways of addressing that is to improve the densification of downtown. So, one of the ways for addressing that is getting more people to go downtown after hours, and to go for dinner, or shows, or that sort of thing, and to have people living downtown, because the more people living downtown, that has a positive impact in terms of reducing crime."

In Sandra's view, however, there is already a "critical mass" of people downtown—who effectively scare away the class of people to whom the city's future truly belongs. When I asked Sandra why her office took an interest in shutting down the St. Regis Hotel's bar, she told me: "What [the St. Regis's bar] contributes to is a whole host of drunken people on the streets of downtown Winnipeg. So that, um, element of people tends to make people feel unsafe. So if you're walking in the middle of the afternoon downtown, and there are a bunch of drunks on the sidewalk, or people are hitting you up for money, it's like, 'I don't even...I wouldn't live down there.'" "There has been criticism that just doing that just moves the problem out of the downtown, and there's some validity to that complaint," Sandra continued, "except that because of the critical mass of the number of these beverage rooms, you get more of this kind of, um, activity, than you would if it was dispersed throughout the city." Of course, the keystone of the NDP's new city—the MTS Centre—could well be the single largest concentration of public intoxication between Calgary and the Great Lakes. Thousands of drunken men regularly spill onto city-centre sidewalks from the MTS Centre, which it should go without saying, also tends to make people feel unsafe.

"Urban Indian" removal was a clear objective for Sandra. When I asked her what she thought CentreVenture meant when it talked about "social issues" downtown, Sandra replied: "One is that critical mass of people that go to the beverage rooms, and the number of single-room occupancy hotels that we have." "Some of the social issues are homelessness, and, um, we have a very transient Aboriginal population," Sandra continued. "We have an urban Aboriginal population that's higher than any other city in Canada, and the interesting thing about that population is that they're not a stable population. ...So there will be people from a reserve who move to town, and maybe are here for a year, or six months, and then they move back to the reserve." "And all of the social supports exist in the downtown. ...So, homelessness shelters, housing, social service agencies, they all have services in the downtown, so that tends to put everybody in the same physical space," said Sandra, erasing both the rich and enduring Indigenous presence in Winnipeg and the role of previous urban apartheid regimes in producing such a landscape. It was the physical concentration, but also the emotions of poor and Indigenous peoples downtown, that troubled Sandra. I asked Sandra what the difference was, in her view, between intoxicated people at the St. Regis Hotel and 15,000 intoxicated hockey fans at the MTS Centre. "I would say it's a quick, sort of happy crowd," Sandra said of the MTS Centre crowd. "There's not a lot of fighting or things like that. Whereas people who start drinking at ten in the morning, and, you know, by midnight they're just not people you want to mix with."

When I asked provincial planners and economists why the Manitoba government was so interested in manipulating the demographics of Winnipeg's downtown, I hoped to hear a more coherent and substantive plan for the region's economic future than the vague, jargon-filled documents on the public record. But what I heard was a nearly identical regurgitation of those documents. The same old metaphors were rolled out to explain Winnipeg's exceptional importance to the provincial economy: "Winnipeg is frankly the backbone of the province"; "the heartbeat of Manitoba is the city of Winnipeg"; "Winnipeg needs to be a healthy, vibrant community, and the downtown is key to that." I was informed that the specific historical and geographical conditions that led the province to invest in city-centre redevelopment included "a decline in vibrancy of the downtown"; "a lot of vacant windows"; and the slightly more revealing, "you know, we were losing head offices to Calgary and Toronto and Vancouver and everywhere else."

I pressed Mike, the trained economist, to explain how exactly CentreVenture—or developer subsidies, hotel shutdowns, and police in general—contribute to the economic well-being of Manitobans. He offered several ways in which he believed the authority bolstered the regional economy. The first was that CentreVenture, in his view, could help to reduce urban sprawl, saving the state money in infrastructural expenditures. "So if you have a situation where you have more businesses locating in downtown Winnipeg, more people living in downtown Winnipeg," said Mike, "I guess it can to some degree mitigate the urban sprawl, which from an economic standpoint would mean building fewer roads, and installing less infrastructure in the far-reaching areas of the city." Mike even suggested that CentreVenture could make the city more environmentally friendly. "If you have a situation where more people are living downtown, you have potentially less car congestion, which leads potentially to less greenhouse gas emissions." Indeed, the urban wing is adept at turning criticisms of suburban sprawl and car culture—often citing the work of urbanists Jane Jacobs and Richard Florida—into a selling point for luxury condos, and at justifying their thefts as crucial to the moral, social, and environmental health of the city.

Eventually Mike settled, perhaps more substantively, on CentreVenture's role in attracting tourist spending. "From an economic development and a tourist aspect, if you can get your downtown to a point where it becomes a destination for outside folks, that can have positive impacts too," he said, going on to cite the expanded convention centre, the then forthcoming Canadian Museum for Human Rights, and the return of the NHL. "When you pair all these things together," Mike continued, "a vibrant downtown has the ability to generate positive economic benefits from tourist draws, both within Canada and even just within the province. …If you have your capital city that's exporting and generating a lot of jobs, that has direct benefits in terms of increased tax revenue, which allows the government to do more things, to invest in health care, to invest in education, downtown redevelopment, so it's very important from that standpoint."

Apparently unsatisfied with this rationale, Mike summoned an additional economic explanation that amounted to positing a kind of psychological trickle-down effect. "At the end of the day, these things are a point of pride for people who live in the city," he said. "Your overall psyche's improved when you see cranes in the downtown. It just makes people feel better, and it provides a positive thing for people, which quite often translates into economic success as well." Mike reiterated this point later, saying that "slowly, progressively, the downtown is evolving to a place where people want to be again…it's a point of pride for people, I think, that does translate into tangible economic benefits." Without apartheid, police, and notions of Indigenous disposability, in other words, the good vibes necessary for the city's economic revival would remain elusive.

Even if there were a substantive economic rationale—something beyond padding real estate profits—for the dominant agenda of bulldozing, policing, and swamping the existing city-centre community, it would remain a fundamentally racist process of sacrificing some for the benefit of others. There is no substantive economic basis, however—only buzzwords and vague assertions—for the idea that subsidizing city-centre real estate profits materially benefits all members of the community. For all mainstream political parties, this idea is simply the unquestioned common sense that has been solidified in the minds of planners, politicians, and bureaucrats through decades of insistent organizing by the urban wing. For actual city-centre residents dealing with staggering levels of unmet human need, however, it is anything but common sense.

THE PEOPLE'S ANALYSIS

When momentum is built for a development vision that prioritizes human life over real estate profits, it seems likely that it will come not from existing planners and politicians—whether they have social-democratic allegiances or not—but from long-time residents and organizers of city-centre neighbourhoods. The history of struggle in these neighbourhoods against decades of neglect, disinvestment, and demonization has produced a development analysis that rejects the trickle-down theories of the past 30 years and beyond.

Throughout the winter of 2014, I spoke extensively with six community organizers in Winnipeg's Centennial neighbourhood—a tree-lined district of small houses, duplexes, apartment blocks, and warehouses where a railway spur line used to run. Centennial is a community of nearly 2,500 people on the northwestern edge of CentreVenture's jurisdiction. Centennial has a median household income of $24,093—Winnipeg's citywide median household income is $57,925—and 60 percent of its residents are considered "low income." Statistics Canada estimates that 41 percent of Centennial residents are Indigenous, but these counts are typically considered low; one organizer I spoke with estimated 80 percent of the community was Indigenous. Thirty percent of Centennial residents are non-Indigenous people of colour—"visible minorities"—according to Statistics Canada.[3]

I spoke with Garth, whose family has lived in the area for more than 50 years (they were displaced by city council's 1960s Main Street urban renewal schemes). Garth was friendly, mild-mannered, and straightforward. At the time, he held a top position at the small grassroots Centennial Community Improvement Association (CCIA), and years earlier he had been involved with the slightly larger Central Neighbourhoods Development Corporation (CNDC). Garth got involved in neighbourhood organizing in the early 2000s when the Winnipeg Foundation—a multimillion-dollar philanthropist organization then experimenting with a five-year neighbourhood-based community development model—identified him as a potential "neighbourhood leader" and he got involved in the foundation's "Centennial Project."

Garth and I spoke over coffee in the dining room of the downtown hotel where he works. He told me he viewed the Centennial Project as the first time the broader city had significantly paid attention to conditions in Centennial. "[The Winnipeg Foundation] wanted to find a neighbourhood that was somewhat neglected throughout the times," said Garth. "We are one of the poorest neighbourhoods in Winnipeg...and so the city really hasn't put a lot of money back into the community."[4] Almost a decade later, Garth was ambivalent about the legacy of the Centennial Project. "It has been good and it has been bad," he said. "In those five years, actually, there was a lot of money funnelled into the Centennial Community." But by the end of the project, "everyone that was hired to do the work pretty much disappeared, so from that point on we were left to struggle and survive on our own." The relatively new CCIA has only one full-time staff member, a neighbourhood housing coordinator, and the organization struggles to get things done. To Garth, the CCIA's lack of resources was a stark indicator of how the state has abandoned Centennial.

I met with Chris, a community organizer who works with parents of school-age children, in the Family Room of a school in Centennial. Family Rooms have been established in several schools in Winnipeg's Indigenous neighbourhoods with the aim of building trust between parents and their children's school, Chris told me, something made extremely difficult by the impact of Indian Residential Schools on many parents' lives. The Family Room is a highly active community space where parents and children eat lunch, drink coffee, read, watch TV, use the computer, and work with Chris to navigate a variety of issues from finding childcare to filling out Manitoba Housing applications.

Chris spoke quickly and intently about neighbourhood struggles. Like Garth, Chris was emphatic that Centennial had long been neglected by the city's dominant development visions. "We always seem to be overlooked," Chris told me. "I see things happening in the South End all the time, but what's happening here?"[5] "People think they don't have a voice," Chris explained, describing a sense of powerlessness built up over years by outside forces—landlords, politicians, planners—with the power to dictate neighbourhood change.

The palpable sense of unjust abandonment in Centennial—of being "neglected," "overlooked," and "left to struggle and survive on our own"—is rooted in a severe decline in access to the basic necessities of life, most pressingly food and shelter. "There's no housing here," said Chris, who told me that much of her time is spent helping parents navigate the housing application process or fighting with landlords, sometimes in court, to be treated with fairness. "The biggest issues are always with the housing," said Garth, "whether it's affordable, whether it's liveable." Chris told me that most parents she knows strongly want to remain in Centennial—to maintain social ties and keep their kids in the same school—but housing is so scarce that families are often forced to move away. "Landlords are handing out evictions like candy these days," she said, noting that several parents at her school had been given eviction notices in the middle of the school year. (It is illegal in Manitoba to evict families with school-age children during the school year.) Chris believed the intent of such evictions is often to raise rents and replace them with higher income tenants.

Part of the problem is that landlords have allowed a large portion of Centennial's original housing stock to become uninhabitable. "There are so many boarded-up houses around here," said Chris, pointing out the window, "that people started saying, 'Why are these houses boarded up when the thing we need most is more housing?'" She told me that residents organized a neighbourhood housing audit, counting boarded-up houses and trying to find out who owned them. Many of the houses turned out to be owned by landlords in Alberta, British Columbia, and the US who were impossible to track down. Much of the housing that is available, Chris told me, is too small for neighbourhood families—many if not most of whom have several children, often three or more. It is essentially impossible, she said, to find a place that is both large enough as well as affordable, even from Manitoba Housing, where large units are in extremely high demand. This is not a matter of mere comfort; if parents are unable to obtain the correct ratio of bedrooms to children, the fear is authorities will take custody of their children due to inadequate housing conditions.

Homelessness is a major issue in Centennial. Aideen, who runs a popular adult drop-in, primarily for solvent users, out of a former bank building, told me that most of the people who come in are homeless.[6] Many spend winter days in Portage Place, the MTS Centre lobby, or some other segment of the city's heated indoor skywalk and tunnel complex. When they are evicted from these spaces, Aideen said, they often spend the night in underground parking garages or other out-of-view public places. Part of this is because solvent users in particular are banned from one of the city's largest homeless shelters (just outside of Centennial) and are often picked on in other shelters—having their shoes stolen, for instance. On the day I visited—in the middle of one of the coldest winters in decades—Aideen told me she knew that at least four people had slept under a nearby bridge that week.

Centennial faces another, more recent process of neglect in the mass exodus of grocery stores from the neighbourhood, and from more or less the entire city centre. Chris narrowed her eyes in frustration as she listed, one by one, the nearby grocery stores that had closed in the past year or two: "Riediger's on Isabel," "Extra Foods on Notre Dame," "Zellers in the Bay basement," and so on.[7] "Where's the closest place you can walk for groceries, if you didn't have your vehicle?" Chris asked a woman who was heating something up in the kitchen of the Family Room. "Nowhere," the woman said bluntly, telling us that she usually drives to a big chain grocery store in the suburbs. "There aren't any mom and pop stores?" Chris asked. The woman in the kitchen said she preferred not to shop at stores like that because of the limited selection and higher prices. That preference is something many in the neighbourhood—without access to a vehicle or effective public transportation—cannot afford.

There are several food banks in and around Centennial, and I asked Garth if people in the neighbourhood rely on them. Garth hesitated at first. "Mmm, I wouldn't like to say that," Garth answered, "but I know, I know there is." "We have Freight House, which is our community centre," Garth continued, "and there are actually food banks I think twice a week there, whether the people actually require it or not, I don't know, but I know it's put to use." Garth's hesitations—"I wouldn't like to say that" and "whether the people actually require it or not"—was striking. The indignity of the situation made him uneasy, but at the same time, he felt a responsibility to acknowledge the reality of the situation.

Organizers in Centennial are doing what they can in the face of the grocery store exodus, but it's an uphill battle. A mainstay of the drop-in Aideen runs is a two-dollar Sunday brunch, which attracts neighbourhood families in addition to the usual drop-in crowd. "For most families here, it's been years since they've been able to take their kids out for breakfast, if ever," said Aideen. "Now they can." Julie, from the CNDC, told me she helped to organize a forum at Portage Place about the dearth of grocery options downtown. "There were so many people at the forum," Julie told me. "There were so many people around the periphery that didn't have a chance to come in and actually participate in the break-out sessions."[8] A petition had been drafted to press City Council to address the problem. "I took some of the petitions to talk to people in the food court about the grocery situation downtown," said Julie, "and I talked to maybe two or three people before security told me I had to leave the food court. They said I would have to get permission from management if I wanted to do that." The petition, so far, has come to nothing.

Warehousing the poor. Homeless shelter, Centennial neighbourhood, Winnipeg, ca. 2014.

The neighbourhood organizers I talked to view the fact that CentreVenture's jurisdiction overlaps with Centennial as more of a threat than an opportunity. As a community organizer for more than ten years in Centennial, Garth said he has had zero contact with the City's development authority. I told him I found that a bit surprising, given CentreVenture's broadly defined mandate to pursue "the economic, physical, and social revitalization of downtown Winnipeg."[9] "CentreVenture itself is more based towards businesses as opposed to the social and economic well-being of the residents itself," Garth explained matter-of-factly. "Their budgets are based on businesses, not the people themselves," he continued. "It doesn't really translate into any social or economic [benefits to] the community itself." Garth was being understated and diplomatic, but he couldn't have been clearer.

The organizers I talked with in Centennial refused to acknowledge any possibility that the neighbourhood would benefit from the $2 billion attracted by CentreVenture to the downtown, especially that invested in luxury condos. This is how I posed the question to Garth, paraphrasing what Mike, the government economist had said to me: "There's a hope that increased investment in the downtown built environment—places like the MTS Centre, the Convention Centre expansion, this new condo and hotel development on Portage—will improve the local economy and improve the economic circumstances of all different kinds of people. Do you feel like that is happening at all, in Centennial?" To this, Garth replied:

> Well, Centennial is, again, a different type of place. If we were looking at the same type of residents that would be living in these condos, we would definitely be talking about gentrification then. Because again, the people that would be living in that newest condo...I believe they're selling for about $160,000, $170,000 for 500 square feet. And that's basically enough for a single person. We're talking all families in Centennial right now. There's very, very few single people living in Centennial.

As it turns out, most of the downtown residential development brokered by CentreVenture looks particularly unfriendly to families. Even new housing advertised as "affordable" is usually out of the reach of Centennial families. "There's a condo development going up down the street," Chris told me. "The sign says, 'CONDOS $120,000'—parents can't afford that, with condo fees and everything." And yet, billboards outside this particular condo development advertise it as "AFFORDABLE." At one point, Chris asked me: "Have they [CentreVenture] done anything that is supposed to be affordable for everyone, or for the community here?" While there have been one or two developments CentreVenture has worked with non-profit organizations to build, the first thing that came to mind was the Avenue Building on Portage Avenue, which

Bethany from CentreVenture told me included eight affordable rental apartments as a result of conditions placed on a provincial government grant the developers received. "Okay," Chris replied, "so my question is, what is the application process like? And also, how big are these units? Because families here need three, four bedrooms." Before this, Chris told me about the process of applying to Manitoba Housing—how families never know when they'll be selected to receive housing, or where in the city it will be, so they sometimes end up leaving the neighbourhood when they'd rather stay. The Avenue Building might have been an attractive, nearby source of affordable housing for people in Centennial, except that CentreVenture and the developer never thought to inform people in Centennial about it.

In the Family Room with Chris, I had a list of the development projects that CentreVenture and the provincial planners I had spoken with routinely cite as the best examples of the city's improving fortunes. I asked Chris if she thought any of them had benefitted people in Centennial. "Let me see this list," she said keenly, and went down the page with her index finger. First up was "Main Street redevelopment." I mentioned the new WRHA and United Way headquarters on Main. Chris slowly shook her head. "The families are unaware of what programs/services are happening in this building." "Waterfront Drive?" "Hmm, nope," said Chris. "We do go to the Forks sometimes, or to a baseball game when we receive complimentary tickets from an organization." The new hockey arena was on the list. "Yeah, the MTS Centre. I am not sure how many families can afford to go there," said Chris, "unless, of course, the hockey program receives a donation of tickets for games maybe through our school resource officer [a police officer]." "I was thinking about the Convention Centre," said Chris as she went down the list. "We went to a career expo there a few months ago with several interested parents, but other than that, not really. ...Maybe if they had more family-orientated programs that would be the kind of thing we would go to," she added. "And what's CentrePoint?" When I told her Chris laughed a bit, and quickly said "nope." "Like, who is that for?" she asked, facetiously.

Aideen had a somewhat novel theory about how the dominant development vision might improve the economic circumstances of people in Centennial. "A lot of people around here," Aideen told me, "are employed in the underground economy, or what I like to call the secondary economy." She said that crowds attending Jets games, or coming downtown for dinner and a show might increase the business of "kids on bikes" who sell weed downtown. Or, Aideen said, she wouldn't be surprised if there was a "posse of kids" that take game and concert nights at the MTS Centre as opportunities to break in to the influx of parked cars from the suburbs.

If I was really looking for people who benefitted from the dominant development vision, Garth suggested I speak to a group called Residents of the Exchange District (RED), which many condo owners on Waterfront Drive are associated with. "We've never really been in touch," said Garth, "but they're our direct neighbours, and demographically they're very, very different from what we have in our community." "They're the upwardly mobile," Garth explained. "They're the ones who live in the condos and everything, right on Princess [Street] itself. They're not the ones that would venture deep into Centennial." I asked Garth if he viewed RED as a potential ally for the CCIA. "Their concerns are a little bit different than what our concerns would be," Garth told me. "You know, their December was having a dinner at one of these furniture stores for $150 a person." Garth chuckled. "That's beyond what the concerns of our residents are. A lot of our residents are concerned with getting a hamper, you know," said Garth, referring to a Christmastime tradition of charities donating food to poor families.

Garth's reference to Princess Street marked that thoroughfare as the place where the luxury-condo neighbourhood formed by Waterfront Drive and the city's warehouse district—the Exchange District—encroaches on Centennial, which Garth contrasted as "a lot more social housing, like Manitoba Housing, there is affordable housing…there are some rooming houses. Again, demographically, it's a very different group of people." At times Garth didn't seem to put too much stock into the accelerated construction of luxury condos and other development nearby. When I asked him about the "divide" between RED and the CCIA, Garth said, "I wouldn't necessarily call it a divide—it is what it is. They developed all these condos for almost $200,000 on Princess itself. Is there any need for them to come into Centennial? I wouldn't think so." At other times, though, he seemed more concerned. "There's always consideration for gentrification in our communities; there's always concerns," he said. "I see all the money being put into downtown, and it's a trickle-down effect into Centennial. We'll see some advantages to it, but…like I said, we really don't want to see a lot either because of the gentrification effect." "Housing values have risen almost by triple" in the past ten years, Garth added with concern.

Nor was the increased policing of the city centre welcomed by the Centennial community organizers I spoke with. I asked Garth about the police presence in the neighbourhood. "For a while there it was a little bit unfriendly," he said. "I'd have to say, you know, tension. …The police chief at the time wouldn't really want to listen to your concerns. He just kind of gave in, at times, to the city council." While Garth was hopeful that a new police chief would treat the neighbourhood more fairly, Aideen was not. The WPS is not typically friendly to the people who frequent the drop-in, according to Aideen. "People talk about the new police chief and his 'community policing,' how he listens, and everything, but he's no different from the rest," she said. "I've seen him, when he was just a beat cop. I've seen him kick girls off the block, when I used to work at [a drop-in for neighbourhood sex workers]…I've seen him drop girls off at the edge of town and steal their shoes." Aideen told me she was fed up with the constant demonization of the neighbourhood, especially the stigmatization of the solvent users she works with. She told me about doing an interview recently with a supposedly progressive online magazine. Aideen was disappointed by the resulting article, which she described as "sensationalistic." The author sent her a link to the article. "That's great," Aideen responded, "but I read the same thing in the *Sun* three months ago." One of the author's arguments was that solvent use should be criminalized. "Did that work for other drugs?" said Aideen. "They had a war on drugs, how did that go? I know teenagers who are locked up at Rockwood for weed." Aideen suggested an alternative approach: "Try asking why there's no housing for people, why there are no resources." A significant part of the answer to Aideen's questions is that city-centre residents' grassroots development agendas have been disregarded for more than 50 years while ideas of a progressive urban future have been monopolized by a development agenda based strictly on capitalist profits.

COUNTER FUTURES

While questions such as Aideen's—questions surrounding resource distribution and unmet human needs—are evaded by the dominant development agenda for the city, they are taken up by a diversity of radical and progressive struggles rooted in Centennial and Winnipeg's broader city centre. Just as the dominant development agenda relies on visual placeholders of its desired urban future, existing city-centre residents articulate counter development agendas through the physical environment. In some cases, CentreVenture has come under more or less direct critique. "YOUTH AGAINST CHRIST" appeared in black spray paint on the side of a West End building in the days following the unsuccessful challenge to the Youth For Christ development in 2010. "CULTURE NOT CONDOS" read the marquee of a Main Street bar following a failed attempt by CentreVenture to give $10,000 apiece to anyone buying a new downtown condo. Other grassroots place-making activities challenge the North-West's history of settler colonialism. A large poster featuring the word "TREATY" in the style of Obama's "HOPE" poster appeared throughout the city centre at the height of Idle No More. On Main Street, "NATIVE LAND ALWAYS" is written over top of a commercial realtor's "FOR SALE" sign in a vacant lot. "GET RIEL!" is spray-painted in bright colours everywhere. On a wall right behind the "affordable" $120,000 condos in Centennial is written the reply, "FTP FUCK THE POLICE 4 LIFE." Throughout the city centre, a butterfly emblem reading "NO MORE STOLEN SISTERS" spreads its wings.

By far the most powerful counter-development agenda organized in Winnipeg in 2013 and 2014 was that forged by Idle No More, a movement that has been called the most "sustained, united, and coordinated nationwide mobilization of Indigenous nations against a legislative assault on our rights since the proposed White Paper of 1969."[10] While Idle No More organizing in Winnipeg did not openly target the dominant urban development vision, it did make extensive use of urban space—mostly but not entirely in the city centre—to articulate opposition to dominant capitalist extraction-based development agendas that threatened Indigenous lands, communities, and the earth itself. In Winnipeg, Idle No More brought together a wide range of Indigenous and non-Indigenous peoples in unified opposition to the privileging of capitalist profits—in the

Geography of refusal. Wellington Avenue and Victor Street, West End Winnipeg, ca. 2010.
(Photo by Ian Whetter, used with permission)

    Geography of refusal. North End Winnipeg, ca. 2013.

Geography of refusal. Times Changed High and Lonesome Club, Main Street at St. Mary Avenue, Winnipeg, ca. 2018.

form of oil, gas, mining, hydro, and timber interests—over all other collective objectives, including sustaining human life, honouring Indigenous sovereignty, and preserving the existence of the earth. In the process, activists and organizers countered the divisiveness and racism of reactionary conservatives with a concerted effort to reach across the processes of othering and demonization that racial capitalism thrives on.

Urban Idle No More actions highlight the degree to which everyday life in the racial-capitalist city isolates and individualizes. Instead of attempting to overcome these dynamics—suburban anti-Native racism, for instance—CentreVenture empowers feelings of fear and suspicion through its strategy of eradication, policing, and surveillance of the existing city-centre community for the comfort of suburbanites. Perhaps the most central place-making activity of the Idle No More movement is the act of dancing with strangers in public. The "Round Dance Revolution," as it has been called, breaks down the prevailing isolation, literally connecting masses of people who hold hands, form one big circle, and dance to the beat of hand drummers.[11] People can be anxious and self-conscious at first, smiling awkwardly at each other as they grasp hands. By the end, people are at ease, talking and laughing with each other, feeling energized and joyful, the way it feels to glimpse other ways of being in the world and to begin building the power to stretch glimpses into lifetimes.

Idle No More round dances challenge the specific divide between Indigenous and non-Indigenous peoples in the city, something that dominant development visions work hard to solidify. Many Idle No More callouts in 2013 and 2014 included the message "ALL WELCOME," while some featured an emblem with red, yellow, black, brown, and white fists encircling the words "IDLE NO MORE." "We are all one" was a popular chant. Among other things, Idle No More created space for a variety of groups and movements in the city to broach the possibility of new or reinvigorated alliances.

Many large labour organizations, for example—including the Canadian Union of Postal Workers, the Canadian Union of Public Employees, and the Winnipeg Labour Council—expressed solidarity with Idle No More in written statements and joined in marches and round dances in Winnipeg and across the country. Urban spaces created by Idle No More organizers became places of spontaneous solidarity. One day, an event organized by local prison abolitionists—to gather and sing songs in front of the Remand Centre, a 289-person jail in downtown Winnipeg, in a show of support for the people imprisoned there—was joined by a crowd of Idle No More demonstrators from a separate event. The two groups joined in a spontaneous round dance that filled the entire street as people watched from the jail's windows. In the summer of 2013, Idle No More organizers convened a weekly gathering called "Water Wednesdays"—organized in response to federal bill C-45 and "the Canadian Government's reckless stewardship of our water resources"[12]—in a park beside the daunting provincial government campus that includes the Manitoba Legislature, Land Titles building, Law Courts, and Remand Centre. The park became a meeting place for organizers and activists of all stripes. The anti-violence organizers of "Meet Me at the Bell Tower" mixed with people wearing the red squares of the anti-austerity movement; anti-homelessness activists that share bannock and other food on Main Street mixed with members of the local Copwatch. People from Shoal Lake 40 First Nation—where Winnipeg extracts its drinking water—visited to speak about how the community had been literally turned into an island by the infrastructure built to send water to Winnipeg and how Shoal Lake itself does not have access to clean tap water. Indigenous radio stations, university radio stations, and other alternative media were regularly on hand. In this way, Idle No More began to activate the potential for "unexpected consolidations" in Winnipeg's city centre, as diverse struggles against racial capitalism took small steps toward joining forces.

Through Idle No More, this latent coalition brought a counter analysis of the dominant regional bloc into the streets. Activists occupied important economic spaces—major downtown intersections, shopping malls, the MTS Centre, the airport, and the street in front of the *Winnipeg Sun*'s offices—to highlight a series of connections between historical, economic, and cultural dynamics that work against social and environmental justice. "1812–2012 SAME FIGHT SAME GOVERNMENT" read one sign in a march down Portage Avenue; "RAISE CORPORATE TAXES NOT CARBON LEVELS" read another at an Elsipogtog solidarity rally in front of Portage Place; "RACISM IS HATE—THE SUN SELLS HATE," activists in front of the *Sun* offices pointed out; others wore hoodies and shirts featuring the simple reminder: "GOT LAND? THANK AN INDIAN."

Occupying the stolen city. Idle No More demonstration, (R) Percy Ballantyne, Portage Place shopping mall, Winnipeg, ca. 2012. Photo by John Woods. Winnipeg Free Press, December 22, 2012. (Courtesy of Winnipeg Free Press)

Resisting captivity. Idle No More round dance and Caroling With Conviction action, Remand Centre, Winnipeg, ca. 2012. Photo by John Woods. Winnipeg Free Press, December 23, 2012. (Courtesy of Winnipeg Free Press)

As if to confirm that Idle No More activists had gotten a thing or two correct about the regional racial order, local reactionary backlash to the movement was widespread and often brutal. CSIS and the WPS monitored the movement closely. One organizer found leaflets with the text "I'LL HANG WITH RIEL" on the steps of a bank at Portage and Main during a New Year's Eve round dance there. (The message eerily echoes a nineteenth-century action at the same corner, where an effigy of Riel was strung up alongside a racist slogan). Rumours circulated that a North End statue of Chief Peguis had been vandalized. The *Sun* sponsored a contest in which readers were invited to find the most fitting descriptor for Attawapiskat Chief Theresa Spence, a prominent figure of the Idle No More movement then on a hunger strike in Ottawa. Winnipeg-based Aboriginal Peoples Television Network (APTN) reported that entries published by the *Sun* included a number of racial slurs.[13] A *Free Press* poll, responding to a proposal from activists, asked its readers, "Should Victoria Day be renamed to honour aboriginals?" to which 89 percent of respondents answered "No." The editor-in-chief of a small town newspaper—the *Morris Mirror*—in southern Manitoba made national headlines when he gave a year-in-review "thumbs down" to "Canada's native community...who are demanding unrealistic expectations of the government and who in some cases are acting like terrorists in their own country." At the Chipmans' MTS Centre, Idle No More activists were ejected from a pre-season Winnipeg Jets game for chanting and displaying signs related to the movement.

The regional tradition of anti-Native racism that reared its ugly head in reaction to Idle No More was incubated by, among many other things, the dominant bloc's promotion of an urban future cleansed of Native people, which reached a rare level of intensity in the same years. The dominant bloc's decision to deepen, rather than abolish a contradiction of its own making—the racial vilification of people in an area it now needed to lure moneyed white people to—built anti-Native racism into the new urban identities that suburbanites will make for themselves. This is signalled first and foremost by the fact that the suburb-to-city-centre migrations arranged by the dominant bloc are structured for suburbanites to *replace*, rather than associate with, listen to, and align with existing inhabitants. The new state-promoted urban identities are made through the acts of—or even vague desires to participate in—replacement, silencing, and ultimately land theft, which the dominant bloc simultaneously hides and misconstrues to feel good, proper, progressive, cosmopolitan, environmentally friendly, adventurous, and futuristic.

If this cycle continues, the next 150 years will be more of the same: the stealing of Indigenous lands and social wealth by millionaires and billionaires; redistribution of some of this wealth to a selection of already prosperous white people; the serial delineation of new frontiers where these people can remake themselves, where new commodities can be produced and sold; and the perpetual drawing of new lines to keep out the dispossessed, keep them poor, justify silencing and stealing from them, and pathologize, police, and imprison them.

In this context, alternative futures rooted in the people's development tradition face many challenges. One challenge is for people to take to heart—to feel deeply—that the dominant urban agenda is in fact bad, conservative, backwards, played out, boring, toxic, based on lies, beneficial only to narrow special interests, and taking us even further down a path that tends toward genocide. This will require a true rejection of all racial order—including both vilification and uplift tendencies—and the mentalities that view apartheid, eviction, and policing as effective solutions for anything. Interwoven with this task is the challenge of taking to heart the fact that the dominant agenda can be overtaken by something radically different, a vision based on the thrill—the one that Idle No More sparks—of associating with, rather than replacing, each other. In other words, the challenge is to truly feel that we can remake regions and selves by turning our immense collective capacity—the same capacity that today raises tower after tower for corporations and luxury condo buyers—to build homes, food distribution networks, transportation infrastructure, daycares, schools, clinics, hospitals, community centres, and safe spaces for all. Finally, this will require taking to heart the fact that the only way to finally install such a development agenda will be to understand and grapple with things—institutional capacities, cultural imaginations, political relationships—as they exist here and now. Integral to this taking to heart will be the practice of rooting the new agenda in the spirit of past visions—the Manitoba Treaty, Treaty 1, and their offspring—and shaping it, in the spirit of Marvin Francis' *City Treaty*, according to current conditions.[14]

1   Mike, interview with author, Winnipeg, MB, July 18, 2013.

2   Sandra, interview with author, Winnipeg, MB, July 11, 2013.

3   Statistics Canada, *2011 Census Data – Centennial*.

4   Garth, interview with author, Winnipeg, MB, January 3, 2014.

5   Chris, interview with author, Winnipeg, MB, January 17, 2014.

6   Aideen, interview with author, Winnipeg, MB, January 2, 2014.

7   After sitting vacant for two years, Loblaws reopened the Extra Foods on Notre Dame under a new name in 2015.

8   Julie, interview with author, Winnipeg, MB, August 2, 2013.

9   Hilderman, Thomas, Frank, Cram Landscape Architecture, Planning and Property & Services Department, Planning & Land-Use Division, *CentrePlan Development Framework*.

10   Coulthard, *Red Skin White Masks*, 161.

11   Idle No More is revolutionary, at least insofar as Idle No More organizers "see themselves as responsible for reorganizing the society, which is what revolutionary social forces must do," as distinguished from rebellions in which people are engaged simply in "protesting their condition" (Boggs and Boggs, *Revolution and evolution in the twentieth century*, 17).

12   onewinnipeg.ca, "Winnipeg Water Wednesdays Have Returned for 2014!"

13   Piapot, "Racial Tensions Rise along Edges of Idle No More Rallies."

14   Robin D.G. Kelley (*Hammer and Hoe*, 231) theorizes Alabama's history of Black Reconstruction, 1930s Communist organizing, and 1950s civil rights activism as "movement(s) rooted in the past and shaped by the present."

ENDNOTES

NEW TIMES

During the 2014 Winnipeg civic election, the campaign of the leading right-wing mayoral candidate was effectively ended by comments made by Lorrie Steeves, the candidate's wife, in a Facebook post from 2010. The post contained a series of expletive-laden, derogatory comments about Native people, specifically those forced to panhandle for a living in the city centre, casting them as aggressors who ought to be silenced and removed from the path of "honest people."[1] Almost immediately after the comments became public, Winnipeg news media and public opinion cast Gord Steeves—a wealthy, white South End lawyer—as an unworthy mayoral candidate, sending him plummeting to the bottom of the race. Steeves's fall paved the way for the ascendance of Brian Bowman—another wealthy South End lawyer and former chair of the Winnipeg Chamber of Commerce—who became Winnipeg's 43rd mayor on October 22, 2014.

Bowman—whom the Toronto *Globe and Mail* described as a "business-friendly conservative with progressive ideals"—campaigned on a neoliberal agenda of "fiscal conservatism" and was supported by the city's South End and suburban constituencies.[2] Winnipeg's largely Native city centre did not support Bowman's agenda, siding instead with Judy Wasylycia-Leis, a North End left-wing candidate of Ukrainian ancestry.[3] Bowman revealed little about his own ethnic identity during the campaign, but once elected he frequently identified as Métis and described himself as "Canada's first Aboriginal mayor." "He rarely mentioned his indigenous [sic] background during the campaign," observed the *Globe*, "but he's now being cast as a politician who can help bridge a racial gulf in what by some measures is Canada's most indigenous [sic] city."[4]

On January 22, 2015, Bowman was pressed into this duty more dramatically than perhaps any Winnipeg mayor before him. In front of a throng of television cameras at a staged media event, Bowman wept in response to the cover story of a national magazine—a publication found in almost every corporate lobby or doctor's office in the country—that had just named Winnipeg "Canada's most racist city."[5] "We're not going to end racism tomorrow, but we're sure as hell going to try," Bowman told reporters, promising that his words would soon be followed by "action." Two weeks later, however, several city-centre councillors leaked to the *Free Press* a proposal, apparently circulated by Bowman, to dispense with numerous community centres and youth recreation facilities in the city's Native neighbourhoods as a proposed cost-cutting measure. Bowman denied having anything to do with the proposal, but the councillors stood by their accounts.[6]

Whether or not Bowman was behind the proposed cuts is almost beside the point. Rather, the story matters insofar as it highlights a key dynamic of Canadian political life in the current age of reconciliation: the contradiction between the requirements of capital accumulation—in this case, austerity—and rising pressures to address the material needs and aspirations of Indigenous peoples. With racial vilification and open colonial presumptions of Indigenous death, disappearance, and inferiority increasingly off the table, present-day old-guard urban politics in Winnipeg offers key insights into new formations of liberal settler colonialism. As the case of "Canada's first Aboriginal mayor"—brought to you by the Chamber of Commerce—indicates, the dominant regional bloc is now compelled to package its deadly agenda in terms that purport to embrace Indigenous survival. How this will play out in the near future depends on our ability to recognize it as a true *contradiction*—rather than a "gulf" that can be bridged by more enlightened agents of the same old interests.

In this sense, the mayor's tears are part of the problem. As many have pointed out, the sorrowful settler colonialism that politicians such as Bowman and Prime Minister Justin Trudeau push, which expends so much energy encouraging Canadians to feel that racism is a matter of unfortunate attitudes and misunderstandings—"gulfs," "tensions," and "divides"—is a strategy for *protecting* structures of dispossession and racial order.[7] Defining racism as an attitude problem leads only to friendlier, at times "redwashed"[8] structures—organized abandonment, child theft, eviction, apartheid, homelessness, hunger, policing, imprisonment, and pipelines—that perpetuate systemic racism. Indeed, CentreVenture and its decades of Urban Indian removal was initiated and supported by governments otherwise staunchly committed, so they said, to "bridging the gap" between Indigenous and non-Indigenous peoples. Radical reconciliation, which is to say the process of restoring stolen Indigenous land and self-determination, is something that capitalism and its dominant regional blocs—with their constant need to accumulate, steal, and enforce inequalities—cannot accommodate.

To help take this contradiction to heart, it is worth repeating that Canadian capitalism *is* settler-colonial capitalism, and Canadian settler colonialism *is* racial capitalism. To be clear, this is not to say that capitalism is the sole cause of racism or colonialism, only to say that capitalism can't do without them.[9] With this in our hearts and minds, we might be able to finally turn away from friendly liberal capitalist agendas and structures—including but not limited to "fiscal conservatism"—knowing that they are not only fruitless terrain for solving problems, but that they also actively delay and thus deny meaningful reconciliation by requiring, innovating, and defending new mechanisms of racist extraction, including Indigenous dispossession and new feelings of anti-Native racism.

In the same vein, rejecting fiscal conservatism, austerity, and neoliberalism without reference to their racial and colonial dynamics is not enough. As Cedric J. Robinson wrote, "There was the sense that something of a more profound nature than the obsession with property was askew in a civilization that could organize and celebrate—on a scale beyond previous human experience—the brutal degradations of life and the most acute violations of human destiny."[10] The racial mentalities—which go far beyond the overt expressions of racism that currently, though not consistently, disqualify individuals from holding prominent positions—mined and emitted by capitalism insinuate themselves into every aspect of today's world, including the Left. One result is the unintentional persistence of racial uplift agendas even within the political visions of those who intend to resist, but at times unwittingly reinforce, capitalism, racism, and barriers to movement building. In order to move forward based on an understanding of racial capitalism, it is important to keep reflecting on the ways we think about urban and colonial problems. How do certain progressive-seeming explanations of the city accidentally bring us back to the idea that violent institutions—like imprisonment or homelessness—would disappear if dispossessed people just got their shit together? How do we end up distancing struggles and selves that are, in fact, intimately connected?

RACIAL UPLIFT IN "DECOLONIZING" AGENDAS

Winnipeg's problems are often defined by progressive people in ways that unintentionally weaken the possibility of radical reconciliation and at times play into the hands of new colonial agendas. Over the past two decades, forward-thinking explanations of Winnipeg's racism problem—in particular, the unacceptable conditions in which Indigenous Winnipeggers are forced to live—have been shaped to a great extent by what has been called the CCPA school of social research. The CCPA-Manitoba is an interdisciplinary group of scholars established in 1997, with long-standing connections to the Manitoba NDP, organized labour, and Winnipeg's city-centre community-based non-profit organizations.[11] CCPA-school researchers, assisted in recent years by several million-dollar federal research grants, have published over one hundred books, articles, and reports about Winnipeg's city centre—often addressing an audience of non-academic suburbanites, particularly those who wield state power—including the CCPA-Manitoba's annual *State of the Inner City Report*. The way this body of work, which is far from homogenous, tends to describe the forces shaping the Indigenous city centre has had a significant impact on the orientation of political action in the city. Feelings about what colonialism, and thus decolonization, is and how it specifically shapes urban lives in the present are particularly critical.

A 2013 book on Indigenous street gangs in Winnipeg, *"Indians Wear Red,"* is perhaps the most celebrated and widely read of the CCPA school's publications.[12] At the heart of the book is the incisive and undoubtedly true claim that Winnipeg's North End and broader city centre are "colonized spaces." However, while *"Indians Wear Red"* includes a number of brief assertions that colonialism is "a living phenomenon" that continues to shape the city centre, the bulk of the book nevertheless promotes the feeling that colonialism is a force that either occurred in the past, occurs outside of the city (through processes such as oil exploration and hydroelectric development), or occurs in the city primarily if not entirely through the intergenerational trauma, unhealthy lifestyles, and sometimes predatory actions of Indigenous peoples themselves.[13]

Critically, contemporary urban structures of colonialism, dispossession, and disenfranchisement are not the focus of *"Indians Wear Red,"* nor are they the focus of CCPA-school research in general. The urban institutions—police, prisons, child welfare agencies, landlords, developers, bosses, school administrations, and so forth—that plan, carry out, defend, and/or benefit from contemporary forms of dispossession, eviction, occupation, exploitation, and violence in the city appear throughout *"Indians Wear Red,"* but they are rarely implicated as sources of harm or as targets for reform.[14] The book's main interlocutors, former Winnipeg gang members, identify these institutions and the structural violence they commit—from literal torture to caging, child theft, wage theft, eviction, expulsion, and withholding the necessities of life—as crucial to the arcs of their lives. The CCPA school, however, regularly treats such racial-capitalist structures as more or less innocent, passive, and even proper responses to Indigenous peoples' colonially induced behaviour.[15]

In large part, this is a function of the CCPA school's political commitment to imploring the Canadian state to fund Indigenous communities predominantly on the basis of those communities' need to heal themselves from the traumas of Canadian colonialism. By presenting city-centre people as objects of repair to an audience of structural power—and not vice versa—CCPA-school research often unintentionally contributes to the region's long tradition of racial uplift. The "Urban Indian" industry that emerged in the 1950s lives on in modified form, as "cultural heritage" is replaced by "colonial trauma" as the primary force supposedly preventing Indigenous peoples from obtaining acceptable standards of living in the city. Indeed, the bulk of *"Indians Wear Red"* presents damage-centred, frequently pathologizing, and at times demonizing portrayals of Indigenous peoples and communities, inadvertently distracting from and playing into the narratives that uphold contemporary urban racial vilification, dispossession, and apartheid agendas.[16]

Accordingly, *"Indians Wear Red,"* like much CCPA-school research, envisions "decolonization" in very narrow terms, as traditional education and ceremonies funded by the Canadian state for Indigenous peoples who want to put their lives back together.[17] Crucially, long-standing Indigenous imperatives to reclaim stolen lands and sovereignties, and to do so in resistance to contemporary urban forms of oppression, are not presented as integral to this decolonial future. Neither does this work produce a robust basis for solidarity between Indigenous and non-Indigenous peoples differently dispossessed by capitalism and struggling for new worlds. In line with the narrative of the "inner city" that emerged in the 1970s, the Indigenous city centre is represented as a unique place cut off from the rest of the city and from other struggles. Accordingly, it is depicted as the primary location of the problem and the primary object of repair, as opposed to the centres of dominance—the Chamber of Commerce, Manitoba Club, CentreVenture, City Hall, the provincial legislature, Ottawa, the G20, and so forth—where problems truly lie, or the more quotidian places where loyalty to empire has been purchased with small pieces of the stolen pie. Since the problem is not defined as the prevailing racial capitalist order, in other words, we are made to feel that there is little shared material interest—beyond a moral commitment to righting wrongs—from which to take action together. Indigenous peoples are positioned as the only ones whose identities and human potential have been profoundly damaged by settler colonialism and capitalism, and non-Indigenous peoples are placed in the role of supporting them in piecing themselves back together. This definition of the problem does not prepare us very well to come together as people who all stand to benefit from new structures based on reciprocity, equality, and life itself, whether or not our current pay packet includes the "paltry dividend" of white supremacy.[18]

Pointing out the unintended effects of our own work and that of our comrades in this way matters, for one, because historical change is not linear, the current spirit of reconciliation will not be with us forever, and it feels important to make the most of times like these while doing everything possible to avoid being dragged into new times of intensified white supremacy. Indeed, the reality is that many contradictory historical forces advance simultaneously, in relation to one another, as can be appreciated today by considering that the first Black president of the United States has given way to a KKK-endorsed president, and that the age of reconciliation on Turtle Island is also the age of Trumpism.[19] Racial uplift narratives, whether they are pushed by compassionate capitalist politicians—whose best intentions go forever unrealized due to contradictions that seem like lies[20]—or by leftist scholars and non-profits, in fact keep the cultural groundwork alive for the blossoming of new types of racial vilification and fascist tendencies. At the end of the day, these narratives do what capitalism needs racial regimes to do: attribute its inequalities and predations to the inferiority of the—supposedly under-educated, unambitious, unassimilated, unprepared, unreasonable, or overly traumatized—poor.[21]

In this sense, Lorrie Steeves could be forgiven for thinking little of those hateful comments, coming as they did at a time of renewed civic vilification of city-centre Indigenous peoples—orchestrated by CentreVenture and supported by all mainstream Canadian parties—since they, like much hate speech, simply took widely accepted liberal racism to its logical conclusion. Aligned with capital in dominant blocs, "socially liberal" politicians had for decades embraced—the NDP might say "compromised" to—colonial, apartheid, fascist-tending impulses when it came to gentrification, policing, prisons, borders, pipelines, dams, and many other things. Steeves' transgression was to express the spirit of the prevailing capitalist development agenda in an exaggerated, unmasked way that offended the liberal sensibilities of a city that still prefers to "hide its hate."[22] Interestingly, Steeves' comments oscillated from racial vilification to racial uplift—"we need to get these people educated"—and back again, confirming the compatibility of the two narratives. More interestingly still, in the spring of 2018, Bowman kicked off his run for re-election by trumpeting increased policing of city-centre panhandlers as his top campaign promise.[23]

TIME FOR *CITY TREATY*

How can we strengthen our ability to imagine the cities we need, when the burial of alternative visions means that many of us have been deskilled in this line of work? Our capacity to be confident in remaking places and selves may benefit if we take to heart that solutions to serial dispossession already exists in the rich portfolio of decolonial blueprints—which can be implemented today in both spirit and letter—produced over decades of hard work by peoples' development traditions. In Winnipeg, this means being guided by the Anishinabe Treaty 1 and the Métis Manitoba Treaty development visions, by the agenda of land reform, community control, and prioritizing human need advanced by city-centre organizers throughout the twentieth century, and by the ways of thinking, feeling, and acting that these struggles have left for us.

Emboldened by the past and responding to the specific challenges of the present—the agenda Marvin Francis proposed in *City Treaty*—one way to imagine the path forward could be to think about how existing capacities for making and remaking the world might be radically rearranged.[24] CentreVenture—which names a particular set of capacities currently oriented toward a conservative political vision—or at least the precedent it sets, is one small example of contemporary world-making capacity that could be reconfigured to start the process of building decolonial cities and regions. Through CentreVenture, which is not unique to or even within Winnipeg in this respect, the capacity has been established for shifting control over resources—including land and social wealth in the form of tax revenue—from the Canadian state to autonomous organizations that possess significant freedom to redistribute those resources according to their own principles and visions. Organizations such as CentreVenture have the capacity to craft development plans for specific places and to attach specific land-use requirements to specific lands. They have the capacity to draft policies for governments and to push, from a position of moral and civic authority, governments to adopt those policies, to release resources from the control of the state for specific projects, and to take other concrete actions in support of their vision. Crucially, they have the educational capacity to promote certain ways of feeling about the future of the city and the material capacity to demonstrate that such a future is possible.

The capacity for land control that CentreVenture represents—designed specifically for a moment of crisis in which a large amount of land was abandoned by capital—could also be expanded in numerous directions to transfer far more urban land and resources back to Indigenous nations and communities. Some version of a "use it or lose it" bylaw could be applied to reclaim vacant land and buildings. Similar mechanisms could be used to apprehend land from "slum" landlords who are unfit to provide safe, healthy, or acceptable housing; to confiscate land from dangerous, polluting, or otherwise harmful uses such as rail yards or Christianizing complexes; and to reclaim publicly funded developments such as shopping malls and luxury condos currently held by private interests. Protective designations, in the style of current "heritage"-based policies, could be applied to prevent the demolition of buildings that serve critical social purposes, such as hotels for health care–seeking families. TIF models could be reworked to divert property tax revenues directly to community control.

The purpose of the above list is not to prescribe a specific agenda but to start thinking about ways to make durable what before was ad-hoc—in other words, to imagine structures that can stretch what people already do in piecemeal fashion over time and space.[25] Successfully creating these structures, of course, requires clout. If Glen Murray, Bowman, and seventeen years of NDP rule in Manitoba, not to mention Trudeau and the current Liberal MP for Winnipeg's city centre, have taught Winnipeg something, it might be that we would benefit from focusing less on the tempting shortcut of *taking* power—electing enlightened politicians who we know will bend, more often than not, to the considerable power of dominant blocs—and focusing more on *making* power.[26]

Forming organizations and doing things—a rich 70-plus-year tradition in Winnipeg's city centre—is one way people make themselves more powerful than they were before. Bringing organizations together in coalitions, movements, and united fronts—an equally long, if perhaps more sporadic tradition—is a way to increase that power exponentially. The Winnipeg General Strike, Neeginan, rail relocation, the Winnipeg Native Child Welfare Coalition, and the Community Inquiry into Inner City Revitalization are just a few moments when city-centre Winnipeggers and their organizations, focusing on building trust, reciprocity, and political education *within* their communities, have joined forces to make new kinds of power.[27] While these movements tended toward the creation of standalone legislation and development projects, we can imagine coalitions aimed at creating permanent structures for the reclamation of stolen land, labour, and control over our lives; structures, that is, endowed with the capacities necessary to facilitate, in perpetuity, the litany of plans and projects—"twenty Thunderbird houses," and much, much more—that a decolonial city would encompass.

The history of racial capitalism and resistance in Winnipeg is full of lessons for how movements, if they are flexible enough, can act strategically to make the most of their power. Times of crisis, when there is widespread feeling that things cannot go on in the same way and when the character of the solution is up for grabs, are moments when underlying contradictions might be highlighted and transcended. Capitalist crises of overaccumulation, such as those that contributed to Canadian expansion, suburbanization, and post-industrial redevelopment, could be opportunities to make claims on surpluses—which capitalism perpetually produces—in resistance to agendas that require the state to fund newly profitable outlets. The same goes for moments of especially intense competition between capitalists with different geographical ties—such as inter-imperial competition, inter-urban competition, and intra-urban competition between suburban and urban developers—that give momentum to various forms of conquest. Fissures like these—tensions, conflicts, splits, and contradictions—within dominant blocs can be exploited to weaken them or to delay or thwart the ascendance of conquest agendas.

On the flip side, dominant structures and agendas that silence the aspirations of various communities can form the bases of new alignments and solidarities, the way suburbanization produced the rail relocation movement and the CAI produced the Community Inquiry into Inner City Revitalization. Tactically speaking, the struggles that have gained traction over the years—such as those that led to the Manitoba Treaty and Treaty 1, or gains made by the Winnipeg Native Child Welfare Coalition or the students who fought for Children of the Earth High School—demonstrate the power of direct action and civil disobedience, combined with petitions and legal challenges, to force Canada and its institutions to relinquish some of their power. The repository of deep grassroots analysis passed on from organizers who doubled down on earlier struggles—in the style of *Wahbung* or the Community Inquiry—could be a foundation for avoiding co-optation when capitalist-committed actors such as Lloyd Axworthy, the Liberal party, or Canada itself purport to steward grassroots movements that threaten to exceed the narrow horizons of racial capitalism.

The point is that the structures tying regional survival everywhere to racial hierarchy and dispossession were pieced together in fits and starts by coalitions of human beings who honed feelings and capacities over decades and centuries, regularly abandoning old ones and building new ones. They can be abolished and replaced in the same way. They likely won't be, however, unless we manage to build the feelings and capacities necessary to recognize and trash white supremacy as it exists here and now—in all its forms, from liberal uplift to conservative vilification—on the way to building new and revolutionary alliances.

1   Kives, "Steeves' Wife Complains about Harassment by 'Drunken Native Guys' in Facebook Post."

2   Friesen, "Winnipeg's First Native Mayor Seen as Bridge Builder."

3   Mackinnon, "Will Winnipeg's First Indigenous Mayor Bridge the City's Divide? It's Complicated."

4   Bowman, "Bio"; Friesen, "Winnipeg's First Native Mayor Seen as Bridge Builder."

5   Macdonald, "Welcome to Winnipeg: Where Canada's Racism Problem Is at Its Worst."

6   Santin, "Poor to Bear Brunt of City Cuts." In the years following, Bowman has maintained the city's neoliberal status quo of stunted property and business taxes (with the exception of introducing a new fee for suburban developers), a bloated police budget, and inadequate funding for social services such as public transit, affordable housing, women's centres, community centres, and youth recreation programming (Kives, "Pain for Winnipeg"; Marcoux, "16 Years of Winnipeg Budgets Show Gains by Police at Expense of Other City Departments"). He has also used his Métis identity to deny the existence of well-known structural racisms, including systemic police mistreatment of Indigenous peoples (O'Brien, "Mayor Faces Long Learning Curve").

7   Audra Simpson refers to such spectacles as "the performance of empathetic, remorseful, and *fleetingly* sorrowful states…states that are built upon violence and still act violently" (Simpson, "The State is a Man," 2).

8   *Redwashing* has been used to describe capitalist attempts to cover up harms against Indigenous communities by sponsoring Indigenous education, art, and culture. See Thomas-Müller, "We Need to Start Calling Out Corporate 'Redwashing'."

9   As Coulthard writes in *Red Skin White Masks*, 173, "For Indigenous nations to live, capitalism must die."

10   Robinson, *Black Marxism*, 308.

11   Dobchuk-Land, "'Tough on Crime, Tough on the Causes of Crime'."

12   *"Indians Wear Red"* won the Manitoba Book Award for Non-fiction in 2014.

13   For colonialism as "a living phenomenon" in Comack et al., *"Indians Wear Red,"* see pages 17, 35, 59, 137, and 146. The wording of the third sentence in this paragraph is intentional: In *"Indians Wear Red,"* colonialism shapes only the city centre, obscuring its role in creating the wealth, power, and hindered humanity of the city's South End, affluent suburbs, and beyond. For the feeling that colonialism is a force of the past in Comack et al., *"Indians Wear Red,"* see pages 3, 16, 35, 37, and 144. "The past impacts on the present," Comack et al. quote from Monture, "Race and Erasing," 207. The concept of "trauma trails," used throughout *"Indians Wear Red,"* compares colonialism to "a stone cast into a pond," describing trauma as "the point of penetration" and "[trauma's] wake" as "the psychosocial repercussions," ignoring the reality that colonial stone after colonial stone continues to be thrown. For instances of colonialism occurring outside of the city in Comack et al., *"Indians Wear Red,"* see pages 36 and 39. For colonialism occurring inside the city primarily through the intergenerational trauma, unhealthy lifestyles, and sometimes predatory actions of Indigenous peoples themselves, in Comack et al., *"Indians Wear Red,"* see Chapters 3, 4, and 5, specifically pages 83, 87, 106, 110, 131, 132, 133, and 137.

14   Comack et al., *"Indians Wear Red,"* 5, 6, 16, 39, 69, 90, 137, and 140.

15   Comack et al., *"Indians Wear Red,"* 5, 6, 69, 70, and 139.

16   This follows Eve Tuck's caution against "damage-centered research" and Dian Million's critique of research that constructs Indigenous people as needing "therapy" and "inclusion" rather than social and economic justice, and Bronwyn Dobchuk-Land's application of the latter critiques to the CCPA school. Million, *Therapeutic Nations*; Tuck, *Suspending Damage*; Dobchuk-Land, "Tough on Crime, Tough on the Causes of Crime." For pathologization of Indigenous peoples in Comack et al., *"Indians Wear Red,"* see Chapters 3 and 4, specifically pages 24, 39, 63, 67, 69, 70, 83, 87, 105, 106, and 132. Throughout the book, Indigenous peoples are portrayed as broken, hopeless, desperate, addicted, dying, chaotic, destructive, hyper-masculine, and prone to violence. For demonization of Indigenous peoples in Comack et al., *"Indians Wear Red,"* see page 105.

17   Comack et al., *"Indians Wear Red,"* 142. To its credit, *"Indians Wear Red"* has been somewhat successful in encouraging people to leave gangs and to become politically active. It is also worth noting that the primary source cited for the book's decolonization agenda derives from comments made by an Indigenous elder who prefaces them explicitly by saying they apply only to herself: "You see—and I'm going to speak for myself—my life is like a shattered puzzle..."

18   Robinson, *Forgeries of Memory and Meaning*, 126.

19   Kurashige, Paper presented at the Annual Meeting of the American Studies Association.

20   "Many things that seem like lies are actually contradictions." Gilmore, Paper presented at the Annual Meeting of the American Studies Association.

21   Kelley, "Births of a Nation," 121.

22   Mercredi, "This City is Red."

23   Thorpe, "Mayor's State of City Address Outlines Vision of 'New Winnipeg.'"

24   "The historically specific arrangement of these capacities—how they are combined and to what end—indicate the 'balance of power relations' in the society as a whole" (Gilmore, *Golden Gulag*, 78).

25   Gilmore, *Golden Gulag*, 78.

26   Gilmore, *Golden Gulag*, 248.

27   "When the performance of charismatic leadership stands in for building movements and relationships, for grassroots political education, and for a practiced commitment to disassembling social hierarchies, the promise of social justice and political empowerment is endangered by a formation of authority that limits our capacities to remake the world" (Erica R. Edwards, as quoted in Kelley, "Births of a Nation," 132).

Adams, H. (1989). *Prison of grass*. Markham: Fifth House Publishing.

Adams, H. (1992). Causes of the 1885 struggle. In G. Melnyk (Ed.), *From Riel to reform: A history of protest in western Canada*. Markham: Fifth House Publishing.

Alfred, T. (2009). Colonialism and state dependency. *Journal of Aboriginal Health*, November 2009, 41–60.

Andersen, C. (2014). *"Métis": Race, recognition, and the struggle for indigenous peoplehood*. Vancouver: UBC Press.

Antwi, P. (2015). Faithful bodies and their affective currencies in the black Atlantic. [Presentation]. *Paper presented at the Annual Meeting of the American Studies Association*. Toronto.

Artibise, A.F.J. (1975). *Winnipeg: A social history of urban growth 1874–1914*. Montreal: McGll-Queen's University Press.

Artibise, A.F.J. (1977). *Winnipeg: An illustrated history*. Toronto: James Lorimer & Company.

Avila, E. (2004). *Popular culture in the age of white flight*. Berkeley: University of California Press.

Axworthy, L. (1974). *A test case for institutional innovation: Winnipeg's unicity*. Winnipeg: Institute of Urban Studies, University of Winnipeg.

Ballantyne, B. (1996). We had a good life. In Raymond M. Beaumont (Ed.), *Grand Rapids Stories Volume I*, June 1996. Winnipeg: Frontier School Division No. 48.

Bannerji, H. (1997). Geography lessons: On being an insider/outsider to the Canadian nation. In *Dangerous territories: Struggles for difference and equality in education*. New York: Routledge.

Bantjes, R. (2000). *The dominion survey as imperial panorama: Inscriptions and counter-inscriptions*. Aberdeen, Scotland. http://people.stfx.ca/rbantjes/WritingConf.pdf.

Bantjes, R. (2005). *Improved earth: Prairie space as modern artefact, 1869–1944*. Toronto: University of Toronto Press.

Barkwell, L. (2008). *The reign of terror against the Métis of red river*. Winnipeg: Louis Riel Institute.

Barkwell, L. (2016). *20th century Metis displacement and road allowance communities in Manitoba*. Winnipeg: Louis Riel Institute.

Barron, F. L. (1988). The Indian pass system in the Canadian west, 1882–1935. *Prairie Forum* 13 (1), 25–42.

Begg, A. (1869). *Begg's red river journal*. November 26, 1869.

Begg, A. & W.N. Nursey. (1879). *Ten years in Winnipeg*. Winnipeg: Times Printing and Publishing House.

Bellan, R. (1978). *Winnipeg first century: An economic history*. Winnipeg: Queenston House Publishing Co. Ltd.

Benell, P., Feduniw, T., Kroeger, A., Malinowski, D. & Sikora, W. (1979). *The building abandonment study: Winnipeg's inner city*. Winnipeg: Institute of Urban Studies.

Benjamin, W. (1940). Ninth thesis on the philosophy of history. In *Illuminations*. New York: Penguin Random House.

Bercuson, D.J. (1990). *Confrontation at Winnipeg: Labour, industrial relations, and the general strike*. Revised edition. Montreal: McGill-Queens University Press.

Berger, C. (1970). *The sense of power: Studies in the ideas of Canadian imperialism, 1867–1914*. Toronto: University of Toronto Press.

Bertrand, J. (1979, August 31). Judge claims police can't lock up drunks. *Winnipeg Tribune*.

Best, M. (1955, November 2). Province Will Build 3 Bridges in City Area. *Winnipeg Free Press*.

Black, D. (2013, February 15). The history of Canada's immigration policy has been one of exclusion. Today, the country continues to welcome some, but not others. *Toronto Star*.

Blomley, N. (2004). *Unsettling the city: Urban land and the politics of property*. Hove: Psychology Press.

Boggs, J. & Boggs, G.L. (1974). *Revolution and evolution in the twentieth century.* New York: NYU Press.

Borrows, J. (1992). Negotiating treaties and land claims: The impact of diversity within First Nations property interests. 12 *Windsor Y.B. Access. Just.* 179.

Bower, D. (1957, November 26). South Bypass Road to Be in Use Next Fall. *Winnipeg Free Press.*

Bowman, B. Bio. [Facebook page.] *Brian Bowman: Politician.* Retrieved from https://www.facebook.com/MayorBrian-Bowman/info?tab=page_info.

Boyens, I. & Rosner, C. (1982, May 12). Native groups call for disbanding. *Winnipeg Free Press.*

Brandon, J. (2014). *Winnipeg and Manitoba housing data.* Winnipeg: Canadian Centre for Policy Alternatives–Manitoba Office.

Brenner, N. & Theodore, N. (2002). Cities and the geographies of 'actually existing' neoliberalism. *Antipode* 34 (3), 349–79.

Brown, J. (1980). *Strangers in blood: Fur trade company families in Indian country.* Vancouver: UBC Press.

Brown, J. & Grey, S.E. (Eds). (2010). *A. Irving Hallowell – Contributions to Ojibwe studies: Essays, 1934–1972.* Lincoln: University of Nebraska Press.

Bryce, G. (1906). *A history of Manitoba: Its resources and people.* Toronto: Canada History Company.

Bumsted, J.M. (1994). *Winnipeg general strike of 1919: An illustrated history.* Winnipeg: Watson Dwyer Publishing Limited.

Bumsted, J. M. (1999). *Dictionary of Manitoba biography.* Winnipeg: University of Manitoba Press.

Burley, D.G. (2003). *City and suburb: Housing in twentieth century Winnipeg.* An Exhibition Sponsored by the Winnipeg Real Estate Board.

Burley, D.G. (2010). The emergence of the premiership, 1870–1874. In B. Ferguson & R. Wardhaugh (Eds), *Manitoba premiers of the 19th and 20th centuries.* Regina: Canadian Plains Research Centre.

Burley, D.G. (2013). Rooster town: Winnipeg's lost Métis suburb, 1900–1960. *Urban History Review,* XLII (1), 3-26.

Byrd, J. (2015). The settler colonialism analytic: A critical reappraisal. [Presentation]. *Comments on a panel at the Annual Meeting of the American Studies Association.* Toronto.

Canadian Broadcasting Corporation. (2007, August 31). Bell tolls for downtown Winnipeg hotel. CBC. Retrieved at http://www.cbc.ca/news/canada/manitoba/story/2007/08/31/bell-hotel.html.

Canadian Broadcasting Corporation. (2013, April 1). Canada buys Rupert's Land. *CBC.* Retrieved at http://www.cbc.ca/history/ry/EPCONTENTSE1EP9CH1PA3LE.html.

Canadian Broadcasting Corporation. (2015, November 6). Brown Town Muddy Water documents Winnipeg's early indigenous music scene. *CBC.* Retrieved at http://www.cbc.ca/radio/unreserved/drums-throat-singing-and-what-many-hope-is-a-new-era-of-reconciliation-1.3305417/brown-town-muddy-water-documents-winnipeg-s-early-indigenous-music-scene-1.3307967.

Canadian Broadcasting Corporation. (2015, November 24). Winnipeg downtown in period of unprecedented growth, study finds. *CBC.* Retrieved at http://www.cbc.ca/news/canada/manitoba/winnipeg-downtown-in-period-of-unprecedented-growth-study-finds-1.3335462.

Canadian Broadcasting Corporation. (2015, May 28). CentreVenture sells St. Regis hotel, plans for parkade and retail. *CBC.* Retrieved at http://www.cbc.ca/news/canada/manitoba/centreventure-sells-st-regis-hotel-plans-for-parkade-and-retail-1.3090052.

Canadian Broadcasting Corporation. (2015, December 10). Donald Trump invited to Winnipeg to learn 'compassion'. *CBC*. Accessed on March 19, 2018 at http://www.cbc.ca/news/canada/manitoba/donald-trump-brian-bowman-invitation-1.3359788.

Canadian Broadcasting Corporation. (2017, October 25). Winnipeg's indigenous population highest in Canada, but growth rate is slowing. *CBC*. Accessed on April 4, 2018 at http://www.cbc.ca/news/canada/manitoba/aboriginal-population-statistics-canada-1.4371222.

Canadian Business. (2018). Canada's richest people 2018. *Canadian Business*. Accessed on February 24, 2018 at http://www.canadianbusiness.com/lists-and-rankings/richest-people/top-25-richest-canadians-2018/image/26/.

Canadian Centre for Justice Statistics, and Statistics Canada. (2012). *Adult correctional services survey 2011/2012 and national household survey 2011*.

Canadian Indian Workshop. (1966). *Nish Nawh Be*. [Newsletter of the Canadian Indian Workshop] Carol Wabegijig (Ed.).

Canadian Press. (2012, December 3). Canadian business tax rate among world's lowest. *Canadian Press*. Retrieved at http://www.cbc.ca/news/business/canadian-business-tax-rate-among-world-s-lowest-1.1173662.

Canad Inns Corporate Office. (2011, June 29). Canad Inns to rejuvinate MET as vibrant downtown destination funding assists with costs unique to historical building.

Cardinal, H. (1969). *The unjust society*. Vancouver: Douglas & McIntyre.

Cariou, W. 2008. Introduction. In M. Francis, *Bush Camp*. Winnipeg: Turnstone Press.

Carter, S. (1990). *Lost harvests: Prairie Indian reserve farmers and government policy*. Montreal: McGill-Queen's University Press.

Carter, S. (1999). *Aboriginal people and colonizers of western Canada*. Toronto: University of Toronto Press.

Carter, S. (2015). 'They would not give up one inch of it': The rise and demise of St. Peter's Reserve, Manitoba. In Z. Laidlaw & A. Lester (Eds.), *Indigenous communities and settler colonialism: Land holding, loss and survival in an interconnected world*. Toronto: Palgrave Macmillan.

Cash, M. (2011, June 29). North Portage gets makeover. *Winnipeg Free Press*. Retrieved from https://www.winnipegfreepress.com/business/north-portage-gets-makeover-124695919.html.

Cash, M. (2013, May 1). New structure to be king of downtown? *Winnipeg Free Press*. Retrieved from https://www.winnipegfreepress.com/business/new-development-king-of-core-205538121.html.

Cash, M. (2013, November) Good To grow. Winnipeg is an investor's dream: Stable, diversified and growing. *Delta Sky Magazine*. Retrieved at http://www.economicdevelopmentwinnipeg.com/uploads/document_file/winnipeg_profile.pdf?t=1397601473.

Central Neighbourhoods Development Corporation. (2014, November 19). *Communities*. Retrieved at cndc.ca/communities.htm.

CentrePlan Committee. (1997). *CentrePlan action plan, 1997–99*. Winnipeg: CentrePlan Committee.

CentreVenture. (2007). *Heart of gold strategic business plan 2007–2009*. Winnipeg: CentreVenture.

CentreVenture. (2007, August 24). Revitalization of Main Street expected with Centreventure's strategic purchase of Bell hotel properties. *CentreVentre*. Retrieved at http://www.bridgmancollaborative.ca/uploads/9/4/6/5/9465877/revitalization_main_street.pdf.

CentreVenture. (2010). *2010 annual report*. Winnipeg: CentreVenture.

CentreVenture. (2011, June). *Bell hotel supportive housing RE: IDA downtown achievement awards*. Retrieved at https://www.ida-downtown.org/eweb/docs/2011%20Awards/Centre%20Venture%20Development%20Corp.,%20Bell%20Hotel%20Supportive%20Housing.pdf.

CentreVenture. (2011, June 28). CentreVenture Development Corporation announces major development in the sports hospitality and entertainment district (SHED). Retrieved at https://www.newswire.ca/news-releases/centreventure-development-corporation-announces-major-development-in-the-sports-hospitality-and-entertainment-district-shed-508507061.html.

CentreVenture. (2012, September 27). Ringing the bell. Retrieved at www.youtube.com/watch?v=QIZckOcLpEw.

CentreVenture. (2012, November 15). Revitalization efforts of Portage avenue continue with CentreVenture's strategic purchase of St. Regis hotel and surface parking lots.

CentreVenture. (2012). *2012 annual report*. Winnipeg: CentreVenture.

Césaire, A. (2001). *Discourse on colonialism*. New York: Monthly Review Press.

Champagne, L. (2013). Interview by Darrell Chippeway. Research interview for Preserving the History of Institutional Development in Winnipeg. [Video]. Winnipeg, MB.

Chartrand, P.L.A.H. (1991). *Manitoba's Metis settlement scheme of 1870*. Saskatoon: Native Law Centre University of Saskatchewan.

Chippeway, L. (2012). In Meadmore, Interview by Darrell Chippeway. Research interview for Preserving the History of Institutional Development in Winnipeg. [Video]. Winnipeg, MB.

City of Winnipeg. (1995). *CentrePlan: Working together for Winnipeg's downtown*. Retrieved at http://winnipeg.ca/ppd/Documents/Planning/DowntownUrbanDesignReview/CentrePlan.pdf.

City of Winnipeg. (2010, February 24). *Hansard of the Council of the City of Winnipeg Wednesday, February 24, 2010*. Winnipeg: City of Winnipeg.

City of Winnipeg. (2010, July 21). *Hansard of the Council of the City of Winnipeg Wednesday, July 21, 2010*. Winnipeg: City of Winnipeg.

City of Winnipeg, Corporate Services Department. (1995). *Plan Winnipeg...toward 2010*. Winnipeg: City of Winnipeg.

City of Winnipeg Executive Policy Committee. (2012, April 18). *Minute no. 218 establishment of a tax increment financing zone to support strategic public investments consistent with the Portage avenue development strategy and sports hospitality and entertainment district*. Winnipeg: City of Winnipeg.

Clatworthy, S., Hull, J. & Loughran, N. (1994). *Urban aboriginal organizations: Edmonton, Toronto, and Winnipeg*. Ottawa: Department of Indian Affairs and Northern Development.

Comack, E., Deane, L., Morrissette, L. & Silver, J. (2013) *"Indians wear red": Colonialism, resistance, and aboriginal street gangs*. Halifax: Fernwood.

Community Inquiry Board to the Urban Futures Circle, Inter-Agency Group. (1990). *Community Inquiry into Inner City Revitalization: Final Report*. Winnipeg.

Connors, D. (2011, July 21). 'They killed it man.' *Winnipeg Free Press*.

Cooper, S. (2013, February 26). *Excuse me, Canada, your homelessness is showing*. Ottawa: Canadian Centre for Policy Alternatives.

Coulthard, G. (2007). Subjects of empire: Indigenous peoples and the 'politics of recognition' in Canada. *Contemporary Political Theory* 6 (4), 437–60.

Coulthard, G. (2014). *Red skin white masks: Rejecting the colonial politics of recognition*. Minneapolis: University of Minnesota Press.

Coulthard, G. (2015). The misery of settler colonialism. Roundtable on Glen Coulthard's *Red skin, white masks* and Audra Simpson's *Mohawk interruptus*. [Presentation]. Comments on a panel at the *Annual Meeting of the American Studies Association*, Toronto.

Courchene, D. (1973). Problems and possible solutions. In D.B. Sealy & V.J. Kirkness (Eds.), *Indians without tipis: A resource book by Indians and Metis*. Winnipeg: William Clare Limited.

Courchene, V. (2005). Treaty 1. *Elders Treaty Video Series*. Winnipeg: The Manitoba First Nations Education Resource Centre.

Craft, A. (2013). *Breathing life into the stone fort treaty*. Saskatoon: Purich Publishing.

Czuboka, M. 1986. *Juba*. Winnipeg: Communigraphics.

Dafoe, J.W. (1906, June 16). The day of the anglo-saxon. *Manitoba Free Press*, 16 June.

Damas and Smith Limited. (1975). *Neeginan: A feasibility report prepared for Neeginan (Manitoba) Incorporated*. Winnipeg: Damas and Smith Ltd.

Daschuk, J. (2013). *Clearing the plains: Disease, politics of starvation, and the loss of aboriginal life*. Regina: University of Regina Press.

Decter, M. & Kowall, J. (1990). *The Winnipeg core area initiative: A case study*. Ottawa: Economic Council of Canada.

Dennison, W. (1972, October 21). Native peoples will hold protest march on Legislature. *Winnipeg Free Press*.

Dennison, W. (1972, October 28). Indians march in protest. *Winnipeg Free Press*.

Dennison, W. (1973, March 7). Native groups support occupation demands. *Winnipeg Free Press*.

Department of Agriculture. (1874). *Information for intending emigrants*. Ottawa: The Government of Canada.

Dickason, O.P. (2006). *A concise history of Canada's First Nations*. Oxford: Oxford University Press.

Distasio, J. & Kaufman, A (Eds.). (2015). *The divided prairie city*. Winnipeg: Institute of Urban Studies.

Distasio, J. & Mulligan, S. (2005). *Beyond a front desk: The residential hotel as home*. Winnipeg: Institute of Urban Studies.

Dobchuk-Land, B. (2016). "Tough on crime, tough on the causes of crime": Liberal carceral logics and the reproduction of settler colonial violence in Winnipeg, MB, Canada. *PhD Dissertation*, City University of New York Graduate Center Sociology Department.

Douglas, M. (2002). *Purity and danger*. London: Routledge.

Du Bois, W.E.B. (1935). *Black reconstruction in America, 1860–1880*. Cleveland: World Publishing.

Dupuis, M. (2014). *Winnipeg's general strike: Reports from the front lines*. Charleston, South Carolina: The History Press.

Economic Development Winnipeg, Inc. (2014). *Winnipeg: Overview of key sectors*. Winnipeg: Economic Development Winnipeg Inc.

Edmonds, S. (2011, December 7). Downtown development gets kickstarted by return of the NHL to Winnipeg; NHL renews interest in downtown Winnipeg. *The Canadian Press*.

Elkins, C. & Pedersen, S. (2005). Settler colonialism: A concept and its uses. In C. Elkins & S. Pedersen (Eds.), *Settler colonialism in the twentieth century: Projects, practices, legacies*. New York: Routledge.

Eyford, R. (2016). *White settler reserve: New Iceland and the colonization of the Canadian west*. Vancouver: UBC Press.

Fanon, F. (1963). *The wretched of the earth*. New York: Grove Atlantic.

Fernandez, L. & Silver, J. (2018). *Indigenous people, wage labour, and trade unions: The historical experience in Canada*. Winnipeg: Canadian Centre for Policy Alternatives – Manitoba.

Fletcher, A. (1958, February 27). Winnipeg's Traffic: Blueprint for Action. *Winnipeg Free Press*.

Fletcher, A. (1960, February 17). Council Gets Sweeping Powers Over Planning. *Winnipeg Free Press*.

Fontaine, J. (2012). Interview by Darrell Chippeway. Research interview for Preserving the History of Institutional Development in Winnipeg. [Video]. Winnipeg, MB.

Food Banks Canada. (2013). *Hungercount 2013: A comprehensive report on hunger and food bank use in Canada, and recommendations for change*. Retrieved at www.foodbankscanada.ca/FoodBanks/MediaLibrary/HungerCount/HungerCount2013.pdf.

Food Banks Canada. (2016). *Hungercount 2016: A comprehensive report on hunger and food bank use in Canada, and recommendations for change*. Retrieved at https://www.foodbankscanada.ca/getmedia/6173994f-8a25-40d9-acdf-660a28e40f37/HungerCount_2016_final_singlepage.pdf.

Ford, T. (2008, May 5). Respect the locals when it comes to Main Street. *Winnipeg Free Press*.

Francis, M. (2002). *City treaty*. Winnipeg: Turnstone Press.

Francis, M. (2003). Voices from dark rooms: Winnipeg's new occidental hotel and the spectre of Main street. Marvin Francis fonds. University of Manitoba Archives & Special Collections.

Francis, M. (2004). Duncan's worlds: The change of environment in Duncan Mercredi's poetry. Marvin Francis fonds. University of Manitoba Archives & Special Collections.

Francis, M. (2008). *Bush camp*. Winnipeg: Turnstone Press.

Freeman, E.A. (1873). *Comparative politics*. London.

Friesen, G. (1979). Homeland to hinterland: Political transition in Manitoba, 1870 to 1879. *Historical Papers* 14, (1), 33.

Friesen, G. (1987). *The Canadian prairies: A history*. Toronto: University of Toronto Press.

Friesen, G., Hamilton, A.C. & Sinclair, C.M. (1996). Justice systems and Manitoba's aboriginal people: An historical survey. In G. Friesen (Ed.), *River road, essays on Manitoba and prairie history*. Winnipeg: University of Manitoba Press.

Friesen, J. (1999). Magnificent gifts: The treaties of Canada with the Indians of the northwest 1869–1876. In R.T. Price (Ed.), *The spirit of the Alberta Indian treaties*. Edmonton: University of Alberta Press.

Friesen, J. (2003). Morris, Alexander. *Dictionary of Canadian biography*, 11. University of Toronto/Université Laval. Retrieved at http://www.biographi.ca/en/bio/morris_alexander_11E.html.

Friesen, J. (2014, November 9). Winnipeg's first native mayor seen as bridge builder. *The Globe and Mail*. Retrieved at http://www.theglobeandmail.com/news/national/winnipegs-first-native-mayor-seen-as-bridge-builder/article21514131/.

Fulham, S.A. (1976). *In search of a future: A submission on the migration of native people*. Winnipeg: Manitoba Métis Federation.

Gaetz, S., Dej, E., Richter, T. & Redman, M. (2016). *The state of homelessness in Canada 2016*. Toronto: Canadian Observatory on Homelessness Press.

Gaudry, A. (2014). 'Free men consenting to unite with Canada': Métis-Canadian negotiations and the Manitoba treaty of 1870. [Presentation]. Paper presented at *Native American and Indigenous Studies Association*, Austin, Texas.

Gaudry, A. (2016). Fantasies of sovereignty: Deconstructing British and Canadian claims to ownership of the historic north-west. *Native American and Indigenous Studies*, 3 (1).

Gerson, W. (1957). *An urban renewal study for the City of Winnipeg: The CPR-Notre Dame area*. Winnipeg: City of Winnipeg.

Gibney, M. (2008). *The age of apology: Facing up to the past*. Philadelphia: University of Pennsylvania Press.

Gilmore, R.W. (2007). *Golden gulag: Prisons, surplus, crisis, and opposition in globalizing California*. Berkeley: University of California Press.

Gilmore, R.W. (2008). Forgotten places and the seeds of grassroots planning. In C.R. Hale (Ed.), *Engaging contradictions: Theory, politics, and methods of activist scholarship*. Berkeley: University of California Press.

Gilmore, R.W. (2015). Paper presented at the *Annual Meeting of the American Studies Association*, Toronto.

Gilmore, R.W. (2016). Comments on a panel at the *Annual Meeting of the American Studies Association*, Denver.

Gilmore, R.W. (2017). Abolition geography and the problem of innocence. In G.T. Johnson and A. Lubin (Eds.), *Futures of black radicalism*. Brooklyn: Verso Press.

Giroday, G. (2007, August 19). Bell hotel gave them a home. *Winnipeg Free Press.*

Goeman, M. (2013). *Mark my words: Native women mapping our nations.* Minneapolis: University of Minnesota Press.

Goeres, U.B., and Buchwald Pitblado Asper Barristers and Solicitors. (1999, November 17). *Asset Agreement between the City of Winnipeg and CentreVenture Development Corporation.*

Goldstein, A. (2015). Settlement and its disavowals: Relations of colonization and differential racialization. [Presentation]. Paper presented at the *Annual Meeting of the American Studies Association,* Toronto.

Goldstein, A. (2016). Critical ethnic studies committee I: Colonial unknowing and criminality. *Comments on a panel at the Annual Meeting of the American Studies Association,* Denver.

Gonick, C. (1990). The Manitoba economy since World War II. In J. Silver & J. Hull (Eds.), *The Political Economy of Manitoba,* 25–48. Regina: Canadian Plains Research Centre, University of Regina.

Gordon, W. (1992). Radio program, *Not Vanishing,* flourishes. *Women in Action,* special issue: "Indigenous women: Taking control of our lives, 2. Manila: Isis International. Retrieved at http://www.isiswomen.org/phocadownload/print/isispub/wia/WIA1992-2.pdf.

Gramsci, A. (1971). *Selections from the prison notebooks.* London: Lawrence & Wishart.

Green, J. & Fleury-Green, V. (2015). *Brown Town Muddy Water.* [Film].

Green, J. & Fleury-Green, V. (2015, November 7). Interview. On Deerchild, R (interviewer), *Unreserved.* Canadian Broadcasting Corporation.

Greenberg, M. & Schneider, D. (1994). "Violence in American cities: Young black males is the answer, but what was the question?" *Social Science and Medicine* 39 (2), 179-187.

Gregory, S. (1998). *Black corona: Race and the politics of place in an urban community.* New Jersey: Princeton University Press.

Gregory, D., Johnston, R., Pratt, G., Watts, M. & Whatmore, S. (2011). *The dictionary of human geography.* John Wiley & Sons.

Greyeyes, T. (2001). The strip. In *Urban Kool.* Winnipeg: Aboriginal Writers Collective.

Greyeyes, T. (2012). *Mary Richard.* Retrieved at https://www.youtube.com/watch?v=f5P-BH7K_Ry8.

Guilbault, M. (2012). Interview by Darrell Chippeway. Research interview for Preserving the History of Institutional Development in Winnipeg. [Video]. Winnipeg, MB.

Gutkin, H. & Gutkin, M. (1997). *Profiles in dissent: The shaping of radical thought in the Canadian west.* Edmonton: NeWest Press.

Haliburton, R.G. (1869). *The men of the north and their place in history: A lecture delivered before the Montreal literary club, March 31st, 1869.*

Hall, D.J. (1984). 'A serene atmosphere'? Treaty one revisited. *Canadian Journal of Native Studies* 4, 2.

Hall, D.J. (1985). Clifford Sifton: Immigration and settlement policy 1896–1905. In R.D. Francis & H. Palmer (Eds.), *The Prairie West,* 281–308. Edmonton: Pica Pica Press, Textbook division of The University of Alberta Press.

Hall, L.E.M. (2004). 'A place of awakening': The formation of the Winnipeg Indian and Métis Friendship Centre, 1954–1964. *University of Manitoba Master's thesis,* Department of History.

Hall, L.E.M. (2009). The Early History of the Winnipeg Indian and Métis Friendship Centre, 1951-1968. In E.W. Jones & G. Friesen (Eds.), *Prairie metropolis: New essays on Winnipeg social history,* Winnipeg: University of Manitoba Press.

Hall, N.J. (2010). *A history of the legislative assembly of Assiniboia.* Winnipeg: Manitoba Métis Federation, Province of Manitoba, Indian and Northern Affairs Canada. Retrieved at http://www.gov.mb.ca/ana/major-initiatives/pubs/laa%20essay%20eng.pdf.

Hall, N.J. (2015). *A casualty of colonialism: Red river Métis farming, 1810–1870.* Retrieved at https://casualtyofcolonialism.wordpress.com/

Hall, N.J. (2015b). *Aftermath: The 'reign of terror'.* Retrieved at https://hallnjean2.wordpress.com/chronology-after-the-resistance-1870-1871-2/aftermath/

Hall, S. (1980). Race, articulation, and societies structured in dominance. In UNESCO (Ed.), *Sociological theories: Race and colonialism.* Paris: UNESCO.

Hall, S. (1996). The meaning of new times. In D. Morley and K-H Chen (Eds.), *Stuart Hall: Critical Dialogues in Cultural Studies.* Abingdon: Routledge.

Hall, S. (2017). Racism and reaction. In *Selected Political Writings: The Great Moving Right Show and Other Essays.* Durham: Duke University Press.

Hall, S., Critcher, C., Jefferson, T., Clarke, J. & Roberts, B. (1978). *Policing the crisis: Mugging, the state, and law and order.* London: The Macmillan Press Ltd.

Hammond, C. (2013, January 10). Carlton Inn finds itself on CentreVenture buyout chopping block. *The Uniter.*

Hanke, L. (1959). *Aristotle and the American Indians: A study in race prejudice in the modern world.* Bloomington: Indian University Press.

Harper, E. (2004). What Canada means to me. In J. Oakes, et al. (Eds.), *Aboriginal cultural landscapes.* Winnipeg: University of Manitoba Press.

Harper, S. (2008, June 11). Statements by Ministers: Apology to Former Students of Indian Residential Schools, House of Commons Debates." presented at the 39th Parliament, 2nd Session, No. 110. Retrieved at http://www.parl.gc.ca/HousePublications/Publication.aspx?DocId=3568890&Language=E&Mode=1&Parl=39&Ses=2.

Harris, C. 1993. Whiteness as property. *Harvard Law Review* 106 (8).

Harris, C. (2003). *Making native space: Colonialism, resistance, and reserves in British Columbia.* Vancouver: UBC Press.

Harris, C. (2004). How did colonialism dispossess? Comments from an edge of empire. *Annals of the Association of American Geographers* 94 (1), 165–82.

Harvey, D. (1992). *The condition of postmodernity: An enquiry into the origins of cultural change.* John Wiley & Sons.

Harvey, D. (2015). Consolidating power. Interview with AK Malabocas. *ROAR Magazine,* 0, 16. Retrieved at https://roar-mag.org/magazine/david-harvey-consolidating-power/.

Hauch, C. (1985). *Coping strategies and street life: The ethnography of Winnipeg's skid row.* Winnipeg: University of Winnipeg Institute of Urban Studies.

Healy, W.J. (1927). *Winnipeg's early days.* Winnipeg: Stovel Company.

Helgason, W. (2013). Interview by Darrell Chippeway. Research interview for Preserving the History of Institutional Development in Winnipeg. [Video]. Winnipeg, MB.

Hendry, L. (2001, November 7). Main Street hot spot for growth. *Winnipeg Free Press.*

Herron, S. (1973, March 19). There is no way back. *Winnipeg Free Press.*

Highway, T. (2008). *Kiss of the fur queen.* Norman: University of Oklahoma Press.

Hilderman, Thomas, Frank, Cram Landscape Architecture, Planning, and Property & Services Department, Planning & Land-Use Division. (1999). *CentrePlan Development Framework.*

Hirst, N. (2004, August 7). Waterfront drive is the future. *Winnipeg Free Press.*

Horsman, R. (1981). *Race and manifest destiny: The origins of American racial anglo-saxonism.* Cambridge: Harvard University Press.

Howard, J. (1952). *Strange empire: Louis Riel and the Métis people.* Toronto: James Lewis and Samuel.

Hugill, D. & Toews, O. Born again urbanism: New missionary incursions, aboriginal resistance and barriers to rebuilding relationships in Winnipeg's north end. *Human Geography* 7 (1), 69–84.

Hunt, S. (2015). Violence, law and the everyday politics of recognition. Comments on Glen Coulthard's *Red skin, white masks* presented at *Native American and Indigenous Studies Association*, Washington, D.C.

Hutton, J. (2013, February 19). More jail cells won't solve overcrowding. *Winnipeg Free Press*.

INCITE! Women of Color Against Violence. (2007). *The revolution will not be funded: Beyond the non-profit industrial complex.* Boston: South End Press.

Indian Métis Friendship Centre and the Institute of Urban Studies. (1971). *The Indian-Métis urban probe.*

Indigenous and Northern Affairs Canada. (2010). *Fact sheet – urban aboriginal population in Canada.* Retrieved at http://www. aadnc-aandc.gc.ca/eng/1100100014298/11 00100014302.

Institute of Urban Studies. (1973). Kinew Housing Incorporated. Winnipeg: Institute of Urban Studies.

Jafri, B. (2015). Imagining decolonization: Indigenous and diasporic mediations on the future. Paper presented at the *Annual Meeting of the American Studies Association*, Toronto.

Janzen, L. (2000, August 30). Committee pulls plug on historic Savoy hotel. *Winnipeg Free Press*.

Johnson, G.T. & Lubin, A. (2017). Introduction. In G.T. Johnson & A. Lubin (Eds.), *Futures of Black Radicalism*. New York: Verso.

Johnston, B. (2003). *Honour earth mother: Mino-Audjaudauh Mizzu-Kummik-Quae.* Cape Croker, Ontario: Kegedonce Press.

Jones, G. (1968, March). Outlook in city – bleak. *The Prairie Call.*

Kaye, F.W. (2011). *Goodlands: A meditation and history on the great plains.* Edmonton: Athabasca University Press.

Kelley, R.D.G. (1990). *Hammer and Hoe: Alabama communists during the great depression.* Chapel Hill, NC: UNC Press.

Kelley, R.D.G. (2017). Introduction: Race, capitalism, justice. *Boston Review*, 1, 5-8.

Kelley, R.D.G. (2017). Births of a nation: Surveying trumpland with Cedric Robinson. *Boston Review.* Retrieved at http://boston-review.net/race-politics/robin-d-g-kelley-births-nation.

Kiernan, M. (1987). Intergovernmental innovation: Winnipeg's core area initiative. *Plan Canada* 27 (1).

Kirbyson, G. (2011, November 19). City to get a touch of glass. *Winnipeg Free Press*.

Kirbyson, G. (2013, May 10). Downtown soaring with the Jets. *Winnipeg Free Press*.

Kirkness, V, et al. (2012, March 8). *Women of Wahbung: The role of women in the development of the 1971 document of the Manitoba Indian Brotherhood's WAH-BUNG – OUR TOMORROWS.* Assembly of Manitoba Chiefs. Retrieved at http:// amc.manitobachiefs.com/images/pdf/ women%20of%20wahbung.pdf.

King Jr., M.L. (1967). *Where do we go from here: Chaos or community?* Boston: Beacon Press.

Kives, B. (2010, July 7). New plan to save downtown. *Winnipeg Free Press*.

Kives, B. (2010, September 1). Hotel buyouts in core for fewer drunks? *Winnipeg Free Press*.

Kives, B. (2010, October 21). More feet on street best core fix: Poll. *Winnipeg Free Press*.

Kives, B. (2014, August 8). Steeves' wife complains about harassment by 'drunken native guys' in Facebook post. *Winnipeg Free Press*.

Kives, B. (2017, March 22). Winnipeg city council approves True North Square tax rebates. *Canadian Broadcasting Corporation*.

Kives, B. (2017, May 15). St. Regis Hotel plans to lay off staff, close as prelude to redevelopment. *Canadian Broadcasting Corporation*.

Kives, B. (2017, May 26). Pain for Winnipeg: Mayor says that provincial funding changes will lead to cuts. *Canadian Broadcasting Corporation.*

Klos, N. & Douchant, C. (1998). 'Development at the core': A brief outline of downtown Winnipeg development over the last 35 years. Winnipeg: Institute of Urban Studies.

Knight, E. (2012, October 2). *Tax increment financing and social enterprise: Promoting equitable community revitalization in Winnipeg.* Winnipeg: Canadian Centre for Policy Alternatives – Manitoba.

Kramer, R. & Mitchell, T. (2010). *When the state trembled: How A.J Andrews and the citizens' committee broke the Winnipeg general strike.* Toronto: University of Toronto Press

Krotz, L. (1977, April 2). Down and out on Main Street. *Winnipeg Free Press.*

Knowles, V. (2007). *Strangers at our gates: Canadian immigration and immigration policy, 1540–2006* (revised edition). Toronto: Dundurn Press.

Korneski, K. (2007). Britishness, Canadianness, class, and race: Winnipeg and the British World, 1880s–1910s. *Journal of Canadian Studies, 41* (2), 161-184.

Kulchyski, P. & Neckaway, R. with the assistance of McKay, G. & Buck, R. (2007). The town that lost its name: The impact of hydroelectric development on Grand Rapids, Manitoba. In J. Loxley, J. Silver & K. Sexsmith (Eds.), *Doing community economic development.* Winnipeg: Fernwood Publishing.

Kurashige, S. (2016). Grace Lee Boggs: American revolutionary. Comments on a panel at the *Annual Meeting of the American Studies Association,* Denver.

Lagassé, J. (1959). *A study of the population of Indian ancestry living in Manitoba: Main report.* Winnipeg: Manitoba Department of Agriculture and Immigration, Social and Economic Research Office.

Lambrecht, K.N. (1991). *The administration of dominion lands, 1870–1930.* Canadian Plains Research Center, University of Regina.

Layne, J. (2000). Marked for success??? The Winnipeg core area initiative's approach to urban regeneration. *Canadian Journal of Regional Science 23* (2).

Lefebvre, H. (1992). *The production of space.* John Wiley & Sons.

Lemieux, T. & Riddell, C. (2014). *Top incomes in Canada: Evidence from the census.* IRPP Paper.

Leo, C. & Brown, W. (2000). Slow growth and urban development policy. *Journal of Urban Affairs, 22* (2), 193–213.

Lett, D. (2012, February 29). Day of reckoning on the horizon. *Winnipeg Free Press.*

Levasseur, J. (2018, April 18). Future of Winnipeg's SkyCity condos questioned after RCMP raid. *Canadian Broadcasting Corporation.* Retreived at http://www.cbc.ca/news/canada/manitoba/skycity-condos-winnipeg-fortress-raid-1.4619641.

Levin, E. (1972). *Neeginan: A Proposal for the Urban Indians and Metis.*

Lewycky, D. (2009, May 31). Property and public access. *Winnipeg Free Press.*

Lewys, T. (2011, June 11). Its ship has come in. *Winnipeg Free Press.*

Lezubski, D., Silver, J. & Black, E. (2003). High and rising: The growth of poverty in Winnipeg. In J. Silver (Ed.), *Solutions that work: Fighting poverty in Winnipeg.* Halifax: Fernwood Publishing.

Little Bear, L. (1986). Aboriginal rights and the Canadian 'grundnorm.' In J.R. Pointing (Ed.), *Arduous journey: Canadian Indians and decolonization.* Toronto: McLelland and Stewart.

Loewen, R. and Friesen, G. (2009). *Immigrants in prairie cities: Ethnic diversity in twentieth-century Canada.* Toronto: University of Toronto Press.

Logan, J. R. & Molotch, H. L. (2007). *Urban fortunes: The political economy of place.* Berkeley: University of California Press.

Lyon, D. & Fenton, R. (1984). *The development of downtown Winnipeg: Historical perspectives on decline and revitalization.* Winnipeg: Institute of Urban Studies.

Macdonald, N. (2015, January 22). Welcome to Winnipeg: Where Canada's racism problem is at its worst. *Maclean's Magazine*. Retrieved at https://www.macleans.ca/news/canada/welcome-to-winnipeg-where-canadas-racism-problem-is-at-its-worst/.

Mackinnon, S. (2009). Tracking poverty in Winnipeg's inner city, 1996–2006. *State of the Inner City Report 2009*. Winnipeg: Canadian Centre for Policy Alternatives–Manitoba.

Mackinnon, S. (2014, November 7). Will Winnipeg's first indigenous mayor bridge the city's divide? It's complicated. *Rabble*. Retrieved at http://rabble.ca/blogs/bloggers/policyfix/2014/11/will-winnipegs-first-indigenous-mayor-bridge-citys-divide-its-compl.

MacLeod, M.A. (1960). *Songs of old Manitoba*. Toronto: The Ryerson Press.

Manitoba. (1991). *The red river settlement*. Winnipeg: Manitoba Culture, Heritage and Citizenship, Historic Resources.

Manitoba Collaborative Data Portal. (2018). Community Data Map, Winnipeg Health Region. Accessed at https://mangomap.com/cgreenwpg/maps/75242c36-1a2e-11e7-835a-06c182e4d011/community-data-map-winnipeg-health-region?preview=true#.

Manitoba Historical Society. (2014). Walking tour of north Point Douglas. Retrieved at http://www.mhs.mb.ca/docs/features/walkingtours/pointdouglas/#tour_b.

Manitoba Historical Society. (2009). *Memorable Manitobans: Huntley Douglas Brodie Ketchen (1872–1959)*. Retrieved at http://www.mhs.mb.ca/docs/people/ketchen_hdb.shtml.

Manitoba Historical Society. (2015). *Memorable Manitobans: Alfred Joseph Andrews (1865-1950)*. Retrieved at http://www.mhs.mb.ca/docs/people/andrews_aj.shtml.

Manitoba Historical Society. (2015). *Memorable Manitobans: David John Dyson (1863–1949)*. Retrieved at http://www.mhs.mb.ca/docs/people/dyson_dj.shtml.

Manitoba Indian Brotherhood. (1971). *Wahbung: Our tomorrows*.

Manitoba Indian Brotherhood. (1971b). *Urban housing study*.

Marable, M. (2011). *Malcolm X: A life of reinvention*. New York: Penguin Books.

Marcoux, J. (2016, March 21). 16 years of Winnipeg budgets show gains by police at expense of other city departments. *Canadian Broadcasting Corporation*. Retrieved at http://www.cbc.ca/news/canada/manitoba/16-years-of-winnipeg-budgets-show-gains-by-police-at-expense-of-other-city-departments-1.3500207.

Martin, C. (1973). *Dominion lands policy*. Montréal: McGill-Queen's Press.

Maunder, M. (2015). Winnipeg's developers: The birth of the suburbs, 1946–1991. In Distasio & Kaufman (Eds.), *The divided prairie city*. Winnipeg: Institute of Urban Studies.

Marx, K. (1973). *Grundrisse*. New York: Penguin Books.

Marx, K. (2004). *Capital: A critique of political economy, volume 1*. New York: Penguin Books.

Maynard, R. (2017). *Policing black lives: State violence in Canada from slavery to the present*. Halifax: Fernwood Publishing.

McArthur, K. (1999, April 27). People at heart of city plan. *Winnipeg Free Press*.

McCallum, M.J.L. (2014). *Indigenous women, work, and history, 1940–1980*. Winnipeg: University of Manitoba Press.

McGowan, R. (2012, November). *Speech to Winnipeg realtors*. Retrieved at http://www.winnipegrealestatenews.com/Resources/Article/?sysid=1726.

McGowan, R. (2013, February 25). CentreVenture door always open. Retrieved at http://www.centreventure.blogspot.ca/ on February 25, 2013.

McGowan, R. (2013, May 15). McGowan to talk downtown development at News Café. Retrieved at www.winnipegfreepress.com/local/McGowan-to-talk-downtown-development-at-News-Ca-207605301.html.

McKenzie-Jones, P. (2015). Removing imagined borders: American Indian and Canadian First Nations activism from the red power era to the present day. Retrieved at http://www.academia.edu/15579196/Removing_Imagined_Borders_American_Indian_and_Canadian_First_Nations_Activism_from_the_Red_Power_Era_to_the_Present_Day.

McKittrick, K. (2006). *Demonic grounds: Black women and the cartographies of struggle.* Minneapolis: University of Minnesota Press.

McLeod, A. (2013). Interview by Darrell Chippeway. Research interview for Preserving the History of Institutional Development in Winnipeg. [Video]. Winnipeg, MB.

McNeill, M. (2008, March 18). North Main getting major facelift. *Winnipeg Free Press.*

McNeill, M. (2009, July 27). Full steam ahead for Main Street. *Winnipeg Free Press.*

McNeill, M. (2016, December 24). True North Square towers to rise in spring. *Winnipeg Free Press.* Retrieved at https://www.winnipegfreepress.com/business/soon-to-rise-expected-to-shine-408102196.html.

Mcquillan, D. A. (1980). Creation of Indian reserves on the Canadian prairies 1870–1885. *The Geographical Review*, 70 (4).

Meadmore, M. (2012). Interview by Darrell Chippeway. Research interview for Preserving the History of Institutional Development in Winnipeg. [Video]. Winnipeg, MB.

Mental Health Commission of Canada. (2015). "Initiatives: Winnipeg." *Mental Health Commission of Canada.* Retrieved at http://www.mentalhealthcommission.ca/English/initiatives-and-projects/home/winnipeg?routetoken=27e2684b-c37883a5ac43734683d52150&terminitial=66.

Mercredi, D. (1997). *The Duke of Windsor: Wolf sings the blues.* Winnipeg: Pemmican Publications.

Mercredi, D. (2017). This city is red. *Prairie Fire*, 38 (1), 103-105.

Metropolitan Corporation of Greater Winnipeg, Planning Division. (1963). *Draft development plan: Metropolitan Winnipeg.*

Metropolitan Corporation of Greater Winnipeg, Planning Division. (1967). *Downtown Winnipeg.* Winnipeg: City of Winnipeg.

Metropolitan Corporation of Greater Winnipeg, Planning Division. (1970). *Charleswood detailed area plan.* Winnipeg: City of Winnipeg.

Metropolitan Corporation of Greater Winnipeg. (1971). *The end of the metropolitan.* Souvenir Issue December 1971. Winnipeg: City of Winnipeg.

Metropolitan Planning Committee and Winnipeg Town Planning Commission. (1946). Greater Winnipeg tax forfeited lands (1946). In *Background for Planning Greater Winnipeg* (Winnipeg, 1946), plate 9. Retrieved at https://www.flickr.com/photos/manitobamaps/3130341037.

Metropolitan Planning Committee and Winnipeg Town Planning Commission. (1948). *Preliminary report on residential areas.* No.7 of Master Plan Reports. Winnipeg: City of Winnipeg.

Milgrom, R. (2011). Slow growth versus the sprawl machine: Winnipeg, Manitoba. In *In-between infrastructure: Urban connectivity in an age of vulnerability.* Praxis (e)Press.

Mill, J.S. (1869). *The subjection of women.* London: Longmans, Green, Reader and Dyer.

Miller, J.R. (1996). *Shingwauk's vision: A history of native residential schools.* Toronto: University of Toronto Press.

Miller, J.R. (2009). *Compact, contract, covenant: Aboriginal treaty-making in Canada.* Toronto: University of Toronto Press.

Million, D. (2013). *Therapeutic nations: Healing in an age of indigenous human rights.* Tucson: University of Arizona Press.

Minister of the Interior. (1905). Twentieth century Canada and atlas of western Canada. Department of the Interior.

Minister of the Interior. (1909). *Prosperity follows settlement in any part of Canada: Letters from satisfied settlers.* Department of the Interior.

Mochoruk, J. (2004). *Formidable heritage: Manitoba's north and the cost of development, 1870–1930*. Winnipeg: University of Manitoba Press.

Monture, P. (2007). Race and erasing: Law and gender in white settler societies. In Hier & Bolaria (Eds.), *Race & racism in 21ˢᵗ-century Canada*. Peterborough: Broadview Press.

Morgensen, S.L. (2011). *Spaces between us: Queer settler colonialism and indigenous decolonization*. Minneapolis: University of Minnesota Press.

Morris, A. (1880). *The treaties of Canada with the Indians: Including the negotiations upon which they were based, and other information relating thereto*. Toronto: Coles Publishing Company.

Morrissette, V. (2013). Interview by Darrell Chippeway. Research interview for Preserving the History of Institutional Development in Winnipeg. [Video]. Winnipeg, MB.

Mulaire, M. (2017, January 30). How do we do business with Trump's America? *The Winnipeg Chamber of Commerce blog*. Accessed on March 19, 2018 at http://www.winnipeg-chamber.com/chamber-blog/opinion-how-do-we-do-business-with-trumps-america

Mungai, L. (1984). Citizen participation and the renewal of a declining inner city neighbourhood: A case study of Winnipeg's north logan neighbourhood. University of Manitoba Political Studies Master's Thesis.

Munroe, G. (2012). Interview by Darrell Chippeway. Research interview for Preserving the History of Institutional Development in Winnipeg. [Video]. Winnipeg, MB.

Murch, D. (2017). History matters. *Boston Review*, 1, 32-38.

Murray, G. & Stephens, G. (1999, April 26). *CentreVenture working draft*. Winnipeg: City of Winnipeg.

Nabess, A.J. (1972, October 26). Indians on the march. *Winnipeg Free Press*.

Nelson, C. (1992). RCAP submissions, December 8, 1992, Roseau River First Nation.

Nepinak, D. (2013). Interview by Darrell Chippeway. Research interview for Preserving the History of Institutional Development in Winnipeg. [Video]. Winnipeg, MB. Retrieved at https://www.youtube.com/watch?v=EJAs8-x8a1I.

Nepinak, D. (2005). Main Street. In *Bone memory*. Winnipeg: Aboriginal Writers Collective of Manitoba.

Nepinak, D. (2006). Indians. *Contemporary Verse 2*, winter 2006.

Nerbas, D. (2004). Wealth and privilege: An analysis of Winnipeg's early business elite. *Manitoba History*, 47.

Nguyen, L. (2014, January 2). Top Canadian CEOs earn annual worker's salary by lunchtime on Jan. 2. *Ottawa Citizen*.

Nicolaides, B. & Wiese, A. (2006). *The suburb reader*. New York: Routledge.

North Main Task Force. (1997). *Our place: North Main task force*. Winnipeg: Winnipeg Development Agreement.

O'Brien, D. (1999, September 30). City "open for business." *Winnipeg Free Press*.

O'Brien, D. (1999, November 18). CentreVenture becomes busy player. *Winnipeg Free Press*.

O'Brien, D. (2014, November 26). Mayor faces long learning curve. *Winnipeg Free Press*.

Oleson, T. (2009, June 7). Walking down Main. *Winnipeg Free Press*.

Oliver, E. (1915). *The Canadian North-West, its early development and legislative records: Minutes of the councils of the Red River Colony and the Northern Department of Rupert's Land*. Ottawa: Government Printing Bureau.

Omi, M & Winant, H. (1994). *Racial formation in the United States*. New York: Routledge.

onewinnipeg.ca. (2014). Winnipeg water Wednesdays have returned for 2014! *Winnipeg Water Wednesdays*. Retrieved at https://www.onewinnipeg.ca.

Owram, D. (1980). *Promise of eden: The Canadian expansionist movement and the idea of the west, 1856–1900*. Toronto: University of Toronto Press.

Owram, D. (2007). The promise of the west as settlement frontier. In *The prairie west as promised land*, 3–28. Calgary: University of Calgary Press.

Pasternak, S. (2017). *Grounded authority: The Algonquins of Barriere Lake against the state*. Minneapolis: University of Minnesota Press.

Penner, N. (1975). *Winnipeg 1919: The strikers' own history of the Winnipeg general strike*. Toronto: James Lorimer & Company, Publishers.

Perry, A. (2007). Whose world was British? Rethinking the "British world" from an edge of empire. In Darian-Smith, Grimshaw, and Macintyre (Eds.), *Britishness abroad: Transnational movements and imperial cultures*. Melbourne: Melbourne University Press.

Perry, A. (2015). *Colonial relations: The Douglas-Connolly family and the nineteenth century imperial world*. Cambridge: Cambridge University Press.

Perry, A. (2016). *Aqueduct: Colonialism, resources, and the histories we remember*. Winnipeg: ARP Books.

Perry, A. (2016). Drinking dispossession: Winnipeg, water, and settler colonialism, 1913–1919. Paper presented at *University of Manitoba Native Studies Colloquium*, Winnipeg.

Peters, E.J. (2002). "Our city Indians": Negotiating the meaning of First Nations urbanization in Canada, 1945–1975. *Historical Geography*, 30, 75–92.

Peters, E.J. (2007). First Nations and Métis people and diversity in Canadian cities. In T. Courchene and K.G. Banting (Eds.), *Belonging? Diversity, Recognition and Shared Citizenship in Canada*. Montréal: McGill Queens University Press.

Peters, E.J. & Andersen, C. (Eds.). (2013). *Indigenous in the city: Contemporary identities and cultural innovation*. Vancouver: UBC Press.

Peters, E.J. & Barkwell, L. (2010). Rooster town: A Métis road allowance community. Winnipeg: Louis Riel Institute. Retrieved at http://docshare01. docshare.tips/files/2929/29295136.pdf.

Peters, E.J., Stock, M. & Werner, A. (2018). *Rooster town: The history of an urban Métis community, 1901–1961*. Winnipeg: University of Manitoba Press.

Piapot, N. (2013, January 3). Racial tensions rise along edges of Idle No More rallies. *APTN National News*. Retrieved at aptn. ca/news/2013/01/03/racial-tensions-rise-along-edges-of-idle-no-more-rallies/.

Piché, J., Kleuskens, S. & Walby, K. (2016). The front and back stages of carceral expansion marketing in Canada. *Contemporary Justice Review* 19, (4).

Pratt, D., Bone, H. and the Treaty and Dakota Elders of Manitoba with contributions by the Assembly of Manitoba Chiefs Council of Elders and Courchene, D.H. (Date unknown). *Untuwe Pi Kin He – Who We Are: Treaty Elders' Teachings, Vol.1*. Winnipeg: Treaty Relations Commission of Manitoba and the Assembly of Manitoba Chiefs.

Province of Manitoba. (2004, May 20). Tri-level agreement to invest $75 million into City of Winnipeg. Retrieved at http://www. gov.mb.ca/chc/press/top/2004/05/2004-05-20-04.html.

Province of Manitoba. (2006). *Aboriginal people in Manitoba*. Retrieved at http://www. gov.mb.ca/ana/pdf/pubs/apm2006.pdf.

Province of Manitoba. (2006, April 18). Sustainable funding of operation clean sweep announced by Macintosh and Katz. Retrieved at news.gov.mb.ca/news/index. html?item=28452&posted=2006-04-18.

Province of Manitoba. (2009, November 1). *The community revitalization tax increment financing act*. Province of Manitoba.

Quality Construction Co. (1960, September 16). Parade of Homes. *Winnipeg Free Press*.

Ray, A., Miller, J. & Tough, F. (2000). *Bounty and benevolence: A history of Saskatchewan treaties*. Montréal and Kingston: McGill-Queens University Press.

Razack, S.H. (2000). Gendered racial violence and spatialized justice: The murder of Pamela George. *Canadian Journal of Law and Society* 15.

Renaud, A. (1957). *The Indian in the community.* Toronto: National Commission on the Indian Canadian.

Richard, M. (2002). Interview with Kurt Sargent, re: History of Urban Aboriginal Organizations.

Riel, L. (1869, December 7). Agreement of surrender. In R. Huel & G. Stanley (Eds.), *The collected writings of Louis Riel, volume 1.* Edmonton: The University of Alberta Press.

Riel, L. (2000). You are like the trembling seed. In G. Campbell (Ed.), *Selected poetry of Louis Riel.* Toronto: Exile Editions.

Robinson, C. (1983). *Black Marxism: The making of the black radical tradition.* Chapel Hill: The University of North Carolina Press.

Robinson, C. (2007). *Forgeries of memory and meaning: Blacks and the regimes of race in American theatre and film before World War II.* Chapel Hill: The University of North Carolina Press.

Rosner, C. (1978, October 11). Indians angered by inner city report. *Winnipeg Free Press.*

Roussin, D. & Christensen, T. (2010). *Public funds for Youth For Christ: Have our politicians learned nothing from past mistakes?* Winnipeg: Canadian Centre for Policy Alternatives–Manitoba.

Royal Commission on Aboriginal Peoples. (1996). *Report of the Royal Commission on Aboriginal Peoples, volume 1.* Ottawa: Government of Canada.

Said, E.W. (1994). *Culture and imperialism.* New York: Vintage Books.

Saldaña-Portillo, M.J. (2015). Can the settler colonialism paradigm account for indigenous America today? Presented at the *Annual Meeting of the American Studies Association,* Toronto.

Saldaña-Portillo, M.J. (2015). The settler colonialism analytic: A critical reappraisal. Comments on a panel at the *Annual Meeting of the American Studies Association,* Toronto.

Santin, A. (2015, February 5). Poor to bear brunt of city cuts. *Winnipeg Free Press.* Retrieved at https://www.winnipegfreepress.com/local/poor-to-bear-brunt-of-city-cuts-290883091.html.

Schlesinger, J. (2013, March 18). Jets effect heats up Winnipeg's commercial real estate market. *The Globe and Mail.* Retrieved at https://www.theglobeandmail.com/report-on-business/industry-news/property-report/jets-effect-heats-up-winnipegs-commercial-real-estate-market/article9871232/.

Schwartzkopf, S. (2013, July 29). Top 5 cities with the most Native Americans. *Indian Country Today* Retrieved at April 4, 2018 at https://indiancountrymedianetwork.com/news/native-news/top-5-cities-with-the-most-native-americans/

Scofield, G. (2011). *Louis: The heretic poems.* Gibsons, B.C.: Nightwood Editions.

Scott, W. (1913). Immigration and population. In A. Short & A. Doughty (Eds.), *Canada and its provinces,* 7, 517-590. Toronto: Publisher's Association of Canada.

Selinger, G. (1985). *Viable policy and plan making: the fight in Winnipeg to stop the Sherbook-McGregor overpass and relocate the C.P.R. yards.* Prepared for delivery at the Canadian Urban Studies Conference, University of Winnipeg.

Sharpe, E. (2013, February 24). New doubts about CentreVenture. *Winnipeg Free Press.*

Silver, J. (1990). Plant closures in Manitoba, 1976–1986. In *The Political Economy of Manitoba,* 228–48. Regina: Canadian Plains Research Center, University of Regina.

Silver, J. (2002). *Inner-city priorities for a renewed tri-level development agreement.* Winnipeg: Urban Future Group, Canadian Centre for Policy Alternatives - Manitoba.

Silver, J. (2004). Community development in Winnipeg's inner city. *Canadian Dimension,* 38 (6).

Silver, J. (2006). *In their own voices: Building urban aboriginal communities.* Halifax: Fernwood Publishing.

Silver, J. (2014). *About Canada: Poverty.* Halifax: Fernwood Publishing.

Silver, J., McCracken, M. & Sjoberg, K. (2009). *Neighbourhood renewal corporations in Winnipeg's inner city: Practical activism in a complex environment.* Winnipeg: Canadian Centre for Policy Alternatives-Manitoba.

Silver, J. & Toews, O. (2009). Combating poverty in Winnipeg's inner city, 1960s–1990s: Thirty years of hard-earned lessons. *Canadian Journal of Urban Research* 18 (1), 98–122.

Sim, R.A. (date unknown). *What is meant by "urban Indians."* Canada Department of Citizenship and Immigration. National Archives of Canada Record Group 29, Portion of 60 File 2-38-6 1.

Simms, T. (1987). *Arresting urban decline: The community economic development alternative.* Winnipeg: University of Manitoba Master's Thesis, Faculty of Social Work.

Simpson, A. (2009). Captivating Eunice: Membership, colonialism, and gendered citizenships of grief. *Wicazo Sa Review* 24 (2), 105–129.

Simpson, A. (2016). Whither settler colonialism? *Settler Colonial Studies*, 6 (4).

Simpson, A. (2016). The state is a man: Theresa Spence, Loretta Saunders and the gender of settler sovereignty. *Theory & Event*, 19 (4).

Simpson, L. (2015). Comments at a roundtable on Glen Coulthard's *Red skin, white masks* and Audra Simpson's *Mohawk interruptus.* Presented at the *Annual Meeting of the American Studies Association*, Toronto.

Simpson, L. & Klein, N. (2013). Dancing the world into being: A conversation with Idle No More's Leanne Simpson. *Yes Magazine.* Retrieved at http://www.yesmagazine.org/peace-justice/dancing-the-world-into-being-a-conversation-with-idle-no-more-leanne-simpson.

Sinclair, N. & Cariou, W. (Eds). (2011). *Manitowapow: Aboriginal writings from the land of water.* Winnipeg: Portage & Main Press.

Smith, A. (2005). *Conquest: Sexual violence and American Indian genocide.* Boston: South End Press.

Smith, K.D. (2009). *Liberalism, surveillance, and resistance : Indigenous communities in western Canada, 1877-1927.* Edmonton: University of Alberta Press.

Smith, N. (1996). *The new urban frontier: Gentrification and the revanchist city.* New York and London: Routledge.

Smith, Wilbur & Associates. (1957). *Report on traffic, transit, parking, metropolitan Winnipeg.* New Haven, Connecticut.

Spillet, L. (2012). Interview by Darrell Chippeway. Research interview for Preserving the History of Institutional Development in Winnipeg. [Video]. Winnipeg, MB.

Sproat, G.M. (1872). Letter to J.H. Pope. Letter 'A,' 27 March 1872, LAC, RG 17, "Immigration Branch" series, vol.2397. As cited in Eyford 2016, 66.

Stanger-Ross, J. (2008). Municipal colonialism in Vancouver: City planning and the conflict over Indian reserves, 1928–1950s. *Canadian Historical Review*, 89 (4), 541-580.

Stanley, G. (1963). *Louis Riel.* Toronto: Ryerson Press.

Stanley, G. (1985). Forward. In *The collected writings of Louis Riel, volume 1.* Edmonton: University of Alberta Press.

Statistics Canada. (2006). *2006 census data – Centennial.* Retrieved at https://www.winnipeg.ca/census/2006/Community%20Areas/Downtown%20Neighbourhoods/Centennial/Centennial.pdf.

Statistics Canada. (2006). *2006 census data – inner city.* City of Winnipeg. Retrieved at http://winnipeg.ca/census/2006/City%20of%20Winnipeg/.

Statistics Canada. (2012). *Police resources in Canada.* Retrieved at https://www.statcan.gc.ca/pub/85-225-x/85-225-x2012000-eng.pdf.

Statistics Canada. (2013). *Police resources in Canada.* Ottawa: Minister of Industry.

Stevenson, T. (1961, July). The importance of defending our culture. *The Prairie Call.*

Stewart, D.G. (1993). A critique of the Winnipeg core area initiative: A case study in urban revitalization. *Canadian Journal of Urban Research*, 2 (2).

Swainson, D. (1992). Canada annexes the west: Colonial status confirmed. In G. Melnyk (Ed.), *From Riel to reform: A history of protest in western Canada.* Fifth House Publishing.

Swan, R. (2010). Robert A. Davis: 1874–1878. In B. Ferguson & R. Wardhaugh (Eds.), *Manitoba premiers of the 19th and 20th centuries*. Regina: Canadian Plains Research Centre.

Taylor, S. (2017, February 2). Bowman says 'no' to sanctuary city status for Winnipeg – for now. *Metro Winnipeg*.

The Canadian Encyclopedia. (2013). Tommy Douglas. Retrieved at http://www.thecanadianencyclopedia.com/en/article/tommy-douglas/.

The Manitoban. (1871). *The Manitoban* (as transcribed by the Manitoba Treaty and Aboriginal Rights Research Centre, 1970). Winnipeg: Provincial Archives of Manitoba.

The New Nation. (1870, January 7). Our Canadian heroes. *The New Nation*. Retrieved at https://www.manitobia.ca/content/en/newspapers/NNT/1870/01/28/1/Ar00100.html/Olive.

Thiessen, J. (2009). Winnipeg's Palliser Furniture in the context of Mennonite views on industrial relations, 1974–1996. In E.W. Jones & G. Friesen (Eds.), *Prairie metropolis: New essays on Winnipeg social history*. Winnipeg: University of Manitoba Press.

Thomas-Müller, C. (2017, March 20). We need to start calling out corporate 'redwashing'. *Canadian Broadcasting Corporation*. Retrieved at http://www.cbc.ca/news/opinion/corporate-redwashing-1.4030443.

Thompson, J.H. (1998). *Forging the prairie west*. Don Mills: Oxford University Press.

Thorpe, R. (2018, March 24). Mayor's state of city address outlines vision of 'new Winnipeg'. *Winnipeg Free Press*. Retrieved at https://www.winnipegfreepress.com/local/mayors-state-of-city-address-outlines-vision-of-new-winnipeg-477791383.html.

Toews, O. (2017). *Winnipeg free for all: Towards democracy at city hall*. Winnipeg: Canadian Centre for Policy Alternatives–Manitoba.

Tough, F. (1996). *As their natural resources fail*. Vancouver: UBC Press.

Trouillot, M-R. (1995). *Silencing the past: Power and the production of history*. Boston: Beacon Press.

Truth and Reconciliation Commission of Canada. (2015). *Honouring the truth, reconciling for the Future: Summary of the final report of the Truth and Reconciliation Commission of Canada*. Retrieved at http://www.trc.ca/websites/trcinstitution/File/2015/Honouring_the_Truth_Reconciling_for_the_Future_July_23_2015.pdf.

Tuck, E. (2009). Suspending damage: A letter to communities. *Harvard Educational Review, 79*(3), 409-428.

Tully, J. (2000). Aboriginal peoples: Negotiating reconciliation. In J. Bickerton & A-G Gagnon (Eds.), *Canadian politics*. Toronto: University of Toronto Press.

Turner, J. (2010, July 7). Licensing mayhem. *Winnipeg Sun*.

Tyman, J.L. (1972). *By section, township and range: Studies in prairie settlement*. Assiniboine Historical Society.

United Nations. (2014, July 10). World's population increasingly urban with more than half living in urban areas. Retrieved at March 28, 2018 at http://www.un.org/en/development/desa/news/population/world-urbanization-prospects-2014.html.

Urban Futures Group. (1990). *Community inquiry into inner city revitalization*. Winnipeg: Institute of Urban Studies.

Valverde, M. (1991). *The age of light, soap, and water: Moral reform in English Canada, 1885–1925*. Toronto: McClelland and Stewart Inc.

Vanstone, R. (2012). Winnipeg community members prevent overpass construction, 1979-1981. *Global Nonviolent Action Database*. Swarthmore College. Retrieved at http://nvdatabase.swarthmore.edu/content/winnipeg-community-members-prevent-overpass-construction-1979-1981.

Vowel, C. (2016). *Indigenous writes*. Winnipeg: Portage and Main Press.

Walker, R.C. (2008). Aboriginal self-determination and social housing in Canada: A story of convergence and divergence. *Urban Studies* 45 (1), 185-205.

Warnock, J.W. (2007). The national policy and 19th century imperialism and colonialism. In *The prairie agrarian movement revisited*. Regina: Canadian Plains Research Centre, University of Regina.

White-Harvey, R. (1994). Reserve geography and the restoration of native self-government. *Dalhousie Law Journal* 17, 587–611.

Whittier, J.G. (1878). *Poems of John Greenleaf Whittier*. Boston: James R. Osgood and Company.

Williams, R. (2001). *The long revolution*. Peterborough: Broadview Press.

Wilson, G. & University of Regina Canadian Plains Research Center. (2007). *Frontier farewell: The 1870s and the end of the old west*. University of Regina, Canadian Plains Research Center.

Winnipeg City Council Executive Policy Committee. (2010, July 7). Item No. 8 Portage Avenue Action Strategy. Agenda – Winnipeg Executive Policy Committee.

Winnipeg Free Press. (1941, June 14). A muskrat Venice. *Winnipeg Free Press*.

Winnipeg Free Press. (1953, August 18). Huge shopping area to cost $10 million. *Winnipeg Free Press*.

Winnipeg Free Press. (1954, March 10). Plan Urged On Highway Approaches: C of C Report Suggests Ways to Relieve Congestion. *Winnipeg Free Press*.

Winnipeg Free Press. (1955, October 21). 38 Builders Set to Work on Big 1,300 Home Project. *Winnipeg Free Press*.

Winnipeg Free Press. (1956, September 13). To Display Latest Homes. *Winnipeg Free Press*.

Winnipeg Free Press. (1958, March 11). Biggest Yet Road Plan Unveiled By Province. *Winnipeg Free Press*.

Winnipeg Free Press. (1958, April 14). Realism in Traffic. *Winnipeg Free Press*.

Winnipeg Free Press. (1960, September 16). And A Commerce Degree Helps. *Winnipeg Free Press*.

Winnipeg Free Press. (1960, September 19). Residential Construction Ranks as One of Main City Industries. *Winnipeg Free Press*.

Winnipeg Free Press. (1968, March 26). Indians here have to live in slums, city council told. *Winnipeg Free Press*.

Winnipeg Free Press. (1972, October 25). Photograph of vandalized Louis Riel statue. *Winnipeg Free Press*.

Winnipeg Free Press. (1972, October 25). Native policy outlined. *Winnipeg Free Press*.

Winnipeg Free Press. (1972, November 1). Indian party possible. *Winnipeg Free Press*.

Winnipeg Free Press. (1974, January 23). Opposes Indian village in city. *Winnipeg Free Press*.

Winnipeg Free Press. (1974, January 30). City contributes $7,500 for study. *Winnipeg Free Press*.

Winnipeg Free Press. (1979, April 12). Metis reject negotiation session; occupation continues. *Winnipeg Free Press*.

Winnipeg Free Press. (1985, March 14). Council blamed for decay. *Winnipeg Free Press*.

Winnipeg Free Press. (1991, July 12). Why Kill it Now? *Winnipeg Free Press*.

Winnipeg Free Press. (1999, May 9). Politicians on downtown. *Winnipeg Free Press*.

Winnipeg Free Press. (1999, May 9). People, people, people. *Winnipeg Free Press*.

Winnipeg Free Press. (1999, November 2). Politicians Talk as Winnipeg Burns. *Winnipeg Free Press*.

Winnipeg Free Press. (2007, January 16). It's our downtown. *Winnipeg Free Press*.

Winnipeg Free Press. (2007, August 28). Last call at the Bell. *Winnipeg Free Press*.

Winnipeg Free Press. (2011, March 9). Let's make it happen. *Winnipeg Free Press*.

Winnipeg Free Press. (2012, November 19). The hotel domino effect. *Winnipeg Free Press.*

Winnipeg Free Press. (2012, December 29). Faces of the aboriginal community. *Winnipeg Free Press.*

Winnipeg Into the Nineties. (date unknown). Winnipeg into the nineties fonds. Winnipeg: City of Winnipeg Archives. Retrieved at http://nanna.lib.umanitoba.ca/atom/index.php/winnipeg-into-nineties-win-fonds.

Winnipeg Police Service. (2016, December 15). Winnipeg Police Service Announces Downtown Safety Strategy. Retrieved at February 21, 2018 at http://www.winnipeg.ca/police/press/2016/12dec/2016_12_15.aspx.

Winnipeg Tribune. (1942, January 28). Unknown. *Winnipeg Tribune.*

Woodsworth, J.S. (1911). *My neighbor: Urban ills and urban reform.* Toronto: University of Toronto Press.

Woodsworth, J.S. (1913). *Report on living standards, city of Winnipeg, 1913.* Appendix D. In A.F.J. Artibise (Ed.), *Winnipeg: A social history of urban growth, 1874–1914* by Montreal: McGill-Queens University Press.

Wolfe, P. (2006). Settler colonialism and the elimination of the native. *Journal of Genocide Research* 8 (4), 387–409.

Woods, C.A. (1998). *Development arrested: The blues and plantation power in the Mississippi Delta.* New York: Verso.

Yalnizyan, A. (2010). *The rise of Canada's richest 1%.* Ottawa: Canadian Centre for Policy Alternatives.

Young, D. (1992). Northern Manitoba hydro electric projects and their impact on Cree culture. In Lithman, et al. (Eds.), *People and land in northern Manitoba: 1990 conference at the University of Manitoba.* Winnipeg: Department of Anthropology at the University of Manitoba.

Young, D. (2012). Interview by Darrell Chippeway. Research interview for Preserving the History of Institutional Development in Winnipeg. [Video]. Winnipeg, MB.

INDEX

OWEN
TOEWS

Owen Toews is a postdoctoral fellow at the University of Alberta. He received his PhD in geography from the City University of New York (CUNY) Graduate Center and has worked as an instructor at the University of Manitoba Department of Environment and Geography, Brooklyn College Honors Program, and the Hunter College Department of Urban Affairs and Planning. He is a founding member of the DIY museum collective Winnipeg Arcades Project, a member of the abolitionist prisoner solidarity group Bar None, and acquisitions editor for ARP Books' Semaphore series. Born and raised in Winnipeg, he is descended from Russian Mennonites.